M

The · Master · Musicians

LISZT

Series edited by Stanley Sadie

The · Master · Musicians

LISZT

Derek Watson

J.M. Dent & Sons Ltd
London

First published 1989

© Derek Watson, 1989

Made and printed in Great Britain by
Butler & Tanner Ltd, Frome and London for
J. M. Dent & Sons Ltd
91 Clapham High Street London SW4 7TA

This book is set in 10½ on 12 pt Sabon by
Butler & Tanner Ltd

Music examples set by Tabitha Collingbourne

British Library Cataloguing in Publication Data

Watson, Derek
    Liszt.—(The Master musicians series).
    1. Hungarian music. Liszt, Franz, 1811–1886
    Critical studies
    I. Title   II. Series
    780′.92′4

    ISBN 0–460–03174–0

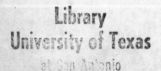

For
Ronald Stevenson

Preface

When my predecessor Dr Walter Beckett wrote *Liszt* for the Master Musicians Series three decades ago, the composer's reputation had long been at a low ebb. That volume, and Humphrey Searle's book on the music, stimulated interest among a new generation, including myself. Music is nothing without performance: when starting serious work on Liszt twenty years ago I could expect to find half-a-dozen LPs of his music in a good record shop, mostly of the popular pieces. Browsing in a London store this year I counted over 200 recordings covering every aspect of his *œuvre*. This astonishing upsurge of interest by artists, the listening public and the recording industry reflects a significant change in Liszt's standing. Thirty years ago he was seen as a peripheral and rather extreme figure of the Romantic age. Now he is counted a central, even *the* central figure of mid-nineteenth-century music. My aim has been to provide the fullest introduction to his life and work available to date in a single volume.

For encouragement and help I fondly remember my late colleagues Humphrey Searle, Friedrich Schnapp and Douglas Peroni. For further advice and answers to many questions I thank Eunice Mistarz, Maurice Hinson, Alastair Hardie, Patrick Douglas-Hamilton, Stewart Spencer, Lennart Rabes, Ulrike Seeberger and Miklós Forrai. For help in translations, Alpin Smart and T. J. O'Donnell. To Adrian Williams very special thanks for many thoughtful and constructive criticisms which helped shape the biographical chapters. To Ronald Stevenson I acknowledge both a debt of scholarship and, through his playing, a creative insight upon Liszt. And to Robert David MacDonald for yards of Lisztiana borrowed from his shelves and much perceptive discussion, my gratitude. For their generosity, patience and interest in the progress of my manuscript, I am grateful to Eileen Skinner, Will Scott and Flora Watson, and to Lyn Pullen who typed it.

Edinburgh, 1988.

D.W.

Contents

Liszt

List of illustrations

11 Liszt with some pupils, Weimar 1884. From left to right (back row) Moritz Rosenthal, Victoria Drewing, Mele Paramanoff, Liszt, Frau Friedheim, Hugo Mansfeld; (front row) Georg Liebling, Alexander Siloti, Arthur Friedheim, Emil Sauer, Alfred Reisenauer, A. W. Gottschalg. Photograph, Louis Held.

Key to sigla

AL   *Correspondance de Liszt et de Madame d'Agoult*, ed. D. Ollivier

BHZ   *Briefe hervorragender Zeitgenossen an Franz Liszt*, ed. La Mara

FLB   *Franz Liszts Briefe*, 8 vols., ed. La Mara

GM   *Gazette musicale*, Paris

GS   *Franz Liszt: Gesammelte Schriften*, 6 vols., ed. L. Ramann

JALS   *Journal of the American Liszt Society*

LCA   *Briefwechsel zwischen Liszt und Carl Alexander*, ed. La Mara

LLOM   *The Letters of Franz Liszt to Olga von Meyendorff*

LSJ   *The Liszt Society Journal*

NE   New Edition of the Complete Works. Series I, Works for Piano Solo. 18 vols., Kassel & Budapest, 1970–85.

NHQ   *New Hungarian Quarterly*

SAE   *Liszt Saeculum*

The wonderchild (1811–27)

The genius of Liszt is by its very complex nature hard to define. Claims made for his greatness as pianist, composer, teacher, writer, champion of music old and new, and most generous musical spirit of the nineteenth century are legion. Born in Hungary and yet much nearer to Vienna than to Pest, at home and at work in France, Germany and Italy – he can be claimed by a handful of nations as their son. From Lisbon to Moscow and from Dublin to Constantinople the records speak of his versatility and his victories. The reaction created by genius is, as Marcel Proust put it, 'like those extremely high temperatures which have the power to disintegrate combinations of atoms which they proceed to combine afresh in a diametrically opposite order, following another type'.[1] The traditional opening for the biographer is to explain genius by way of geography.

The little town of Raiding lies in the Austrian Burgenland, a long strip of land on Austria's eastern frontier with Hungary. It is about a hundred kilometres from Vienna and about fifty kilometres from the district capital, Eisenstadt. Prior to 1919 Raiding and Eisenstadt were part of Hungary. Today's visitor to this region of central Europe is confronted with a very different map from that of 1811. At the time of Liszt's birth Raiding was a village in a predominantly sheep-farming area on the estates of the Esterházy family. Its nearest cultural centres were Oedenburg and Eisenstadt. The boy Liszt gave his first public concerts in Oedenburg and Pressburg, both then in Hungary. Today Oedenburg is Sopron in Hungary, Pressburg is Bratislava in Czechoslovakia, and although Raiding and Eisenstadt are now in Austria, the reader may encounter their Hungarian names (Doborján and Kismarton respectively).

This geographical complexity is the consequence of events long after Liszt's death. In his lifetime his birthplace was in Hungary and he reiterated from his years of youthful travel until

[1] Proust, À l'Ombre des Jeunes Filles en Fleurs: 'Elstir'.

his old age of yearly wanderings: 'I am a Hungarian'. In one sense, then, there is no problem of nationality. Yet he did not speak Hungarian, his youth was spent largely in France, his tours as a virtuoso spanned all Europe, he settled in Germany for the middle period of his career, he retired for some years to Rome, and his old age was spent in ceaseless travel between Italy, Germany and Hungary. There is therefore a good case for proclaiming Liszt as the first pan-European, the first internationalist in music. The case is two-fold: his influence upon, and his absorption of, the cultures with which he came into contact.

Hungary did not exist as an independent country during Liszt's lifetime; it remained annexed to Austria. He was born in the near-feudal era that preceded the uprisings of 1848–9. In the wake of that war for national independence a period of severe reaction and retribution set in, only gradually easing before a degree of compromise was instituted in 1867 under the dual monarchy of Austria and Hungary. (The country eventually became independent in 1919.) Also in Liszt's lifetime, France passed through the dictatorship of Napoleon, the restoration monarchy of Louis XVIII and Charles X, the 'citizen kingship' of Louis Philippe, the presidency and Second Empire of Napoleon III, and the Third Republic. Both Italy and Germany achieved unification under King Victor Emmanuel (1860) and Emperor Wilhelm I (1871). When Liszt died the continent was in a condition of relative stability, but through subsequent turbulence of war the Europe and the society he had known were to be thoroughly reshaped.

Liszt's descent on the paternal side is rooted in German-speaking migrants to western Hungary in the late seventeenth century. The earliest identified ancestor is Sebastian List (*c.* 1703–93), a crofter in Ragendorf (today Rajka, Hungary). By his first wife, Anna Maria Roth (1713–86), he had three children of whom Georg Adam List (1755–1844) was the grandfather of Franz Liszt. A glance at the longevity of Liszt's grandfather and great-grandfather indicates a hardy, sturdy stock. But the reality of a harder, more pitiable way of life is evident from the history of the marriages and progeny of this Catholic family. Sebastian, to comfort the last few years of his life, took a second wife when he was about eighty-four. Of the children of the first marriage, one son died in infancy and a daughter, Ursula, married a crofter and day-labourer: their ten children all died in infancy. But Georg Adam List lived to the grand old age of nearly eighty-nine. He in turn had three marriages and produced twenty-five children, most of whom died in infancy.

Liszt's grandfather Georg first married in 1775. He was 19; his bride, Barbara Schlesak, two years younger. Their second son Adam, Franz Liszt's father, was born on 16 December 1776 in Edelsthal, where Georg was schoolmaster from 1774–85. Adam learned music – piano, violin and elementary composition – from his father, who had in turn been trained as cantor, organist and choirmaster to prepare him for the extra duties expected of a schoolmaster in a small community. Around the start of 1787 the family moved to Kittsee, where Georg was village teacher, and from 1795 to 1801 we find them in St. Georgen. Here Adam's mother died, having borne Georg thirteen children. Little more than a month later he remarried.

Meanwhile Adam had left the family fold. From 1790 he studied at the Royal Catholic Gymnasium in Pressburg. After his final examinations he entered a Franciscan order at Malacka near Pressburg, as a novice (21 September 1795). So began the important thread of St. Francis that runs through the lives of Adam and Franz (baptised Franciscus) Liszt. Adam, however, proved unsuited to the life of the cloister: in late July 1797 he was urged to leave on account of his 'unsteady and inconstant nature'. Despite this failure, he never lost his warm attachment to his friends who remained friars in the order. In the autumn following his dismissal, Adam enrolled at the University of Pressburg and was entered in the register of the philosophy faculty as 'Adamus Matthäus Liszt, natio et locus natalis Germanus, Edelsthal, aetas 22'. Note the statement of his German nationality and the spelling of his name: 'List' has become 'Liszt'. Adam, like his father, spoke no Hungarian. German was the language of his home and his education. The change in spelling of the surname 'List', a fairly common German name in the area, was almost certainly made to avoid the Hungarian pronunciation – 'Lischt'.

While studying in Pressburg Adam supplemented his musical knowledge by taking lessons from Franz Paul Riegler. In addition to the piano it seems he was proficient in flute, guitar, violin and cello. Occasionally he joined the cello section of the court orchestra at the Esterházy palace in Eisenstadt and he played under Haydn who, although he had ceased regular duties there in 1790, returned periodically to direct festive events. At the very end of his life Franz wrote of his father's activities of ninety years earlier:

He often took part, as an amateur, among the violoncellos in the prince's frequent court concerts, under the conductorship of the happy great *master* Joseph Haydn. My father often told me about his dealings with Haydn and the daily parties he made up with him.[2]

Shortage of cash drew Adam's university career to a premature close after one term. He had now to find employment and there was only one direction in which he could seek it: the rich and powerful Esterházy family.

In thanks for their part in clearing the realm of the Turks following the siege of Vienna in 1683, the Austrian emperor greatly improved the already high fortunes of the Esterházy family, bestowing large gifts of land, a degree of autonomy and the title of prince for the head of the house. The name of these fabulously wealthy rulers is not principally remembered for their political, diplomatic or military achievements but for the lasting impression they made on the arts through their patronage. Above all Prince Nicholas I (1714–90), called the Magnificent, is immortalised through the life and work of the man who served him as Kapellmeister: Joseph Haydn. In 1764 Nicholas was in Paris as the ambassador of the Empress Maria Theresa. Mightily impressed by Versailles and not content with his own magnificent palace in Eisenstadt, he returned home to build his own Versailles – the palace of Eszterháza (now Fertöd, Hungary). Between these two great houses, Eisenstadt and Eszterháza, Haydn worked to provide music for divertissements of all kinds, while Nicholas attracted to them the artistic and aristocratic lights of Europe. No visit to Vienna was complete without a journey to savour the luxury, the glitter and the grandeur of his hospitality. In 1794 his grandson Nicholas II succeeded to the title. Less musical, but no less expansive and extravagant, this prince reshaped and enlarged the Eisenstadt palace (1794–1805), laid out a fine park and amassed a priceless collection of books and art treasures. Two other anecdotes complete the picture of the power and ostentatiousness of the Esterházys. In 1809 Napoleon invited Nicholas II to accept the throne of Hungary and end the Hapsburg rule: the offer was spurned. And in 1821 at the coronation in London of George IV, the sensation next in significance to the plight of Queen Caroline was the appearance of Prince Paul Esterházy, in a dazzling suit made of diamonds.

[2]FLB, II, 379f.

Adam Liszt obtained a post from Nicholas II, beginning work on 1 January 1798 as an apprentice estate manager in Forchtenau. But his ambitions were set upon Eisenstadt. An appointment there would bring him to the heart of the musical and theatrical life of the court. Accordingly he submitted an application and, to prove that he possessed the culture and musical ability to warrant a post in the capital of the princely domain, sent with it a *Te Deum* of his own composition, scored for 2 oboes, 2 clarinets, 2 horns, 4 trumpets, timpani, strings, mixed chorus and organ. At length his hopes were realised, but four long years elapsed from the date of his application till the happy month of February 1805 when he moved to Eisenstadt.

Less pleasant fortunes attended his father during these years. Georg's abrasive character led to a quarrel with his superiors in St. Georgen and in October 1801 he was removed from his teaching duties there to a post in the lumberyards on the Esterházy estates at Marz. The salary was a pitifully small one to support his ever-growing family. After some time he moved to supervise a sheep farm near Mattersdorf but little more than a year later, in December 1806, his second wife died. With twelve children and no spare time to tend them, Georg married for the third time seven weeks later. This wife bore him seven more children. The tragedy and poverty of Georg's existence was exacerbated by his sloppiness in book-keeping and he was more than once called to task for irregularities in accounts. Over-taxing the horses was another misdemeanour; apparently he took his wife for joy rides all the way to the Vienna Prater in the estate's horse and carriage while pretending to be on official duties. A series of brushes with his employers led to his ultimate dismissal in 1812.

Meanwhile in Eisenstadt Adam had enjoyed the happiest years of his young manhood. Whenever free from his duties as a clerk, he made music, joining the orchestra and singing bass in the choir. An unforgettable experience was taking part in the first performance of Beethoven's Mass in C, conducted by the composer in Eisenstadt on 13 September 1807, the name-day of Princess Marie Esterházy. He formed a friendship with the Kapellmeister, Mozart's pupil Hummel (whom he often joined in a hand of cards), and with his assistant, Johann Nepomuk Fuchs (1766–1839). He may also have met Cherubini who paid a visit shortly after Adam's appointment; and he would certainly have heard with keen interest all news from Vienna about international musical life.

But by the age of thirty-two Adam sought a better paid and more independent position. A post had recently been created at Raiding for an administrator and book-keeper to supervise the Esterházy sheep farms there. Most writers have described Adam's move to Raiding as a banishment from music. But he himself applied for the post; Raiding was only three hours ride from Eisenstadt, from Oedenburg much less; Fuchs and other friends from the court orchestra often visited young Liszt, and thus he was hardly stranded unwillingly in a cultural desert.

Better pay and being the master of his own house (albeit a one-storey tied cottage) were all the more to be valued when in 1810 he became engaged to Anna Maria Lager. Born in Krems, Lower Austria, on 9 May 1788, her parents were Matthias Lager (1715–96), a fairly prosperous baker with a substantial house, and Franziska Romana, née Schuhmann (1752–97), daughter of a Bavarian clockmaker. Thus on his mother's side, too, Franz Liszt's ancestry is Austro-German. Anna was eight when her father died, and six months later was an orphan. The family house was sold to provide for the children and Anna stayed in Krems with relatives until old enough to make her own living, when she moved to Vienna and worked as a chambermaid.

She first met Adam either there or in Mattersdorf, where in 1810 she stayed with a brother employed in soap-manufacture, and where Adam visited his father. They were married in the parish church of Unterfrauenhaid, two miles from Raiding, on 11 January 1811. Anna brought with her a dowry from the Lager estate of 1500 gulden. During the summer, when five months pregnant, the young bride fell down an old well on the estate. Luckily she was only soaked and slightly hurt. There must however have been great anxiety for the safe delivery of the child. But on 22 October a boy, their only child, was born in the cottage at Raiding (preserved today as a Liszt museum). On the next day he was baptised by Father Georg Mersits at Unterfrauenhaid: the parish register names the godparents as Franciscus Zambothy and Julianna Szalay. The latter was the mother of Adolf Frankenburg, childhood playmate of Liszt's and later a well-known Hungarian writer. Records prove that the great comet of 1811 burned bright in the sky just prior to the birth. Legend has it that gypsies camped nearby read this as a sign that a great one had been born.

Franzi, or Zischy, as he was called at home, spent his earliest years in the quiet rural household of a practical, hardworking, dutiful mother and a father who, despite industrious application to his duties supervising income, rents, pensions and the welfare of both workers and livestock on the estate, devoted much of his time to music. Since knowing Hummel, a great keyboard virtuoso, it was the piano that most attracted Adam. His father's playing was the sound most often in the baby's ears, but two other musical influences – church music and the bands of itinerant gypsies – also made an early impression. Franzi caused his parents much anxiety as he was frail and delicate, often subject to fainting fits. Once they thought him dead and even had a coffin made.

Another worry for Adam was the continuing plight of his father. In the summer of 1812, having been dismissed his post, Georg, his wife and their brood descended upon Raiding. But Adam's means were not great enough to provide for his pitiful relations. As a result of entreaties and petitions Georg eventually moved on to various jobs, among them dairy farming at Nebensdorf, then a post in Lower Austria, and finally at the age of sixty-four we find him labouring in a cloth factory in Pottendorf. By 1821 however, his little grandson Franzi had attained such fame that fate finally smiled on the old man. He was appointed organist and choirmaster in Pottendorf and held this post for seventeen years. He and his wife were awarded pensions and so Georg died, not rich, but with dignity. Incidentally, this new degree of prosperity enabled Georg's last child Eduard (1817–79) to acquire an education that was to lead to a most distinguished career. Technically the composer's uncle, but always called 'cousin Eduard' by Liszt, he was a great friend and counsellor in later years.

These rays of fortune had their origin in the events described in Adam's diary.[3] When Franzi was in his sixth year, wrote Adam:

> He heard me play a concerto by Ries in C sharp minor. He leant over the piano and listened with all ears. In the evening he came in from the garden after a short walk, and sang the theme of the concerto. We made him repeat it. He did not know what he was singing. That was the first indication of his genius. He begged unceasingly for me to teach him the piano.

And so Adam became the boy's first teacher. He seems to have fulfilled this role admirably, particularly in his choice of rep-

[3] The diary is lost but parts of it were published in the *Revue et Gazette Musicale*, Paris, 14 June 1835.

ertoire – from a groundwork of Bach to the modern pieces of Beethoven. Beethoven's picture hung on the cottage wall and so from infancy Liszt looked to Beethoven as a model to follow. Franzi made astonishing progress: he had a keen ear, an instinctive grasp of harmony and a remarkably good memory, and was a fluent sight reader. Adam's journal discovers his own frustrated musical career coming to new life:

> My son, you are marked for destiny! You will achieve all the artistic hopes that fascinated me in vain as a youth. What was only a presentiment in me, will in you be fulfilled. The genius, born out of season in me, will in you bear fruit. In you I will again become young and will give forth.

Anecdotes abound of the enthusiasm the boy created. Neighbours gave him a new piano. When frustrated by his inability to stretch a big chord he would bring his head forward and use his nose as an eleventh finger. By 1819 he began to show talent for composition.

With increasing time devoted to music, it is hardly surprising that Liszt's general education was seriously neglected: a lack he felt keenly in later life and then took steps to remedy. He often remarked that he could read musical notation before he learned the alphabet. His teacher at the little *Volksschule* in Raiding was the exclusively German-speaking Johann Rohrer (1783–1868) who was also village sacristan, organist, cantor and clerk. On a visit to his birthplace in 1840 Liszt paid this early mentor handsome thanks for his grounding in the 'three Rs'. On another visit in 1881 Liszt told the story of the old stove, and of how as a youngster he had been fascinated by the contents of his father's gunpowder pouch, used for hunting expeditions. His childish curiosity sought to experiment with a combination of this magical powder and the hot iron stove. The resulting explosion blew the oven apart and threw Franzi to the floor. He was uninjured but soon given a sound thrashing by Adam who hurried home to view the destruction.

A strong religious sense also became apparent during his early years, a trait inherited from Adam the former Franciscan novice. He learned from him the beliefs and rituals of the Catholic faith; they visited the Franciscan community and worshipped regularly at their local parish churches.

Such was the boy's progress by the summer of 1819, when he was nearly eight, that Adam realised the need for a teacher of the first rank. His old acquaintance Hummel would have been a natural choice but he had just moved from Vienna to Weimar, and in any case charged a huge fee for lessons. But there was another teacher in Vienna, a young man but already of great renown: Carl Czerny. Adam humbly petitioned Nicholas II to allow him a transfer to Vienna where he could continue to work for the Esterházys and simultaneously supervise the welfare of his son. This request fell on deaf ears for the moment. However, Adam took Franzi to visit the Austrian capital and asked Czerny to hear him play. The great pedagogue wrote in his memoirs:

> He was a pale sickly-looking child who swayed about on the stool while playing as if he was drunk, so that I often thought he would fall to the ground. His playing too was quite irregular, untidy and confused, and he had such little knowledge of fingering that he simply threw his fingers all over the keyboard in a quite arbitrary way. But despite this, I was astounded at the talent with which Nature had endowed him. He played at sight one or two things I gave him with such a natural instinct, that this showed all the more clearly that here Nature had herself created a pianist. It was just the same when ... I gave him a theme on which to improvise: without the smallest knowledge of harmony, he still put a touch of genius into his delivery.[4]

Czerny gladly agreed to take on the child at a later date and meanwhile gave Adam advice on technical exercises for him. Another appeal was then made to Prince Esterházy who now agreed to hear the boy, indeed interrupted a hunting party in September 1819 to do so. Nicholas was impressed but not yet willing to let Adam leave his post in Raiding. On 13 April the determined father wrote again and pointed out his son's phenomenal achievements: 'In the space of 22 months to overcome with ease all difficulties in Bach, Mozart, Beethoven, Clementi, Hummel, Cramer, etc., and to play the hardest piano pieces at sight, in strict tempo, without mistakes and with precision, is in my musical opinion giant progress.'[5] Adam was firmly set on Vienna and the lessons with Czerny, and if the prince would not respond to his petitions then he would attract support for his young genius from other quarters, through public concerts.

Liszt's first public appearance was in Oedenburg in October 1820, as part of a concert presented by a young blind flautist, Baron Sigismund von Braun. Liszt played a concerto in E flat by

[4] Czerny, *Erinnerungen aus meinem Leben*, Strassburg, 1968, 27f.
[5] Horvath, *Franz Liszt*, I, 46.

Ries and improvised on themes suggested by the audience. The nine-year-old's debut was a triumph and the concert was repeated some days later. The second town to hear him was Pressburg, on 26 November: Liszt, dressed in braided Hungarian costume, created a sensation with his playing. Six Hungarian magnates who were attending a meeting of the Diet in the town (Counts Amadé, Apponyi, Erdödy, Szapáry, Viczay and Michael Esterházy) approached Adam afterwards and offered the boy an annual stipend of 600 florins for the ensuing six years to enable him to study abroad.

During the following eighteen months many a family council must have been held to plan the move to Vienna. The sum offered was barely sufficient and the good businessman Adam took care in the sale of his effects and livestock to supplement the travelling fund, further augmented by their savings, including Anna's dowry. Would the boy's health stand the strain? Would the hopes placed in him be fulfilled? For they were leaving the security of a good job, with food, fuel and a home taken for granted. In Vienna these things had a high price. Young Liszt, patiently guided by his father according to Czerny's instructions, gave them growing confidence. Arrangements had to be made with the prince for Adam's departure and the appointment of a replacement. Most writers assert that the family moved to Vienna in 1821. This was not so: it was the spring of 1822 before all the arrangements were made and young Liszt left his native village with his parents. He was not to see it again for eighteen years, and when he returned he was the most famous living Hungarian.

Czerny, who had been Beethoven's pupil, was the most celebrated Viennese piano teacher of the age. An indefatigable composer of more than a thousand works, the best remembered being his hundreds of valuable studies and exercises, he brought to his teaching the same energy and painstaking care for perfection. With the ten-year-old Liszt he was assiduous in imposing a hitherto unknown discipline on his playing – a dose of mechanical medicine which the boy resented at first but later greatly appreciated. Czerny recalled:

> I never had such a diligent, gifted and ardent pupil. As I knew from previous experience that just such geniuses, whose gifts of mind outstrip their physical strength, neglect to take care of a thorough technical grounding, it seemed to me above all necessary to make use of the first few months to regulate and to strengthen his physical

dexterity so that he would never take a wrong path in later years. In a short time he played the scales in every key with all the masterly fluency which his fingers, very favourably shaped for piano playing, permitted. Through a study of the Clementi sonatas ... I got him accustomed to keeping strict time, previously a deficiency, to a fine attack and beautiful tone, to the correct fingering and proper musical phrasing, although these pieces seemed academic and dry at first to the exceptionally lively boy. This method produced the result that when, a few months later, we studied the works of Hummel, Ries, Moscheles and then Beethoven and Bach, it was no longer necessary to keep an eye on the mechanical rules, but we could enter at once into the spirit and style of these very different authors. Because he had to learn each piece very quickly he acquired the ability to read at sight very difficult works as if he had studied them a long time.[6]

Czerny taught Liszt for about a year from May 1822, and never charged him a fee. The two men later corresponded and Liszt always praised his teacher's outstanding qualities.

For composition lessons Liszt went to the veteran Antonio Salieri, distinguished composer and former teacher of Beethoven, Moscheles and Schubert. He too taught Liszt free of charge and wrote a petition on the boy's behalf in August 1822 urging Prince Esterházy to help the family find accommodation in central Vienna as he feared for the delicate condition of his pupil making the long journeys from his lodgings in Mariahilf in all weathers. By October, when the Liszts moved to the inner city (conveniently to the street in which Czerny lived, Krugerstrasse), his lessons with both teachers were on a daily basis. Salieri's tuition included score reading and analysis. A *Tantum ergo*, now lost, was a product of this period but another work of 1822 exists as Liszt's first published composition. That year the publisher Diabelli invited fifty composers to contribute a variation upon a humble little waltz he had composed. A fifty-first composer spurned the suggestion, but shortly afterward published his own set of thirty-three variations on the waltz. That work, Beethoven's opus 120, ranks as one of the greatest variation sets of all time. Diabelli's collaborative publication ranks merely as a curiosity; a fascinating miscellany of the styles of the period with contributions by a few names that are remembered: Czerny, Hummel, Kalkbrenner, Schubert, Sechter, Tomášek and the youngest of the composers – 'Liszt Franz

[6] Czerny, op. cit., 28.

(a boy of 11 years) born in Hungary'. The boy's variation is a
bravura exercise straight from the world of Czerny's schoolroom.

Liszt's Viennese debut took place on 1 December 1822 in the
town hall when he appeared with two other young artists: the
singer Caroline Unger (1803–77) and the violinist Léon de Saint-
Lubin (1805–50). It was the little pianist who stole the show,
particularly with his performance of Hummel's A minor concerto.
'A young virtuoso has again dropped from the clouds and compels
us to the highest admiration' wrote the correspondent of a Leipzig
musical paper, who ended his review: '*Est Deus in nobis*'. Rossini
was all the rage at that time: Mlle Unger sang an aria by him
and Liszt improvised on a theme from his new opera *Zelmira*,
combining it with the andante theme of Beethoven's Seventh Symphony.

Rossini was greatly to interest Liszt in the next few years. But
his own 'Deus in nobis' remained Beethoven. With his father, he
called on the great man. In the conversation books of the deaf
composer there is an entry (probably written for Franz by Adam):
'I have often expressed the wish to Herr von Schindler [Beethoven's
secretary] to make your high acquaintance and am rejoiced to be
able now to do so. As I shall give a concert on Sunday the 13th, I
most humbly beg you to give me your high presence.'[7] The reference is to Liszt's final Vienna concert in April 1823. The young
virtuoso's name appears several times in the conversation book.
Schindler asked Beethoven on Liszt's behalf for a theme on which
to improvise at the concert.

The long-deaf Beethoven was virtually unapproachable by
visitors; he also had a deep antipathy to child prodigies. Nor was
he in the habit of attending concerts. The notoriously unreliable
Schindler gave different accounts of the episode in the first and
third editions of his Beethoven biography, finally stating that
Beethoven did not attend the concert. Indeed most recent commentators have concluded that he did not. Certainly he did not
supply Liszt with any theme on which to improvise. But Liszt
never denied the truth of the story which became current that
Beethoven climbed upon the stage at the end of the concert, lifted
him in his arms and kissed him. This *Weihekuss*, the master's kiss
of consecration, is a vexed issue in the Liszt literature. d'Ortigue,
Ramann and La Mara, the scholar Ludwig Nohl and Liszt's pupil
Göllerich all maintain that Beethoven attended the concert. Göl-

[7] *Ludwig van Beethovens Konversationshefte*, III, Leipzig, 1983, 168.

lerich quotes Liszt's words: 'Beethoven appeared at my second Viennese concert for Czerny's sake and kissed me on the forehead. I never played at his house but I visited him twice. There was a piano with torn-out strings there.'[8] As Sitwell remarked, Liszt's personal testimony cannot be lightly contradicted and the *Weihekuss*, whether it took place in private or in public, 'was the consecration so to speak of Liszt's career, and . . . his extraordinary life, that extended over nearly the whole of the nineteenth century, would not be complete if he had not known Beethoven'.[9]

Liszt's veneration for Beethoven led him to become the foremost nineteenth-century exponent of his piano music (especially the late sonatas) and his last three concertos. With Berlioz and Habeneck he must be given credit for introducing Beethoven's music in an unadulterated form to Paris. Through his pupil Hans von Bülow this Beethoven tradition was extended for a further generation. Liszt's transcriptions of Beethoven rank among his most important arrangements and include the nine symphonies, the septet, three concertos and many songs. His devotion to his spiritual mentor is illustrated by his cherished possession of Beethoven's Broadwood piano. He also owned Joseph Danhauser's death mask of Beethoven and, for a time, the Heiligenstadt Testament. One of his greatest tributes to Beethoven was his part in bringing about the Bonn monument to her most famous son, which still stands today. Interestingly there is no evidence to prove that Liszt met the other contemporary Viennese composer for whose works he was later to be so ardent an ambassador – Franz Schubert.

Liszt gave other concerts in Vienna, mostly of a private or semi-private nature. Among the notables who befriended him an important contact for Adam was the powerful Prince Metternich, Chancellor of Austria, who was to supply letters of reference for the boy's future travels. Adam, with the classical precedent of Mozart always in his mind as a triumphant example, now determined to take Franz in the footsteps of Wolfgang Amadeus: through Germany to Paris and then to London.

Before beginning the great westward tour however, an important visit was made to Pest so that the boy could say farewell to the capital of his homeland. Adam emerges as a concert manager of surefire diplomacy; a victory in Pest would guarantee that his

[8] Göllerich, *Franz Liszt*, 160. See also LSJ, VIII, 1983.
[9] Sitwell, *Liszt*, 11.

son was viewed everywhere else as the artistic ambassador of Hungary who brought glory to his native land. Posters in German lined the streets of Pest:

> High and gracious nobility! Praiseworthy officers of the Royal and Imperial Army! Honourable members of the public! I am Hungarian and know no greater joy than to offer my homeland, before I set out for France and England, the first fruits of my learning, as a first pledge of my heartfelt gratitude and devotion.[10]

Reviewing the concert of 1 May a Hungarian newspaper took up the theme:

> This handsome blonde youth displayed such skill, lightness, accuracy, feeling and strength, such signs of mastery that the whole audience was delighted and astounded. Everyone was filled with the hope that, through his splendid playing, he will bring honour to his fatherland.[11]

It is said that instead of people greeting each other in the street with a 'good morning' or 'good evening' the phrase on every lip was 'Have you heard the little *Wunderkind* yet?' The great impression made by his first appearance in Pest led to four further concerts before he left for Pressburg to give another performance on 27 May.

In chronicling Liszt's ever-widening repertoire it is noteworthy that his Pest concert of 19 May included Weber's *Momento Capriccioso* op. 12 and an improvisation on the *Rákóczy March*.[12] This march, one of the most famous pieces of Hungarian music, is closely connected with the proudest chapters of the nation's history. Its origins and development are complex but have their roots in the national uprising against the Hapsburgs (1703–11) led by Ferenc Rákóczi II. By the time of Liszt's youth the tune attracted a patriotic fervour which was as inflammatory as the sentiments evoked by the *Marseillaise*. The composer later made several arrangements of the march and this early performance shows how deeply it was rooted in him. Another source of Liszt's enthusiasm for popular Hungarian melody was the gypsy violinist-composer and leader of a well-known band, János Bihari (1764–1827), whom he met in Vienna in 1822. Bihari's interpretative skill left on the

[10] Horvath, op. cit., 89ff.
[11] Domestic and foreign reports, 3 May 1823.
[12] Walker, *Franz Liszt: the virtuoso years*, 87n.

boy a deep impression which was fully recalled decades later in his book *The Gypsies and their music in Hungary*: 'I have not only retained an impression of his inspirations, but they must have distilled into my soul like the essence of some generous and exhilarating wine.' He never lost this wonder for the qualities of dreamily free improvisation, rich ornamentation and sparkling fury that he admired in the playing of Bihari and in the gypsy bands that camped on the hillside near Raiding in his earliest childhood. He wrote of his longing to hear them again when he returned to Hungary: those rhythms and harmonies that seemed almost to emanate from another planet, so unlike were they to anything else in his European musical experience.

The family left Vienna en route for Paris on 20 September 1823. Following Mozart's route, Liszt gave concerts in Munich, Augsburg, Stuttgart and Strassburg. The famous pianist Moscheles was in Munich: Liszt heard him play but waited until his departure before making his own first appearance. The comparison with the recently heard Moscheles was in Liszt's favour. On being presented to the Bavarian king, His Majesty asked 'And you, little one, have dared to play after Moscheles?' The *Augsburger Allgemeine Zeitung* was also impressed:

> A new Mozart has appeared among us. That prodigy we know was only seven years old when he attracted the admiration of the world by his artistic talent. It is true that young Liszt is now four years older. But when one considers the difference in the times and the demands the public now makes on artists, one has to admit that we are justified in exclaiming: 'a new Mozart has appeared' ... We have heard Hummel and Moscheles and are not afraid to assert that this child is not a whit inferior to them in performance.[13]

After his Stuttgart performance the *Schwäbischer Merkur* reported:

> Facility, expression, precision, interpretation, etc., in fact all qualities which denote an exceptional pianist are possessed by this boy to a high degree. He has also a profound knowledge of counterpoint and fugal structure which he displayed in a free fantasia for which a local artist had given him a written theme at the end of the concert. All this justifies the claim that this boy already ranks among the first pianists of Europe, perhaps already surpassing many of them.[14]

[13] Horvath, op. cit., 98f.
[14] ibid., 100.

The Liszts arrived in Paris on 11 December, an unwelcoming wintry day. Promptly next morning they presented themselves at the Conservatoire to meet the imposing director Luigi Cherubini. Franz was extremely nervous, but Adam was confident that his former connection with Eisenstadt and his letter of introduction from the mighty Metternich would open any door. Cherubini received them formally and gave his answer: the piano classes of the Conservatoire were over-subscribed and the rules forbade him to admit any foreigners. The interview was over; Liszt was turned away.

Other doors quickly opened in the French capital however. By good fortune the family had rented rooms in an hotel opposite which lived the piano manufacturer Sébastien Erard and his family. This leading instrument maker had lately perfected and patented the 'double-escapement' piano action, an important development which enabled notes to be very rapidly repeated by the player without the key having to return fully to the keyboard surface. Sébastian and his nephew Pierre were to prove invaluable friends of Liszt. They presented him with one of their new seven-octave grands, and Adam arranged a mutually beneficial business deal by which Erard would supply pianos in advance to Franz's tour destinations, and the boy's much publicised concerts would promote the firm's products wherever he played.

Within weeks of the young prodigy's arrival he was the subject of glowing press articles; within months Parisian journals rivalled each other in the chorus of eulogy. He was elected an honorary member of the Société Académique des Enfants d'Apollon. He attended thirty-six elegant soirées in three months, was lionised by society ladies, and among his patrons were the Duc d'Orléans (later King Louis Philippe) and the Duchesse de Berry in whose house he played to the royal family. Franz Gall, the inventor of phrenology, took a cast of his head for study. Prints of him appeared in shop windows and an original portrait hung in the Louvre. Advertisements for his public debut on 7 March 1824 heralded him as 'the wonder of the day'. The concert itself at the Théâtre Italien was his greatest achievement to date and the ovations seemed endless. Next day the critic of *Le Drapeau Blanc* declared himself a believer in the transmigration of souls and hailed Liszt as the reincarnation of the soul and spirit of Mozart. The only faint dimming of the radiance of his success was the inability of the French to get his name right. They tried every permutation of List, Leist, Listz – and eventually he was dubbed 'le petit Litz'.

Adam could not turn back now: London was the next port of call. Pierre Erard accompanied Franz and Adam on their first visit to England in May 1824 and they stayed at Erard's London premises in Great Marlborough Street. On 5 June he played for the first time at a gathering of the Royal Society of Musicians in the Argyll Rooms and, after a few private appearances, he gave his public debut in the same hall on 21 June before a distinguished company of composers and pianists, including Clementi, Cramer, Kalkbrenner, Cipriani Potter and Ries, the conductor being Sir George Smart. Playbills for another concert on 29 June at the Theatre Royal Drury Lane announced that 'For this Night only, the incomparable Master Liszt has in the most flattering manner consented to display his inimitable powers on the New Patent Grand Piano Forte invented by Sébastien Erard'. At the end of July he played to George IV at Windsor, pieces by Handel and Mozart, and at the king's request improvised on the minuet from *Don Giovanni*. The warm reception at Windsor was arranged by the Austrian ambassador, Nicholas II's son, Paul Esterházy. The visit ended with two concerts at the Theatre Royal, Manchester (2 and 4 August), where for once the twelve-year-old Liszt was outshone by a 'baby harpist', the Infant Lyra, 'not yet four years old'.

Father and son returned immediately to France and from Adam's many letters to Czerny it is clear that during the English tour and afterwards Franz had been busy with composition. Late in 1824 he became the pupil of Ferdinando Paer (an arrangement effected by a letter from Metternich, formerly Austrian ambassador in Paris). The works of this period which survive are bravura pieces designed to display his extraordinary ability and include the *Huit Variations* (published in Paris, 1825, as his opus 1) and the *Sept Variations brillantes sur un thème de G. Rossini* (published in London and Paris, 1824, as his opus 2). An opera was also begun and Paer encouraged this particular project, *Don Sanche, ou le Château d'Amour*, and assisted with the instrumentation.

Some Paris concerts in the Spring of 1825 were followed by a second English tour in June. Again Liszt played to the king at Windsor and at Drury Lane Theatre, and made another visit to Manchester where his 'New Grand Overture' was performed – undoubtedly that to *Don Sanche*. At a private concert in London an amusing incident occurred when a flautist, Mr. Nicholson, was about to play a composition of his own accompanied by Cipriani Potter. The piano was found to be a semitone flat. Nicholson could not flatten his flute and Potter would not risk a transposition from C major to C sharp. An embarrassing deadlock ensued until Potter asked Liszt if he could transpose. Without delay the boy sat at the piano and played the work at sight, transposed into the difficult key, even improving the accompaniment here and there.

After a short break in Boulogne-sur-Mer 'to wash away the exertions of England' they were back in Paris, when suddenly a request arrived for the score of *Don Sanche* for scrutiny by the jury of the Académie Royale within eight days. After a hectic effort of copying, the work was duly submitted and the jury (including Cherubini and Boieldieu) declared themselves satisfied: the première was announced for 17 October, just before Liszt's fourteenth birthday. The boy took a lively interest in the rehearsals, in the interpretation of the conductor Rudolphe Kreutzer, and in the tenor who sang the role of the eponymous hero – Adolphe Nourrit (later a close friend). *Don Sanche* was cast in one act by its librettists who based the story on one by the French writer of fairy tales Claris de Florian (1755–94). The aim of the authors would seem to have been to provide Liszt with an opportunity for writing effective music in every possible dramatic context: chivalrous love music, a romantic serenade, a thunderstorm, a spirited jealousy duet, Cupid descending from the clouds, a sleep aria, an attempted abduction, a duel, a funeral march, village merrymaking, ballets and interludes. Cluttered into a conventional and simply framed plot, this opera illustrates a healthy melodic gift and his absorption of the Italian-French idioms from the time of Gluck. It was indulgently received for a mere four evenings. The score was long thought to be lost but was rediscovered in 1903. It was to be Liszt's only opera and as such remains a youthful curiosity; but later we will find his thoughts turning to many operatic projects, all destined to remain incomplete.

At some point late in 1825 Liszt's mother returned to Graz in Austria to stay with a sister. Little is known about Anna in these years; only later in Liszt's life through correspondence and involvement with his children do we learn more about her solid, sensible and kindly nature. It may have been that she felt out of her depth socially in the glamorous world in which her little boy now moved. Sadly she was never to see her husband again.

Early in 1826 Liszt toured to Bordeaux, Toulouse, Montpellier, Nîmes, Avignon, Aix, Marseilles and Toulon. After a triumphant appearance in Lyon there were the first press references to his magnetic attraction for female members of the audience. Late in the year he visited Switzerland, touring from Dijon to Geneva, Lausanne, Berne, Lucerne and Basel. But the most significant event of the year was his period of study with the composer Antonín Reicha. Liszt had met him briefly, shortly after his arrival in Paris, and it is possible that Adam had long ago encountered him in Esterházy circles (Reicha was in Vienna from 1802 to 1808). Childhood friend of Beethoven, teacher of Berlioz and later of Gounod and Franck, Reicha is principally remembered for his chamber works for woodwind. But in the realms of orchestration and counterpoint he was a revolutionary. His experiments in string and woodwind scoring, also with chords for timpani, influenced Berlioz. His thirty-six fugues for piano (dedicated to Haydn) exploit unconventional key relationships between subjects and answers, widely leaping parts, and an example of quintuple metre (Fugue no. 20) which was derived from Lower Rhine folk dances. How many of Reicha's unconventional ideas on tonality, melody and instrumental layout penetrated to Liszt we may never know. But it is not too fanciful to see his influence on the extraordinary little piece in G minor (entitled *Scherzo* in Busoni's edition) which Liszt wrote during another visit to London in May 1827 (see Ex. 1).

This third and final London visit of Liszt's boyhood evoked a pen sketch by Charles Salaman:

> I visited him and his father at their lodgings in Frith Street, Soho, and young Liszt came to early dinner at my home. He was a very charmingly natural and unaffected boy, and I have never forgotten his joyful exclamation, 'Oh, gooseberry pie!' when his favourite dish was put upon the table. We had a good deal of music together on that memorable afternoon ... Liszt played some of his recently published *Études* ...[15]

These Études are the most important of his early compositions and are the basis of the later *Transcendental Études* (1837; revised 1851). They may date from as early as 1824 and were published in Paris in 1826 as *Étude en 48 Exercices dans tous les Tons Majeurs et Mineurs*, although only twelve studies appeared. Remarkably

[15] Huneker, *Franz Liszt*, 305.

Ex. 1

Allegro molto quasi presto

skilful products for a boy of fourteen, they are in themselves worthy of study and are the best introduction for players of the later set of Études (with which they will be discussed in Chapter 11).

His concert in the Argyll Rooms on 9 June 1827 included a Piano Concerto in A minor which, along with another early concerto by Liszt referred to in Adam's letters to Czerny, is lost. Moscheles attended the performance and wrote of the concerto's 'chaotic beauties; as to his playing it surpasses in power and mastery of difficulties everything I have ever heard'.[16] The concert ended with 'Master Liszt's Brilliant Variations on *Rule Britannia*'.

Father and son stopped again in Boulogne to recuperate after their English visit. Here tragedy struck. Adam had contracted

[16] *Aus Moscheles Leben*, Leipzig, 1872–3, I, 138.

typhoid fever and he died on 28 August. A letter urgently written by Franz to his mother in Austria, warning her of the seriousness of the illness and of the possible need for her to come to France, arrived too late. Adam was buried in a cemetery on the outskirts of the town. (During the First World War his remains were disinterred and reburied in a mass grave.) According to a letter of Liszt's old age, Adam on his deathbed

> told me my heart was good and I didn't lack intelligence, but he feared that women would trouble and dominate my life. This premonition was strange for, when sixteen years old, I had no idea of what a woman was – and in my simplicity I asked my confessor to explain to me the sixth and ninth Commandments, as I was afraid that I might have broken them unwittingly.[17]

Franz had lost not only a father but, leaving aside the prophetic claims of the last quotation, a man of far-sighted and sure business acumen who had devoted twenty years to a single task: the guiding and shaping of the career of his wonderfully gifted only son. Firm and ambitious, but never unkind or selfishly greedy, his hand had led Franz on a blazing path of success from an obscure corner of eastern Europe to the highest acclaim of the most cultured capital cities. He had also instilled in him a religious reverence for his art which would never die. But now Liszt stood alone: he was not yet sixteen.

[17] FLB, VII, 82.

2

Years of pilgrimage (1828–39)

Anna Liszt joined her son in Paris and they set up home in Montmartre. A decade later Liszt described his revulsion for the career of the travelling prodigy:

> When death robbed me of my father and I returned to Paris alone, I began to foresee what art *could* become and what the artist *must* become; and I was overwhelmed by the awareness of insuperable obstacles all around me which barred the direction that my thoughts led me. Above all, finding no sympathetic word from any kindred soul ... I developed a bitter aversion to art as I saw it: more or less debased to the level of trade for profit, labelled as a source of amusement for fashionable society. I would rather have done anything else in the world than be a musician in the service of a great lord, patronised and paid like a juggler or a performing dog.[1]

Although written retrospectively, these lines indicate that he had become aware of the inferior position of performing artists. In certain salons they were roped off from the guests and they arrived and departed by the servants' stairs. Still, in April 1828 Liszt appeared at least eight times before the public and took part in an eight-hand performance of Beethoven's Seventh Symphony.

Teaching became his principal source of income and there were plenty daughters of the aristocracy eager to become his pupils. Soon his peripatetic existence began to lack discipline: he practised at odd hours, his lessons were of unequal length and at varying times; he would slip into a coffee house or meet friends rather than take a proper lunch; he would arrive home late and hungry and revive himself with wine or spirits as his long-suffering mother re-heated his supper. The pedagogue's life re-emphasised his humble status in circumstances that profoundly upset and shocked him. One of his pupils, Caroline de Saint-Cricq, a girl of his own age and daughter of a government minister, soon began

[1] GS, II, 127f.

to receive more visits than the others and lessons became progressively longer. They read the poetry of Chénier, Hugo and Lamartine together, and Caroline's ailing mother, watching over this tender friendship, reputedly pleaded with her husband 'If they love one another, let them be happy'. But the Comte de Saint-Cricq adhered to the traditions of the *ancien régime*. When his butler, whom Liszt had failed to tip, complained of the very late hour at which the pianist left the house, Liszt was barred from further meetings with Caroline and the unhappy girl was soon married off to a member of the only class her father considered suitable: Bernard, Comte d'Artigaux – a landowner at Pau.

Liszt never forgot Caroline. He met her again while on a tour in 1844 and dedicated to her his arrangements of folk tunes of Béarn (*Faribolo Pastour* and *Chanson du Béarn*). One of his most memorable songs of farewell, *Ich möchte hingehn*, was inspired by their bitter-sweet re-encounter. In 1860, when making his will, he bequeathed her a ring. In deep depression in 1828, he suffered a nervous collapse and by his own account[2] fell ill for two years, thrusting himself into a crisis of religious fervour. He frequently lay on the damp stone floor of his church, Saint-Vincent-de-Paul, in ecstatic prayer. A longing to enter the priesthood was resisted by both his mother and his confessor. Cataleptic attacks such as he had experienced as a child returned and the rumour of his death went abroad, *Le Corsaire* even printing his obituary on 23 October. Shop windows exhibited his boyish portrait with the words 'Né le 22 Octobre 1811, mort à Paris 1828'.

At the end of the year Wilhelm von Lenz arrived in Paris, intending to take lessons from Kalkbrenner. He was distracted by a poster announcing a performance by Liszt of Beethoven's E flat concerto. Anyone playing the music of this legendary titan in Paris was certain to be of a different breed from Kalkbrenner. So Lenz made for the Liszt residence.

> He was at home. That was a great rarity, said his mother, an excellent woman with a true German heart, who pleased me very much; her Franz was almost always in church and no longer occupied himself with music at all. In Liszt I found a pale haggard young man with infinitely attractive features. He was on a broad sofa, lost in thought and smoking a long Turkish pipe. Three pianos stood nearby. He made not the slightest movement on my entrance but rather appeared not to notice me at all. When I explained to him

[2] Ibid., 128.

that my family had directed me to Kalkbrenner but I came to *him* because he dared play a concerto by Beethoven in public, he seemed to smile. But it was only as the glint of a dagger in the sunlight.[3]

One of the three pianos had a specially heavy touch; a device ordered by Liszt so that he could 'play ten scales when he played one'.

That Liszt no longer occupied himself with music was not true. A letter of 23 December 1829 speaks of 'so many lessons that each day, from 8.30 in the morning till 10 at night, I have scarcely breathing time'.[4] But in the years 1828 to 1830 he partially withdrew into a realm of gloom and resignation and fed his spirit with literature imbued with *le mal du siècle*: Chateaubriand's *René*, Benjamin Constant's *Adolphe* and Senancour's *Obermann* – all pervaded with melancholy. He explored mystical theology, Byron's poetry and further curious admixtures of secular and sacred themes: Montaigne and Lamennais, Voltaire and Lamartine. A close friend was the strange figure Chrétien Urhan, violinist and mystic. The composer of works of a personal, romantic tendency (entitled *Auditions*), ardent lover of Beethoven, Weber and Schubert, organist at Liszt's church and most devout of Catholics, he was designed to attract Franz's friendship. His favourite instrument was the viola d'amore – extremely unusual for the period but characteristically individual. Always dressed in light blue in honour of the Blessed Virgin, Urhan sat with his back to the stage during the ballets at the Opéra so that he never saw the abominations of female dancing.

The years following his father's death saw a dearth of compositions by Liszt. One work of 1829, a *Grande Fantaisie* on the 'Tyrolienne' from Auber's *La fiancée*, illustrates his re-awakened interest in the theatre and his uncompromisingly virtuoso style. Another stimulating opera, Rossini's *William Tell*, was premièred in Paris on 3 August 1829 and its theme of patriotism, liberty and deliverance of the oppressed greatly attracted him. A year later he was penning the words *indignation, vengeance, liberté*, on a work of his own. In the 'three glorious days', 27 to 29 July 1830, the cannons roared and Liszt stirred from his lassitude to share in the spirit of revolution. The autocratic Charles X fled to England: the citizen kingship of Louis Philippe began. 'The guns cured him' was Anna's comment on her son's awakening. Europe seemed to

[3] Lenz, *Die grossen Pianoforte-Virtuosen unserer Zeit*, Berlin, 1872, 8–12.
[4] FLB, I, 4f.

24

be grasping a new future, and this thought prompted his sketch of a *Revolutionary Symphony* in which he scrawled feverish themes and words of fervour which expire in a heat of *enthousiasme, enthousiasme, enthousiasme!*

A new generation of writers, artists and musicians emerged in the wake of *Les Trois Glorieuses*. Their means of expression and their enthusiasm may seem naive today, but there is no doubting their fervour. Liszt's circle of friends soon included leading spirits of the Romantic literary movement. He admired the theme of liberty in the works of Hugo; the heroic gusto of Dumas *père*; the humanitarianism of Eugène Sue; the acute satire and social observation of Balzac; the infectious Romanticism of Gautier; the aristocratic de Vigny, poet of disillusion and solitude; the passionate personal mysticism of Lamartine; the sensuality of de Musset; the brothers Deschamps who mirrored European poetry in their translations; the influential Goethe-translator Gérard de Nerval; the poet-novelist Sainte-Beuve who turned literary critic; and George Sand whose first successful novel, *Indiana*, asserted a woman's right to love and independence. The political hopes of the citizen kingship proved a dead letter but the era witnessed an immensely prolific literary and artistic revolution. Liberal refugees from oppressed nations flocked to France: the Italian patriot Princess Belgiojoso, the Polish poet Mickiewicz, the German-Jewish writer Heine. The hostesses of the Faubourg Saint-Germain and the Faubourg Saint-Honoré vied with one another to create salons of the liveliest and most stimulating *literati*. They were joined by painters, Delacroix, the Devérias, Ary Scheffer; by stars of the Opéra, Malibran, Pasta, Rubini, Nourrit; by great names of the stage, Lemaître, Rachel and Marie Dorval; by composers, Rossini, Bellini, Donizetti, Meyerbeer and Halévy.

Amidst this galaxy Liszt found himself fêted as virtuoso and as handsome young dandy. Life was a curious mixture of social intoxication and social concern. By October 1830 he regularly attended meetings of the foremost group of religious humanitarians, the Saint-Simonists, and came to know their leader, Prosper Enfantin. Only in his last years did the Comte de Saint-Simon attract a group of young followers who, on his death in 1825, took up his neglected ideas of abolishing privilege of birth, inherited land and income from peasant labour; of ending economic competition and establishing co-operation and classless solidarity. A reform of the banking system to enhance industrial growth was an essential tenet. These early idealistic socialists saw the role of the artist as servant of the new society. The growing movement underwent a change in emphasis around 1828–30 when, taking their cue from Saint-Simon's last essay, *Le Nouveau Christianisme*, the members formed a religious hierarchy. They viewed the artist as a priest-figure who would persuade people, classes and governments to abandon traditional rivalries and to work jointly in a spirit of association.[5] Liszt's consciousness of the social inferiority of the artist (rooted in his child-prodigy travels and his experience in the Saint-Cricq household) together with his absorbing interest in the connection between music and religion, found tangible expression in the doctrines of Saint-Simon. Other musicians (Berlioz, Nourrit, Félicien David) and many of his literary friends (Sainte-Beuve, Heine, Sand) were much affected by the movement. But the essence of its creed touched Liszt most profoundly and may be viewed as a motto of his life: seeking a new role for the artist in a society that treats art as an ephemeral luxury, not as a serious expression of the spirit. The Saint-Simonian movement degenerated and disintegrated, assisted by a series of trumped up charges brought by the government. Liszt dissociated himself from the scandals and fanatical excesses of the sect in its heady last days and often stressed that he was never an actual member. But his denials must be viewed in the light of the opprobrium and public ridicule Saint-Simonism evoked in its decline. Its basic tenets resounded deeply within him. In his copy of Ramann's *Franz Liszt* (1880) the elderly composer noted in the margin these maxims of Saint-Simon:

> All social institutions must aim at improving the moral and material condition of the most populous and poorest class.

> To all according to their abilities, and all according to their means.[6]

Liszt and his mother moved to the rue de Provence where he continued teaching an endless but lucrative procession of fashionable young ladies. Caroline Boissier, mother of one such girl, kept a detailed account of Liszt's lessons (December 1831 to March 1832). This diary of Valérie Boissier's dutiful parent is one of the most readable accounts of Liszt's methods and style of teaching. It is of value to today's student with descriptions of his recommended

---

[5] R. P. Locke, 'Liszt's Saint-Simonian Adventure', *19th Century Music*, IV/3, 1981.
[6] Raabe, *Leben*, 205.

exercises, studies in flexibility and finger equalisation. It is refreshing to read hints such as singing a passage to feel its natural phrasing, or his teaching by metaphor:

> We found that with Liszt, Bach's fugues were to music what the gothic style is to architecture. All these parts that spring, clash, meet, cross, mingle and yet constitute a regular whole, are the fine and marvellous lacings which make up, taken as a whole, such magnificent cathedrals. In the fugues all these phrases must be expressed, felt, played with clarity . . .[7]

There are reflections on his character too. He is a wonderful teacher: kindly, frank and tirelessly patient in correcting a nuance. Yet sometimes he is not witty or benign, but whimsical, quibbling and rough. We receive sudden insights into his deeper concerns:

> He struggles with a suffering nature and so he analyses the language of all pains. He visits hospitals, gambling casinos, asylums for the insane. He goes down into dungeons, and he has even seen those condemned to die! He is a young man who thinks a great deal, who dreams, who excuses everything; his brain is as trained, as extraordinary as his fingers – and had he not been a skilled musician, he would have been a philosopher or a distinguished literary figure.[8]

The four essential influences on Liszt's musical nature in these years were Berlioz, Paganini, Chopin and Fétis. According to his *Memoirs* Berlioz first met Liszt on the eve of the première of the *Symphonie fantastique*. 'I spoke of Goethe's *Faust*, which he confessed he had not read, but which he soon came to love as much as I.'[9] After the concert (5 December 1830) Liszt 'literally dragged me off to have dinner at his house and overwhelmed me with the vigour of his enthusiasm'.[10] A firm friendship was cemented and Liszt was one of the very few outside his family that Berlioz addressed with the intimate 'tu'. The orchestral score of the *Symphonie fantastique* did not appear until 1845, but in 1834 Liszt (at his own expense) published his transcription of it – an extraordinary feat of symphonic piano writing and an invaluable task of propaganda for his friend. It may seem strange that a work so associated with instrumental colour and effect should make its way in the world through a piano 'reduction', but this full and

[7] Transl. by E. Mach, *The Liszt Studies*, New York, 1973.
[8] ibid.
[9] Berlioz, *Memoirs* (transl. D. Cairns), 166.
[10] Berlioz to his father, 6 Dec 1830.

faithful rendering of the orchestral textures, with all the scoring indicated, was the text on which Schumann based his lengthy, influential review (1835). Charles Hallé heard Liszt give a memorable performance of one movement:

> At an orchestral concert ... conducted by Berlioz the 'Marche au supplice' from the 'Symphonie fantastique', that most gorgeously instrumented piece, was performed, at the conclusion of which Liszt sat down and played his own arrangement, for the piano alone, of the same movement, with an effect even surpassing that of the full orchestra and creating an indescribable furore.[11]

Liszt made other important arrangements of Berlioz: *Harold in Italy*, the overtures *Les Francs-juges* and *King Lear* and his first extant work for piano and orchestra, a *Grande fantaisie symphonique* on themes from *Lélio*.

Paganini, that tall, gaunt wizard, with his pale, cadaverous features, lank dark hair, sunken eyes and uncannily sinister reputation, cast a spell over Parisian musical life following his first appearance there on 9 March 1831. When Liszt heard him the achievements of his own twenty years seemed as nought: he strove like a madman to re-create on the piano the same degree of transcendental virtuosity that Paganini displayed on the violin.

> For a whole fortnight my mind and my fingers have been working like two damned souls: Homer, the Bible, Plato, Locke, Byron, Hugo, Lamartine, Chateaubriand, Beethoven, Bach, Hummel, Mozart, Weber, are all around me. I study them, meditate on them, devour them with fury; in addition I practise four to five hours of exercises (3rds, 6ths, octaves, tremolos, repeated notes, cadenzas, etc.). Ah! provided I don't go mad you will find an artist in me! ... 'And I too am a painter!' cried Michelangelo the first time he saw a masterpiece. Your friend ... cannot stop repeating those words of the great man ever since Paganini's last performance ... What a man, what a violin, what an artist! Heavens! what sufferings, what misery, what tortures in those four strings![12]

The immediate product of this frame of mind was the grand fantasy on *La Clochette* of Paganini, a work of almost superhuman difficulty and the ancestor of the well-known *Campanella* study in the Paganini Études (1838, revised 1851). The other studies of

[11] Hallé, *Autobiography*, 57.
[12] FLB, I, 7f. Correggio, not Michelangelo, made the remark on seeing Raphael's 'St. Cecilia'.

that set draw on Paganini's 24 Caprices for solo violin, and are models of what the art of transcription should be: a re-creation in terms of another instrument, not just of the notes and harmonies, but of the texture and technical difficulty of the original.

Chopin's Paris debut on 26 February 1832 was attended by Liszt along with many other composers and pianists: Mendelssohn, Pixis, the Herz brothers, Kalkbrenner and Hiller. Although their characters and style of playing were utterly different, Liszt conceived a great enthusiasm for his Polish contemporary, and this warm personal sympathy was reciprocated at first. Liszt introduced Chopin to Heine and Berlioz. In a cheerful tripartite letter to Hiller, also signed by Liszt and the cellist Franchomme, Chopin remarked: 'I am writing without knowing what my pen is scribbling, as Liszt is at this moment playing my Études and banishing all suitable thoughts from my head. I should like to rob him of the way he plays my studies.'[13]

In 1832 Liszt attended a series of lectures on the philosophy of music by Fétis – remembered today not for his many compositions, but for his historical and theoretical writings. The Romantics loved distant horizons and took a serious interest in the publication and performance of music of former ages. Fétis played an important role in the scholarly aspect of this but unfortunately his reputation has been tarnished on account of the partiality of his judgements of contemporary music, and successively Berlioz, Liszt and Verdi suffered from his critical antipathy. But Liszt maintained that in understanding the progress of harmony Fétis was the greatest authority.[14] Fétis defined four harmonic periods: *unitonique* (early modal), *transitonique* (simple major/minor), *pluritonique* (more modulatory) and *omnitonique* (constantly modulatory and tonally ambiguous). In this last, he saw clearly the trend in modern music, and the concept of a free system of harmonic movement replacing the laws governing classical tonality fascinated Liszt who composed a *Prélude omnitonique* (apparently lost).

Among other significant contacts were Charles Alkan, whom he saw frequently during the 1830s, and John Field whom he heard in 1832. Liszt also came to know Mendelssohn who spent the winter of 1831 to 1832 in Paris.

Towards his twentieth birthday Liszt's entanglements with a

[13] ibid., 8ff.
[14] ibid., II, 111f.

number of women took a more serious turn. He referred later to 1831 as

> an epoch when my mother and Madame D . . ., hoping to calm my excited soul, wanted at any cost to marry me to this dear young lady [Charlotte Laborie] . . . It was also the time of Hortense and to a small extent Madame G . . ., a time of struggle, of anguish, of solitary torments, when I was trying violently to smash, destroy, annihilate the love of Adèle.[15]

Adèle, Comtesse Laprunarède (later Duchesse de Fleury) was the most important of these loves; they spent some months of 1831 together in her home in the Swiss Alps.[16] Mme Boissier's diary for 23 March 1832 refers to another affair:

> He saw, once again, a certain young lady by the name of Fräulein von Barré with whom he had made a journey to Savoy one year ago; it was said at the time that he was insanely in love. For three-and-a-half hours the other day he wrote music for her.

The romantic fortunes of both Berlioz and Liszt took decisive turns at the same period. Liszt attended a performance of the *Symphonie fantastique* and the première of its sequel, *Lélio*, on 9 December 1832. In the audience was the actress Harriet Smithson, astounded to find herself the heroine of both works. Next day Berlioz was introduced to her and from that moment struggled against all hindrance (including some wise counsel from Liszt) to make her his wife. In March Harriet broke a leg – a grievous blow to a theatrical career already in financial ruins. Chopin and Liszt together gave a benefit concert for her, and in October Liszt was a witness at the wedding of Harriet and Hector in the British Embassy chapel. Meanwhile Liszt had encountered the woman who was to be intimately bound up with his life for more than a decade. At a soirée of the Marquise le Vayer early in 1833 he entered the salon and met the gaze of Marie, Comtesse d'Agoult.

Marie Catherine-Sophie de Flavigny was born in Frankfurt-am-Main on 31 December 1805. Her father, Vicomte de Flavigny (1770–1819), an exile from the time of the revolution, fought loyally for the Bourbon cause. While in Frankfurt in 1797 he met and married Marie-Elisabeth Bethmann, daughter of a rich and respected banker whose Dutch ancestors had converted from

---

[15] AL, I, 39; and *cf.* 83.
[16] JALS, XI, June 1982, 14, 17.

Judaism to the Protestant faith. The marriage did not take place easily. Marie-Elisabeth's mother, by all accounts an awesome matriarch of strict Swiss Protestant background, opposed any liaison with the Catholic Flavigny. To cool her daughter's ardour she arranged for a fault to be investigated in the Frenchman's papers and to have him spend a spell in prison. With a determined independence that was to be inherited by her daughter and her grand-daughter (Cosima Wagner) Marie-Elisabeth took herself to the prison, gained admittance somehow, and spent the night with her lover. Faced with this *coup d'audace* Frau Bethmann not only agreed to the wedding but urged it at the earliest possible date.

The child Marie and her elder brother Maurice spent most of their youth in France. But in 1815, back at the Bethmann country house near Frankfurt, an old gentleman paid a visit and stroked the long, curly blonde hair of little Marie. He was Goethe, and in later years she recalled this fleeting encounter as a moment of benediction. Marie's education included a wide range of reading and an introduction to piano playing which she was allowed to continue in her convent 'finishing school'. The heiress on her father's side of the Catholic ultra-royalist line, and on her mother's of a proudly Protestant middle-class tradition, Marie was conscious of her French and German traits. She had a tendency to high-mindedness, an aloof nature, and was prey to loneliness. She viewed the salons of the Faubourg Saint-Germain with an independent and analytical eye. There is no reason to doubt that at twenty she differed from the frank self-analysis given in her *Souvenirs*, written in old age:

> I am silent for fear of giving myself away. I then seem to be icily cold: 'Six inches of snow on twenty feet of lava' has been said of me, and not without reason. If one adds to this impassioned but reserved disposition my horror of the commonplace and my distaste for imitating anyone else, it will be easily understood that my conversation was not at all the kind needed to fill social gaps or to amuse a salon ... I cannot come to terms with what bores me.[17]

With her riches, striking beauty, culture and fine command of languages, young men were eager to play suitor, but her cold exterior repelled them all. Conscious none the less of her obligation to make a good marriage, she abdicated a personal decision and left it for her mother to arrange. The choice fell on Charles,

[17] d'Agoult, *Mes Souvenirs*, 349.

Comte d'Agoult, fifteen years her senior: a kind, unpretentious and unintellectual ex-soldier. They had nothing in common. The wedding on 16 May 1827 was a grand social occasion attended by Charles X, the royal family, the Duchesse de Berry and the Duc d'Orléans and his family. Two daughters were born of this hopeless union and, having thus fulfilled her social and marital obligations, the countess stepped out into the social rounds of fashionable salons. She acquired a personal country home, the Château de Croissy, with an exquisitely laid-out park. Here she could enjoy the company of her children and indulge in elegant entertaining. In Paris she began her own fledgling salon and attracted such notables as Rossini and de Vigny.

At their first meeting Marie was aware that Liszt was regarded as a social inferior in such salons, yet his artistic talent and his original and thoughtful personality placed him well above his surroundings. Writing to him afterwards to invite him to one of her own receptions, she had the greatest difficulty in drafting words which would not imply that she was just another wealthy and ambitious hostess, or on the other hand reveal too clearly the personal interest she felt in him. He called on her the next day without even replying to the letter. Because of her independent way of life they were able to meet frequently and hold long discussions on religion, the social position of artists, the literary movements of the day. These themes are echoed in their correspondence which, in published form, begins with a long series of mostly undated letters mainly from Liszt, of 1833 to 1834. Part of this time Marie was in Paris, where they met clandestinely at his mother's home; during summer months she was at Croissy, six leagues away, and he visited her there. His letters were often addressed to a go-between and they wrote phrases in English or German to arrange secret meetings. As early as May 1833 she wrote: 'On your knees, Franz, on your knees, pray for me, save me ... Sometimes I love you foolishly and at these times I realise that I could not, would not and ought not to be so absorbing a thought for you as you are for me.'[18] A year later, he wrote: 'Yesterday I had no evening prayer to offer. It seemed that we had not parted. Your glance was still radiating magically in the sky. Your breath was still on my lips, the beating of your heart still echoed with mine, prolonging to infinity this new intense life

---

[18] AL, I, 57.

which we have revealed to one another'.[19] Much of the correspondence deals with literary and musical friends including Chopin, with whom Liszt took part in a Ferdinand Hiller concert on 15 December 1833. Marie's jealousy of Liszt's other lady friends, mutual confessions of inner longing, declarations of rapturous joy – these themes crowd the pages. 'Not an angel's, not God's, but thine' becomes a motto in Liszt's letters. After a happy week at Croissy he spent the autumn of 1834 with the Abbé Félicité de Lamennais at La Chênaie in Brittany.

This priest had achieved fame with his *Essai sur l'indifférence en matière de religion* (1817) in which he appeared as the advocate of papal supremacy and champion of the faith against the errors of eighteenth-century agnosticism. But in the ensuing decade his concern for the plight of the poor led him to declare that the Church must align herself with progressive social trends. He criticised hereditary monarchy and predicted the triumph of universal suffrage. Eventually his influential liberal newspaper *L'Avenir* was suspended and in 1832 a papal encyclical explicitly condemned the freedom of expression which Lamennais advocated. His retort was the moving and resoundingly written book *Paroles d'un croyant* (1834) which achieved immense prestige among French intellectuals and was attacked by the pope as 'detestable for its impiety and audacity'. Harold Laski aptly called it 'a lyrical version of the Communist Manifesto'; de Musset hailed Lamennais as 'our modern Luther'; George Sand called him 'Christ's sole apostle on earth'. Liszt read the book on its publication and wrote enthusiastically to the author, receiving in turn an invitation to La Chênaie. Lamennais became Liszt's spiritual mentor and confirmed in him the views of the artist, society and the church that he had responded to in the Saint-Simonist movement.

The friendship bore important fruits in musical and literary ways. The three *Apparitions* and the single piece *Harmonies poétiques et religieuses* (the latter originally conceived for piano and orchestra; the title is from Lamartine, to whom it is dedicated) are among the most important of Liszt's earlier works and show many features of his mature harmonic style, melodic fingerprints and formal structure. Earlier in the year a serious uprising of silk weavers occurred in Lyon. Lamennais was much concerned with the fate of the workers (he had witnessed a similar revolt in 1831) and subsequently defended some of them at their trial.

[19] ibid., 76.

Liszt certainly would have discussed the affair at La Chênaie. His remarkable piano piece *Lyon* is traditionally dated 1834 but there is evidence that it may have been composed as a result of Liszt's visit to Lyon three years later, when he was forcibly struck by the appalling poverty and misery and wrote a harrowing account of his experience (see Chapter 11). Whatever the date, *Lyon* is one of the products written under the stimulus of Lamennais and his social philosophy. Another is the 'instrumental psalm' *De Profundis* for piano and orchestra, unfinished and unpublished, ideas from which occur in *Totentanz* and *Pensées des morts*.

Liszt's essays *On the Future of Church Music* (1834) and *On the Position of Artists and their Place in Society* (1835) also bear the stamp of Lamennais. A passage in the first of these reads:

> Today, when the altar trembles and totters, when pulpit and religious ceremonies serve as subjects for the mocker and doubter, art must leave the sanctuary of the temple and expand into the outside world to seek a stage for its glorious manifestations ... Music must recognise God and the people as its living source; must go from one to the other to ennoble, to comfort, to purify man, to bless and praise God ... To attain this the creation of a new music is indispensable. This music, which ... we would call *humanitarian*, must be inspired, strong and effective, uniting, on a colossal scale, *theatre* and *church*: at the same time dramatic and sacred, splendid and simple, solemn and serious, fiery and wild, stormy and calm, clear and tender ... Yes, banish every doubt, soon we shall hear in fields, in forests, villages and suburbs, in the factories and in the towns, national, moral, political and religious songs ... which will be composed *for* the people, taught *to* the people and sung *by* the people; yes, sung by workmen, day-labourers, handicraftsmen, by boys and girls, by men and women of the people![20]

The subsequent article is even bolder and a good deal more practical. Arguing for raising the status of the artist from a sort of superior servant to a respected member of the community, Liszt demanded state funds for performance and publication of the best new works; the introduction of musical education in primary schools and its expansion in other schools; the reorganisation of choral societies and the reformation of church music, especially plainchant; the establishment of philharmonic societies modelled on the music festivals of England and Germany; model performances of the best operas, chamber and orchestral works; an

[20] GS, II, 56.

academy for advanced music studies independent of the Conservatoire, staffed by eminent artists, with a department for the history and philosophy of music and with branches extended to provincial towns; finally, the necessity for a cheap but scholarly edition of important musical works from the Renaissance to the present day. Such ideas were not unique; they are echoed in Lamennais, d'Ortigue, Berlioz, de Vigny and Balzac. But Liszt was the first musician to codify such an all-embracing set of demands and to couch them in such vehement language.

In October 1834 Marie suffered a tragedy. Her elder daughter Louise, just six years old, fell seriously ill with a cerebral disorder and, despite every medical attention, died in December. Liszt called many times to see Marie, but was always turned away. After the death she suffered a nervous collapse, retired to Croissy, became suicidal and could not endure the sight of her other daughter who was placed in the care of a convent.

Meanwhile, in early November, Alfred de Musset had introduced Liszt to George Sand, just at the time that the stormy affair of poet and novelist was entering its final crisis. There was a mutual attraction between George and Franz (strong enough to arouse de Musset's jealousy), but she felt instinctively that Liszt loved 'no one but God and the Holy Virgin, who does not resemble me in the slightest degree'.[21]

Slowly recovering at Croissy, Marie glanced through the pile of letters of sympathy which had arrived and found several from Franz, passionately thanking God for their love and expressing his fear of losing her. When she can forgive and forget all the sadness and misery of the past 'we will fly far from the world, we will live and love and die together'. By March 1835 Marie had joined him in Paris and by May they had planned to leave France, for she knew she was pregnant. At a concert on 9 April at which he and Madame Vial gave the première of his two-piano *Konzertstück* on Mendelssohn's *Songs Without Words*, Liszt collapsed at the keyboard: an indication of the stress he was enduring. However, other concerts with Berlioz and Chopin at this time were free of any such incident. Lamennais now hastened from Brittany to dissuade Franz and Marie from any rash action, but their plan proceeded. Marie left for Switzerland at the end of May; Liszt joined her in Basel a few days later. She left behind a remarkably

---

[21] *The Intimate Journal of George Sand* (transl. M. J. Howe), London, 1929, 35.

good-natured and forgiving husband, a five-year-old daughter and, above all, a scandal.

After ten days in and around Basel, the lovers made a journey of five weeks through the most spectacular Swiss landscapes, via Lake Constance, Wallenstadt, the mountain passes and lakes of the William Tell country, down the Rhone valley, and arrived at Geneva on 19 July.[22] This trip was the initial inspiration for the Swiss pieces of the *Album d'un voyageur*, later revised in the first volume of *Années de pèlerinage* (see especially the *Chapelle de Guillaume Tell, Au lac de Wallenstadt, Un soir dans les montagnes, Les cloches de Genève*). Liszt knew Geneva well, having stayed there in 1831 and 1832 with his pupil Pierre-Etienne Wolff, with whom they now lodged until finding a flat of their own which had views of the mountains on one side, the lake on the other. Liszt's mother sent his possessions including his books and his piano from Paris.

A diversely talented group of friends soon gathered round them. The botanist Pyrame de Candolle; the archaeologist and orientalist Alphonse Denis; the politician James Fazy, owner of a liberal newspaper; the writer and philologist Adolphe Pictet, a retired army officer; the economist, historian and aesthetician Sismonde di Sismondi; and the young poet Louis de Ronchaud, later a close confidant of Marie. Living in Geneva was Madame Boissier whose daughter Valérie Liszt had taught in Paris, and in whose diary we sense something of Calvinist Geneva's attitude towards Liszt's morals:

> He was friendly and is basically a good child. But the poor young man is horribly spoiled by the world and by success ... He has had the misfortune to live among literary people of the day who have fed him with their dangerous doctrines, their false ideas and their incredulity. He ... adheres to a very immoral system connected with the Saint-Simonians on the one hand and with Madame Dudevant [George Sand] on the other. He shrugs his shoulders at the blessings of marriage and other bagatelles of that sort.[23]

Later she observes that 'He has improved in some respects since Paris: he has more ease in his manners and in the ways of society'.

Marie suffered from society's disapproval and the many friends Liszt attracted did not suit her. Especially irritating was

---

[22] On Liszt's Swiss period see JALS, XI, June 1982, 10–17 and XII, Dec. 1982, 182f; also R. Bory, *Une Retraite romantique en Suisse*.
[23] Bory, op. cit., 31.

the appearance, within a month of their arrival, of Liszt's pupil Hermann Cohen. This bright fifteen-year-old Jewish boy, nick-named Puzzi, could not bear to be parted from his master who, with characteristic generosity, invited him to join their household. Marie felt wounded at the failure to take account of her feelings. More trouble occurred when Liszt played in public, as on 3 October for Prince Emilio Belgiojoso's concert in aid of Italian émigrés. Marie's dislike of his virtuoso appearances and the admirers who flocked to them resulted in part from her fear that, having abandoned her family to be with her genius, he would fail her by pursuing social rather than creative success. These seeds of discontent were eventually to blight their love.

As Liszt settled in Geneva a conservatoire of music opened with Wolff one of the founder-professors. Liszt taught there during its first session. His notes on some students survive:

Julie Raffard:
Very remarkable musical feeling. Very small hands. Brilliant execution.
Amélie Calame:
Pretty fingers; the work is diligent and very careful; almost too much so. Capable of teaching.
Marie Demellayer:
Vicious technique (if technique it be); extreme zeal and mediocre talent. Grimaces and contortions. Glory to God in the highest and peace to men of good will.
Ida Milliquet:
Artist from Geneva; flabby and mediocre. Fingers good enough. Good enough posture at the piano. Enough *enoughs* the total of which is not much.
Jenny Gambini:
Beautiful eyes.[24]

In letters of late 1835, Liszt's ideas for composition and future concerts were clearly defined.[25] The set of pieces *Harmonies poétiques et religieuses*, the *Transcendental Studies*, and his intention of touring throughout Europe are discussed, and yet these plans have hitherto been accredited to a much later date. His ambitions as pianist and composer were mapped out system-atically, well in advance. Works which did not appear in their final versions until the 1850s thus had a long gestation.

On 18 December a daughter, Blandine-Rachel, was born to

[24] ibid., 48f.
[25] JALS, V, June 1979, 75–9 and XII, Dec. 1982, 63ff.

Marie and Franz. On the birth certificate the mother appears as 'Cathérine-Adelaïde Meran, a lady of property, aged 24 years, born at Paris'. This falsification of facts was made, not to deceive the citizenry of Geneva, but to prevent Blandine legally being considered Charles d'Agoult's child. The baby was placed in the care of a wet-nurse and later, as the parents continued their travels, she was looked after by a local pastor's family.

Liszt travelled to Lyon in April 1836 to give some concerts; Marie remained in Geneva and so, usefully, their letters exist to show that he still saw her as the centre of his life and was profoundly sad to be without her – sentiments echoed in her replies. From Lyon he continued to Paris with the object of seeing her brother Maurice to reassure him of his honourable intentions toward Marie and their child. Liszt had been away from the capital for a year but his name had remained constantly before the public. Joseph d'Ortigue's biography of him appeared in the *Revue et Gazette Musicale* in June 1835. From May to October the same journal printed his essay *On the Position of Artists* in instalments, and in December the first of his *Bachelor of Music* essays, 'To George Sand'. These *Lettres d'un bachelier-ès-musique* were modelled on Sand's *Lettres d'un voyageur*, one of which (summer 1835) had been addressed to Liszt.

There is a problem of great magnitude concerning Liszt's literary output. Without doubt Marie assisted in writing his essays of the period to 1840, and similarly Princess Wittgenstein was his collaborator on the later prose works. Indeed his two periods of literary activity, 1834 to 1840 and 1849 to 1859, coincide exactly with his closest relations with the two women. The problem is: which passages belong to Liszt and which to his collaborators? Every item would have to be examined on its own merits. Most of the manuscripts have been lost since the time of their publication. But the British Library possesses a twelve-page draft in Liszt's hand of the article *On the Position of Artists*,[26] and in Weimar there are a few holographs of essays of the Wittgenstein era. The issue is compounded by the fact that both d'Agoult and Wittgenstein became authors themselves. But it can safely be assumed that when music is the topic then the views are Liszt's own, as neither collaborator was qualified to discuss the subject. Similarly personal experiences recalled in detail (in which neither

[26] Add. MSS: 33965 Folio 234. Published in LSJ, IX, 1984, 29f.

lady participated) must originate with Liszt. In the last analysis his literary output *is* important, for reasons both of biography and of general nineteenth-century musical thought.[27]

Liszt the author was of interest to the Paris he returned to in 1836, but this was eclipsed by interest in Liszt the pianist. During his absence it was not unnatural that the habitués of the concert world looked for other pianists who might rival Liszt's powers. In Sigismund von Thalberg, who first played in Paris in the autumn of 1835, they seemed to have found one. News of Thalberg's success reached Liszt in Geneva. In letters to Marie from Lyon he pours scorn on Thalberg's compositions and hints that he would have rushed to Paris to prove for himself that Thalberg is as impoverished in talent as his predecessors like Kalkbrenner and Herz, but Thalberg has left and so the temptation is over.[28]

At one of two concerts in the Salle Erard in May Liszt played Beethoven's *Hammerklavier* sonata. Berlioz wrote:

> Until now this has been the enigma of the sphinx for almost every pianist. Liszt, another Oedipus, has solved it in a manner that would have sent quivers of joy and pride through the composer, could he have heard it in his grave. Not a note was omitted, not one added (I followed, score in hand), no inflection lost, no change of tempo permitted ... Liszt in thus making comprehensible a work not yet comprehended, has proved that he is the pianist of the future.[29]

Liszt was anxious to maintain contact with his Paris friends and to ascertain how the affair with Marie was regarded, should they return to Paris. His guests at one dinner party included Chopin, Meyerbeer, Delacroix, Nourrit, Gautier, the philosopher Pierre Ballanche and the prominent Saint-Simonian Emile Barrault. He was clearly still in favour and he proudly reported to Marie his encounter with Princess Belgiojoso: 'She is always charming to me, comparing me to no one else at all and deriding the *Thalbourgeois*.'

After concerts in Lausanne and Dijon he returned to Marie in July and they set out for the Alpine resort of Chamonix. George Sand had long expressed a desire to join them in Switzerland and she arrived in Geneva late in August (with her two children, a

---

[27] The problem of Liszt's authorship is discussed in Walker, *Franz Liszt: the virtuoso years*, 20–3 and in Gut, *F. Liszt: les éléments du langage musical*, 29–42; and *cf.* M. Eckhardt, *New Documents on Liszt the Author*, NHQ, XXV/95, Autumn 1984, 181–94 (reprinted in JALS, XVIII, Dec. 1985).
[28] AL, I, 140, 146f, 156.
[29] GM, 12 June 1836.

maid and a friend picked up en route) to find a note inviting her
to Chamonix. Pictet (nicknamed 'the Major') would escort her
there. Both he and Sand wrote amusing accounts of the bohemian
days which followed.[30] Finding Liszt's hotel, George read his
flamboyant entry in the register:

> Place of birth: Parnassus
> Profession: Musician-Philosopher
> Coming from: Doubt
> Going to: Truth

Taking her pen, she embroidered along the same lines:

> Names of travellers: Piffoël family
> Domicile: Nature
> Coming from: God
> Going to: Heaven
> Place of birth: Europe
> Occupation: Loafers
> Date of passport: Eternity
> Issued by: Public opinion

As the chambermaid opened the door of Room 13, George could
see little in the dark and tripped over Puzzi lying on the floor. He
wore a blouse over which fell his long hair, so that his sex must
have been as confusing to the staid hotel proprietor as that of the
cigar-smoking Sand dressed, like her daughter, in male attire.
Joyous hugging and delighted shrieks ensued as Franz and Marie
emerged from the gloom and recognised George. The chambermaid, aghast at such goings on, dropped her candle and fled to
report the invasion of Room 13 by a troupe of gypsies. The Major
arrived meanwhile and was approached by an anxious landlord.

'Have you come to arrest them sir?'

'Arrest whom?'

'Why, that family of gypsies up there, with long hair and
smocks.'

On entering the room Pictet found Marie at one end of a sofa
holding a scent bottle to counter the fumes from George, seated
at the other end and smoking a long Turkish pipe. Liszt lay at
their feet.

Jokes, absurdities and nicknames, the nocturnal philoso-

---

[30]Bory, op. cit., 70–8; Pictet, *Une Course à Chamonix: Conte fantastique*, Paris,
1838; Sand, 'Lettre d'un voyageur à Charles Didier', *Revue des Deux Mondes*, 1
Nov. 1836.

phising of the Major on such propositions as 'the absolute is identical with itself'; getting drunk on punch, smoking drugged cigars and scandalising the other residents of the hotel (mainly impeccably respectable Englishmen with their demure spouses) – thus were the evenings spent at Chamonix. By day the band of vagabonds explored the surrounding countryside. They quarrelled and laughed, argued and sang, rejoicing in their youth, their exotic garb, the breathtaking country they traversed. At Fribourg Liszt played on the new Mooser organ at the cathedral of St. Nicholas, improvising at length on the *Dies Irae* from Mozart's *Requiem*: a powerful, trance-like meditation on the Apocalypse vividly recalled by Sand and Pictet. The holiday ended with George staying ten more days in Geneva where she loved to lie *under* the piano as Liszt played, 'enveloped' by the music. His recent Rondo *El Contrabandista* evoked her story *Le Contrebandier*.

She was not separated long from her friends. In mid-October Franz and Marie returned to Paris and took a suite at the Hôtel de France, where George joined them at the end of the month and where a salon celebrating 'humanitarian art' was established. Sainte-Beuve wrote of its atmosphere as 'a mass of affectations, vanities, pretentiousness, of bombast and uproar of every kind', but it regularly attracted Lamennais, Princess Belgiojoso, Charles Didier, Heine, Mickiewicz, Meyerbeer, Berlioz, Nourrit, the violinist Massart and Chopin. That autumn Liszt introduced George Sand to Chopin: although there was in no sense love at first sight, it was a fateful meeting.

By the new year the Hôtel de France ménage dispersed. In January and February 1837 Liszt gave four remarkable chamber concerts with Urhan and the cellist Alexandre Batta, including five piano trios of Beethoven, then unknown in Paris, and a selection of Schubert *Lieder* (with Nourrit). Liszt had every reason to consider himself 'the pianist of the future', not only for his championship of Beethoven but through his technical advances of recent years and the evidence of his new compositions – mostly not yet made public. This was his mood when Thalberg again became the talk of the town as his supposed rival. Unfortunately Liszt involved himself in a sordid campaign of smear and counter-smear in the press, and his attacks on Thalberg were unnecessarily vindictive and belittling. In defence it can be said that his published review of Thalberg's compositions was in fact written by Marie, that the hyper-charged competitive atmosphere of pianistic rivalry at that time in Paris provoked such heady remarks, and that Liszt was really countering what he saw as the reactionary view of Fétis (Thalberg's leading champion) who had claimed Thalberg as the creator of a new school and Liszt the representative of one that was out of date and had no future. Thalberg was undoubtedly a player of distinction and a master of *cantabile* playing. He astonished audiences with his effect of seemingly playing with three hands: the melody was sustained in the middle register with alternate hands while surrounded by a filigree of arpeggiated chords (a device derived from the English harpist Elias Parish-Alvars). His manner was aristocratic, self-assured and without excessive movement of arms or body – in contrast to Liszt's outward impetuosity. Thalberg was also a transcriber of merit and later he and his works achieved great success on both sides of the Atlantic. In future years Liszt showed his admiration by playing Thalberg's arrangements, meeting and corresponding with him and penning a tribute to him on his death. But posterity tends to remember only their duels of 1837.

On 12 March Thalberg gave a successful concert at the conservatoire, playing his fantasy on Rossini's *Moses* and his variations on *God Save the King*. A week later Liszt upstaged him by renting the Opéra, filling every seat, and playing his fantasy on Pacini's *Niobe* and Weber's *Conzertstück*. But the climax of their rivalry was the result of a charity event, lasting several days, organised by Princess Belgiojoso in aid of Italian refugees. Her stroke of genius was to invite Liszt *and* Thalberg to contest their powers in her salon, which became a veritable lions' den on 31 March. The princess's verdict has withstood the test of time: 'There is only one Thalberg in Paris, but there is only one Liszt in the world'. A work commissioned for this occasion (but not completed in time) was a set of six variations, *Hexaméron*, on a theme from Bellini's *I Puritani*. In the opera it is a patriotic cry for freedom. The choice was probably that of Belgiojoso herself, ardent republican and former friend of Bellini. The sextet of composers involved in this work were Thalberg, Pixis, Henri Herz, Czerny (then spending a year in Paris at Liszt's suggestion), Chopin and Liszt, who himself arranged the theme, wrote an introduction, the second variation, three extended interludes and the finale. It was subsequently a great favourite in his recitals and he donated the royalties on its sale to the princess's Italian cause.

After concerts in April (in which he included some Chopin

studies, op. 25, a set dedicated to Marie) the couple arrived at George's estate at Nohant in early May and stayed for three months. Liszt worked at transcriptions of Schubert songs and Beethoven symphonies. This was an idyllic interlude before their move to Italy, where the next two years were spent. Before leaving France Liszt visited Lyon and gave a concert with Nourrit for the benefit of the unemployed. The fashionable opera star Nourrit also trained vast choirs of working men in Paris: the choruses they sang included some with texts by Lamartine, and Liszt now paid a visit to that poet-politician at Saint-Point near Mâcon.

After visiting little Blandine in Geneva, the lovers reached the shores of Lake Maggiore on 17 August and explored the dramatic mountainous landscape around there and Lake Como until settling at Bellagio for two months 'in a delicious little inn' where Liszt spent much of his time at a bad piano composing his *12 Grandes Études*. With Marie imminently expecting their second child, they moved to an hotel in Como. From there Liszt often travelled alone to Milan where the publisher Ricordi offered him the use of a villa, a carriage, his box at La Scala, access to his vast library and helped arrange concert appearances. Also in Milan was an old friend, Rossini, whose delightful *Soirées musicales* Liszt had been busily transcribing.

At Como Liszt received a parcel of compositions by Schumann, whom he had not met and whose music was unknown to him. The discovery of this new piano music prompted an enthusiastic review for the *Gazette Musicale*. That journal also now printed his 'Bachelor of Music' letters which embrace many subjects: the plight of the artist, the state of music in Italy, the Italian ignorance of solo piano playing (plus an attack on standards at La Scala for which he was forced to apologise), the wonder of the visual arts in Italy, travel notes and comments on modern music.

On Christmas Eve 1837 Marie gave birth to another daughter, christened Francesca Gaetana Cosima Liszt ('Cosima' is derived from St. Cosmas). Leaving Marie in Como to convalesce, Franz returned to Milan, its glittering society and the company of friends who were there, including Nourrit and Hiller. Marie joined him in late January (having left Cosima in the care of a nurse) and at once loathed the city and its frivolities. In mid-March they travelled through Verona, Vicenza, Padua and settled in Venice where Marie felt tired and unwell. In her diaries there is a new note of disillusionment and unhappiness caused by more than post-natal depression: the tension of the relationship, the feeling that she could live neither with Franz nor without him, an irritation that he was enjoying himself rather too much in these cities – all these thoughts tortured her. But Liszt was adoring Italy, and Venice especially.

His love of Italy was to be profound and lifelong. Forty-five years later he wrote that his love of Venice was undiminished. The roots of his feelings for the country were two-fold. Firstly the engendering of a passion for Italian music in the Paris of his youth, where Rossini was idolized, Paganini released unknown magic, and Bellini's lyric *bel canto* and coloratura style made a deep impression. Secondly his eyes now feasted on treasures of art and architecture in a profusion that crowds and colours the pages of his essays. Italy is reflected in the Paganini *Études*, in many transcriptions, in the Italian volume of *Années de pèlerinage* and its supplement *Venezia e Napoli*, in his early songs and in subsequent orchestral works.

While in Venice he learned of events in his homeland which profoundly stirred him into an awareness of being Hungarian and moved him to action. In March 1838 a disastrous flooding of the Danube almost wiped out the city of Pest and caused huge losses of life, homes and livelihoods throughout the land. In response to an international appeal by the Hungarian authorities Liszt made speedy arrangements to travel to Vienna where he gave eight public concerts in April and May, the first of which raised a considerable sum for the flood victims. His Viennese appearances caused a sensation and letters to Marie are full of his triumphs, press cuttings, news that he has now quite eclipsed Thalberg, of the many prints of him on sale everywhere, of royal and aristocratic patrons and the possibility of his appointment as court pianist. He met Czerny and his old patrons Count Amadé and Prince Metternich, and came to know his Viennese 'cousin' Eduard for the first time. He asked Marie to join him but she declined and remained in Venice, ill, miserable and frustrated. He writes as devotedly as ever and may be forgiven the giddy list of his Viennese achievements, which understandably went to his young head. What nagged at Marie was the realisation that her aim of encouraging Liszt to work in blissful seclusion was now threatened by his apparent desire to communicate as a performer with a growingly ardent public.

A significant Vienna encounter was with the eighteen-year-old Clara Wieck, staying with her pedagogue father, Friedrich, in Liszt's hotel. Her diary records the incomparable effect of Liszt's playing, his generous and passionate artistic nature and his originality. In turn he praised Clara's playing and was delighted to be introduced to more works of her beloved: Schumann's *Carnaval* and *Fantasiestücke*. He wrote warmly to the composer, 'To be absolutely frank and precise, only Chopin's compositions and yours interest me strongly. The rest do not deserve the honour of being mentioned by name...' Liszt dedicated his Paganini Studies to Clara. A year later he wrote to Schumann giving the highest praise to his C major *Phantasie*, op. 17, which he had dedicated to Liszt. Friedrich Wieck's account of Liszt's concert on 18 April was excitedly conveyed to his wife the next day:

> We have heard Liszt in concert! That must be an unforgettable experience for a pianist. Although the public understood only half of his 'Puritani' fantasy, a quarter of his Devil's Waltz and even less of his so-called Étude, Weber's *Concertstück* came across. It was excellent; very fast to be sure, but extraordinarily spirited, original and creative in delivery ... After he had destroyed Thalberg's Erard ... he played the Fantasy on a C. Graff, burst two brass strings, personally fetched a second C. Graff in walnut wood from the corner and played his Étude. After breaking yet another two strings he loudly informed the public that 'since it didn't satisfy him he would play it again'. As he began he vehemently threw his gloves and handkerchief on to the floor...[31]

Liszt played mostly from memory and his Vienna repertoire was impressively varied, including major works of Hummel, Beethoven, Weber and Chopin; Handel and Scarlatti fugues; and, with several singers, Schubert songs. Between 1837 and 1840 Liszt made no less than forty-four transcriptions of Schubert *Lieder*.

The weeks in Vienna became a visit of almost two months and might have been extended further, even to Pest, but for a desperate letter from the sick Marie in Venice: 'I am still unable to leave my room. In the name of heaven, delay no more'.[32] After a final concert and farewell banquet he hastened to her. An unpleasant row ensued and among the jealous phrases she cast at him was the epithet of 'Don Juan parvenu' (an insulting phrase neither Liszt nor his biographers forgot). Somehow things were

[31] Quoted and transl. by C. Suttoni: JALS, XII, Dec. 1982, 12f.
[32] AL, I, 233.

patched up and when Marie was well they left Venice for Genoa, Liszt renting a villa and a carriage to take her for drives. The summer was spent by the shores of Lake Lugano, Liszt making frequent trips to Milan. Not only was the scenery and artistic heritage of Italy a powerful stimulus for him but also its literature, and this summer the couple studied Dante together. Liszt kept a diary[33] which reflects this reading, as well as his emotional conflicts.

In the autumn he gave concerts in Bologna, Padua, Pisa and Florence, where they settled for the winter. (Marie was aware that she was again pregnant.) Here they met the painter Henri Lehmann, who executed well-known portraits of both of them, and the sculptor Lorenzo Bartolini to whom they also sat. In January 1839 Blandine, now three years old, was returned to them, to Marie's joy. The stifling tension of the relationship now eased somewhat. Marie's diary notes Liszt's plan to dedicate four months of each year to concert tours and 'to live the rest of the time alone with me'.[34] With the lifting of emotional clouds Liszt saw in a clear and confident air a vista of future aims and activities:

> If I feel within me the strength and life, I will attempt a symphonic composition based on Dante, then another on Faust – within three years' time – meanwhile I will make three sketches: the *Triumph of Death* (Orcagna), the *Comedy of Death* (Holbein), and a *fragment dantesque*. The *Pensiero* [*sic*] also bewitches me.[35]

This vitally important statement of intent casts light on the works of art which stimulated musical composition. The macabre four-teenth-century fresco *The Triumph of Death* is in the Campo Santo, Pisa (where it was badly damaged in World War II) and is now attributed to Francesco Traini (or sometimes to Bonamico Buffalmacco): the figure of Death is seen on the Day of Judgement cutting down victims with a scythe as the blessed ascend to heaven and the damned are cast into a fiery hell. Ramann maintained that this was the inspiration for Liszt's *Totentanz* for piano and orchestra. But there is evidence that the impulse for that work was in fact the Holbein woodcut series, known in Germany as *Der Todtentanz*. At the time of the first performance, German musical

[33] *Journal des Zyi*. Quoted in d'Agoult, *Mémoires*. New light is shed on these months in Italy by S.Winklhofer, 'Liszt, Marie d'Agoult and the "Dante" Sonata', *19th Century Music*, I/1, July 1977, 15–32.

[34] d'Agoult, *Mémoires*, 168.

[35] *Journal des Zyi*, Feb. 1839; d'Agoult, *Mémoires*, 180.

writers close to Liszt named Holbein as the source of his *Totentanz* and Liszt wrote amusingly to Bülow (who first played it) that if there was a fiasco 'we'll blame it on Holbein for corrupting the public taste'. It has therefore been suggested that the Pisa *Triumph* might be the inspiration for quite another work, the uncertainly dated *Malédiction* for piano and orchestra.[36]

Il Pensieroso is the informal title of Michelangelo's statue of Giuliano de' Medici in Florence. The piano piece is the second in the Italian book of *Années de pèlerinage,* and is prefaced by another 1839 piece *Sposalizio,* inspired by Raphael's *Marriage of the Virgin* in the Brera, Milan. The *fragment dantesque* referred to above is, or rather was to become, the 'Dante Sonata' properly called *Après une lecture du Dante; Fantasia quasi Sonata.* Its genesis has confused scholars who, again following Ramann, date its conception to 1837. It was actually sketched in September 1839 and performed in its early version in Vienna in November. Along with *Totentanz* and the other pieces of the Italian *Année* it was revised in the early Weimar years when the *fragment* became a *Fantasia quasi Sonata.* It is notable that most of these works share the common theme of death, a subject to which Liszt often returned: it forms a vein of symbolic importance in works after the Weimar years.

Rome, where the couple moved early in 1839, entranced Liszt: it lured him until his last years. Marie's fears and depressions were dispelled a little by the friendship of the painter Ingres (who left a fine drawing of Liszt) and by a visit from Sainte-Beuve. But they were both deeply saddened by the suicide in March of their friend, the tenor Nourrit. Also during this Roman stay Liszt first had the daring to devote an entire concert to a solo performance. The impact and audacity of this innovation are hard to conceive today. But it was entirely characteristic of Liszt to pioneer the solo *recital* (a term first ever used at his London concerts of 1840). He could truly 'affect the Louis XIV style and say *Le concert c'est moi*'.[37]

On 9 May Marie gave birth to a son, Daniel, who was left with a nurse at Palestrina and later with Henri Lehmann's sister (where he remained until 1841). The following month Franz, Marie and Blandine left the Eternal City first for Lucca and then for the fishing village of San Rossore, where they stayed until the autumn. There he learned that the scheme for a Beethoven monument at

[36] Winklhofer, op. cit.
[37] Letter to Princess Belgiojoso, 4 June 1839.

Bonn had foundered owing to lack of support, particularly from France, and he saw this as a slight to his most revered master which he, following his Vienna successes of 1838, could set right. His offer to provide the sum still outstanding for the monument gave him the impetus to return to concert touring. Against Marie's wishes he announced concerts in Vienna for mid-November and made arrangements for her to travel with the two little girls to Paris. It was not the end of their relationship, but it was the vital turning point. To Marie it seemed that Dante was abandoning his Beatrice. She and Blandine bade adieu to him in Florence and sailed from Livorno to Genoa where they were reunited with Cosima for the rest of the journey. Three days later Liszt marked his twenty-eighth birthday: he was travelling north to embark on the most glamorous period of his career.

3

Lisztomania (1839–47)

Liszt's *Glanzperiode*, when the term 'Lisztomania' was coined by Heine, conjures up images of him that have remained most to the fore in popular imagination. A dazzling wizard, a showman and superman of the keyboard who thrilled audiences in musical capitals and far-flung regions of Europe and whose works matched the glitter and even the vulgarity of that era of hysterical adulation. An artist who travelled at times like a monarch without need for passport and who inspired an adoration many a monarch might envy; who at other times sought out obscurity and determined to be a musical ambassador to regions where concerts were novel; who was good-looking, charismatic and heralded by legends of his saintly generosity, demonic powers and romantic entanglements. This is the stuff on which a more recent 'star' system has thrived: Liszt was the first of that particular constellation and its aura both attracted and repelled, for he acquired detractors as energetic as his admirers.

His journeys encompass so many people and places that any account of them is in danger of reading like a mixture of travelogue, gazetteer and social almanac. This table shows at a glance where he was and when; it is a broad guide and shows only the principal towns and regions visited:

NOV.–DEC., **1839**, Vienna; DEC.–JAN., **1840**, Pressburg, Pest; FEB., Vienna, Brno, Oedenburg, Raiding; MAR., Prague, Dresden, Leipzig; APR., Metz, Paris; MAY–JUNE, London; JULY, Baden; AUG.–SEP., tours southern England; OCT.–NOV., Hamburg; NOV.–JAN., **1841**, tours England, Ireland, Scotland; FEB., Brussels, Liège; MAR.–APR., Paris; MAY–JUNE, London; JULY, Hamburg, Kiel, Copenhagen; AUG.–OCT., Nonnenwerth, Cologne, Bonn, Coblenz, Frankfurt; NOV., Cassel, Weimar; DEC., Dresden, Leipzig; DEC.–MAR., **1842**, Berlin; MAR., Baltic towns; APR.–MAY, St. Petersburg; JUNE–JULY, Paris, Liège, Brussels; AUG.–SEP., Nonnenwerth; OCT., Weimar; NOV.–DEC., Holland; DEC.–FEB., **1843**, Berlin, Breslau, Posen; MAR.–APR., tours Poland; APR.–JUNE,

Moscow, St. Petersburg; late JUNE, Hamburg; JULY–SEP., Non-nenwerth; OCT.–DEC., southern Germany; DEC.–FEB., **1844**, Weimar; late FEB., Dresden; MAR., northern Germany; APR.–JUNE, Paris; JUNE–SEP., tours southern France; OCT.–DEC., Madrid; DEC.–JAN., **1845**, Córdova, Seville, Cádiz, Gibraltar; JAN.–FEB., Lisbon; MAR.–APR., Malaga, Valencia, Barcelona; APR.–JULY, southern France, Alsace, Switzerland; AUG., Bonn and other Rhine towns; SEP.–DEC., Baden, Freiburg, Strassburg, Lux-embourg, eastern France; DEC.–JAN., **1846**, tours France; FEB., Frankfurt; MAR., Vienna, Brno; APR., Prague; MAY, Pest; MAY–JUNE, Grätz; JULY, Zagreb; AUG., Oedenburg, Raiding; SEP.–OCT., tours Hungary; NOV.–DEC., tours Transylvania; late DEC., Bucharest; JAN., **1847**, Jassy, enters the Ukraine; FEB.–MAR., Kiev, Woronince; APR., Lemberg; MAY, Czernovtsy, Jassy, Galatz; JUNE–JULY, Constantinople; JULY–AUG., Odessa; SEP., Elisa-betgrad.

In eight years he played extensively in twenty-one modern countries: England, Scotland, Ireland, Belgium, Holland, France, Spain, Portugal, Switzerland, Austria, Italy, Germany, Luxembourg, Denmark, Hungary, Czechoslovakia, Romania, Yugoslavia, Turkey, Poland and Russia. A list of all his concerts would be tedious, indeed no one has yet supplied a total for the years 1839–47, many of the sources being obscure. Three examples give an idea of his energy and taxing schedule. Throughout the British Isles in mid-winter 1840–41 he gave 45 concerts in 31 towns within 67 days and travelled 2,222 miles.[1] The next winter in Berlin, in addition to conducting, he gave 21 public concerts, played 80 works (50 from memory) and made many other private and social appearances within ten weeks. In widely scattered towns between Pest and Bucharest he gave 20 concerts from mid-October to the end of 1846 as well as attending ceremonies and banquets. Difficult terrain, old-fashioned transport, late nights, frequent recourse to tobacco and alcoholic stimulants, and yet also the composition of a significant body of works, add to the wonder of the geographical and artistic achievement coldly summarised in the above table.

Only a robust constitution could have survived; but he did have periodic attacks of a 'fever' which affected him at the outset of his travels. After the first of six Vienna matinée recitals in aid of the Beethoven Monument (an impressive event, 19 November 1839, patronized by the dowager empress and at which Liszt first played his *fragment dantesque* and his transcription of Beethoven's

[1] LSJ, VI, 1981, 2, quoting John Orlando Parry.

Pastoral symphony) he was laid low and the concert dates were disrupted. In his hotel he met Marie Pleyel with whom he had been on intimate terms about five years previously. (A displeased Chopin discovered they had been using his Paris apartment for their intimacies!) His Viennese association with this notoriously amorous pianist took careful explaining in a letter to Marie d'Agoult, as did an affectionately flowery dedication of his *Norma* fantasy to her some years later. A similar encounter with Caroline Unger at a Trieste concert (26 October) had also required diplomatic elucidation to pacify the countess's growingly jealous mind.

At the height of his Vienna successes he announced his intention to visit his homeland. The return of her most famous son was celebrated and is remembered in Hungary as an event of historic national importance. He gave three concerts in Pressburg where he had last been heard sixteen years before, including a rendition of the subversive Rákóczy March. On 23 December he travelled to Pest in a carriage procession escorted by Hungarian magnates including Count Casimir Esterházy and Liszt's host Count Leo Festetics. Whenever in public he was greeted as a timely and triumphant hero who had brought a new sense of pride to his country and had come to the rescue in her moment of crisis a year before. This culminated in the solemn presentation of a jewelled sabre of honour after a concert (4 January 1840) in which he had again played the Rákóczy March. The sword was a noble symbol given to one whose appearance seemed to symbolise downtrodden Hungary's heritage and hopes: the land needed heroes. Outside afterwards Liszt found

> an immense crowd blocking the square and two hundred young people carrying torches, led by a military band, crying 'Eljen! Eljen! Eljen!' ... Impossible to give you an idea of the enthusiasm, the respect, the love of this people! At eleven o'clock at night the streets were full. In Pest everybody, even the most elegant, is in bed by ten ... Yet the shouting never stopped. It was a triumphal march such as La Fayette and a few men of the revolution experienced.[2]

He proposed the foundation of a conservatory of music in Pest and gave a concert to establish funds, an event (11 January) also significant as Liszt's first ever appearance as a conductor. (The National Conservatory opened in 1845.) At a banquet afterwards he met the distinguished poet Vörösmarty who, a year later,

[2] AL, I, 351f.

addressed a famous patriotic ode to Liszt (a poem finely set by Kodály). He also met two leading political spirits of the tidal surge of nationalism, István Széchenyi and Lajos Batthyány. At the Franciscan monastery in Pest he saw some of his father's former friends. An important musical result of his homecoming was renewed contact with gypsy musicians and a turn to 'Magyar' themes in composition. The series of pieces *Magyar Dallok* (Hungarian National Melodies; 1839–47) were the basis of the first fifteen Hungarian Rhapsodies (begun 1846), and several other 'Hungarian' works belong to 1840.

Moravia beckoned next (two concerts in Brno) and then Oedenburg, scene of his first concert as a boy. He revisited his native village, Raiding, where many of the older inhabitants were overjoyed that their prophecy of his returning one day in a grand coach was fulfilled. He bestowed a sum to restore the village organ, made a gift to his old teacher Rohrer and visited his grandfather, old Georg Adam, in Pottendorf. Within two weeks he was in Prague, where he had been eagerly awaited, for six concerts in eight days. There he was joined by Hermann Cohen and made contact with leading musicians such as Tomášek and Kittl. A boy aged sixteen listened to Liszt's concerts unaware that one day the great man would be his friend and mentor: Bedřich Smetana sat enraptured. Again the aspirations of an oppressed nation caught Liszt's imagination and in his *Hussitenlied* he transcribed what he believed to be a fifteenth-century Hussite song, *Těšme se blahou nadějí* (Let us celebrate in blissful hope). In fact the words and music are nineteenth century.[3]

Schumann came from Leipzig to Dresden to greet Liszt on his arrival there. It was their first meeting. They travelled to Leipzig, Liszt spending much time with Schumann and playing his *Carnaval* in public. Following their warm correspondence and with their concern for the philosophy of music, the status of artists, a mutual passion for Beethoven and for poetry in music, the two seemed set to be friends. In 1840 Schumann was spellbound by Liszt's playing and wrote flattering reviews of his Dresden and Leipzig concerts. Yet a hint of the difference in their natures is contained in Robert's letter to Clara (18 March):

[3] The composer Josef Theodor Krov (1797–1859) wrote it in the 1820s.

How extraordinarily he plays – boldly and wildly, and then again
tenderly and ethereally! I have heard all this. But, Clärchen, this
world – his world I mean – is no longer mine. Art, as you practise
it, and as I do when I compose at the piano, this tender intimacy I
would not give for all his splendour – and indeed there is too much
tinsel about it.[4]

Clara was dismayed by Liszt's refusal to send her father tickets
for his recitals. In this Liszt was taking Schumann's side in his
legal battle with Friedrich Wieck (over permission to marry Clara).
Wieck abused Liszt and Hermann Cohen in the press; Liszt ignored
the libels but Puzzi took Clara's father to court and won his case.
In these upsetting experiences lie the roots of Clara's antipathy to
Liszt, and over the next few years she and Robert began to view
his phenomenal virtuoso success as a distasteful betrayal of genius
for popular glory.

Liszt's debut in conservative Leipzig was not a success; movements from the *Pastoral* transcription failing to make an effect.
He suffered from a combination of the return of his 'fever' and an
unfriendly audience. Mendelssohn arranged a private concert for
him which improved the atmosphere, and together with Hiller
they performed Bach's triple keyboard concerto. At a final charity
concert he included music by Hiller and Mendelssohn's D minor
Concerto, a work he had first seen only a few days before.

During his separations from Marie letters flowed vigorously
between them. She complains of illness, her awkward social
position, and of his lifestyle and supposed infidelities. Ironically
her own letters are crowded with the names of men who flocked
to her new salon: Hugo, Sue, de Vigny, Lamennais. Some were
more than merely friendly: de Ronchaud, Sainte-Beuve, de Girardin, Henry Lytton Bulwer (diplomat brother of the novelist
Edward), Bernard Potocki (a Polish expatriate). The last two both
proposed marriage. Meanwhile at Marie's (or her family's) desire
and with Liszt's agreement, Blandine and Cosima now stayed with
Anna Liszt. If Marie considered Liszt's mother to be common and
intellectually inferior,[5] the little girls adored her and found real
love in her home for the first time. Liszt sent regular sums to Anna
for their upkeep and education. These commitments explain why
he sometimes undertook artistically unrewarding tours. In April
1840 Liszt was with Marie in Paris. He gave private concerts and

[4] B. Litzmann, *Clara Schumann* (transl. G. E. Hadow), London, 1913, 285.
[5] AL, I, 325.

looked up old acquaintances including Princess Belgiojoso whose deep friendship with him over many years has been underestimated by Liszt biographers. In their long, lively and affectionate correspondence[6] Cristina emerges as a wise, intelligent counsellor for whom Liszt had high regard, turning to her (at moments of crisis with Marie) for sympathy and advice, although the exact degree of their intimacy remains obscure. Needless to say, Marie's opinion of her was low indeed.

A grossly defamatory misrepresentation of his recent acclaim in Hungary, and particularly a series of mocking jibes concerning the presentation of the sabre, deeply offended Liszt. The patriotic aspect of the event was misunderstood in Paris where it was viewed as an exhibition of ridiculous dandyism. He was lampooned and caricatured: cartoons often depicting him in Hungarian garb with a huge sabre, bent over concert grands in warlike posture. It was ammunition for the barbed wit of Heine; even Berlioz thought the gift an odd one 'for a man of peace'. In a dignified, modest reply[7] to one cheap smear Liszt pointed out that the sword was the reward of a nation given in national form. The reward, he felt, was beyond his due at present, but symbolised the *hope* Hungarians had in him, a hope he was proud to attempt to justify.

Between May 1840 and June 1841 Liszt made no less than four visits to Britain. London audiences were appreciative, if muted in comparison to his childhood appearances. The sensational liaison of Lady Blessington and Count d'Orsay was no barrier to their home, Gore House, becoming the mecca for artists wishing to impress the highest society, and when Henry Reeve introduced Liszt he met Louis Bonaparte, Lords Castlereagh and Chesterfield, Monckton Milnes (later Lord Houghton), the tenor Rubini and Charles Macready. The actor noted in his diary: 'Liszt, the most marvellous pianist I ever heard. I do not know when I have been so excited.' Socially the visit was spectacular: he went on to meet Lady Beresford, Lady Jersey, the Duchess of Cambridge, the Duke of Beaufort, and was received by Queen Victoria and Prince Albert with the Duchess of Kent at Buckingham Palace. But financially and artistically this first visit, and the other three, were considerably less profitable. English musical taste was not well cultivated and Liszt was not thrilled by remarks like Lady

[6] See *Autour de Mme d'Agoult et de Liszt*, ed. D. Ollivier; and B. A. Brombert's biography of Belgiojoso, *Cristina: Portraits of a Princess*.
[7] *Revue des Deux Mondes*, Oct. 1840.

Blessington's 'What a shame to put such a man at a piano'. The critic Henry Chorley was one of the few enthusiastic voices raised in Liszt's favour, many newspapers being far from polite. *The Musical Journal* observed that he 'has been presented by the Philharmonic Society with an elegant silver breakfast service for doing that which would cause every young student to receive a severe reprimand – viz., thumping and partially destroying two very fine pianofortes'. Despite the efforts of notable advocates of his music, Liszt and conventional British taste did not marry easily. For the remainder of the century various factors – Victorian moral disapproval of his affairs with married women, an ingrained dislike of heart-on-the-sleeve Romanticism and of excessive virtuosity, a bias against the composer of Catholic church music in the land where the Protestant oratorio reigned supreme, a distrust of continental revolutions in harmony and form – contributed to the failure of Liszt's works, a failure which, through ignorance and misconception, thwarted the progress of his music in this century and can still be detected in provincial criticism today.

Over a dozen letters reported his society successes to Marie who observed: 'I am a little afraid that the trouble is you can no longer stand the truth or any restraint. Surrounded by Puzzis of various degrees, the language of the most absolute flattery is all you can listen to.'[8] She arrived in England on 6 June 1840, their intention being to have a quiet holiday after his concerts. Not wishing to appear in society, she stayed at Richmond while he attended the professional round of dinners and receptions, and was often too tired to travel back to Richmond. When he did he found her irritable and ready to squabble. In one note he complains, 'Yesterday (to recall only one occasion), all the way from Ascot to Richmond, you didn't utter a word that wasn't a wound or an insult.'[9] The unhappy sojourn ended with their return to France early in July.

Six weeks later he was back for the first of two extended British tours which had been arranged by an impresario, Louis Lavenu. On the first Lavenu and Liszt were joined by a composer-pianist, Frank Mori, two lady singers and a remarkable entertainer, John Orlando Parry, who was by turns visual artist, harpist, pianist, organist, singer, actor, comedian, mimic and composer (notably of humorous songs like 'Wanted, a Governess'). Posterity

[8] AL, I, 425f.
[9] AL, I, 450.

must be grateful for one more talent: he kept a diary. This document, detailed and delightfully written, is a valuable record of an otherwise obscure corner of Liszt's life.[10] Between 17 August and 26 September the motley group gave fifty concerts, averaging audiences of about 140 (as low as 30 in Coventry; as high as 400 in Brighton) and Parry computed the miles covered at 1,167. This was the itinerary:

Chichester, Portsmouth, Ryde, Newport, Southampton, Winchester, Salisbury, Blandford, Weymouth, Lyme Regis, Sidmouth, Exmouth, Teignmouth, Torquay (no concert owing to Liszt's indisposition), Plymouth (where a second concert was cancelled as only 7 people turned up), Exeter (2 concerts), Taunton, Bridgwater, Bath (3 concerts), Clifton, Cheltenham (2 concerts), Leamington, Coventry, Northampton, Harborough, Leicester, Derby, Nottingham, Mansfield (Liszt visiting Byron's ancestral home, Newstead Abbey, nearby), Newark, Lincoln, Horncastle, Boston, Grantham, Stamford, Peterborough, Huntingdon, Cambridge, Bury St. Edmunds (2 concerts), Norwich (2 concerts), Ipswich, Colchester, Chelmsford, Brighton (2 concerts).

All the sorrows and joys of touring were recorded by Parry: the awful roads, unreliable diet, strange hotels, unpredictable audiences, problems with pianos; the exhaustion of travel, late nights, worsening weather, yet none the less a good amount of fun and high spirits. Several quotations from the diary best give the flavour of the second tour:

23 November (Reading). M. Lizst [sic] had not arrived from Calais in consequence of the winds which prevailed! Went to Town Hall – 140 people. When they heard Liszt was not come, great many left! We were obliged to go on with the CONCERT tho' to only a few persons. Everything went flat.

The celebrated pianist joined them for concerts in Oxford, Leamington, Birmingham, Wolverhampton, Newcastle-under-Lyme and Chester. En route to play in Liverpool they stopped at Birkenhead:

1 December. Had Oysters, Pickles, Bread & cheese in *the open air* at the Hotel Gardens!! We enjoyed it very much – Liszt treated us all. Boat arrived – crossed to Liverpool – Liszt all alive on board – put on his Hungarian *great* bear skin cloak! Everybody thinking he was a little touched – great Fun tho'.

[10] Parry's diary was first published in LSJ, VI (1981) and VII (1982).

Preston, Rochdale, Manchester, Huddersfield, Doncaster, Sheffield, Wakefield, Leeds, Hull, York and again Manchester, before they sailed on 16 December from Liverpool to Dun Laoghaire ('the vessel rolled dreadfully') and a month in Ireland. On his first night in Dublin

> Liszt went to the Theatre Royal, & saw Charles Kean in 'Macbeth' until 9 o'clock. Then he went to the *Rotunda* (where the concert is tomorrow) ... He played over his Concert Stück (Weber) wth a very fair *band* chiefly composed of Amateurs & men from the Regiments quartered here. The *Duke of Leinster* played principal double bass, & there were in the band 'Sir Frederick' this & 'Sir John' the other, with 'Lord' so & so, Colonels & Captains & c. & c!! They were so pleased with Liszt that they *encored* his March in the Concert Stück!

Of their seven Dublin concerts the first and last were exceptionally well attended ('*at least* 1200 people!!!') and of the third Parry notes:

> 23 December. Tonight Liszt played for the first time here *extemporaneously*, & a most wonderful performance it was. When Lewis [Lavenu] asked the audience if they had any Themes ready written, one was handed only, but Mr. Pigott gave him 'The Russian Hymn' in addition. It was not enough, so after *talking to the audience in the most familiar manner, & making them laugh* very much because he had got no *lively* air to work on, he turned round suddenly and said – 'I play de *Wanted Governess!*' And off he started, with the Irish Air & then the Russian Hymn & last my Song, which he played most wonderfully, not all the way thro' but the Waltz part in ... at least 12 different ways & then wound up with the 3 together in a manner truly extraordinary! 'Twas rec'd as it deserved with tumultuous applause.

Christmas was celebrated in Dublin whence they journeyed to Cork for three concerts. They saw the old year out and the new year in over Irish whiskey, and gave a concert in Clonmel, where Liszt had to perform on a small Tomkinson square piano. 'So funny to see Liszt firing away at *Guillaume Tell* on this little instrument – but it stood his powerful hand capitally.' The wandering minstrels completed more Dublin engagements and played in Limerick and Belfast, reaching Donaghadee on 16 January. The crossing next day to Portpatrick in Scotland was rough and wet. After landing and dining they set off on the nine miles to Stranraer

& then as we could only get *one* pair took the same leaders (poor things) on 6 miles further. But on our arrival there – *Lochraen* (or some such place) – there was not a horse to be had! So after a deal of rumpus we all got out of the carriage not knowing what to do. The road before us was over a dreadful place – where we were likely to have rocks and stones roll on our heads! The Snow was so deep in this part that they (only *this* morning) found a man frozen to death! At last one of the post boys – an intelligent Scotchman – said there was a packet going at 4 in the morning from the place we *had left* 6 miles off, that went to *Ayr*, & then from there we might go by Railway to Glasgow. So after a deal of pro & con, & angry words – Liszt in a passion – . . . it was decided we should go *back* again (!) . . .

Back in Stranraer they waited half the night to embark, Liszt meanwhile settling down to sleep in the carriage. Eventually

the carriage was brought to the door – with Liszt asleep in it – & having got all our things we prepared for a start. 'Twas now half three & a fine starlight morning! – freezing very hard. As the Quay was very near (that is, a quarter of a mile), the Ostlers and Boots & c. put a rope to the Carriage & proceeded without horses to the Quay. But as our Carriage was very heavy we lent a hand, & a funny procession it was . . . we all tugging the carriage and the 'great Pianist' – who was fast asleep all the while & knew naught of the honour being conferred on him.

At last manoeuvring the carriage aboard over two planks (having to wake the 'great Pianist') they ultimately cast off. As this voyage ended another shock awaited the stalwart troupe:

It was now near 10 & we were in a sad plight – whether we should reach Ayr before the Steamer (*Railway*) started for Glasgow. After . . . partly dressing for the Concert on board to be quite in readiness, we glided into a harbour & to our dismay saw the Railway Train – just leaving! Impossible to catch or stop it, so there we were left in the lurch. No train till 2!! (The Concert begins at 1!! – 40 miles off!) However, on inquiry we found there was a *third class train* (where they carried Pigs & Cattle & c. & luggage!) starting at 11 – & it was proposed we should go in this! . . . We were all perished on the horrible *open train* on the Railway. 'Twas most horrible.

Fortified with porter they spent three hours in this open carriage in the bitter cold, with livestock adjoining. Having missed the Glasgow concert that day (Monday) the agent advised giving a concert on Wednesday (as planned) with an additional one on Friday. This was all very well, except that their Edinburgh appearances were for Tuesday, Thursday and Saturday. Thus the intrepid group had daily to traverse forty-three rough miles in freezing conditions – a coach journey of five or six hours. This in addition to concerts, sight-seeing in Edinburgh and plenty of late-night carousal. On one of the journeys, 'I never remember seeing such hail & terrific sort of sleet – which was impelled by the Wind so that it almost broke the Glass of the carriage windows.' The second Glasgow concert (22 January)

> was not half so good as we expected. Very badly attended indeed. Liszt brought in some very dashing Scotch girls with him ... *He* sat in the room with them – to the great dismay of the poor 'artistes'. For a wonder, I was *not encored* in a Single thing. Everything rather flat. I sang my 'Trio' shamefully – but this was entirely owing to Liszt sitting right under me – made me dreadfully nervous.

Two days later they left the Scottish capital 'with 4 white horses & the Jockeys in Velvet Caps! An immense crowd to see us start. Took a last farewell of Holyrood, Arthur's Seat, Calton Hill & c. in our way and thus we left the great city of Edinburgh.' The southward journey included concerts in Newcastle, Sunderland, Durham, Richmond, Darlington and Halifax. On 30 January they made a twelve-hour railway journey from Leeds and were mightily relieved to reach Euston Station and the end of this 'Grand Tour' of ten adventurous, arduous and uncomfortable weeks. Liszt had been promised the huge fee of 500 guineas a month but Lavenu lost heavily on the tour and his star pianist nobly waived his rights in the face of this financial disaster. His last visit to London (until that of his old age, forty-five years later) was in May and June 1841 for some recitals and a Philharmonic Society concert.

Returning to his continental doings: the last of Liszt's essays of this period was a short obituary of Paganini.[11] It is important for its reflection on the nature of virtuosity and for its final motto-phrase:

> May the artist of the future gladly and readily decline to play the conceited and egotistical role which we hope in Paganini has had its last brilliant representative; may he set his goal within, and not outside, himself, and be the means of virtuosity and not its end. May he constantly keep in mind that though the saying is *Noblesse oblige*, in a far higher degree than nobility: *Génie oblige!*

[11] GM, 23 Aug. 1840.

In acts like the founding of a pension fund for the Hamburg orchestra with a gift of 17,000 francs (1840) and his continued efforts for the Beethoven fund, Liszt showed publicly what he considered to be the obligations of genius.

Included in his first Paris solo recital (27 March 1841) was his fantasy *Valse infernale* from Meyerbeer's *Robert le diable*. He struck a rich vein with operatic fantasies in the years 1840–2 including works based on *Norma, I Puritani, La Sonnambula, Lucrezia Borgia, Lucia di Lammermoor, Parisina* and *Don Giovanni (Don Juan)*. The spectacular success of the *Réminiscences de Robert le Diable* (it sold 500 copies on the first day of publication in Paris) led to an unfortunate incident on 25 April at an all-Beethoven concert in aid of the Monument Fund at which he played the E flat Concerto under Berlioz. But the Parisian public demanded the *Valse infernale*. A scandalized German reviewer wrote:

> All this particular public demands from him is miracles and meretricious rubbish. He gives it what it wants, basks in its favour and plays – in a concert for Beethoven's memorial – a fantasy on *Robert le Diable*. It was done, however, with some reluctance. The programme consisted exclusively of Beethoven's works, but that did not prevent a raving audience from calling thunderously for that fantasy, Liszt's most popular showpiece. It was a point in favour of this very talented man that he threw out a few angry words – *Je suis le serviteur du public: cela va sans dire!* – before sitting down and rattling the favourite piece contemptuously off. So one is punished for one's sins. One day Liszt will be called upon in heaven to play his fantasy on the devil before the assembled company of angels – though perhaps that will be for the very last time![12]

The writer of those lines was the 27-year-old Richard Wagner, then eking out a precarious existence in the French capital. He encountered Liszt twice personally but in these casual meetings there is no hint whatever that they would some day form one of the most remarkable liaisons among artistic giants.

Liszt engaged a secretary, Gaetano Belloni, who managed his tours and other activities for the next six eventful years. In Brussels in February he met the young Prince Felix Lichnowsky who became a close friend and the companion of several tours. Grandson of

[12]Transl. R.L. Jacobs and G. Skelton, *Wagner writes from Paris*, London, 1973, 133f.

Beethoven's patron, young Lichnowsky's liberal politics had caused strains with his family; he was in financial straits, which Liszt gladly helped alleviate.

On 26 April Liszt attended one of Chopin's rare concerts and wrote an admiring review. Its generous spirit contrasts sharply with Marie's sour view: 'a small malevolent coterie is trying to resuscitate Chopin, who is going to play at Pleyel's place. Madame Sand hates me, we no longer see each other...'[13] She even put about the malicious fiction that Sand was encouraging Chopin out of jealousy of Liszt's recent triumphs. The causes of these divisions between George and Marie are as complex as those between Frédéric and Franz.

The two men were utterly different characters. Just as Liszt always admired Chopin's individuality and musical refinement, Chopin was at first overwhelmed by Liszt's technique, his amazing sight-reading, and skill at drawing unusual sonorities from the piano. But Liszt the socialite, the political philosopher, the darling virtuoso of crowded salons, the composer of dazzling fantasias, the scornful duellist with Thalberg, the idealist defender of Beethoven – in other words the public Liszt – Chopin began to dislike. The Pole was by nature a retiring, private individual; a poetic, classically-orientated artist. The Hungarian, in the years Chopin observed him, was the embodiment of Romantic extravagance, and his public and private doings were announced everywhere with the subtlety of a salvo of artillery. Chopin was, as Liszt put it, 'repelled by the furious and frenzied face of Romanticism'. Even Chopin's long affair with the literary epitome of high Romantic ebullience, George Sand, was essentially a withdrawing: they disappeared to Nohant, to Majorca – while Paris gossiped. And Marie d'Agoult led the town-talk.

On her return in November 1839 relations were strained with Sand, owing to indiscretions on the part of both women. Balzac had been George's guest at Nohant in February 1838 and there she filled him with information about her guests of the previous summer. He wrote to Madame Hanska, 'It was *à propos* of Liszt and Madame d'Agoult that she gave me the subject of *Les galériens*, or *Les amours forcés*, which I am going to treat, for in her position she cannot do so herself. Keep this secret.'[14] What Balzac learned was not so much about Liszt, whom he knew, but about Marie;

[13] Letter to Henri Lehmann, 21 April 1841.
[14] Quoted by Newman, *The Man Liszt*, 116n.

and in addition to the story of a lady who gave up husband and high society to follow her lover (which was common knowledge) he now gleaned aspects of her character, her role as protective muse, and her candid views on Liszt. His novel was finally, significantly, called *Béatrix* and the first two parts were published serially in April–May 1839. (The third part, 1844–5, has little bearing on present matters, Balzac's imagination having wrought a very different fate for the characters originally drawn from life.) When it appeared Sand wrote anxiously to Balzac, 'I count on you to clear me of any blame should it occur to her to accuse me of spreading malicious stories.'[15] The portrait of Marie in the book as Béatrix, who leaves her titled husband for the composer-singer Gennaro Conti, is coldly and cleverly accurate in physical detail and in character portrayal. Or character betrayal – for Sand herself is cast in the novel as an authoress with a sexually ambiguous name (Camille de Maupin[16]) who, with venomously feline sharpness, introduces us to the failings and flaws of Béatrix. The portrait of Conti is a less than believable Liszt, but quite in keeping with an eighteen-thirties' view and a d'Agoult–Sand–Balzac composite impression: an artist vain and pretentious, prophetic, demonic, angelic, exuberant, but inwardly cold; who apes and trifles with other men's works. That Marie (and all literary Paris) knew the amusement Balzac was creating is clear from her letter to Liszt of 21 January 1840:

> A week ago Potocki met Balzac at the Opéra. 'Well,' said Balzac, 'I've got those two women to fall out.' (I have not mentioned to you previously that Balzac has a new novel on the stocks, written after a week's tête-à-tête at Nohant.) 'Not really,' replied Potocki, 'for I saw Mme Sand yesterday at Mme d'Agoult's.'[17]

They may well have been seen together, but their relations were no longer those of friends. For Marie's pen, too, had dipped in poison, in letters from Italy during the winter 1838–9 to Carlotta Marliani, Ronchaud and Pictet, which are full of jibes and sarcasm directed at Chopin and Sand (who were in Majorca). Jealousy was the motive, for Marie gives Carlotta an admission that Liszt would have been astounded to read: 'You do well to love Chopin's talent;

---

[15] Sand, *Correspondance*, Paris, 1964– , IV, 711.

[16] A double play on Sand's maiden name, Aurore Dupin, and on Gautier's Mlle de Maupin, also based on Sand.

[17] AL, I, 361.

it's the beautiful expression of an exquisite nature. He is the only pianist I can listen to without being bored, but with a deep sense of composure...'[18] Jealousy, too, of George's literary gift which 'mistakes pebbles for diamonds and frogs for swans ... The only thing that interests me ... is the falling-off of her talent'. Carlotta took the letters to Lamennais who, shocked by their nastiness, advised her to show George all that Marie had written. From that moment George determined to have nothing to do with Franz or Marie. But Marie, unaware of Marliani's breach of confidence, proceeded to write haughty letters complaining of George's long silence and 'betrayal of a sacred friendship'. George eventually replied, pointing out that Marie, and not herself, had wounded the friendship.

Wounded, but not quite mortally. The maintenance of icy reserve allowed them to meet in society. The lingering serpent of jealousy still gnawed at Marie who could not endure George succeeding with Chopin where she had apparently 'failed' with Liszt. She gloated over each of George's literary setbacks. Sand's revenge was a pointedly cruel portrait in her novel *Horace* (published 1841–2) of the 'Vicomtesse de Chailly', a society lady of artificial intelligence who has ambition as a patroness of the arts. On its appearance Liszt told Marie: 'There is no doubt that it is your portrait that Mme Sand attempted to paint in her description of Madame de Chailly's "artificial mind", her "artificial beauty" and her "artificial nobility".'[19] A few days later he urged her not to react adversely: 'I beg you not to take any notice of the insults launched at the Vicomtesse de Chailly. Please do not give Mme Sand the satisfaction of being offended by them ... you must not seek revenge for these little perfidies. No, no; you are too noble, too great – sometimes despite yourself.'[20] In conversation he is reported to have reasoned with her: 'Is your name in it? Did you find your address in it, or the number of your house? No! Well then, what are you crying about? What right have you to feel yourself attacked? Let him whom the cap fits wear it...'[21] Ironically, just at the moment *Horace* appeared, Marie was making *her* literary debut, like Sand under a masculine nom-de-plume. 'Daniel Stern' was to go on to write the most spiteful example of

[18] Sand, op. cit., IV, 721, n. 1.
[19] AL, II, 186.
[20] ibid., 191f.
[21] J. Wohl, *François Liszt* (transl. B. P. Ward), London, 1887, 68f.

life-into-literature, her novel *Nélida*. In 1870 Liszt told Princess
Wittgenstein:

> For my part I always protest, as I did thirty years ago when *Béatrix*
> and *Nélida* were published, against deductions being made from
> characters in novels to characters in real life who resemble them.
> The public can divert itself in this way to its heart's content. As for
> the supposed models, the wisest thing for them to do is to remain
> perfectly indifferent and to grant generously to the author the right
> to maltreat them according to his fancy.[22]

Chopin treated all this with a similar independent disinterest. He
had never been over-enamoured of Marie d'Agoult anyway, and
with Liszt he contrived a coolly diplomatic acquaintance. Chopin
too was to quarrel and break with his mistress and in her novel
Lucrezia Floriani the fragile, morbid and tormented character of
Prince Karol is a fictionalized Chopin. He never acknowledged
this, just as Liszt never admitted seeing himself as the anti-hero of
Nélida. With the obvious parallels of two female writers publicly
dissecting the natures of their pianist-lovers, it is interesting to
note that Sand began writing her book immediately after *Nélida*
had been serialized (March 1846).

For one pair of fateful lovers the island of escape was Majorca;
for the other, Franz and Marie, it was Nonnenwerth. On this
picturesque islet in the Rhine near Bonn, where legend has it that
Roland died of love, there were only a few fishermen's cottages,
a chapel and half-ruined convent, part of which was let as a guest
house. In this peaceful sanctuary Marie spent three holidays with
Liszt and the children (1841–3); summers that stretched into
autumns, the last idylls of a dying love. Lichnowsky was a frequent
visitor; Liszt set his poem *Die Zelle in Nonnenwerth*, and a visit
to the Lorelei's rock inspired his famous setting of Heine's ballad.
These years saw his first flowering of song composition: from 1839
onwards he composed about forty-five songs in a decade, the best
of them (Heine, Goethe, Petrarch and Hugo settings) being revised
in the Weimar period.

At nearby Cologne he committed himself to yet another fund-
raising project: the completion of the cathedral. In Frankfurt he
was initiated into Freemasonry (18 September 1841); Lichnowsky
was present and Liszt's sponsor was Wilhelm Speyer, for whose
choir he wrote several male-voice choruses. (He contributed nearly

[22] FLB, VI, 247.

thirty works to this *genre* during the 1840s.) Liszt's Freemasonry was symptomatic of a broadminded and undogmatic religious outlook: he received his second degree in Berlin (February 1842), was subsequently elected an honorary member of Lodges in Iserlohn and Zurich, and joined a Lodge in Budapest, 1870.[23] As late as 1884 he encouraged a pupil, Berthold Kellermann, in his wish to become a Freemason, and on Liszt's death there were many masonic obituaries.

The climax of his tours of German towns and cities was an extended stay in Berlin which followed visits to several musical centres including Cassel (where he met Spohr) and Leipzig (where he took part in a Clara Schumann concert, including his 2-piano arrangement of *Hexaméron*). The thirty-year-old Liszt's debut in the Prussian capital marks the high point of his *Glanzperiode*. No single artist had ever evoked such scenes of wild public enthusiasm, a veritable orgy of *Lisztomanie*.[24] In addition to his twenty-one concerts with their vast repertoire, the patronage of royalty and his election to the Prussian Academy of Sciences, he appeared again as a conductor with Beethoven's *Pastoral* Symphony and Spontini's *Olympia* overture. In Berlin he saw much of Spontini, Meyerbeer and also Mendelssohn, whose opinion of his playing contrasted with that of the delirious crowds. He found it scrappy, unfaithful to the score, careless in dynamics and even harmonies. 'He has forfeited a considerable part of my esteem through the idiotic pranks he played, not only with the public – which matters little – but with the music itself.'[25] This is proper criticism, but it should be noted that faithfulness to the text was not the rule at the time, and Mendelssohn's remarks are not echoed in statements by Berlioz and Wagner (at both ends of Liszt's career) who spoke of his model interpretations of Beethoven.

Of female admirers in Berlin, two were especially notable. The great actress and celebrated beauty Charlotte von Hagn fell under his spell. Some cryptic verses of hers were the basis of his song *Was Liebe sei?* Liszt also treasured the hours he spent in the company of Bettina von Arnim, that imaginative spirit of German Romanticism, essayist and letter-writer, who had known Goethe and Beethoven. The departure from the city which had talked of

---

[23] A full account of Liszt's Freemasonry is given in Philippe Autexier's *Mozart and Liszt Sub Rosa*, Poitiers, 1984.

[24] The events were recorded by the critic Rellstab in *F. Liszt*, Berlin, 1842.

[25] Letter to F. David, 5 Feb. 1842.

nothing but Liszt for two months was of appropriate pageantry: our hero, accompanied by Lichnowsky, in a carriage drawn by six white horses, escorted by thirty carriages-and-four, and followed by hundreds of private coaches. Along Unter den Linden there were students in uniform and crowds calling 'Vivat!' while Friedrich Wilhelm IV and his queen acknowledged the procession from their palace windows. 'Not *like* a king but *as* a king did he march out, surrounded by a rejoicing crowd.'[26]

The progress towards Russia was no less magnificent and his first appearances there were glamorous affairs, news of his colossal Berlin triumphs having preceded him. En route he played in various Baltic towns, and in Königsberg received an honorary degree of Doctor of Philosophy. Russian contacts dated from Rome in 1839 and a recital organized by Count Mikhail Vielgorsky, a noted amateur composer, at the house of Prince Galitsin, Governor-General of Moscow, who was wintering in Italy. The next year, at Ems, Liszt was presented to the Czarina and the idea of a Russian tour with imperial patronage agreed upon. Thus on the day after his arrival in St. Petersburg (16 April 1842) he was received by Czar Nicholas I:

> 'We are almost compatriots, Monsieur Liszt?'
> 'Sire?'
> 'You are Hungarian, aren't you?'
> 'Yes, Majesty.'
> 'I've a regiment in Hungary.'

This chillingly inauspicious prelude did not dampen Liszt's enthusiasm for the nationalist awakening in Russian music. On the contrary his aristocratic demeanour and his musician's common sense kept a tactful if precarious balance. When Nicholas arrived late at a private concert and struck up a conversation, Liszt stopped playing and sat with head bowed. Eventually noticing the silence, the Czar asked the reason. 'Music herself should be silent when Nicholas speaks,' was Liszt's immortal reply. Other remarks of this sort probably tempered the enthusiasm of the nobility on his subsequent visits to Russia and Poland. But Liszt was lastingly more concerned with the stirrings of new music. His championship of Glinka was significant at a time when the Russian was under-valued both at home and abroad. At his fifth Petersburg concert he improvised on themes from *A Life for the Czar*, and on his

[26] Rellstab, *F. Liszt*, 37.

second visit to the city one year later, he saw *Ruslan and Ludmila* and made a transcription from it. He also transcribed a setting of Delvig's *Solovey* (The Nightingale) by another Petersburg composer, Alyabyev.[27] On the 1843 visit he arranged works by Bulgakov and Vielgorsky. In his lifelong regard for Glinka (whom he called 'the patriarch-prophet of music in Russia') Liszt was one of the first to assess the importance of Russian nationalism. He responded with enthusiasm to the strikingly original scores of Dargomizhsky and, later, to those of a new generation, including Balakirev, Borodin, Cui, Glazunov, Liadov, Mussorgsky and Rimsky-Korsakov. His second Russian tour (1843) included Moscow, where he gave seven concerts and spent evenings listening to Muscovite gypsy musicians.

His victorious receptions in Prussia and Russia provoked another series of acid press comments in Paris; however, none of the important future events of Liszt's career was to centre on the French capital. He found plenty of acclaim elsewhere; at Liège in July 1842 at a Grétry Festival, for instance, where he encountered the young César Franck and subscribed towards the publication of his opus 1, a set of three trios. (In gratitude Franck dedicated his Piano Trio op. 2 to Liszt, whose music was to have a profound influence on him.) He was also acclaimed in Germany – particularly in Weimar, capital of the small Grand Duchy of Saxe-Weimar-Eisenach. Geographically small, but in German culture a major landmark, for Bach had worked there (1708–17) and Weimar had been the famous home of Goethe (from 1775) and Schiller (who held the chair of history at nearby Jena from 1789). Wieland and Herder were other writers who flourished in Weimar's great Classical Age under the patronage of the Grand Duke Carl August (1757–1828). This duke's son, Carl Friedrich (1783–1853), married Maria Paulovna (1786–1859), grand-daughter of Catherine the Great, daughter of the assassinated Czar Paul and sister of two Czars, Alexander I and Nicholas I. She was interested in music and had taken lessons from Hummel. Liszt first played before the ducal pair in November 1841, gave a charity concert in the town and received a decoration from Carl Friedrich. He returned almost a year later when the Hereditary Grand Duke Carl Alexander (1818–1901) married Princess Sophie Wilhelmina (1824–97), daughter of the King of the Netherlands. Maria

---

[27] No. 1 of *Deux mélodies russes*, G250.

Paulovna and her son Carl Alexander (Grand Duke from 1853) were the moving forces behind Liszt's appointment as 'Kapellmeister in ausserordentlichem Dienst' (2 November 1842) – a 'special musical directorship' with a small nominal salary and a stipulation that he spend three months of the year there. The contract also noted that 'Herr Liszt wishes to remain Herr Liszt for life, without accepting any other title'. He fulfilled his duties there in the winter of 1843–4 (conducting in Weimar for the first time) but, apart from a brief call early in 1846, he did not settle in the town until 1848, when it became his permanent home. Why, then, did Liszt accept the ducal patronage in 1842? Firstly, he was attracted to Weimar and would have endorsed Berlioz' enthusiasm, expressed on his visit early in the following year:

> Here I breathe! I feel something in the very air that proclaims Weimar a cultivated, an artistic town. It looks just as I imagined: calm, luminous, contemplative, full of air and light, and set in a landscape of streams, wooded hills and charming valleys. How my heart beats as I walk through it. So that was Goethe's summerhouse over there – where the late Grand Duke liked to go and take part in the learned discussions of Schiller, Herder and Wieland! This Latin inscription was carved in the rock by the man who wrote *Faust!*[28]

Secondly, Liszt sensed the desire of the Grand Duchess and her son to recreate the glories of the Classical Age. The idyllic combination of an enlightened court, lively artistic and theatrical life and the scholarship of the nearby university appealed to the idealist in Liszt, and in letters to Marie and to Carl Alexander over the next years he elaborated these ideas.[29] He already looked forward to settling down from his constant travels and, although that time had not yet come, he pondered over ideas for large-scale composition, especially various opera projects. For the realisation of many schemes Weimar seemed perfect. Working with the court orchestra, he could study and perfect orchestration as well as improve his conducting technique. Here were the means for creating a workshop for new music, for bringing neglected works to performance, for developing opera and choral music, gathering together young talents and, above all, finding peace for composition. 'I have come to the conclusion that I must soon give up the

[28] *Memoirs*, 350f.
[29] AL, II, 323; LCA, 1–3, 7–12.

virtuoso career,' he wrote to Marie from Breslau,[30] where on 1 February 1843 he made his debut as operatic conductor with *Die Zauberflöte*.

Five years were to pass before he took his final bow from the concert platform, and within that time his relations with Marie came to an end. Some have attributed this break to the supposed succession of amorous relations Liszt indulged in during their long months of separation. Of these, no name attracted more public scandal than that of a notorious adventuress, the Irish, pseudo-Spanish Lola Montez in whose company he was seen frequently in 1844. Lola, who danced and flirted her way to become the mistress of the King of Bavaria two years later, accompanied Liszt to a Dresden performance of *Rienzi* by the local Kapellmeister, Wagner. Liszt had encountered Wagner again in Berlin fourteen months previously and had promised to see *Rienzi* as soon as he could. A performance (29 February) was specially mounted for him. The two composers met in the tenor Tichatschek's dressing room but Wagner felt repelled by the seductive Lola and hurriedly withdrew. La Montez proceeded to Paris, anticipating Liszt's annual spring visit there, and rumour of their attachment alarmed and antagonized Marie.

Her indignation loses something of its force when it is remembered that she herself was closely involved with a number of men during his absences (most recently with the poet Georg Herwegh), and that she had already committed to paper much of her novel *Nélida* (begun in November 1843; completed the following summer). Marie's transformation into the author Daniel Stern had been encouraged by another male admirer, the journalist and editor de Girardin, who published various critical essays by her.[31] As Daniel Stern she was to attain distinction in later years with her fine *Histoire de la Révolution de 1848* (published 1850–3) and various essays including *Dante and Goethe* (1866). But in Liszt literature she is remembered for *Nélida*, in which the heroine (Nélida is an anagram of Daniel) is a beautiful blonde heiress who emerges from her convent education into the glittering world of the Faubourg Saint-Germain and whose marriage to the Comte de Kerväens is the event of the season. The anti-hero is Guermann, an artist of inferior social rank with whom she elopes to Switz-

---

[30] AL, II, 253.

[31] Her debut as Daniel Stern was in reviewing a Delaroche exhibition, *La Presse*, 12 Dec. 1841.

erland and (after he returns briefly to Paris to establish his supremacy over a hated rival painter) they settle in Milan. But dazzling society and the lure of great commissions elsewhere attract him more than Nélida's Beatrice-like devotion and inspiration. Guermann abandons her in Florence and shortly afterwards accepts the patronage of the Grand Duke of W–. However the great works he has long dreamed of creating prove too much for him. He stares at the blank walls where his frescoes ought to be, in broken-hearted despair. Finally he falls ill, sends for Nélida and dies in her arms, confessing his guilt and error in abandoning her. She returns to Paris and devotes the rest of her life to good works.

This transparent concoction of fact into feeble fiction did not see the light of print until 1846.[32] Not until then did Liszt know of its existence. But in Paris in April and May 1844 there was no doubt that the final break had come. Her disinterest in, even disgust at, his virtuoso tours, the mutually realised impossibility of her sharing life with him at the Weimar court, her shattered vanity at the failure of her 'mission', and her jealousy of his real or imagined love-affairs, now fatally sundered their relationship. She wrote suggesting they communicate only through a third party. On 11 April he replied,

> I am deeply sad and profoundly distressed. I count one by one all the sorrows I have put into your heart, and nothing and no one can save me from myself. I do not want to speak to you, or to see you, even less to write to you.[33]

Forgetting his last avowal he wrote again next day, but apparently to no avail. By 7 May he had agreed to let his friend the violinist Massart act as intermediary. Liszt reassured Marie as to pecuniary arrangements: 'The interest on the capital I shall invest will all but cover the upbringing of the two girls'. Blandine was to go to boarding school; Cosima and Daniel were to remain with Liszt's mother. The rupture was complete. As is the way of the world, the children became pathetic pawns in the lovers' crisis and its bitter aftermath. The published correspondence of Liszt and d'Agoult breaks off for a year and when it resumes she is addressed coldly as 'Madame' and the subject is the sorry wrangle over the children. Alarmed at reports that she intends to have them live

---

[32] Serialized in *La Revue Indépendante* 25 Jan.–10 Mar. 1846; pub. in book form, 2 vols., later that year.
[33] AL, II, 338.

under her roof, he objects to this, knowing that her view of him was so antagonistic that he feared a permanent breach with his children. 'Can you really think it would suit me to have Blandine brought up in your home as long as you remain armed for battle at any price against me?'[34] To this she rejoined

> You are capable of the worst cowardice: that of threatening from a *distance* and *on grounds of legality*, a mother who claims the fruit of her womb ... I am aware, monsieur, that I have lost a desperate struggle in which I could only invoke your heart, your reason and your conscience. But I protest before God and before mankind, I protest before all mothers at the violence done to me ... Henceforth, monsieur, your children have no mother; that is what you wanted. Their fate lies in your hands; no amount of heroic devotion will ever be strong enough to fight against your madness and wild egotism ...[35]

The indignation can be justified on both sides, but there is nothing less edifying in the story of Franz and Marie than their attitude to the children. They were neglected and abandoned as babies, separated from their parents during their formative years and as a result bewildered and emotionally battered. Yet thanks to the love of Anna Liszt and an extraordinary, worshipping wonder they conceived for both parents, they survived the storms with remarkable resilience.

While Marie retired to the country at the end of May 1844 to put the finishing touches to *Nélida*, Liszt also left Paris – a city soured for him not only by the quarrel with Marie but also by a spiteful journalistic attack on him by Heine.[36] He made first for the country home of Princess Belgiojoso and then for the south of France where he busied himself with a flurry of concerts in Lyon, Dijon, Marseilles, Toulon, Nîmes, Montpellier, Sète, Béziers, Toulouse, Montauban, Agen, Angoulême, Bordeaux and Bayonne. At Marseilles he met the poet Joseph Autran and Liszt's setting for male voices of his *Les Aquilons* was performed; three later Autran choruses were added to form the set *Les quatre éléments*. On this journey he also made a poignant visit to Pau and to his first love, the unhappily married Caroline d'Artigaux, née Saint-Cricq. Each was now the victim of an ill-fated relationship, and this re-

---

[34] Vier, *Franz Liszt: l'artiste, le clerc*, 78.
[35] ibid., 155.
[36] 25 April, 'Musikalische Berichte aus Paris', in Heine *Sämmtliche Werke*, XI, Hamburg, 1862, 404ff. *Cf.* E. Newman, *Life of Richard Wagner*, I, 276n.

encounter brought forth his fine song of renunciation, *Ich möchte hingehn*.

When Liszt crossed into Spain and began a six-month tour of the Iberian peninsula, he was the first great pianist ever to make such a journey.[37] His companions throughout were the baritone Ciabatta, who acted as his secretary and sang in several concerts, and Louis Boisselot, son of a Marseilles piano-maker whose instruments Liszt used during the tour. There was no possibility of reaching Weimar that winter as the stay in Spain and Portugal was extended beyond expectation owing to his outstanding successes during nine public and charity concerts in Madrid, a similar number in Lisbon and, in between, ten-day stays each in Córdoba, Seville (where he was immensely impressed by the huge Gothic cathedral) and Cádiz (where he fell for the charms of a señorita called Emilia). At the accustomed round of private soirées and banquets he met local musicians and absorbed many Spanish musical folk idioms. He played to royalty: the fourteen-year-old Queen Isabella II of Spain bestowed a title and a jewelled gift upon him, only to be outdone in munificence by the gifts lavished on him by Queen Maria II of Portugal. The latter was especially impressed by Liszt's latest transcription (November 1844) of the *Marche funèbre* from Donizetti's *Dom Sébastien de Portugal*, an opera about to receive its first Portuguese production. Of Liszt's arrangement (dedicated, like the opera, to the queen) Donizetti marvelled to a friend: 'it will make your hair stand on end!'[38] Other work during the Iberian tour included a Lamennais setting *Le forgeron*, sketches for the *Ballade No. 1*, a transcription of an elegy by one of his hosts in Córdoba, Soriano Fuertes, and the *Grosse Conzert-Phantasie über spanische Weisen* (February 1844; published posthumously 1887): a work of formidable technical complexity and contrapuntal dexterity which, despite its daunting density of texture, amply proves Liszt's devotion to the popular, colourful local dances – fandango, jota and cachucha. His most famous (much later) Spanish work is the *Rhapsodie Espagnole* (*Folies d'Espagne et Jota Aragonesa*): a light-filled evocation of Spain which has justifiably achieved lasting performance both in its solo piano version and in Busoni's arrangement for piano

[37] On his Iberian tour: Robert Stevenson in *Musical Quarterly*, LXV, Oct. 1979, 493–512; JALS, IV, Dec. 1978, 11–17 and JALS, XII, Dec. 1982, 6–13. See also LSJ, VI, 29f.
[38] G. Zaradini, *Donizetti*, Bergamo, 1948, 802.

and orchestra (premièred by Bartók in Manchester, 1904). More evidence of Spanish influence is found in the Hugo bolero song-setting *Gastibelza* (published 1844) and in reports of Liszt's improvisations on Valencian and Catalan folk music during his concerts in Valencia and Barcelona. In Granada he had another vivid encounter with gypsy musicians by the Alhambra. Together with Glinka, Liszt was a pioneer among 'outsiders' who drew on the Spanish style. It is a neat historical resolution that the two founding fathers of the later Spanish and Portuguese nationalist schools were both Liszt pupils: respectively Isaac Albéniz and José Vianna da Motta.

The prolonged stay in Spain was also a psychological retreat from family worries; other reactions to the d'Agoult crisis are seen in his loving letters to his daughters and anxious ones to Massart.

Following concerts in France and Switzerland, Liszt arrived in the third week of July 1845 at Bonn for the long-awaited Beethoven Festival and unveiling of the monument. The idea for a statue had originated as long ago as 1828; the first public appeal had been made in December 1835 and, owing to poor response, another followed three years later. The failure of this in turn drew the sorry affair to Liszt's attention in 1839. He personally contributed 10,000 francs and sacrificed much time and artistic energy arranging and performing fund-raising events. Arriving in Bonn three weeks in advance of the festival he was astonished to find the preparations in considerable disarray. After ten years of planning it was only in the final ten days that the committee hurriedly erected a temporary hall large enough to accommodate the expected thousands. Apart from the mismanagement, various cabals arose and attacked Liszt for taking too prominent a part in the proceedings! The event was attended by the King and Queen of Prussia, but, coinciding as it did with the arrival of their guests Queen Victoria and Prince Albert, the resultant fuss and confusion detracted from, rather than contributed to, the memory of Beethoven. Invitations were bungled, hotels hopelessly crowded, the weather intolerably hot, and pickpockets abounded. Beethoven no doubt would have found wry amusement in the fact that when the veils fell from his bronze likeness he was discovered with his back firmly turned upon the royal spectators.

Berlioz had previously participated in Liszt's Beethoven Fund concerts and attended the festival as a reviewer. His entertaining eye-witness account is matched by those of Sir George Smart,

Moscheles, Chorley and Hallé.[39] 'It seemed as if it had been fated that ... in the arrangement of this "Apotheosis" there should be trouble, jealousy, intrigue, indifference and ill-report,' noted Chorley, who added that 'the seamy side of artistic life has rarely been so clearly and so coarsely manifest as at that Bonn Festival'. Of the attacks on Liszt, Berlioz wrote

> It will be asked how and why there could be any ill-will against Liszt ... to whom the credit must go for initiating and carrying out whatever has been successful at Bonn ... It is chiefly this deserved credit ... which gave offence. Some had a grudge against him because of his extraordinary talent and success; others because he is witty, yet others because he is generous, because he has written too fine a cantata, because the others' compositions ... were unsuccessful ... because he speaks French too well and knows German too thoroughly, because he has too many friends, and doubtless because he has not enough enemies...[40]

Liszt was slighted by the failure of Mendelssohn, Schumann or Hiller to attend; Schindler (Beethoven's biographer) publicly questioned Liszt's ability as a conductor; and to add scandal to simmering controversy Lola Montez turned up uninvited, broke into a private dinner and danced upon a table.

Of the more sober moments of the festival, the musical direction lay in the hands of Spohr and Liszt; the latter conducted the Fifth Symphony and played the E flat Concerto. Berlioz privately criticized Liszt's conducting but had no such reservations about his concerto playing, which was also extravagantly praised by Moscheles and Chorley. Hallé noted: 'he adhered scrupulously to the text, and a finer and grander reading of the work could not be imagined'. The third and final morning began with the première of Liszt's *Beethoven Cantata*. It was his first choral work with orchestra and the variety and style of his instrumentation were warmly praised by that severe critic of the art, Berlioz. As on the previous day the royal guests were late and Liszt was obliged to begin without them. Just as the cantata drew to a close the royal party appeared. Seizing his opportunity, and to the silent indignation of many in the huge crowd, he raised his baton and

[39] Berlioz, *Evenings in the Orchestra*, 2nd Epilogue. Chorley and Smart in SAE, vol. 25, 104–20; and Hallé, *Autobiography*. Official account of the festival: H. K. Breidenstein in SAE, vols. 25, 27, 31.

[40] Quoted in Barzun, *Berlioz and the Romantic Century* (transl. C. Roche), London, 1951, I, 471f.

conducted it again from start to finish. This was merely the beginning of a very long day. A few Beethoven works and Weber's Concertstück (with Marie Pleyel) were performed at the request of Friedrich Wilhelm and Queen Victoria, and a number of miscellaneous pieces followed on the departure of the royals. After some of the audience had been in their seats for more than five hours the concert was brought to a halt and the farewell banquet commenced. This, in appropriate disharmony with the whole enterprise, ended in chaos and uproar with an unseemly wrangle among the guests, sparked off by Liszt's failure to mention the French in his toast to the participating nations. The day ended for Liszt with a musical evening given by the king at Brühl, at which he and Meyerbeer played, and Jenny Lind and Pauline Viardot-García sang. After the wear and tear of Bonn he retired, ill with jaundice, to take the cure at Baden-Baden. He rested at Princess Belgiojoso's during the autumn, and in Paris. There in November he met Marie Duplessis, the beautiful but tragic model for Dumas' *La Dame aux camélias*. She was already in the grip of her fatal illness and to console her, when she begged that he might take her away with him, he encouraged her to dream of a trip to Constantinople.

For her the dream was impossible, but the last great enterprise in Liszt's *Glanzperiode* was his epic eastern tour. It began in the spring of 1846 when between March and mid-May he gave ten Viennese concerts, three each in Brno and Prague, and five in Pest. He met several composers: Nicolai, Balfe, Vincent Wallace, Johann Strauss II, and, again, Berlioz, who tells in his memoirs of a banquet in Prague at which Liszt became so drunk that he and Belloni had difficulty restraining him from engaging in a duel with an even more intoxicated Bohemian. The pianist was still asleep next morning at eleven-thirty, before a concert at noon. After a hurried awakening 'he climbed into a carriage, arrived at the hall, entered to a triple-barrelled broadside of applause, sat down, and played as I do not believe he has ever played in his life. Verily there is a God ... for pianists.'[41]

After some weeks as Lichnowsky's guest at Castle Grätz he gave concerts in Zagreb (July), Oedenburg (August) and revisited his birthplace nearby. During late September and October he visited several Hungarian towns: Köszeg (1 concert), Dáka (as

[41] *Memoirs*, 506–8.

guest of Leo Festetics), Pest (1 concert), Szekszárd (1 concert), Högyész (as guest of Count György Apponyi sen.), Nádasd, and Pécs (2 concerts). At his Pest concert he first played his paraphrase from the recent opera *Hunyadi László* by his most important Hungarian contemporary, Franz Erkel. He celebrated his thirty-fifth birthday while at Szekszárd in southern Hungary as a guest of his friend Baron Antal Augusz. At Nádasd and Pécs he was in the company of Bishop János Scitovszky, who became a firm ally; Liszt wrote a setting for a local male-voice quartet (*A patakhoz*; 'To the brook') and played the organ of Pécs cathedral. From there he visited Mohács, Eszék (now Osijek), Zimoney, Pancsova (now Pančevo) and Bánlak, en route for Transylvania. The first weeks of November were spent in Temesvár (now Timişoara) where he gave four concerts and visited Arad, Lugos (Lugoj) and Nagyszeben (Sibiu) for further appearances. Two weeks in Klausenburg (modern Cluj) were followed by a journey south-east through Nagyendyed (Aiud) and Nagyszeben to Bucharest, the Wallachian capital, where he spent the last two weeks of the year. During these wanderings Liszt inevitably encountered many gypsy musicians and worked on 'Magyar' pieces including the first 'Hungarian Rhapsodies' as well as finding material for his 'Romanian Rhapsody' (published by Bartók, 1936). Liszt was received with almost adoring affection in eastern Europe by local musicians, artists, intellectuals and radicals. National feelings were running high and the journeying of the virtuoso-composer assumed the importance of a royal progress. Early in 1847 he proceeded to Jassy (Iaşi) in Moldavia for a two-week stay, and in mid-January entered the Ukraine for his last Russian tour.

There, on 2 February, Old Style, at one of his concerts in snow-bound Kiev he received a gift for his charity event of 100 roubles from a lady member of the audience. Seeking out the generous donor he discovered her to be the Princess Carolyne von Sayn-Wittgenstein and at their meeting the whole of his future was altered at a stroke. She had been enormously impressed by his playing and deeply struck on hearing his *Pater Noster* sung in a local Roman Catholic church. He in turn was overwhelmed by her personality. Marie received a letter dated 10 February:

> Do you know a piece of news? It is that I have met at Kiev, by accident, a most extraordinary woman, really very extraordinary and eminent ... to such a degree that I gladly decided to make a detour of twenty leagues to talk with her for a few hours. Her

husband's name is Prince Nicolas Sayn-Wittgenstein, and the name of her family Iwanowska. It is from their house that I am writing to you.[42]

This information neatly conceals three facts: that husband and wife had been separated for several years; that his detour 'for a few hours' was in reality a visit of many days (ten days is usually quoted but Liszt may well have remained there throughout March); and that the 'house' was her own luxurious mansion set on her vast estate of Woronince, an area peopled by her 30,000 serfs. Carolyne's character and her influence on Liszt's most prolific period of composition will shortly be discussed. For the moment their continued union was postponed as she made a visit to St. Petersburg (where she met Berlioz) and he fulfilled his remaining concert obligations. During April and May he appeared in Lemberg (Lvov), Stanislav (Ivano-Frankovsk) and Czernovtsy.

In June his long-cherished desire to visit Constantinople was realised and he sailed from Galatz down the Black Sea and through the Straits of Bosporus. He was not disappointed by the magnificent harbour, the Golden Horn, and the glories of Byzantine art. He wrote to Erard of his excitement at the concerts 'which took place in the splendid rooms of the Russian Embassy, from where the eye could roam as far as the Sea of Marmara, from Pera to Constantinople, from Seraglio Point to Mount Olympus, from Europe to Asia'.[43] Mount Olympus was poetic licence, but Liszt might actually have seen it had he carried out his intention of visiting Greece, then returning to Constantinople before going to Weimar in December. None of these plans materialized. He was weary climbing the Olympian heights of pianism and the end of his virtuoso career was close upon the exotic Turkish adventure. The Sultan received him, heard him play twice at the palace and bestowed costly bejewelled gifts on him. His master-of-music happened to be Giuseppe Donizetti (brother of Gaetano) with whom Liszt made friends; a curiosity among Liszt's transcriptions, the *Grande paraphrase de la Marche composée pour Sa Majesté le Sultan Abdul Medjid-Khan*, was the result of this acquaintance.

On his return to the Ukraine from Asia Minor he gave ten concerts in Odessa and called at other nearby towns. At Elisabetgrad (now Kirovograd), one month before his thirty-sixth birthday, he made his final appearance. He never again accepted a fee

[42] AL, II, 375.
[43] FLB, VIII, 50f.

for playing the piano, and the fortunate few who heard him in private or at a rare charity event during the remaining forty years of his life were well aware that they listened to a living legend. He did not go to Weimar that winter but went into retreat with Carolyne at Woronince from late September 1847. When he emerged it was with new creative ideas and far-reaching plans for life.

4

Weimar (1848–61)

Carolyne Iwanowska was born in 1819 at Monasterzyska in the Ukraine, the only child of an immensely rich Polish couple. From the start her life was eccentric. Her mother preferred to live abroad and her father gave her free rein to keep her own hours, to eat when she liked, to ride her horses over the wild plains. She acquired an early addiction to cigars, a voracious appetite for reading and a deep (Roman Catholic) religiosity which in later years bordered on mania. In 1836 she wed Prince Nicholas von Sayn-Wittgenstein (1812–64), an army officer of modest means and a member of a Russian branch of a Westphalian family of that name. Nicholas and Carolyne produced one child, Marie Pauline Antoinette (1837–1920), and they separated a few years after their marriage. The princess then led an isolated, unorthodox life on the estates she had inherited and was twenty-eight when she first met Liszt.

Small, dark-haired and swarthy, copious in conversation and feared for her analytical wit, this unpretty girl seems an unlikely captor of Liszt, the associate of beautiful, stylish women. It is difficult not to paint her in a slightly ludicrous light, especially in retrospect. Her increasingly periphrastic prose culminating in her immense 24-volume *Causes intérieures de la Faiblesse extérieure de l'Eglise* (Interior Causes of the External Weakness of the Church); her cigars and detestation of fresh air; her graceless manner of dress; her plethora of crucifixes and other pious paraphernalia: all these curiosities have fanned the flames of mockery. Yet the princess who so powerfully attracted Liszt in 1847, who exercised immense energy to encourage his most substantial works, whose love for him was always selfless and devoted, cannot be dismissed frivolously as a caricature blue-stocking. The idealized portrait of her given by Ramann and La Mara on the one hand, and the abuse heaped on her by partisans of the Wagner family or Marie d'Agoult's descendants on the other, must be stripped away to assess her properly. The task is well nigh impossible: the immensity of her largely unpublished correspondence, the jungle of verbiage of her own writings plus those she penned in Liszt's name, make it difficult to penetrate to her real personality. Mere statistics have repelled scholars: Alan Walker cites her nearly 2000 unpublished letters to Liszt, the vast unpublished Ramann–Wittgenstein correspondence and 'the more than fifteen hundred handwritten missives with which [she] bombarded the Russian ambassador to Weimar during the 1850s in connection with her divorce case, some of which are two hundred pages long...'[1] – this in addition to four volumes of Liszt's letters to her, and even they are not complete or free of censorship. Confusion is further confounded by the views of her contemporaries: Bülow and Wagner were alienated by her, yet Berlioz gratefully acknowledged her as the inspiration and stimulus for his masterpiece *The Trojans*. Liszt, whose view is of paramount importance, adored her. In his Testament of September 1860 he wrote:

> Whatever good I have done and thought for twelve years, I owe to Her whom I have so ardently desired to call by the sweet name of wife – which human malignity and the most deplorable machinations have obstinately opposed hitherto – to Jeanne Elizabeth Carolyne, Princess Wittgenstein, born Iwanowska. I cannot write her name without an ineffable thrill. All my joys have come from her, and my sufferings will always go to her to find their appeasement. She has not only associated and identified herself completely and without respite with my existence, my work, my cares, my career – aiding me with her advice, sustaining me with her encouragement, reviving me by her enthusiasm with an unimaginable prodigality of pains, previsions, wise and gentle words, ingenious and persistent efforts; more than this, she has still more often renounced herself, sacrificed what was legitimately imperative in her own nature in order the better to carry my burden, which she has made her wealth and her sole luxury.

Their love cannot be doubted. What remains unclear is *when* it was first seriously mooted that they might wed; and also, ultimately, *why* they did not. There is no evidence that marriage was discussed during Liszt's retreats to Woronince. Indeed Carolyne's move to Weimar apparently took him by surprise.

At Woronince (October 1847 to January 1848) he composed and revised works and sketched future pieces, but wrote tan-

---

[1] Walker, *Franz Liszt: the virtuoso years*, 15n, 28.

talizingly few letters to indicate his imminent intentions. Certainly he basked in the favour of this intellectual Polish-Ukrainian admirer and shared with her a hoard of literary, philosophical and religious enthusiasms. He was flattered by her sensitivity to his genius and doubtless by her bestowal of expensive gifts on him. But there is no hint that he had any plans other than moving to Weimar and, at last, devoting himself to composition and conducting. Gossip, including press reports, began to circulate concerning the marriage of the famous pianist to a Russian princess. Writing from Woronince Liszt vehemently denied the rumours.[2] When he left there and travelled by Lvov, Cracow and Dresden to Weimar he wrote regularly to Carolyne: letters of love and longing but without mention of marriage or of her permanent move to Weimar. He settled down to the busy musical life of the court, and conducted his first opera there, Flotow's recent *Martha*.

Tuesday 22 February 1848 was a momentous date for Liszt and for Europe. On that day the Paris revolt began, heralding a wave of uprisings that were to shake Europe for the next year; and on that day Liszt received a number of delayed letters from Carolyne announcing her plan to leave Russia, ostensibly to take the waters at Carlsbad. He offered to meet her as soon as he was free from Weimar duties (after 24 March). Again there is no clue that he knew her full intentions: she had in fact petitioned the Czar for divorce, converted as much of her property as she could realise into Western currency, and made arrangements to travel with her daughter, the child's Scottish governess Miss Anderson, and as many personal possessions as could be transported. The rendezvous was arranged at Lichnowsky's castle of Krzyzanowitz (today in Poland, on the Czech border) although its proprietor was away on political business. There Liszt waited three weeks until Carolyne and her entourage arrived on 18 April, when they proceeded to Lichnowsky's fortress castle of Grätz (Hradec) near Troppau (Opava). Liszt told his friend Schober that the princess had safely passed the blockaded Russian frontier and was established at the castle with

> her very charming and interesting daughter. As it is still very early
> for the spa season, I should like to persuade her to spend a couple
> of weeks in Weimar before her Carlsbad cure (which unfortunately

[2] *Cf.* Winklhofer, *Liszt's Sonata in B minor*, 29.

is very necessary for her!) ... I will prepare a suitable apartment or house for the princess.[3]

Meanwhile he and Carolyne embarked on a tour that was extraordinary in view of the fiery wave of insurrection that swept central Europe: 'circumstances could not have been less propitious for a grand tour of the Hapsburg Empire'.[4] The Paris disturbances led to the abdication of Louis Philippe and the appointment of Lamartine as leader of a provisional government on 24 February. In March there were revolutions in Vienna, Venice and Berlin; the Hungarian Diet forced Austria to grant new democratic rights, the Croatians and Czechs made similar demands and unrest flared in Poland. On 1 March Liszt noted: 'Belloni is more fortunate than I. As a lieutenant of the National Guard he dated his last letter from the Paris town hall! But I am forgetting that I hate politics, and indeed during the last fifteen years this is the first enthusiasm which has gripped me ...'[5] On 24 March he reacted to news from Pest: 'My compatriots have just taken a step that is so decisive, so Hungarian and so unanimous that it is impossible to withhold a tribute of legitimate sympathy'.[6] On 30 March he enthused to Marie:

> ... my heart is in my mouth whenever the courier brings the newspapers. However it may turn out, I will never retract the opinion I voiced at the time of the first news of the provisional government ... that it will strike at every government of Europe, except England. As a result of that alone the Republic of France would again be the most providential stroke of the century. Lamartine's manifesto ... has given me the most intense satisfaction of my life ... God protect France! And Christ deliver the world by love and liberty![7]

He wrote a *Workers' Chorus* ('Arbeiterchor') which was rejected by a Viennese publisher in 1848.[8] The unnamed author of the words may be Lamennais, as Liszt had set another chorus of social comment and hope to his verses, *Le Forgeron* (1845). The cantata

---

[3] FLB, I, 72.
[4] Winklhofer, op. cit., 30.
[5] FLB, VIII, 55f.
[6] FLB, IV, 29.
[7] AL, II, 393.
[8] *Cf.* preface to the first published edition, Editio Musica, Budapest, 1954. An arrangement for mixed chorus and orchestra was made by Anton Webern, 1930. The cantata *Hungaria* was not published until 1961.

Hungaria (text by Schober), written in the wake of the Hungarian rising, is a hymn to liberty and patriotism. The idea for a *Revolutionary Symphony* was revived (see page 25), 'this time in the form of a five-movement symphony. The first was to be *Héroïde Funèbre*, the second a setting of *Tristis est anima mea*, the third was to be based on the Rákóczy and Dombrowski marches (symbolising Hungary and Poland), the fourth on the *Marseillaise*, and the last movement was to be a setting of Psalm 2, *Quare fremuerunt gentes?* Only *Héroïde Funèbre* was completed, although sketches for the second and fifth movements exist. He later arranged the *Marseillaise* for piano and made several versions of the Rákóczy march, including one for orchestra. (He also introduced the tune to Berlioz who used it in his *Damnation of Faust*.) Liszt and Carolyne visited Vienna at the very time the second uprising there forced the emperor to flee his own capital. Liszt's pupil János Dunkl recalled a vivid boyhood memory:

> In the stormy days of the year 1848 I visited the barricades with Liszt, which were commanded by the well-known bass singer Karl Formes. Liszt presented the workers posted there with cigars and gold. Instead of all his medals he wore a cockade of the Hungarian national colours in the buttonhole of his jacket.[9]

On 6 May he was serenaded by Viennese students and made a fiery political speech. He took Carolyne to see his birthplace in Raiding, and at Eisenstadt saw an old Franciscan friend Father Albach, to whom he dedicated his recent *Pater Noster* and the Mass for male chorus and organ. They reached Weimar in mid-June.

Despite his apparent sympathy for revolution, his popular identification (especially in eastern Europe) with freedom and egalitarianism, and his presence at the Vienna barricades, Liszt's political enthusiasms went no further. Just as the liberal efforts of 1848–9 ended in despair, so Liszt's initial fervent response quickly grew into disillusionment. Without crediting him with political prescience, he seems to have sensed intuitively the demise of the ideals of Romanticism and the death of the colourful, flamboyant hopes of republicanism. This led him to an attitude of resignation, but not to the bitterness, frustration and hopelessness of a Lamartine or a Wagner. Liszt remained at heart a spiritual optimist; a democrat with the patience to wait for saner times. The criticism

[9] J. N. Dunkl, *Aus den Erinnerungen eines Musikers*, Vienna, 1876.

was made by some that he should have fought by the side of his Hungarian compatriots. He was chastised for having recourse to art rather than to action, for fleeing from social responsibility into the arms of religion, or for taking refuge in the safe backwater of Weimar. Such indictments ignore Liszt's constant concern with the universal rather than the particular, the revulsion he felt for the bloody reality of revolution, the peculiar stance of the Church in relation to the conflicts, and the personal circumstances Liszt was bound up in: chiefly his Weimar obligations and his new and awkward ties with Carolyne.

Certainly Weimar was a haven of peace. In 1816 Grand Duke Carl August was the first German ruler to grant a constitution. And in 1848 Carl Friedrich circumvented social unrest by granting a timely civil list of pensions for the citizenry. As Liszt settled in Weimar, the 'June Days' in Paris witnessed the deaths of thousands in a brutal suppression. News of fierce reaction in Poland, in the Danubian states, in Italy, constantly bombarded Liszt and the repression and carnage sickened him. Personal tragedy came with the death of his close friend Felix Lichnowsky, murdered during an insurrection in Frankfurt where the National Assembly was meeting. The sad and painful defeat of Liszt's homeland darkened the year 1849. The piano piece *Funérailles*, subtitled 'October 1849', is a powerful, eloquent tribute to Lajos Batthyány and to thirteen leaders of the Hungarian struggle who were all executed on the sixth of that month. Hungary's greatest poet, Petöfi, died on the battlefield at Segesvár. Liszt declared:

> I would be the first to answer the call to arms, to give my blood and not tremble before the guillotine, if it were the guillotine that could give this world peace and mankind happiness. But who believes that? We are concerned with bringing peace to the world in which the individual is justly treated by society.[10]

The effect of his religion on his attitude is complicated by the individuality of his beliefs, the involvement of church and pope in the upheavals, and by the influence of the intensely pious Carolyne. His Christianity had never been orthodox, as shown by his commitment to the ideas of Saint-Simon and Lamennais. He combined an unshakeable faith in the essential tenets of the Gospels with a blend of personal mysticism and a passionate and universal social

[10] Fanny Lewald, *Zwölf Bildern nach dem Leben*, Berlin, 1888, 341.

concern. When Pius IX became pope in 1846 he was popularly regarded as a reforming figure; liberal Catholics and many democratic republicans held great hopes of him. But the progress of 1848 transformed Pio Nono into an absolutist prince and the scourge of freethinkers. On 29 April he dissociated himself from the Italian nationalists, denounced the war against Austria and the idea of revolution. Forced to flee Rome in November he was not restored until the following July, with the aid of Louis Napoleon's French troops. A papal encyclical of 1849 condemned socialism and communism, and in April 1850 he revoked the liberal constitution in the Papal States that he had granted early in 1848. These events must have affected Liszt's thinking and undoubtedly Carolyne's fervent Romanism strengthened in him the view that Church and pope were the ultimate authorities. Revolution had ended, not in harmony and brotherhood after all, but in disunity, internal and international strife, bloodshed and deeper division. Lamennais had once envisaged a European Republic with the pope at its head; and, prior to the emergence of Victor Emmanuel of Piedmont, many Italian liberals had favoured a united nation under the papacy. Liszt's faith in the pontiff was therefore no more new or naive than these views. Another hero emerged for him in the person of the then republican Louis Napoleon. Liszt's twin passions, Republican France and Catholic Rome, now united in such strong bonds, gave him new hope.

Although the number of his sacred works grew considerably in the next decade, it is wrong to attribute this entirely to his reaction to 1848–9 or to the influence of the princess. A number of religious choruses belong to earlier in the 1840s (notably the Lamartine setting *Hymne de l'enfant à son réveil*); in 1846 he wrote a *Pater Noster* and an *Ave Maria*; and the spiritual imagery of earlier instrumental works like *De profundis* and *Harmonies poétiques et religieuses* is continued in the set of ten pieces, first sketched in 1845, also collectively known as *Harmonies poétiques et religieuses*, several of which are sacred or mystical in content, for example No. 3, *Bénédiction de Dieu dans la solitude*. The ecclesiastical choruses of the 1850s are a continuation of a long, developing thread in Liszt's creative career and, when the ideas for an opera faded from his mind, he embraced the larger forms of psalm, Mass and oratorio. The male-voice Mass of 1848, a fairly substantial work, has been cited as evidence of Liszt's retreat from revolution to religion. But the probability is that it was composed before the disturbances of that year, possibly at Woron-ince.[11]

If Liszt emerges ingloriously or unheroically from 1848, little better can be said for his friends Berlioz, Balzac, Hugo or Sainte-Beuve. Nor could those who actively participated claim much honour: Lamennais, Lamartine, Sand and (in Dresden) Wagner. Only with regard to the Hungarian tragedy is Liszt's dilemma particularly poignant. Eighteen years were to pass before the ideas of freedom, so fleetingly glimpsed, were to be partially fulfilled. Fortunately he was then able to contribute to her artistic heritage and esteem. The persuasive Carolyne certainly played a part in keeping him at Weimar, in creative calm. In an obscure article of 1849, which they wrote jointly, this passage appears in her hand:

> Political passions intrude violently into everyone's life. So many things, so many existences have become questionable that no one knows *where* and *how* to get out of the turmoil, that is *where* and *how* to find the calm necessary for an elaborate creation of works that have to leave a lasting trace.[12]

At Weimar, where her stay of 'a couple of weeks' became a residence of twelve years, she rented two floors of a large and ugly villa, the Altenburg, and from 1851 occupied the whole thirty-roomed house, which Liszt filled with his furniture, books and pictures from Paris; treasures acquired during his tours; and valuable musical instruments including a square piano of Mozart's and Beethoven's Broadwood. For a first year he lived in the Hotel Erbprinz and tactfully kept this as his 'official' address even after he moved into the Altenburg. With perfect pretence and decorum the court sent all communications to his hotel during the dozen years Liszt actually occupied the Altenburg. The liaison (like that of Cosima and Wagner later at Tribschen) was not respectable but it had great style. An exalted atmosphere prevailed and hospitality was lavishly bestowed on a profusion of guests. Into the sleepy world of Weimar came a truly international procession of talented visitors. Liszt's impact on the duchy must have been extraordinary: not least because of his tireless, garrulous, cigar-

---

[11] *Cf.* P. Merrick, *Liszt in 1848: a revolutionary change of heart?*, LSJ, IV, 1979, 6–9.

[12] Quoted by M. Eckhardt in NHQ, XXV/95, Autumn 1984, from a MS in the Bibliothèque nationale, Paris, of an article for *La Musique*, 1 July 1849 (not in GS).

smoking mistress, who kept constant and protective watch over his multifarious activities.

Her hopes that the Grand Duchess, as sister of the Czar, would intercede on her behalf and assist her to obtain a divorce, soon met with disappointment. She was tolerated by the Weimar court at first, but the autocratic Czar Nicholas was not to be swayed by a minor princess over whom he held absolute spiritual and temporal power. Nicholas Sayn-Wittgenstein was close to the Czar and, although he had no interest in his wife's personal life, he was determined not to lose her property. An extraordinarily devious and complex set of intrigues, legal and spiritual machinations, occupied more than a decade. Its intricacies in Weimar, at the Russian court, with orthodox clergy and with Rome, allegations by the Wittgensteins that Carolyne had conspired against the Russian state, struggles over custody of the child Marie, and a thousand other wrangles cannot be unravelled here. In essence, the struggle postponed any idea of wedlock between Franz and Carolyne till 1860, and the legal outcome was her loss of her Russian fortune. On a visit to Weimar in September 1852 by Prince Nicholas, some financial compromise was reached and he agreed to seek a Protestant divorce, remarry, and thus increase Carolyne's hopes for permission to marry Liszt. But when Carolyne refused an order from the Czar demanding her return to Russia to settle her affairs, her property was confiscated and held in trust until her daughter came of age. In a very literal sense then, she sacrificed everything for Liszt. As a result of the Czar's decree she became *persona non grata* at the Weimar court which, together with cold-shouldering from some citizens of the little town owing to her cohabitation with Liszt, placed her in a position that was far from easy. Events were rendered tragi-comic by the fact that Nicholas Wittgenstein now deceived her. He obtained a divorce in 1855 and remarried in 1856 but, almost incredibly, Liszt and Carolyne remained unaware of this until 1860. Nor was this irony the last twist in the saga, for in 1860 Carolyne pursued her case in Rome and the sorry conclusion of that sojourn will be discussed later.

Liszt's attitude throughout the crisis is difficult to fathom, as his letters are nebulous on the subject of marriage, so biographers have fallen back upon hearsay and gossip. Although he was wearied by the protracted dispute, Carolyne had won first place in his heart. When he realised her move to Weimar was permanent he accepted the situation and pledged his troth. His first mention of marriage is in a letter of 1849 to his mother.[13] A strong link in the bond was his warm affection for Marie Wittgenstein. His many letters to Carolyne's daughter evince fatherly wisdom and a touching, tender concern that contrasts wistfully with letters to his own three children in Paris. In the first years of their union his phenomenal achievement and creative output owed much to Carolyne's firm practical management. Even when his affections were transferred elsewhere there was no possibility that she would remain anything other than the central being of his life, as the extent of her sacrifice of energy, wealth and reputation for his sake would have made any thought of sundering their relationship scandalously dishonourable. Throughout the Weimar years she was essential to him, and he responded to her self-denial and unflagging sense of duty, if not with absolute fidelity, with at least an outward and sincere affirmation of devotion.

Liszt disappeared temporarily beyond the horizon when he moved to Weimar and the world took time to adjust to the fact that he had retired as a concert pianist at the age of thirty-five. The meteoric and intrepid tours, along with his sixty waistcoats and 360 cravats, were things of a bygone age. When he emerged as a serious composer many people were slow to recognise the fact. In the late 1840s he was not primarily viewed as a composer at all, but at most as a brilliant arranger. No one could have predicted the colossal creative outpouring of the coming decade. Inwardly, however, he had long envisaged many of the serious Weimar goals. They came to fruition only now as his career acquired a hitherto unknown stability.

One ambition he had held dear for some time was to launch himself as an opera composer. His considerable efforts in this direction were fated to remain incomplete. In understanding Liszt the composer it is essential to realise that his creative mind was never compartmentalised and that he usually worked on several disparate projects at once. But this very gift of versatility, this richly diffuse imagination, partly explains his failure in opera, as most of the great composers in that sphere have had a purer and single-purposed vision. For some years, though, Liszt set his sights upon the stage, telling Carl Alexander in 1846 that the conquest of the theatre was the supreme goal of his artistic thoughts, for which he would soon abandon his virtuoso career.[14] He even

[13] Vier, *Franz Liszt: l'artiste, le clerc*, 95f.
[14] LCA, 9.

expressed interest in succeeding Donizetti in Vienna, a powerful, prestigious operatic post that he might have combined with some months in Weimar, but the possibility of the appointment was not pursued.

Three of his operatic projects were to be based on Byron. As early as 1841 he planned *Le Corsaire* (Dumas at one stage helping with the libretto); *Manfred* was considered as a possibility in 1842–4, and as late as 1862 the idea of setting choruses from *Manfred* still attracted him; in 1845 *Sardanapale* occupied him, and until 1851 he had real hopes of mounting it either at Milan or Vienna or Paris. 111 pages of sketches exist for *Sardanapale*, the style owing much to Bellini and Meyerbeer. With *Sardanapale* and *Le Corsaire* he was encouraged and helped by Princess Belgiojoso at a time (after the crisis with Marie and prior to the advent of Carolyne) when it seemed their friendship would become something deep and permanent. In 1845 he considered a stage work based on Dante's *Divina Commedia* (with a text adapted by Autran), and in 1846 a one-act opera after Walter Scott, *Richard in Palestine*. An opera based on Goethe's *Faust* was first mentioned in 1846 and the idea revived in 1850 when Gérard de Nerval visited Weimar. Dumas became involved in the project which Liszt was keen to pursue. *Faust*-related works were much on his mind: the *Chorus of Angels* (1849) was one of several settings from Goethe's play, and he championed *Faust* works by Schumann, Wagner and Berlioz. But no suitable libretto for Liszt's opera materialized. A Hungarian opera, *Janko*, based on a verse-novel by Carl Beck, also foundered, along with one on a gypsy theme, *Kahma, la Bohémienne* (text, Otto Roquette).[15] In 1858–9 he planned an opera on the subject of Joan of Arc with Friedrich Halm and Emmanuel Geibel, and although this, too, fell by the wayside, Liszt orchestrated at this time his dramatic *scena* to a poem by Dumas, *Jeanne d'Arc au bûcher* (originally set, 1845). Additional discarded ideas were the operas *Spartacus*, *Saint Hubert*, *Semele* and about half-a-dozen others. Reasons for the abandonment of all these ideas are many: the feeble nature of many of the scenarios and librettos; Liszt's growing disillusionment with the Weimar theatre; his realisation that his musico-dramatic gifts were not

[15] On *Faust*: E. F. Jensen, 'Liszt, Nerval and "Faust"', *19th Century Music*, Vol. VI, no. 2, 1982, 151ff. For a summary of all his opera projects and a synopsis of *Janko*: L. Szelényi in LSJ, III, 27–30. The libretto of *Janko* was set by Rubinstein as *Die Kinder der Heide*, Vienna, 1861. On *Sardanapale*: Searle, *The Music of Liszt*, 89f.

directed towards the stage but found their real outlet in instrumental and choral works; and, above all, his steadily increasing admiration for the operatic genius of Wagner.

After seeing *Rienzi* in Dresden in 1844 Liszt created interest in Wagner's work by praising it on his travels, and in 1846 made efforts (for the moment unsuccessful) to have it produced in Vienna. That year he received from Dresden the scores of *Rienzi* and *Tannhäuser* and, at Liszt's request, Wagner sent him his *Faust Overture* in January 1848. Calling at Dresden a few months later,[16] after his visit to the Vienna barricades, Liszt astonished Wagner by suddenly appearing in his room. This meeting set the seal on their friendship. They spent an evening at Schumann's house and, after some music-making, an argument broke out concerning the merits of Meyerbeer and Mendelssohn, which ended with Schumann storming angrily out of the room.

Within the next year Liszt was helping Wagner with his purse, his pen, his baton, his piano arrangements, his international influence and his good advice. The penurious Kapellmeister called at Weimar in August, hoping Liszt would buy over the copyright to his scores (through which Wagner had plunged into a morass of debt). Liszt refused: his own finances were mainly tied up with investments for the welfare and education of his children, and those of the princess were uncertain. But his artistic aid was quickly evident. On 12 November he conducted the *Tannhäuser* overture in Weimar, made a piano transcription of it which delighted Wagner, and then mounted the opera itself on 16 February 1849 (its first performance outside Dresden), following that with a lengthy article on the opera (published in Paris, to help widen Wagner's reputation),[17] and made arrangements of other extracts. Wagner could not obtain leave of absence to attend the Weimar première but wrote in terms of the deepest gratitude to Liszt, who replied that he was the indebted one as he had been greatly struck with the bold and fiery genius of Wagner's score. Wagner noted [1 March]: 'We are getting on nicely together. If the world belonged to us, I believe we should do something to give pleasure to the people living in it.' He promised to attend *Tannhäuser* in May when released from his duties, but none of them could have anticipated the manner in which he would arrive: as a fugitive from the calamitous Dresden revolution, with a price

[16] In June, not March 1848 as so often stated in Wagner literature.
[17] *Journal des Débats*, 18 May 1849.

on his head, and hardly safe anywhere in Germany. The political refugee was harboured for twelve days, was stimulated and heartened by seeing a rehearsal of *Tannhäuser* while hidden in a box, and was even presented to the Grand Duchess, before Liszt supplied him with cash and a false passport and sent him over the border, bound for Switzerland and exile. For safe keeping, Wagner's wife sent Liszt the manuscripts of *The Flying Dutchman* and *Lohengrin*. Forwarding the latter to Wagner in Zurich on 29 July, Liszt expressed regret at parting with a work he had come to understand with increasing enthusiasm the more he studied it. Yet he doubted if it would have a wholly satisfactory effect in performance. Wagner's resultant affirmation of the daring imagination of his work and his conviction that Liszt, alone among musicians in Europe, was the man to mount the first production of the opera, won over his friend. He assured Wagner in July 1850:

> Your *Lohengrin* will be given in the most exceptional conditions, with the most favourable prospect of success. The management is spending about 2000 thalers on the production, a thing that has not been done in Weimar within living memory. The press will not be forgotten, and serious, well-informed articles will appear successively in various papers. All the theatre staff will be aflame with enthusiasm. The number of violins will be slightly increased ... and a bass clarinet has been bought. No requirement of design or music will be lacking. I take charge of all piano, chorus, sectional and orchestral rehearsals. Genast will follow your instructions for the staging with zeal and vigour. It goes without saying that we will not cut a single note, not an iota from your work, and that we shall give it in its absolute beauty to the best of our ability.

The fact that Liszt could give *Lohengrin* with the meagre resources at his disposal was one of the most extraordinary aspects of his ambitious feat, and it drew the gaze of the musical world upon Weimar. His orchestra in 1850 numbered a mere thirty-eight: 11 violins, 3 violas, 4 cellos, 3 basses, double woodwind, 4 horns, 2 trumpets, 1 trombone, 1 tuba and 1 timpanist (in 1851 he asked for two more trombones, harp, organ and extra percussion), with a chorus of only 23. The première took place on 28 August, Goethe's birthday. The famous correspondence of the two men, due to Wagner's enforced absence from Germany, is invaluable for Liszt's Weimar years. He performed many tasks for Wagner in Germany: on 16 February 1853 he introduced *The Flying Dutchman* to Weimar, and for a while the possibility of the

Ring being mounted there was seriously considered. The score of *Lohengrin* is dedicated to Liszt, and from this work, too, he made several transcriptions. An essay on the opera and its first performance was followed by articles on *The Flying Dutchman* and *Das Rheingold*.

Liszt's salary at Weimar was as modest as his orchestral forces: 1500 thalers per annum in 1848.[18] Money therefore cannot have attracted him there; nor was there much prestige in leading the musical celebrations of anniversaries, birthdays and so on in a petty dukedom although, as 'Kapellmeister extraordinary' he could leave these in the hands of the regular conductor, Chélard. Although it was a rich duchy (particularly through the fortune of Maria Paulovna) Liszt had great difficulty in persuading the Grand Duke to part with money for the artistic aspirations he claimed to patronise. Actors, singers and musicians were poorly paid. Liszt's dauntless energy at Weimar is thus all the more creditworthy. Peter Raabe lists forty-three operas conducted by him between 1848 and 1858; twenty-three of these were productions new to Weimar and nine were world premières. Of particular interest, apart from Wagner, were Schubert's *Alfonso ed Estrella*, the revised version of Berlioz' *Benvenuto Cellini*, Schumann's *Genoveva*, Cornelius's *The Barber of Baghdad*, four operas by Gluck (for whom he had a fondness dating from boyhood), and Rubinstein's *The Siberian Hunters*. French grand opera was represented from Grétry to Meyerbeer; the Italian tradition from Rossini to Verdi; and German opera from Mozart to Weber. His concert work included all Beethoven's symphonies, Mozart and Haydn, Mendelssohn and Schumann, Handel's *Messiah* and *Samson* and a large corpus of new works.

Along with Wagner, and his own disciples Bülow, Nikisch and Weingartner, Liszt belongs to the founding fathers of the art of modern conducting.

> The Mendelssohn-Spohr school of orchestral conducting, spirited but inclined to glide over difficulties, was superseded by the dynamic school of Weimar. Liszt ... was not a German, and was not educated in the German school of interpretation. Besides his legendary musicianship – Cornelius and others considered his rehearsals the finest musical education – he brought to his task Habeneck's precision and Berlioz' fire, that is, the best qualities of the French school, undoubtedly superior to the German. But the manner in

[18] Haraszti, *Franz Liszt*, 164.

which he conducted was as much his own as his pianistic technique. He insisted that his orchestra master all the technical details so that during the performance he could concentrate all his attention on phrasing and shaping, leaving the individual artists to their own resources. This is a notable conception and a dignified and high-minded artistic principle ... Liszt's beliefs can be summed up in one remark: he wanted to make the conductor 'seemingly superfluous'. Liszt was the first conductor to indicate, by gestures and facial expression, phrasing, dynamics, and everything that is essential in a spirited performance.[19]

His freedom and flexibility of interpretation led to accusations of incompetency, seemingly borne out at the Karlsruhe Music Festival in October 1853, when the orchestra broke down during the finale of the Ninth Symphony under his direction. His former friend Hiller was quick to attack him for vagueness and inaccuracy of beat. In a published reply Liszt defended his concept of conducting, summed up in his classic phrase 'we are steersmen, not oarsmen'.[20] The bad habits of following mechanical and often sluggish time-beaters were ingrained in orchestras (especially those assembled from here and there as at Karlsruhe), and both Berlioz and Wagner wrote of their frustration with attitudes prevailing in the mid-nineteenth century which were at odds with the very essence of contemporary orchestral writing. Liszt's preface to his published symphonic poems is an admirably concise and precise plea to conductors to spend time (especially in sectional rehearsals) communicating the subtleties of colour, tempo, rhythm, accent, balance, contrast and the art of transition.

Despite the rift in their personal relations Liszt devotedly championed Schumann's music at Weimar. In addition to *Genoveva* he presented Part II of Schumann's *Scenes from Faust* (April 1849), gave the première of his *Manfred* (June 1852), introduced *Paradise and the Peri* in 1857, and included his overtures, chamber music and songs in concerts. Schumann's distrust of Liszt's musical aesthetics, and in Clara's case a dislike that grew into hatred, resulted in the Weimar efforts for his music being viewed with coolness and suspicion. Liszt's dedication of his B minor Sonata (published 1854) to Schumann was received with embarrassment, and on the reissue of Schumann's C major Fantasy as part of the posthumously published collected piano works, Clara struck out the original dedication to Liszt.

[19] Paul Henry Lang, *Music in Western Civilization*, London, 1942, 963f.
[20] *On Conducting*, GS, V, 227–32.

Joseph Joachim led the Weimar orchestra from October 1850 until his resignation in December 1852. From the first he seems to have constantly vacillated in his feelings towards Liszt, whom he first met in Vienna in 1846. Before taking up his Weimar appointment he spent 'several unforgettable days' with Liszt: 'Since I have come to know him better my former antipathy to him has been transformed into an equally strong liking for him.'[21] Antipathy eventually won the day. Joachim tried hard to appreciate Liszt's musical aims, admired his strong control over his players, his generosity to his colleagues, and he benefited from his Kapellmeister's fund of wisdom and encouragement in creative matters. But Joachim's admiration for Mendelssohn, his friendship with Ferdinand David and with Brahms, and above all his intimate devotion to the Schumanns sealed his view of Liszt whom he came to view as confused in mind and repulsive in all he created. In the wake of Robert Schumann's mental collapse (February 1854) Clara bravely resumed her concert career and visited Weimar, where Liszt conducted Robert's Piano Concerto with Clara as soloist, and he was considerate and tender, as befitted the circumstances, during her stay at the Altenburg. He published warmly appreciative articles on Robert and Clara at this time and viewed with concern Schumann's suffering and with grief his demise. Despite this loyalty and Liszt's many past kindnesses to Mendelssohn, David, Brahms and Joachim himself, the violinist wrote to Liszt as follows, a year after Schumann's death:

> ... what is the good of hesitating any longer to tell you plainly what I feel – my passive attitude towards your work would surely reveal it, thinly veiled, to you who are accustomed to meet with enthusiasm, and who know me to be capable of a genuine and active friendship. So I shall remain silent no longer on a subject which, I confess to you, your manly spirit had the right to know long before. Your music is entirely antagonistic to me, it contradicts everything with which the spirits of our great ones have nourished my mind from my earliest youth. If it were thinkable that I could ever be deprived of, that I should ever have to renounce all that I have learned to love and honour in their creations, all that I feel music to be, your strains would not fill one corner of the vast waste of nothingness.[22]

[21] *Letters from and to Joseph Joachim* (transl. N. Bickley), London, 1914, 9.
[22] ibid. 130ff.

This blow, and it was not the last from the same pen, has at least the merit of being honest, and is not untypical of the attitude of many conservative minds towards the music of Weimar.

No such clouds as yet obscured the friendship with Berlioz. Having conducted *Harold in Italy* in April 1851, Liszt then wrote to Berlioz suggesting a Weimar revival of *Benvenuto Cellini* (first produced unsuccessfully, Paris, 1838). The Frenchman was touched and delighted at Liszt's admiration for his 'poor brain-child' and began to make changes to the opera which ultimately resulted in a radical revision. When Liszt's production opened on 20 March 1852 Berlioz was unable to attend. But he was present at three Berlioz Festivals in Weimar (a week each in November 1852, February 1855 and February 1856). At the first, in addition to *Cellini*, his *Romeo and Juliet* and the first two parts of *The Damnation of Faust* were heard; at the second the *Symphonie fantastique* and *Lélio* were given (Liszt playing both piano and Chinese gong in *Lélio*) and Berlioz conducted the first performance of Liszt's E flat Piano Concerto with the composer as soloist. In 1855 the Princess urged Berlioz to pursue his idea for an opera based on the *Aeneid*; by the following festival he had yielded to her persuasion and a long correspondence ensued between them on the progress of *Les Troyens*. His letters to Liszt are effectively via the Princess thereafter. In addition to further Berlioz transcriptions and the dedication of the *Faust Symphony* to him, Liszt wrote a long and important essay, *Berlioz and his Harold Symphony*, which deals with aspects of form and content in symphonic programmatic music.

The names of Berlioz, Liszt and Wagner became linked in a kind of Holy Trinity of new music, a development not actively discouraged by Liszt and positively advocated by his young admirers: the disciples of any school always tending to outstrip the founding fathers in enthusiasm, evangelism and dogma. The 'Weimar' or 'neo-German' school, for good or ill, became polarised as the self-styled progressive and advanced wing of the system of musical 'party politics' in the latter half of the century. To clear his head of a jumble of revolutionary and rather muddled thoughts Wagner had written a series of prose works (1849–51) which were wrongly regarded as a blueprint for 'the music of the future'. His music dramas and his subsequent writings refute a good deal of this supposed theory. Not only was the philosophical basis of the new movement therefore somewhat shaky, but Berlioz was suspicious of Wagner's aesthetics and reluctant to have his name attached to any such 'school'. The Princess attempted to exploit the differences between Wagner and Berlioz to the latter's advantage, perhaps in a vain attempt to dampen Liszt's enthusiasm for Wagner. In one way or another all three men were artistically indebted to each other. A host of parallels could be drawn: orchestral, harmonic, thematic (idée fixe, thematic metamorphosis, Leitmotif), in the use of myth by Liszt and Wagner, and of similar subjects by Liszt and Berlioz (e.g. Liszt's *Hamlet, Faust, Tasso, Ce qu'on entend sur la montagne, Christus* and his planned *Sardanapale, Manfred* and *Le Corsaire*). But on examination the differences between them emerge strongly: all were masters of advanced orchestration, but each in a highly individual way; their melodic styles were dissimilar; the advanced chromaticism of Liszt and Wagner was not shared by Berlioz, and Liszt experimented more freely with tonality than Wagner; lastly, the ultimate formal content of their use of extra-musical subject matter was unique in the case of each man. However, all three had apparently ostentatiously abandoned old-fashioned classical models and this was sufficient for them to be banded together and revered *à trois* by the group of acolytes, many of them talented players, composers and conductors, who converged on Weimar. Liszt jokingly called these devotees the 'Society of Murls': he was 'Padischah' or president, the Murls were 'moors' or 'devil-boys' who waged war on the Philistines.

Liszt's favourite pupil, Hans von Bülow, was one of the most forthright and gifted propagandists of the new 'school'. As a boy in Dresden he came to admire Wagner and in June 1849, aged nineteen, visited Liszt. Then a law student, he began to write articles praising Wagner and Liszt, before deciding, in 1850 and flying in the face of parental opposition, to devote his career to music. After spending some months with Wagner in Zurich he went to Liszt as a piano pupil in June 1851, and lived in the Altenburg. He became one of the most complete artists of his generation and reaped laurels everywhere as a conductor and player renowned for the breadth of his repertory and his prodigious memory. His youthful energy found outlets in composition, transcription and vigorous musical journalism. His stance can be gauged from a letter to Bechstein of as late as 1868:

We Weimarists are going to win, you'll see; we shall rule and our opponents will dissolve in gall and be poured away down the closet of the past! And our art – the true, the noble, the high – will thrive greatly; and Liszt will be hailed ... as the founder of interpretative art, with all its implications, and the initiator of a new era.[23]

Further literary allies were Franz Brendel of Leipzig, Schumann's successor as editor of the *Neue Zeitschrift für Musik*; Richard Pohl, an indefatigable advocate of Liszt, Wagner and Berlioz in his books; and the writer and pedagogue Louis Köhler.

Next to Bülow the prodigious talent held in the highest esteem and affection by Liszt was a wildly exuberant Jewish boy, Carl Tausig, aged thirteen when he arrived in Weimar in July 1855 and already well advanced in piano, composition and unruly behaviour. In 1858 he emerged to a triumphant career as soloist and teacher. Another Weimar student, Karl Klindworth, like Tausig and Bülow, was a brilliant arranger, notably of Wagner scores. A gifted composer, Liszt's pupil Julius Reubke, died in 1858 aged only 24: his organ sonata on Psalm 94 and a remarkable one-movement piano sonata are testimony to a genius cut tragically short. Other notable pupils of these years include Franz Bendel, Hans von Bronsart, Leopold Damrosch, Felix Draesecke, Salomon Jadassohn, Robert Pflughaupt and Dionys Pruckner. Two students left entertaining memoirs: Wendelin Weissheimer and, from New York, William Mason, who became the first to take Liszt's ideas to the new world. 'The boys', as Mason calls them, took part in the entertaining of distinguished guests, such as the violinists Wieniawski and Eduard Reményi. The latter, whose playing and enthusiastic Hungarian personality brought him into close contact with Liszt, arrived in Weimar in June 1853 with the twenty-year-old Johannes Brahms. Mason recounts that the very nervous Brahms declined to play before the group and that Liszt instead sight-read his Scherzo op. 4 and part of the Sonata op. 1. Liszt later honoured the company with a rendition of his own recently completed Sonata, and on glancing round the room during an *andante* section, observed young Brahms to be asleep. He finished the piece and left the room without a word. Not too much should be read into this incident: Brahms apparently called on him again, the meeting was cordial and Liszt saw in him a composer of promise.

[23] *Letters of Hans von Bülow* (ed. Moulin Eckart, transl. H. Waller), London, 1931, 82.

The court orchestra contained several great players. Joachim was succeeded by Ferdinand Laub as leader, and the violinists Edmund Singer, Leopold Damrosch and Alexander Ritter were of the first rank, as were the cellist Bernhard Cossmann and the trombonist Eduard Grosse. Liszt benefited from their experienced advice and had the time of the Weimar orchestra at his disposal in order to test the effectiveness of his instrumentation. In his search for perfection in this craft he employed two young composers as secretaries and amanuenses, August Conradi (from early 1848 until autumn 1849, when he left Weimar to become Kapellmeister at Stettin) and then Joachim Raff. From Liszt's sketch of a work in short score of 3–6 staves (with his orchestral indications) his assistant prepared a full score which Liszt in turn revised; another 'clean' score might then be made and the process repeated perhaps several times over. Thus he saved much precious time in laborious copying and had the opportunity to discuss details of scoring, especially with Raff who was an imaginative and prolific composer of works that attained much popularity, although later suffering virtual eclipse. The compositional process of *Tasso* is a good example of the procedure followed with Conradi and Raff (though not necessarily all the versions are listed here):[24]

(1) Liszt's sketches, 1847 or 1848 [MSS N1 & N9].
(2) Full draft in Liszt's hand on 6 staves with orchestral directions [MS N5].
(3) Orchestral score in Conradi's hand, closely modelled on (2) [MS B22c]. This version performed on 28 August 1849.
(4) Orchestral score in Conradi's hand with many corrections in Liszt's hand [Hs 107016]. Performed on 19 February 1850.
(5) Orchestral score in Raff's hand [MS A2b].
(6) Liszt's extensive corrections to (5) [MS A2c]. Rehearsed in July 1851.
(7) Orchestral score in Raff's hand incorporating the corrections in (6) and containing further corrections in Liszt's hand (MS A2a]. This (final) version performed on 19 April 1854.

Such method and collaboration applies to a greater or lesser extent in Liszt's five other earliest symphonic poems: *Ce qu'on entend, Les Préludes, Prometheus, Héroïde Funèbre* and *Mazeppa*. The whole question of these revisions is complex and still requires much research. To the general reader and listener all this is quite

[24] (1–3) and (5–7): Goethe and Schiller Archive, Weimar; (4): Germanisches Nationalmuseum, Nuremberg.

academic: there is no problem (unlike, say, with Bruckner's symphonies) as to which represents Liszt's definitive thoughts, as the final version was always revised by him before publication. But recent research [25] has revealed the important fact that Liszt was not at all the helpless orchestrator he is often depicted as being in the early Weimar days. There is evidence that he practised instrumentation earlier than has been assumed, and a holograph draft of *Héroïde Funèbre* proves him to have been a competent orchestrator as early as November 1849.[26] Raff later made ambitious claims that he deserved most of the credit for the early symphonic poems; claims subsequently made much of by his widow and by Joachim. Undoubtedly Liszt valued and learned from his advice, but Raff remained no more than 'a rather superior copyist'.[27] Raff also wrote books and articles on the 'Weimar School' as did another young man who came to stay at the Altenburg for some years, Peter Cornelius.

The copious musical and literary facets of his personality were quickly realised when Cornelius arrived in 1852. As poet and composer his gifts are best combined in his many songs. He served Liszt as secretary, translator of prose works from French to German, as a fervently partisan contributor to musical journals; and he furnished posterity with anecdotes about Weimar life in his letters and diaries – in particular the sore trial he endured in having the imperious Princess as literary collaborator. His collected writings fill four stout volumes. Weimar writers friendly with Liszt and Carolyne were the novelist and poetess Fanny Lewald, her husband Adolf Stahr, Hebbel, Dingelstedt and Hoffmann von Fallersleben. Other close associates, from a long list, included the actor Eduard Genast, the painter Wilhelm von Kaulbach and the lawyer Carl Gille of Jena with whom he had a valuable correspondence. Famous musical visitors included Robert Franz (thirteen of whose songs Liszt transcribed in 1848), Pauline Viardot, Alexander Serov, Henry Charles Litolff, and the violinists Vieuxtemps and Sivori.

One more visitor left memorable impressions of her three months in Weimar:[28] Mary Ann Evans, later known to the world

[25] *Cf.* JALS, XI, 90ff; XII, 127ff; XVII, 20–3.
[26] Bibliothèque nationale, Paris: Mus. ms. 158.
[27] Searle in *Franz Liszt: the Man and his Music* (ed. Walker), 280.
[28] Collected together in LSJ, VIII, 26–31.

as George Eliot, arrived in August 1854 with her lover George Henry Lewes who was researching his *Life of Goethe*. She wrote:

> The first time we were asked to breakfast at [Liszt's] house ... we were shown into the garden, where, in a saloon formed by overarching trees, the *déjeuner* was set out. We found Hoffmann von Fallersleben, the lyric poet, Dr. Schade, a *Gelehrter* who has distinguished himself by a critical work on the 11,000 virgins(!), and a Herr Cornelius, an agreeable-looking artist. Presently came a Herr or Doctor Raff, a musician who has recently published a volume called *Wagnerfrage*. Soon after we were joined by Liszt and the Princess Marie, an elegant gentle-looking girl of 17, and last, by the Princess Wittgenstein, with her nephew Prince Eugene and a young French (or Swiss?) artist, a pupil of Scheffer. The appearance of the Princess rather startled me at first. I had expected to see a tall distinguished looking woman, if not a beautiful one. But she is short and unbecomingly endowed with embonpoint; at the first glance the face is not pleasing, and the profile especially is harsh and barbarian, but the dark, bright hair and eyes give the idea of vivacity and strength. Her teeth, unhappily, are blackish too. She was tastefully dressed in a morning robe of some semi-transparent white material lined with orange colour, which formed the bordering, and ornamented the sleeves, a black lace jacket, and a piquant cap set on the summit of her comb, and trimmed with violet colour. The breakfast was not sumptuous either as to the food or the appointments. When the cigars came, Hoffmann was requested to read some of his poetry, and he gave us a bacchanalian poem with great spirit ... My great delight was to watch Liszt and observe the sweetness of his expression. Genius, benevolence and tenderness beam from his whole countenance, and his manners are in perfect harmony with it. A little rain sent us into the house and ... then came the thing I had longed for – Liszt's playing. I sat near him so that I could see both his hands and face. For the first time in my life I beheld real inspiration – for the first time I heard the true tones of the piano. He played one of his own compositions – one of a series of religious *fantasies*. There was nothing strange or excessive about his manner. His manipulation of the instrument was quiet and easy, and his face was simply grand – the lips compressed and the head thrown a little backward. When the music expressed quiet rapture or devotion, a sweet smile flitted over his features: when it was triumphant, the nostrils dilated. There was nothing petty or egoistic to mar the picture.

She also met the 25-year-old Anton Rubinstein who called to discuss with Liszt the forthcoming production of his opera *The Siberian Hunters*.

Liszt first heard Rubinstein when the boy pianist made his Paris debut. He was never Liszt's pupil, but Liszt advised on and encouraged his studies (and took a similar interest in Anton's brother Nicholas, aged seven on Liszt's visit to Moscow) and reputedly said of Anton, 'On these shoulders my mantle will fall'. In 1854 the cub was well on the way to being a fully grown lion. Liszt nicknamed him 'Van II', an allusion to Rubinstein's facial resemblance to Beethoven, and perhaps also to his impetuous individuality. He gave Rubinstein's compositions serious attention but was careful not to overpraise them, realising early that Rubinstein preferred 'to fish in Mendelssohnian waters'.[29] In turn the Russian had little time for Liszt's music and heartily detested Wagner. As a pianist though, when he attained complete maturity, Rubinstein stood with Bülow and Tausig next only to Liszt in the nineteenth-century hierarchy, and the velvet beauty and richness of his tone was universally admired. Their mutual regard is touching amid all the jealousies and rivalries of the age, as is Rubinstein's modesty in his oft-repeated remark, 'Put all the rest of us together and we would not make one Liszt'.

One other significant guest had sent Liszt a parcel of piano pieces and a long letter which he received minutes before leaving Weimar to rendezvous with Carolyne in March 1848. It was from a 24-year-old Czech composer totally unknown to him and contained a desperate plea for help:

> I cannot get my compositions published because I would have to pay, and unfortunately I cannot save up so much ... So far no one has done anything for me. Yes, I must say that I was near to despair when I heard that my parents had sunk so low as to become almost beggars ... In my distress, without any sign of help, without friends, a thought struck me like lightning: the name *Liszt* on a piece of music on my table moved me to turn to you, the incomparable artist whose generosity is spoken of throughout the world, and confide in you ... My present position is – dreadful, may God save any artist from a similar one! ... I am a creative artist and a player, yet possess no instrument. A friend allows me to practise on his: truly my fate is unenviable![30]

Liszt responded immediately by accepting the dedication of the 'Six Characteristic Pieces' by Bedřich Smetana and soon arranged for their publication. This was worth more than money to an

[29] FLB, I, 180.
[30] BHZ, 95ff.

artist struggling for recognition. They met when Liszt passed through Prague in June and, eight years later, on another visit there he saw Smetana every day for more than a week and their friendship deepened. In 1857 and 1859 Smetana came to Weimar and was encouraged and influenced by the ideals and aspirations of Liszt and the young circle around him.

In addition to Reubke (whose father was an organ-builder) Liszt had another organist among his pupils of the 1850s: Alexander Winterberger. The Weimar town organist, Johann Gottlob Töpfer, was also a composer and a writer on theoretical and technical aspects of organ building and playing. In nearby Tieffurt Liszt made friends with the organist Alexander Gottschalg. These men awoke his interest in writing for the organ, which he never regularly played as he did not feel competent in pedal technique. Now he had the opportunity to study the possibilities of the mid-nineteenth-century instrument and, with Gottschalg, explored churches in the Weimar area. An additional stimulus may have been his transcriptions for piano of six of Bach's finest organ Preludes and Fugues (1842–50).[31] Liszt's two most important organ compositions are the monumental variations on a theme from *Le Prophète* by Meyerbeer, Fantasy and Fugue on the chorale *Ad nos, ad salutarem undam* (1850), first performed by Winterberger at Merseburg Cathedral on 25 September 1855; and the *Prelude and Fugue on the name BACH* (1855; revised 1870), first performed on 3 May 1856 also by Winterberger at Merseburg. In 1852 Liszt transcribed for organ a Sacred Festival Overture by Otto Nicolai, *Ein feste Burg ist unser Gott*; and in 1860 movements from Bach's cantatas *Ich hatte viel Bekümmernis* and *Aus tiefer Not*.

Transcriptions for piano take second place to original works in the Weimar era, though mention must be made of the Verdi and Wagner arrangements, the *Illustrations du Prophète* from Meyerbeer (Nos. 1–3 for piano; No. 4 the organ *Ad nos*), the Wedding March and Dance of the Fairies from Mendelssohn's *A Midsummer Night's Dream*, the nine Valses Caprices *Soirées de Vienne*, based on Schubert's waltzes, and six Polish Songs from Chopin's opus 74.

With growing confidence in scoring Liszt made arrangements from three composers for piano and orchestra: *Fantasia on themes from Beethoven's 'Ruins of Athens'*, Weber's *Polonaise brillante*

[31] *Cf.* M. Sutter, 'Liszt and the performance of Bach's Organ Music', *Liszt Studien*, II, 207–19.

and, most importantly, Schubert's *Wanderer Fantasia*. These works, together with his two Piano Concertos, *Totentanz* and the *Fantasia on Hungarian Folk Themes* (i.e. Liszt's total output for piano and orchestra, excepting earlier, abandoned works) were scored in the early Weimar years (1848–52) although revisions were made to the concertos and *Totentanz* later. The first performances took place as follows:

Polonaise brillante: Weimar, 17 April 1851. Jadassohn (soloist) / Liszt (conductor).
Wanderer Fantasia: Vienna, 14 Dec. 1851. J. Egghard / Hellmesberger.
Ruins of Athens Fantasia and *Fantasia on Hungarian Themes*: Budapest, 1 June 1853. Bülow / Erkel.
Piano Concerto No. 1 in E flat major: Weimar, 17 Feb. 1855. Liszt / Berlioz.
Piano Concerto No. 2 in A major: Weimar, 7 Jan. 1857. Bronsart / Liszt.
Totentanz: The Hague, 15 March 1865. Bülow / Verhulst.

Liszt orchestrated a number of his songs during the Weimar years: the three from *Wilhelm Tell* (*c.* 1855), *Die drei Zigeuner*, *Mignons Lied* and *Die Lorelei* (all 1860); he also orchestrated several Schubert songs and marches (1859–60).

If Liszt was merely competent as an orchestrator in 1849, by 1854 he had acquired complete assurance. In Bartók's words, 'as an innovator in instrumentation, with his absolutely individual orchestral technique, he stands beside the other two great orchestrators of the nineteenth century, Berlioz and Wagner'.[32] He imposed his originality on the preliminary scores worked out by Raff. It was Carolyne who, in July 1853, urged him to stop using such assistance. 'I think that you do not put enough emphasis on giving colour to musical thoughts. You content yourself with retouching. It seems to me that this is entirely not enough, and if I compare it with a literary style: correction is never as good as original writing.'[33] In the same year he wrote *Festklänge*, his first symphonic poem scored entirely without assistance, and he never used collaborators again. *Orpheus* followed, and was first heard on 16 February 1854, a year that witnessed the premières (in their final versions) of *Les Préludes* (23 February), *Mazeppa* (16 April),

[32] Bartók, *Essays*, London, 1976, 504.
[33] Raabe, *Schaffen*, 78f.

Tasso (19 April), *Festklänge* (9 November); as well as the composition of the *Faust Symphony* (in the space of two months – a remarkable feat even allowing for earlier sketches and the omission for the moment of the choral finale) and *Hungaria*, and the final versions of *Ce qu'on entend* and *Héroïde Funèbre*. (The last three were premièred respectively on 8 September 1856, 7 January and 10 November 1857.) In 1855 he re-wrote *Prometheus* along with the huge choral-orchestral setting of Herder to which it is a prelude (first performed 18 October), and began the *Dante Symphony*, completing it in July 1856 (first performed 7 November 1857). In 1857 he completed *Hunnenschlacht* in February (first performed 29 December), *Die Ideale* and the choral finale to the *Faust Symphony*. The symphony was first heard (with *Die Ideale*) on 5 September 1857,[34] but Liszt continued to revise it before its publication in 1861: this version heard under Bülow, on 6 August 1861. These revisions and the long gestation of works like *Ce qu'on entend*, *Totentanz* and the first two books of *Années de pèlerinage* should bury forever the foolish notion that Liszt threw out his ideas without sketching or polishing, that he was a hit-or-miss composer. On the contrary, he was a fastidious worker. As late as 1880 he was still altering the published score of the *Faust Symphony* (he added a dozen bars to the 'Gretchen' movement). There is no better example of his craftsmanship than in his songs. From 1854 until he left Weimar Liszt enjoyed another rich phase of song writing and apart from the seventeen *Lieder* of those years he carefully re-wrote more than twenty of his earlier songs: paring down the piano part, altering the word-setting, excising needless repetitions, improving the vocal line, and so on. In some cases there are three published versions of a song and further revisions were made in later years. This does not imply insecurity or self-doubt on Liszt's part but rather a healthy creative honesty that constantly seeks to refine and perfect. Any player of Liszt's scores will have encountered his meticulous notation of *ossia* passages, alternative readings, facilitating differing techniques. When a work by Liszt does miss the mark it is certainly not because of shoddy craftsmanship. The last Weimar symphonic poem, one of his finest, was *Hamlet*, written in 1858, published in 1861, but not performed until 1876; an apt illustration of the sad neglect of even his best works.

[34] All these premières were conducted by Liszt, except *Héroïde funèbre* (Moritz Schön) and *Hamlet* (Max Ermannsdörfer).

The orchestra plays an important part in many of his choral works of this period. Apart from the choruses to Herder's *Prometheus* another major secular work is a Schiller setting for male voices and large orchestra, *An die Künstler*, which Wagner warmly praised. The large-scale sacred works with orchestra are the *Missa Solennis* and Psalm 13. The first, composed in the spring of 1855, is also known as the *Esztergom Mass* (or the *Gran Mass* or in German the *Graner Festmesse*) as it was commissioned for the consecration of the cathedral in that ancient Hungarian city. The construction of this magnificent basilica, set on an imposing height overlooking the Danube, was a protracted affair: Beethoven's *Missa Solemnis* was originally intended for its consecration! Liszt conducted his Mass at the ceremony on 31 August 1856. It was 'more prayer than composition' he confided to Wagner: in it he applies the expressive and dramatic qualities he was developing in his symphonic works, a process continued in Psalm 13 of the same year. Of the other Weimar Psalm settings, no. 23 is for solo voice, harp and organ; no. 137 for soprano, women's voices, violin, harp and organ; and no. 18 for male chorus and orchestra (or organ or wind instruments). Along with the 'Prayer' *To St. Francis of Paola* (for male voices, organ, trombones and timpani) the variety of textures and vocal and instrumental combinations illustrates Liszt's perennial quest for a 'new' kind of church music. The origins of his two great oratorios belong to this time, although their completion took place later in Rome. In 1854 the Austrian painter Moritz von Schwind completed a series of frescoes based on the life of St. Elisabeth of Hungary, in the halls of the Wartburg, a castle near Weimar which had been the home of the early thirteenth-century saint, patroness of the poor and downcast. Her character, nationality and the episodes from her life at once suggested to Liszt a dramatic choral-orchestral work on a large scale. In 1855 he commissioned Otto Roquette to supply a libretto, the first parts of which he received in 1856 and began to set in 1857. Progress was slow but he gained a new impulse the following year on reading a life of St. Elisabeth by a Hungarian writer János Danielik and, after some research into modal, liturgical and folk melody, he worked steadily at the score of *The Legend of St. Elisabeth*. The other oratorio, *Christus*, had an even longer growth to fruition. In July 1853 he met the poet Georg Herwegh in Zurich, and told the Princess: 'I have touched on the subject of *Christus* with Herwegh, the piece I want to compose – it is not impossible that he will try to write the work ...'[35] In 1856 he considered Rückert's *Evangelienharmonie* as the basis for a text, and a year later asked Cornelius to write verses based on ideas by Carolyne. Finally Liszt assembled his own text from the Bible and the Liturgy. Work on the score spanned more than a decade but two sections were completed in the Weimar period, *The Beatitudes* and a seven-part *Pater Noster*, both issued separately with organ accompaniment.

Many of Liszt's piano works of this most fertile period of his life were pieces that had a long ripening to maturity. This is especially true of the set of 10 pieces *Harmonies poétiques et religieuses*, the 9 pieces of the Swiss book and the 7 of the Italian book of *Années de pèlerinage*, the 3 pieces *Venezia e Napoli*, the Hungarian Rhapsodies Nos. 1–15, the 12 *Études d'exécution transcendante* and the 6 *Grandes Études de Paganini*. Works that do not have such long roots into his experiences and peregrinations of previous decades include the 3 Concert Studies (*Il Lamento, La Leggierezza, Un Sospiro*) and the study *Ab Irato*; on a small scale the much-loved *Consolations*, the 2 *Polonaises* and the *Berceuse*. As for the *Liebesträume*, most devotees of the universally famous third *Liebestraum* would be surprised to learn that it was not written for piano, but was originally a song, one of three love songs to poems by Freiligrath and Uhland. On a larger scale his most important new keyboard works were the *Grosses Konzertsolo*, later revised as the *Concerto Pathétique* for two pianos (Liszt's only original work for that combination), the *Scherzo and March*, the 2 *Ballades* and the Sonata in B minor. The Sonata of 1852–3 (first publicly performed by Bülow, Berlin, 22 January 1857) is Liszt's masterpiece, now widely played and admired. But it too was misunderstood, neglected by pianists outside Liszt's circle, and attacked by critics: one reviewer of Bülow's performance dubbing it 'an invitation to hissing and stamping'.

The legacy of Weimar – 12 symphonic poems, 2 huge symphonies, 7 concerto works, over 50 secular vocal items, a large corpus of sacred music, the transcriptions, piano and organ works, the many arrangements made from all these and the various versions and revisions of most of them – is a colossal achievement. Liszt was at the height of his powers and in the best works of each genre he attained mastery. Yet it is not the sheer amount of music

[35] FLB, IV, 147.

that is impressive. His output is all the more staggering when it is remembered that he was forging new musical structures in many of these compositions and that his tonal and harmonic procedures were quite revolutionary. He often joked that in his Weimar works he was 'paying off his debts'. The remark is double-edged. He now largely relied on income from the publication of his music, but the 'debts' also meant his earlier career as wandering pianist and socialite. The Weimar Liszt determined to pay back the glitter and tinsel of those years in works of gold. It seems almost miraculous that he had time for so much composition, given his other activities. The above survey omits the long parade of marches and ceremonial pieces which as Grand Ducal Kapellmeister he fittingly turned out. He was preoccupied with management, rehearsing, conducting, engaging artists, supervising productions, entertaining, teaching, proof-reading and, in addition to an immense personal correspondence, he published articles, analyses, replies to critics, propaganda on behalf of fellow composers and two major books, one on Chopin, and a considerable tome on *The Gypsies and their music in Hungary*. Allowing for the assistance of secretaries, amanuenses and the ever ready pen of the Princess, his industry commands wonder and respect. He also found the energy to travel and appear here and there as guest conductor: Karlsruhe, Ballenstedt, Brunswick, Rotterdam, Düsseldorf, Berlin, Vienna, Pest, Prague, Magdeburg, Leipzig, Aachen, Dresden, Coburg and elsewhere.

Following the Weimar Goethe centenary festival of August 1849, Liszt, Carolyne, her daughter and a group of friends enjoyed a carefree holiday on Heligoland. They then repaired to Bad Eilsen where the Princess, who suffered a rheumatic ailment, took the waters. While there Liszt learned of the death of Chopin on 17 October and at once resolved to write a book in tribute to his old friend. The Princess was his collaborator and as a modern translator notes, the book's 'wordiness, its obfuscations, its ramblings on Polish nobility, on national traits, on the glories of the aristocratic spirit, on the value of Polish dances in their original vigour: all of these excursions away from Chopin and his music must be laid at her door. Page after page after page are devoted to fanciful verbiage and the reader (far from being entertained) wonders when he will again encounter the composer hidden behind this flood of words ... Yet the book contains many sensible things and we can hope that these are the sentiments that Liszt insisted be included'.[36] For all its faults 'F. Chopin by F. Liszt' remains a unique document in which one great artist unselfishly praises and laments the passing of a great colleague. Also at Bad Eilsen Liszt worked on a long essay (completed in 1850), *De la fondation Goethe à Weimar* in which he detailed ideas for a foundation, named after the poet and inspired by his universality of outlook, which would embrace writers, composers, painters and sculptors, encourage their arts by competitions and sponsor a four-yearly festival of all the arts. This laudable if somewhat over-idealistic article is especially interesting as the manuscript is entirely in Liszt's hand.

The following autumn Carolyne and Marie again visited Bad Eilsen but both contracted typhus and their stay was protracted until the summer of 1851. Liszt remained with them as long as he could, but when back in Weimar wrote at length almost daily. Whenever parted from her these regular accounts of his doings flowed to the Princess, providing posterity with a good substitute for the diary Liszt never kept. On visiting Wagner in Zurich in July 1853, their first meeting in over four years, he reports: 'We nearly choked each other with embraces ... He wept and laughed and stormed with joy for at least quarter of an hour at seeing me again'.[37] Liszt noted his host's extravagant lifestyle ('he has a decided taste for luxury'), pointing out that Wagner would need two, if not three times his present income to sustain it. He read the *Ring* poems to Liszt, who in turn played Wagner his latest manuscripts: the first six or seven symphonic poems, sketches for the *Faust Symphony* and various piano works. This was Wagner's first exposure to Liszt the serious composer, and it was a revelation. In October the two friends met up in Basel, along with Bülow, Cornelius, Joachim, Pohl, Pruckner, Reményi, Carolyne and Marie. Wagner took a great liking to the 16-year-old Marie, identifying this charming girl with the figure of the goddess Freia in his *Rheingold*. With her, Carolyne and Liszt he proceeded to Paris, where Liszt introduced him to his children. They must have been overwhelmed by the invasion of their orphan-like seclusion by the father they had not seen for eight years and his entourage – the Wittgensteins, Berlioz and Wagner, who read aloud his poem *Siegfrieds Tod*. Throughout this, Cosima, also aged sixteen, stared

---

[36] E. N. Waters, 'Chopin by Liszt', *Musical Quarterly*, XLVII/2, April 1961, 170–94. See also the preface to his translation of the book.
[37] FLB, IV, 140.

shyly at the floor, weeping silently. Neither reader nor listener could possibly have imagined that fate would one day bind their lives together.

Liszt and Wagner met again in 1856. The year began with Liszt's visit to Berlin to see a *Tannhäuser* production which had been mounted due to his negotiations. Later in January he conducted at the Mozart centenary celebrations in Vienna, at the same time urging a complete and scholarly Mozart edition along the lines of the *Bach-Gesellschaft*, a publication which Liszt also worked on. In August he set out for Esztergom for the première of his Mass, which was repeated in Pest (his first visit there in ten years) and in Prague. He conducted the première of *Hungaria* in the National Theatre in Pest, and in Prague formed a lasting friendship with the music historian August Wilhelm Ambros, who as a critic defended him against the views expressed by Eduard Hanslick of Vienna, whose book *Vom Musikalisch-Schönen* (1854) had attacked the Lisztian ideal of a fusion of the arts and declared music to be a pure, autonomous art, not capable of depiction or expression of feelings or emotions. Hanslick's other target was, of course, Wagner, whom Liszt visited for a six-week stay in Zurich in mid-October, joined by the Princess. Not only did the voluble Carolyne irk and annoy Wagner on this visit, but he found Liszt, too, in ill-humour, quarrelsome and physically run down. The strain of his countless activities at Weimar, worries about his children and the exhaustion of recent tours were taking their toll. An unpleasant row with Wagner's young assistant Karl Ritter resulted in Wagner losing his allowance, which was supplied by Karl's mother. But in musical matters things passed congenially. Liszt was spellbound by the *Ring* music which had progressed as far as the first scene of *Siegfried*, and Wagner listened eagerly to Liszt playing through the *Dante Symphony*. On 23 November the two men gave an orchestral concert in St. Gallen. Wagner conducted the *Eroica*, and Liszt his *Les Préludes* and *Orpheus* which Wagner considered 'a quite unique masterpiece of the highest perfection'.[38] When Liszt departed, Wagner set to work on an essay *On Franz Liszt's Symphonic Poems*, published the following spring.

Liszt's irritability at this time had another emotional cause, the roots of which lie three years earlier. In the autumn of 1853 an attractive widow of twenty-eight, with two small sons, arrived

[38] *Briefe an Hans von Bülow*, Jena, 1916, 75.

in Weimar to seek lessons from Liszt. Agnes Denis-Street (née Klindworth; Karl Klindworth's cousin) was a pupil who would merely have flitted in and out of Liszt literature had it not been for the assiduous search for Liszt letters carried out by La Mara. In 1892 she traced Agnes Street to Paris, found the letters to be in the possession of her son George, who in turn provided her with 133 items for publication, on condition that his mother's identity remain secret. In 1894 La Mara published a volume mysteriously titled *Briefe an eine Freundin*, from which it was clear that the recipient of the letters had been on the closest terms with the composer. Ninety-six of the letters belong to the years 1855–61 and the remainder span the years to Liszt's death; there is a gap between 1869 and 1878. In 1899 Wagner's biographer Glasenapp revealed the identity of the 'Freundin', who had died in 1896. The original letters have disappeared, save a handful, but La Mara's transcriptions of them are extant and recent research[39] has revealed the extent to which she abridged them for publication. The unpublished passages in her transcripts are scored through in blue pencil, but readable. Some deletions were to protect the feelings of persons still living, notably Carolyne's daughter Marie, Cosima and other descendants of Marie d'Agoult. But most of the censorship was designed to conceal the true depth of Liszt's intimacy with his pupil. For financial reasons Agnes left Weimar in April 1855 and subsequently lived and taught piano in Brussels and later Paris. The correspondence begins upon her departure from Weimar and reveals that their love had been consummated at least six months before. Apparently in the previous year they had travelled together, Agnes disguised in male attire. Liszt urged Agnes to destroy his letters (advice she fortunately ignored) and assured her he had consigned her own to the flames, sometimes regretfully as on 10 June 1855: 'This time it will cost me more than ever to burn your letter ... but it must be, my beloved'. Secret codes were adopted in their exchanges; Carolyne was deceived by Liszt having the letters delivered to intermediaries (Cornelius and others); and much of the deleted matter contains arrangements for clandestine meetings in various cities: they met in Düsseldorf in May 1855 and in Berlin the following winter. Thereafter his pleas for further meetings were met by refusals: he hoped to see her at Magdeburg in June, in August at Vienna or Pest, but she declined and failed

---

[39] S. Winklhofer, 'Editorial Censorship in Liszt's letters to Agnes Street-Klindworth', JALS, IX, 42–9.

to join him once more in October. In January 1857 he received a reconciliatory note. Again he begged for a reunion but, although the remainder of the correspondence looks back nostalgically on their love, their future relations were as close friends, no longer as lovers.

Another subject touched on in the Street letters is Liszt's concern for his children and his bitter distrust of Marie d'Agoult. Following the tussle over the children in the mid 1840s, a note of reasonable friendliness returns in the letters of Liszt and the countess. A gap in their published correspondence exists between 1849 and 1854, and in this period Liszt's attitude changed dramatically. Again the children were the unwitting cause. Liszt was hardly a model father but his love for his children was strong enough to realise that Marie was equally ill-qualified for motherhood. The obvious solution of bringing Blandine, Cosima and Daniel to Weimar where Carolyne could look after them was apparently never considered, perhaps because the importation of three illegitimate children as well as a new mistress would have strained an already delicate situation. Instead they were left under Anna Liszt's wing; the girls entered the *pension* of a Madame Bernard, where they made excellent progress, and when Daniel was sent to school he proved a brilliant pupil. A condition was imposed that they should not see their mother. Liszt's edict was as impractical as it was cruel. The girls dutifully wrote to the father they loved but never saw, and all was well until Blandine's letter of February 1850:

I write, my dear Papa, to tell you how happy we are and to tell you how we achieved this happiness which has been denied to us for such a long time. We have seen Mama and this great joy has made us forget the pain of our long separation. Each day I was feeling more and more unhappy at not being able to see her and from time to time I tried to get news of her and was never happier than when I heard someone pronounce her name. During the New Year holidays someone mentioned, in our presence, her address. Next day, while out with Cosima, we were completely preoccupied by what we had heard and in the middle of our walk we had the sudden inspiration to go and see her, and that is how we met her again. We only stayed for a few moments with her. She was very moved and very surprised when she saw us, and she was especially happy to find that our feelings for her were as strong and as tender as ever.

In reply Liszt wrote:

> I have not only to scold you but to blame you severely, for you
> have done wrong. You must know that if your grandmother did
> not take you to visit your mother, she was following my orders,
> and that in deceiving her you have deceived me . . . Precious as your
> affection is to me I must tell you sincerely that I value it only in so
> far as you remain truly daughters after my own heart, whose upright
> will, sound reason, cultivated talents, lofty and steadfast characters
> are such as to bring honour to my name and ensure me some
> consolation in my old age.[40]

This dreadful letter was followed up by another decree under
which the children were to be placed permanently under the care
of a former governess of Princess Wittgenstein, a Madame Patersi.

In 1853 Carlos Davila arrived in Weimar, ostensibly seeking
Liszt's permission to marry Blandine, but in reality sent by Marie
d'Agoult to gather information about Liszt's situation with Carolyne. Marie no doubt gained wry satisfaction upon learning of the
intractable dilemma in which the Altenburg couple were placed.
Several times she vainly attempted to persuade Liszt to meet her
to discuss the children's prospects. She played no part in his visit
to them in 1853, nor in a rendezvous he made with the girls in
Brussels in 1854; Daniel spent his summer holiday of 1854 in
Weimar. In 1855 Liszt decided to bring the children to Germany,
first to Weimar on the pretext of a holiday, and then to place
Blandine and Cosima in the care of Bülow's mother in Berlin.
Anna Liszt was horrified at the exile of her grand-daughters to
Prussia merely on account of their mother. Marie herself could
only give way to impotent rage. Just before the children arrived
in Weimar, the Princess and her daughter left for Berlin and then
Paris. Carolyne's exodus has been attributed both to a guilty
conscience over the arrangements for the girls and to disapproval
of Liszt's devious treatment of them. (Most writers have blamed
her for Liszt's uncharacteristically severe behaviour at this time.)
For Blandine and Cosima the visit to the Altenburg was the eagerly
awaited realisation of a long-cherished dream. Even Berlin was
bearable as it was the wish of their adored Papa. Blandine lasted
a year there and returned to Paris with Cosima in the summer of
1856; but Cosima retraced her steps to Berlin – she had decided
to marry Hans von Bülow. Their wedding, attended by Liszt, was

[40] *Correspondance de Liszt et de sa fille Madame Emile Ollivier*, 42, 44f.

on 18 August 1857. Destiny smiled ironically over their honey-moon: it was spent in Zurich with Wagner. Blandine married the French lawyer and politician Emile Ollivier in Florence on 22 October of the same year. Although she had chosen her father's birthday for the wedding, he could not attend. Daniel's fate was also decided in 1857. Having won every prize at the Lycée Bona-parte he wished to pursue a course in engineering at the Poly-technique. Liszt overruled this and sent him to Vienna to study law as preparation for a diplomatic career. Eduard Liszt looked after the boy; Tausig was a friend worthy of his sharp-witted nature and sense of fun; and the rooms of the Altenburg were his for the holidays. But Daniel loathed stuffy Vienna and pined for the cosmopolitan verve of Paris.

From 1857 press attacks on Liszt increased in frequency and venom, as his new works were more widely performed and pub-lished. The critics savaged an all-Liszt concert in Leipzig in Febru-ary, a performance of the E flat concerto in Vienna by Pruckner was sneered at by Hanslick, and the Dresden première of the *Dante Symphony* in November was a disaster gleefully reported in unsympathetic papers. (Liszt acknowledged that the *Dante* failure was due not only to inaccurate, badly copied parts, but to his own careless conducting.[41] The symphony was favourably received in Prague the following March.) In addition to this adverse criticism, Liszt's position at Weimar became steadily less tenable. It had never been easy, and as early as the spring of 1852 Bülow told his family of Liszt's enemies in Weimar and of his own 'unbounded unpopularity'. When the Duke began to lose interest in Liszt's ideas, and more and more emphasis was placed on the dramatic aspect of the theatre rather than on the musical side of court life, Liszt realised that his hopes of a new golden age for Weimar were increasingly futile. Years of bickering with court officials and theatre intendants, constant struggles over money and mounting hostility to his works and aims deeply affected him. A growing note of weariness and depression colours his letters to Agnes, Carolyne and Wagner. The climax of his disappointment and the triumph of the forces against him came on 15 December 1858 when he conducted the première of *The Barber of Baghdad* by Cornelius. There was an angry, noisy demonstration directed against Liszt, who left the theatre, never conducted an opera there again and handed in his resignation as Kapellmeister.

[41] FLB, II, 22f.

He stayed in the town for another two-and-a-half years and remained on excellent terms with his friend and successor, Eduard Lassen, who joined the circle of enthusiastic young 'murls' who helped sustain Liszt's spirits in these crisis years. A greater leisure for composition was one positive result of his resignation. Songs, transcriptions, choral works and, for orchestra, the *Two Episodes from Lenau's 'Faust'*: continuing the Faust/Mephisto seam that winds its way through Liszt's creative imagination over half a century. The second episode, known separately as the *Mephisto Waltz No. 1*, is famous in both orchestral and solo piano form. A melodrama, or poem recited to piano accompaniment, *Der traurige Mönch* (also a Lenau poem) is remarkable for its use of whole-tone harmonies, an apt illustration of his boldness of language by October 1860:

Ex. 2

Outward events continued to sadden and disillusion him. A growing personal breach with Wagner becomes apparent from the winter of 1859. In August Daniel Liszt arrived in Berlin to spend his vacation with Cosima and Hans. He fell ill and the Bülows nursed him for some months. It seems that the delicate youth succumbed either to acute anaemia or to tuberculosis, but only when his condition seriously worsened in December was Liszt urged to hasten to Berlin. Two days later, late on the evening of the 13th, Daniel died, with his father and his sister at his bedside, and was buried on the 15th in St. Hedwig's Cemetery. In 1860 Liszt wrote an elegiac orchestral oration, *Les Morts*. Throughout the score he wrote words of Lamennais: 'They too have lived on this earth; they have passed down the river of time; their voices were heard on its banks, and then were heard no more. Where are they now? Who shall tell? But blessed are they who die in the Lord.'

To crush him further, 1860 saw the publication in *Das Echo* of the infamous manifesto condemning the tendencies of the Weimar school and the music of Liszt in particular. Joachim was the instigator of this document and Brahms, to his discredit, signed it along with two very minor composers. Some, like Robert Franz, had the decency to decline Joachim's invitation to add their names to this attack on a man who had shown them nothing but selfless generosity. Clara Schumann, though, longed to sign. She told the violinist on 25 April that she despised Liszt from the depths of her soul, and in June refused to attend the unveiling of a statue of Schumann in his native Zwickau because Liszt would be there. Liszt's works were *Unmusik*, 'stilted, impotent weeds'. 'Let us oust the word *Liszt*!' cried the manifesto. The cry was met in Weimar by a dignified silence.

On 15 October 1859 Marie Sayn-Wittgenstein was married in Weimar to Prince Konstantin von Hohenlohe-Schillingsfürst. It was a distinguished match and as a result of it she inherited her mother's Russian fortune, and Carolyne was now free to pursue in Rome her mission for papal consent to marry Liszt. She left Weimar forever in May 1860. In September Liszt made out his Will which, in addition to the tribute to her quoted earlier, contains this statement:

> There is in contemporary art one name that is already glorious and will be more and more so: Richard Wagner. His genius has been a torch to me; I have followed it, and my friendship for Wagner has retained all the character of a noble passion. At one time (some ten years ago), I dreamed of a new epoch for Weimar comparable to that of Carl August, an epoch of which Wagner and I were to be the coryphaei, as Goethe and Schiller once were. The meanness, not to say the villainy, of certain local circumstances, all sorts of jealousies and absurdities elsewhere as well as here, have prevented the realisation of this dream which would have redounded to the honour of the present Grand Duke.

Liszt lingered in Weimar for one more winter. He had arrived there a young man full of energy and zest for conquest. He left, thirteen years later, a grandfather (Daniela von Bülow was born on 12 October 1860), tired in spirit, the face lined, the hair quite grey. As the many rooms of the Altenburg, which had rung with music and bustle and voices, were emptied and shuttered, so closed an era which Liszt had filled with an energy unparalleled in the career of any musician or artist in history.

1 Liszt in Rome, 1839. Drawing
   by Ingres.
2 Liszt, *c.* 1841, from a
   daguerreotype.

3 Marie d'Agoult, 1839. Oil painting
by Henri Lehmann.

4 Carolyne Sayn-Wittgenstein with
her daughter, Marie, *c.* 1844.
Lithograph by C. Fischer.

5 Olga von Meyendorff.

6 Cosima, Blandine and
Daniel Liszt. Drawing
by Friedrich Preller,
1855.

Cosima   Blandine   Daniel

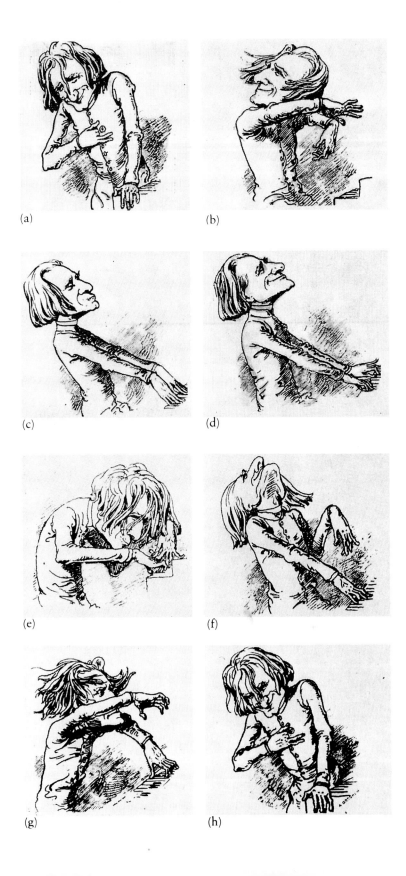

(a)

(b)

(c)

(d)

(e)

(f)

(g)

(h)

8 'The Bayreuth Composing-Steam-Engine': Liszt, the pioneer of the Bayreuth Festival, plays; the piano manufacturer Bösendorfer stokes the furnace; and Wagner materializes (*Humoristische Blätter*, Vienna, 20 August 1876).

7 (*left*) Caricatures of Liszt from a Hungarian journal, 1873.
(a) Liszt appears, his haughty smile tempered by his clerical soutane. Storms of applause.   (b) First chords. He turns his head to make sure of his public . . .
(c) . . . closes his eyes and seems to play just for himself.   (d) *Pianissimo:* St Francis of Assisi talks to the birds.   (e) Hamlet's brooding, Faustian agitation, sighs . . .
(f) Memories: Chopin, George Sand, youth, moonlight, love . . .   (g) Dante's Inferno: the Damned moan, thunderstorms break loose.   (h) He played for *us*: Bravo! Vivat!

9 A page from Liszt's manuscript of *Christus* ('Stabat Mater speciosa') (British Library).

10 Liszt and Cosima, 1867.

11 Liszt with some pupils, Weimar 1884. From left to right (back row) Moritz Rosenthal, Victoria Drewing, Mele Paramanoff, Liszt, Frau Friedheim, Hugo Mansfield; (front row) George Leibling, Alexander Siloti, Arthur Freidheim, Emil Sauer, Alfred Reisenauer, A. W. Gottschalg. Photograph, Louis Held.

5

L'Abbé Liszt (1861–8)

Weimar, for all its exertions, was a conscious withdrawal from the world, so that the world would come to Weimar. Rome was a further withdrawal as Liszt played little part in public musical life (outside the Church), even discouraged performances of his works, and regarded his stay in the city as the third part, and probably the close, of his life. Prior to settling into this voluntary but by no means idle retirement, he went to Paris and enjoyed a whirl of brilliant society, calling on old friends and viewing his visit as a sort of St Martin's summer. Returning to Weimar, a final festival was held at which most of his comrades-in-art gathered and much of his music was heard. These events had a valedictory air, as if he was consciously and forever renouncing the scenes of his triumphs of youth and middle age.

The journey to and from Paris included Brussels in order to see Agnes Street. Wagner was in Paris, in the wake of the *Tannhäuser* fiasco at the Opéra. A certain coolness had entered their relations. Ernest Newman observes that their correspondence from summer 1849 to the autumn of 1859 runs to 570 pages in the second edition; a mere thirty pages suffice for October 1859 to July 1861 and then there is a gap of eleven years. In this strained situation both men 'suffered profoundly, for each, in his heart of hearts, had an unbreakable regard and affection for the other'.[1] The reasons for the breach were not musical (for Liszt never ceased to admire Wagner's works wholeheartedly) but personal. A very revealing letter from Wagner to Bülow of 7 October 1859 throws light on the causes. He laments Liszt's apparent lessening of interest in him, complains of the brevity of his letters, of his delay in sending the dedicatory score of the *Dante Symphony* to him and is aggrieved that when this arrives it is an ordinary 'shop copy' and not specially and beautifully bound like the dedicatory score of *Lohengrin* which he had sent to Liszt. He is annoyed not to

[1] Newman, *Life of Richard Wagner*, III, 136f.

have received a gift of the *Missa Solennis* although it has been published for some time, and is upset by a remark by Richard Pohl in an article on *Tristan*:

> There are many matters concerning which we are quite frank among ourselves (for example that since my acquaintance with Liszt's compositions my treatment of harmony has become very different from what it was formerly), but it is indiscreet, to say the least, of friend Pohl to babble this secret to the whole world.[2]

In a misguided moment Bülow sent this letter to Liszt, who immediately reported its contents to the Princess:

> He seems to insinuate to Hans that you exercise a regrettable influence over me and one contrary to my true nature. If Wagner hasn't the merit for inventing this stupid idea, I on my part don't intend to share its absurdity. Every time he has tried to harp on this theme I have promptly shut him up – considering that he injures me trebly by so false an idea.[3]

Carolyne was in Paris and Liszt urged her to call on Wagner: 'Deal gently with him, for he is sick and incurable. That is why one must just love him and try to serve him as much as one can.' The Princess did not call.

During Liszt's Paris visit of May 1861 Wagner was piqued that he did not see enough of him:

> Liszt was swept up in his usual social routine, and even his daughter Blandine could only manage to get a word with him in the carriage in which he drove from visit to visit. Out of the goodness of his heart however, he found time to invite himself once to my home for a beefsteak party; in fact he even managed to devote a whole evening to me, volunteering to take care of a few obligations on my behalf ... Another day we met for breakfast at the home of Gounod, where we had an uncommonly dull time enlivened solely by the almost desperate humour of poor Baudelaire ... I met Liszt once again at a dinner at the Austrian embassy, an occasion which my friend used quite prettily to demonstrate his sympathy for me by playing some passages from *Lohengrin* in the presence of Princess Metternich. He was also summoned to a dinner at the Tuileries, to which, however, it was not thought necessary to invite me to accompany him ...[4]

[2] *Briefe an Hans von Bülow*, 125f.
[3] FLB, IV, 492.
[4] Wagner, *My Life* (transl. A. Gray), Cambridge, 1983, 647. In fact Blandine enjoyed her father's company on many occasions.

'He was just pitched about from one prince, countess, emperor and minister to another,' Wagner told Mathilde Wesendonck. Liszt played to the Emperor and to the Empress Eugénie. 'I often feel a hundred years old,' Napoleon III is said to have sighed. 'Sire, you *are* the century,' was Liszt's perfect reply. Berlioz reported to his son that 'Liszt has conquered the Emperor: he played at court last week and has been given the Legion of Honour. Ah, if one could only play the piano!'[5]

Charles Baudelaire, whom he took everywhere in the hope of introducing him to influential, wealthy patrons, paid tribute to Liszt in his *Petits poèmes en prose* (*Le spleen de Paris*). The Gounod meeting resulted in another *Faust* work: Liszt's transcription of the waltz and second-act love-duet from Gounod's recent opera. In addition to Tausig, who was then in Paris, he saw Autran, Berlioz, Delacroix, Lamartine, Jules Michelet, d'Ortigue, Rossini, Sainte-Beuve and Pauline Viardot. At a supper given by Halévy on 26 May he met the young Bizet. The tale is told that Liszt played a recent piece and declared that apart from himself, Bülow alone in all Europe could play it properly. At this Bizet read the manuscript through at the piano so brilliantly that an astonished Liszt admitted there were now three men who could master its difficulties 'and the youngest of us is perhaps the most brilliant'.[6]

He had three meetings with Marie d'Agoult: one a luncheon-party to which she invited several guests, and one alone – an intimate talk of three or four hours. According to his letter to Carolyne, he told 'Nélida' that 'Guermann's frescoes are already painted', that he cared nothing for what was said or written about him now, and was content to live and work in solitude. Apparently the painful subject of Daniel was never raised during the long emotional interview. In Liszt's words:

> I kissed her on the forehead for the first time in many long years, and said to her, 'Come, Marie, let me speak to you in peasant's language. God bless you. Wish me no evil!' She could not reply … but her tears flowed ever faster. Ollivier had told me that when he was travelling with her in Italy he had often seen her crying bitterly in places that recalled our youth to her. I told her I had been moved by this. She said, almost stammering, 'I shall always be true to Italy – and to Hungary!' Thereupon I left her quietly.[7]

[5] *Hector Berlioz: A selection from his letters* (transl. Searle), London, 1966, 171.
[6] *Cf.* Winton Dean, *Bizet* (Master Musicians Series), London, 1948; revised 1975, 43f.
[7] FLB, V, 198f.

The final rites at Weimar were three days of music (5–7 August) celebrating three events: the twenty-fifth anniversary of the *Neue Zeitschrift für Musik*; the founding of the *Allgemeiner Deutscher Musikverein* (German Music Union) by Liszt, Brendel and others, the annual festivals of which were to be important outlets for new music; and, of course, to do honour to Liszt on his departure from Weimar. Blandine and Emile Ollivier, Eduard Liszt and (the now amnestied) Wagner attended, along with Bülow (who conducted the revised version of the *Faust Symphony*), Tausig (who played the A major Concerto), the singer Emilie Genast, Cornelius, Gille, Damrosch, Lassen, Weissheimer, Draesecke and Franz Doppler. On 17 August Liszt left Weimar, first for three days with the Grand Duke at Wilhelmsthal, then to Löwenberg for a three-week stay with the Prince of Hohenzollern-Hechingen (an enthusiastic patron of new music), then to Berlin and the Bülows for three more weeks before making his way south through Germany and France to Marseilles, arriving there on 12 October. His plan was to visit the Olliviers at their villa in St Tropez, but instead, having heard from Carolyne that all was prepared for their wedding on his fiftieth birthday, he set sail for Italy on the 17th and arrived in Rome on the evening of 20 October.

But the marriage never took place. As with his early days with Carolyne at Woronince, a veil of mystery descends over Rome on the eve of 22 October 1861. There exists a Will in Carolyne's hand dated 23 October 1861, referring to 'mon mari, Mr François Liszt' and signed 'Carolyne Liszt'. The existence of this extraordinary document was revealed only in 1968[8] and, discounting the virtual impossibility of a secret marriage, it must have been drawn up by Carolyne in the confident expectation of her wedding, and postdated '23 October'. For nearly eighteen months she had been preoccupied in Rome with the continuation of her long struggle to have her first marriage annulled. She had an audience of the pope and conferred with several cardinals. The adroit Cardinal Antonelli, Pius IX's secretary of state, apparently tried to direct her thoughts towards the Church and its needs, so much more important than life with a musician, no matter how celebrated. The legend, repeated in virtually every Liszt biography since Ramann's, is that the couple partook of communion together at six o'clock on the eve of his birthday in the church of San Carlo,

[8] Quarterly Journal of the Library of Congress, Jan. 1968, 87f.

where the wedding was due to take place, the altar already being decorated for the occasion. At eleven o'clock that night a messenger from Cardinal Antonelli came to Carolyne's apartment with the devastating news that as further objections had been raised by her relations, His Holiness was obliged to re-examine the papers and that the ceremony was postponed. This theatrical, eleventh-hour intervention is too good to be true. Was it concocted later by the Princess to save her honour, to protect her from embarrassment and to place Liszt's behaviour in an inculpable light? Did he himself play some part in engineering some obstacle, or did he simply concur with a fiction that conveniently concealed the truth about his intentions? No evidence of the alleged intervention by the Vatican exists; no document substantiates the oft-repeated story. Enquiries pursued by Edward N. Waters[9] elicited the following reply from the Vatican on 1 April 1964:

> We have not excluded absolutely the possibility that documentation regarding the proposed marriage of Franz Liszt to Carolyne von Sayn-Wittgenstein may exist in the Vatican Archives but only, that after careful research, we have not found any reference to that matter.

Unless documentary evidence is some day unearthed, the exact events of that fateful night never will be known. Carolyne accused her Russian and Polish relatives of thwarting the match and also blamed the interference of the Hohenlohe family, especially Prince Gustav Adolph. Gustav, who was ordained a priest in 1849 and held a prominent Vatican post, first met Liszt at the wedding of his brother Konstantin to Marie Wittgenstein in 1859. They became friends and their acquaintance deepened from Liszt's Roman years onward. (Hohenlohe was made a cardinal in 1866.) Again, there is no hint in all the literature appertaining to their friendship that Gustav was involved in any plot to prevent Liszt's marriage. If the tale of the unexpected nocturnal message from the Vatican is untrue, it is intriguing, even questionable, that Carolyne invoked the names of cardinals and even the pope in a fabrication. One thing is certain: Liszt was not displeased by the abandonment of their union, for the sincerity of his intention to wed Carolyne is very doubtful.

Cornelius was convinced that Liszt never really intended to marry her; Cosima viewed the events of October 1861 with sus-

[9] ibid.; and *cf.* JALS, VII, June 1980, 6–16.

picion and doubt, and Tausig later thought that 'Liszt's whole journey to Rome was simply a *blague*.'[10] Adelheid von Schorn, a lady whose books on Weimar and observations on Liszt and Carolyne are abundantly informative, wrote:

> I feel it my duty to repeat what the Princess assured me and others in tones of the utmost sincerity and the deepest sorrow, that during the period when they were separated from each other Liszt had become indifferent; the thought of a legal union with her no longer appealed to him as a necessity. She was conscious of this change in him when he arrived in Rome ... and he himself supplied the confirmation of it, for he never asked her again whether the marriage was possible or not. He was, of course, ready at any time to stand before the altar with her; but her womanly fine feeling sensed that if he did so it would be merely to fulfil a duty. And so she never spoke of it to him again.[11]

Evidence that the failure to marry her hardly troubled Liszt is implied in letters of December to Blandine, Brendel and the Grand Duke. He speaks only of the congenial climate of Rome, his delight in her art treasures and his joy in hours of undisturbed composition. They lived apart, Carolyne becoming more and more concerned with her ecclesiastical researches and hardly leaving her rented apartment in the Via Babuino. When Nicholas Wittgenstein died in 1864 no murmur of any plan to wed Liszt was to be heard. Yet his attentions to her were unflagging for the quarter of a century that remained to them after 1861. He visited her almost every day when in Rome and wrote long, devoted letters whenever he left the city. Her superabundant mental energy never forsook her and many visitors to her rooms reported her stimulating, highly intellectual conversation and her kind hospitality, albeit in curious surroundings:

> The rooms were authentic Roman, but furnished in the most taste-less way imaginable, the colours loud and motley, the furniture all but shabby. But so lofty were the soarings of her mind that the Princess altogether overlooked her aesthetically unbearable sur-roundings. She lived in these selfsame rooms for more than twenty years, without feeling the need to introduce into them any beauty or charm. In all frankness it must be said that she lacked both these qualities herself. But even over her own charmlessness and want of beauty her mind ruled triumphant. She lay constantly on an ottoman, her dress old-fashioned and her strikingly large head

[10] Cf. Newman, *The Man Liszt*, 202.
[11] ibid.

encased in an enormous bonnet, which quite disfigured her, its laces being tied under her chin and causing her naturally sharp features to appear still sharper. Throughout the many years of her sojourn in Rome, this remarkable woman possessed no kitchen of her own, all her food being brought to her from a nearby restaurant. Of the utmost simplicity though they were, the dishes were served with all possible ceremony by her butler. It is well known that the Princess stayed in Rome even during the summer, despite going down with a fever every year at the start of the hot season; and that she worked at a mystical treatise, daily writing one complete proof sheet which was daily printed . . . It grew mightily, and she once told me laughingly that she counted its height in yards.[12]

Liszt's studied behaviour concerning the marital dilemma and his move to Rome concealed, with the aptitude and ease of a long-experienced actor on the stage of life, a distinct moral and spiritual crisis. Fresh-eyed observers penetrated the aura. 'He looked grim, stern and melancholy,' said Alexander Mackenzie, glimpsing him in Sondershausen in 1861, 'quite unlike the genial, kind-hearted old man I was privileged to know so well in after-time.'[13] Liszt aged rapidly in this period. The historian and diarist Ferdinand Gregorovius saw him for the first time in April 1862: 'a striking uncanny figure – tall, thin and with long grey hair. Frau von S. maintains that he is burnt out and that only the outer walls remain, from which a little ghost-like flame hisses forth'.[14]

Far from being 'burnt out', in 1862 alone he composed an *Ave Maria* for piano ('The Bells of Rome'), the 2 Concert Studies *Waldesrauschen* and *Gnomenreigen*, the Variations on a theme of Bach (*Weinen, Klagen, Sorgen, Zagen*: arranged for organ in 1863), the *Cantico del Sol* (Hymn to the Sun of St Francis of Assisi) in its first version for voice and organ, and the Two Legends: *St Francis of Assisi preaching to the birds* and *St Francis of Paola walking on the waves* (for piano; completed and orchestrated in 1863). The Franciscan theme is significant: another aspect of St Francis in his career was his election to honorary membership of the Franciscan order, the Friars Minor, in 1857. A transcription of Allegri's *Miserere* and Mozart's *Ave verum corpus* (combined in a fantasy-like ABAB structure) with the title *Evocation à la chapelle Sixtine* exists in versions for piano and organ (there is

[12] Richard Voss (transl. A. Williams) in LSJ, VII, 1982, 35.
[13] Mackenzie, *A Musician's Narrative*, London, 1927, 38.
[14] Gregorovius, *The Roman Journals 1852–1874* (transl. G. W. Hamilton), London, 1911, 155.

also a duet arrangement and an unpublished orchestral version). The boy Mozart is reputed to have written out from memory the Allegri *Miserere* (the score of which was unpublished and jealously guarded) after hearing it performed by the Sistine Chapel choir. Liszt sent the Grand Duke a programme for this unusual work: 'In the *Miserere* the anguish of Man finds voice; in the *Ave verum corpus* the infinite mercy and grace of God answers in song. This touches upon the most sublime of mysteries, that which reveals the victory of God's love over evil and over death'. In the same letter he spoke of a mystical experience of his own in which he imagined he saw the spirits of Mozart and Allegri in the Sistine Chapel. 'Then, slowly, another shade of unutterable greatness appeared in the background, by Michelangelo's *Judgement Day*. With ecstasy I recognised it at once, for while still an exile in this life he had consecrated my brow with a kiss.' Liszt goes on to draw parallels between certain slow movements of Beethoven and the spirit and harmonic structure of Allegri's *Miserere*.[15] Another product of 1862 which combines transcription with free composition is the *Alleluja and Ave Maria*: the *Ave Maria* is from a hymn attributed to Arcadelt, the *Alleluja* an original work. Also that year he completed *The Legend of St Elisabeth*, a work of about two-and-a-half hours' duration for seven soloists, children's choir, mixed chorus and large orchestra. He told the Hungarian composer Mosonyi that this oratorio, together with the orchestral *Hungaria*, was his musical answer to the faith placed in him by the poet Vörösmarty (see page 51) and that much more will follow, 'whether they understand it or reject it'.[16]

Two pupils of the early Rome years became close friends: Giovanni Sgambati, pianist, conductor and a composer whose later work was admired by Wagner; and Walter Bache, Liszt's foremost English pupil, who later pioneered his master's music in London with tireless fortitude.

Liszt's creative activity in his last twenty-five years has been ignored or greatly underrated by most biographers until recent years. Of Ramann's 1039 pages, about eighty deal with his life and work after 1861. Ernest Newman concluded that 'he produced some fine work ... but on the whole the years from 1861 to 1886 are a lamentable record of disappointment, vacillation, failure'. One biographer actually breaks off her narrative in 1861 without

[15] LCA, 115f.
[16] *Briefe aus ungarischen Sammlungen*, ed. Prahacs, 122ff.

explanation, as if his career ceased thenceforth.[17] In addition to the works mentioned above, the Roman years up to 1868 also saw the completion of the huge oratorio *Christus*, the *Hungarian Coronation Mass*, the *Missa Choralis*, the male-voice *Requiem*, and a number of motets. For orchestra he revised *Les Morts* and wrote *La Notte* and *Le Triomphe funèbre du Tasse*, which together form the *Trois Odes Funèbres*. For piano there are several religious works, a *Funeral March for Maximilian of Mexico*, the *Spanish Rhapsody* and two pieces of the *Fünf kleine Klavierstücke*. He also transcribed works by composers as various as Bach, Beethoven, Gounod, Herbeck, Lassen, Lassus, Meyerbeer, Verdi and Wagner. The magically realised piano version of the *Liebestod* from *Tristan und Isolde* shows his admiration for Wagner the composer at a time (1867) when his feelings for the man were at a low ebb. Beethoven 'arranged by Liszt' might easily be passed over without a realisation of the immense scholarship and profound pianistic knowledge Liszt brought to these careful yet astonishingly bold re-creations for piano. In 1863–4 he revised the transcriptions of Symphonies 5 to 7 that he had made more than quarter of a century earlier and he completed the canon of the nine symphonies.

In addition, with the many versions of these works and with the proof-reading of new and old compositions as they went to press, his Roman years were hardly lazy. Nor was he guilty of idle note-spinning: his vocal, orchestral and piano works of the 1860s contain as many innovations and beauties as the best works of the previous decade. The fact that his sacred works have never found a regular place in the concert or church repertory may explain the perfunctory treatment this chapter of his life has received. Writers who take it for granted that he frittered away his time in Rome usually attribute his assumed indolence to the lack of Carolyne's firm control. Like so many ingrained Liszt legends, this fiction demonstrably denies the facts. In Rome he certainly cut a more solitary, even at times a pathetic and prematurely aged figure, but his desire to recede from the world was deeply sincere. The fact that he embarked later on a final round of ceaseless travel and musical activity of astonishing variety has also been held against him, the implication being that his Roman seclusion was insincere. A less jaundiced view might allow Liszt this period of attempted retreat, which was rich in creativity and from which he emerged

[17] Eleanor Perényi.

inwardly restored for the final and arguably the boldest phase of his life.

His slow renewal and recovery in the early Roman period was overshadowed by another tragedy. In July 1862 his daughter Blandine gave birth to her first child. The boy, Daniel, was quite healthy but his mother never recovered from the birth, grew steadily weaker and died in St Tropez on 11 September. To this sadness was added another within a year or so: his only surviving child, Cosima, was increasingly attracted to Wagner and less and less content in her marriage to Bülow. In 1864 she began an adulterous relationship with Wagner and between 1865 and 1869 bore him three illegitimate children, Isolde, Eva and Siegfried. (Liszt's third grandchild, Blandine, born 20 March 1863, was the last child of Bülow and Cosima.)

Another myth concerning Liszt in Rome is that he sought, and was disappointed not to gain, the post of musical director to the Vatican. Undoubtedly Carolyne desired this for him, but there is no evidence that Liszt had the slightest ambition in that direction. He preferred his isolation, and his deepening relationship with the Church should not be interpreted as an attempt to oust the maestro di cappella at St Peter's. In June 1863 he gave up his flat in the Via Felice and entered the Oratory of the Madonna del Rosario at Monte Mario, where his rooms commanded a view over all Rome, the Campagna and the mountains. His study was simply furnished: a work table, an old, rather decrepit piano, a harmonium and a pair of chairs. Here on 11 July Pope Pius IX visited him and heard him play. The pope received Liszt several times in audience and also enjoyed these private recitals, affectionately referring to him as 'my dear Palestrina'. In November Liszt explained to Brendel that it was not easy to shut out the world:

> In spite of my seclusion and retirement I am still very much disturbed by visitors, social obligations, musical protégés and wearisome, mostly unnecessary correspondence and duties. Among other things the St Petersburg Philharmonic Society has invited me to conduct two concerts of my works ... these good people cannot refrain from prattling on about my 'former triumphal tours, unrivalled mastery of the piano' etc., and this is as utterly sickening to me as flat, lukewarm champagne.[18]

[18] FLB, II, 133.

In July 1864 Gustav Hohenlohe invited him to the beautiful Villa d'Este at Tivoli and placed a suite of rooms at his permanent disposal. Liszt subsequently made frequent use of the Villa d'Este, finding there a true quiet and real privacy which was not possible in Rome.

The wider world saw him again for two months that summer. He was invited to the festival of the *Allgemeiner Deutscher Musik-verein* in Karlsruhe, and Cosima joined him there. She came from Starnberg where Wagner was living under the patronage of his new friend and saviour King Ludwig II of Bavaria, and where her amorous relations with him had begun in June. She probably told her father of her feelings for Wagner, and Liszt almost certainly took her to task. His first thought was to save Cosima's marriage. Bülow should have conducted at Karlsruhe but he was lying desperately ill in a Munich hotel, his nerves shattered and his limbs partially paralysed. Whether this collapse was due to his shock at learning of the liaison of his wife and his hero Wagner is a matter for conjecture. Liszt went with Cosima to Munich and Wagner joined them there at Bülow's bedside. How much Liszt then knew of the depth of Cosima's love for Wagner is also unknown. On 30 July he went with Wagner to the villa by Lake Starnberg and in letters to Carolyne he dwells on Wagner's dazzling change of fortune, on the humour, wit and vivacity of his new score *Die Meistersinger*, and on Wagner's praise of his own Beatitudes from *Christus*. He returned to Munich next day, stayed three more days, and Wagner joined him again before his departure. Liszt knew that the Wagner–Bülow situation was delicate, but had he known the whole truth he would surely not have urged Bülow (as he did in October) to move without delay from Berlin to Munich and accept Ludwig II's invitation to take up a post there. For Wagner was then in Munich, and Cosima proceeded to visit his home every day. The complications of the Bülow–Cosima–Wagner triangle belong to the Wagner story, but Liszt's preoccupation with the unfolding drama is important, as the three of them were, next perhaps to Carolyne, the people he held most dear in the world.

From Munich he called at Stuttgart, Weimar, Löwenberg and Berlin. In late September he stayed at Wilhelmsthal, the Grand Duke's summer residence, and early next month went, with Cosima, to Paris to visit his mother, Emile Ollivier, and his grand-son Daniel. Cosima and her father paid a brief call on Marie d'Agoult. Liszt then proceeded south to St Tropez to visit Blandine's grave and then sailed to Italy. He resumed his sheltered life at Madonna del Rosario on 18 October and worked there through the winter.

A decisive step taken in 1865 was the logical conclusion of a conviction Liszt had long felt. He decided to enter the Church and take minor orders. On 20 April he gave a 'farewell' concert and Gregorovius attended:

> He played the *Invitation to the Dance* and the *Erlkönig* – a curious farewell to the world. No one suspected that he had the abbé's stockings already in his pocket. The following Sunday he received the tonsure in St Peter's and the first consecration at the hands of Monsignor Hohenlohe. He now wears the abbé's frock, lives in the Vatican and ... looks well and contented. This is the end of the gifted virtuoso, a truly sovereign personality. Am glad that I heard him play again; he and the instrument seem to be one, as it were, a piano-centaur.[19]

Liszt's entry to the Vatican was through Hohenlohe's influence, and in his private chapel at the Villa d'Este on 30 July Hohenlohe conferred on him the four minor orders: doorkeeper, reader, exorcist and acolyte. These were nominal orders of a symbolic nature, they involved no binding obligations, nor was the Abbé Liszt entitled to perform any of the major functions of priesthood such as giving Mass or hearing confession. He wrote of the significance of his actions to his mother, and his decision deeply moved and gladdened Anna Liszt in the closing months of her life. She wrote of her tears and her joy at the news and saw it as the fulfilment of a desire she had sensed from the time of his youth. Casual observers were inclined to be cynical. Gregorovius again: 'Yesterday saw Liszt ... he was getting out of a hackney carriage, his black silk cassock fluttering ironically behind him – Mephistopheles disguised as an abbé. Such is the end of Lovelace!'[20]

In August the composer, in his clerical garb, went to Pest, making the journey for the first time by train, to conduct the première of *St Elisabeth*. It was his first visit to Pest since 1858, and the oratorio was given in the new Concert Hall with immense success, strengthening his reputation in Hungary. The Bülows and Smetana were present, Erkel assisted in the rehearsals and distinguished players such as Reményi, Plotényi and Mosonyi took their places in the expanded orchestra of the National Theatre. It

[19] Gregorovius, op. cit., 230.
[20] ibid.

was repeated on the 23rd to equal acclaim, and meanwhile he conducted a triumphant concert that included the *Dante Symphony* and the first performance of his orchestral version of the Rákóczy March. He also played his 2 *St Francis Legends* in a public concert given with Bülow and Reményi. In the following year Smetana arranged a performance of *St Elisabeth* in Prague and Bülow introduced it to Munich. Before leaving Hungary, Hans, Cosima and Liszt visited Esztergom and Szekszárd (home of a close friend and ally Baron Antal Augusz, statesman, art patron and musician). Liszt returned to the Vatican in the second week of September. (Wagner's entries in his 'Brown Book' diary refer to Cosima's absence and reveal how deeply he distrusted Liszt's motives and suspected him of deliberately separating Cosima from himself.[21])

Liszt's mother died in Paris on 6 February 1866. Her last months had been spent in Ollivier's home where her great-grandson Daniel brought her much pleasure, as did her son's actions in faraway Rome. The funeral of this former Austrian chambermaid at the Montparnasse cemetery was attended by a large throng: aristocrats, financial barons, politicians, poets, journalists, artists and actors.[22] A month later Liszt came to Paris for the dual purpose of visiting Anna's grave and to attend a performance of his *Missa Solennis* at the church of St Eustache on 15 March. His larger works, especially with orchestra, were not known in Paris and the poor rendering (under Théodore Dubois) and hostile critical reaction on this occasion were very damaging. The chorus was poorly trained and the circumstances of the performance were deplorable, as Walter Bache reported:

> The execution was tolerable: unfortunately there were no women's voices in the chorus, so that the accents, etc., were not given with much vigour: the orchestra and chorus were unfortunately not raised, which of course lessened the effect in so vast a church ... Just fancy, there was a detachment of soldiers in the church, and occasionally during the music the officer gave the word of command at the top of his voice! During the Sanctus the drummer performed an obbligato! Can you believe me? Before the Mass we had several polkas played by the military band, and the Mendelssohn Wedding March badly played on the organ!! (One of the papers said that Liszt did it.) Directly after the last notes of the *Agnus Dei*, orchestra

[21] *The Diary of Richard Wagner: the Brown Book,* ed. J. Bergfeld (transl. G. Bord), London, 1980, 63f, 71–5, 119.
[22] Horvath, *Franz Liszt,* vol. I, 24.

and chorus began some other piece belonging to the service in a
Donizetti style, all the people believing that it was by Liszt! During
the music, lady patronesses came round rattling money boxes and
upsetting chairs with their crinolines![23]

Other accounts mention a selection of pieces from *Tannhäuser*
played beforehand on the organ, to please the Wagnerites in the
congregation! Liszt later admitted that he should have stopped the
performance under such conditions and, although he put a brave
face on it, this Paris failure rankled in his mind until the last year
of his life. Berlioz, now a sad and embittered man, felt repelled by
Liszt's score, seeing in it a kind of musical religiosity he despised.
He refused to review it, giving d'Ortigue the task instead. Privately
he described the Mass as 'a negation of art'. Later Liszt attempted
to justify himself, score in hand, at a meeting with Berlioz,
Kreutzer, d'Ortigue and others. Berlioz did not even stay till the
end of the discussion. Rossini, however, came to Liszt's defence:
a matinée at his home was one of several Paris encounters that
helped assuage the St Eustache disappointment. At a soirée given
by Gustave Doré he heard Francis Planté and Saint-Saëns give a
two-piano rendering of the *Dante Symphony*. At the church of Ste
Clothilde he re-encountered César Franck and was treated to an
unforgettably impressive performance of Franck's *Six Pièces*. He
also heard the remarkable pianist Teresa Carreño (then aged
twelve) and at once offered her lessons in Rome – an offer she did
not take up. This Paris visit also witnessed the last meeting of
Liszt and Marie d'Agoult, predictably not a happy occasion. He
was less than delighted to hear her read fifty or so pages of her
Mémoires and learn that she shortly intended to publish them;
and he was angered by her tactless (or perhaps cunningly timed)
re-issue of *Nélida* in 1866.

From Paris Liszt went to Amsterdam to hear Bülow conduct
an infinitely more successful performance of the *Missa Solennis*
(27 April). At another concert (25 April) his Psalm 13 was given
and Bülow played the A major concerto. In Amsterdam Cosima
no doubt discussed the Wagner situation with her father. The
crisis was now acute: scandal in Munich had forced Ludwig II to
ask Wagner to leave Bavaria and he was again an exile (but with
a generous royal pension) in Switzerland. In March Cosima had
joined him there – an act that Liszt regarded an abomination. He

[23] C. Bache, *Brother Musicians*, London, 1901, 192f.

accurately foresaw that her behaviour with Wagner would alienate the King and end Bülow's Munich career. But Cosima joined Wagner at his new home, Tribschen, a week after the Amsterdam visit.

Liszt was back in Rome in mid-May and remained there for a full year, completing *Christus* and the *Hungarian Coronation Mass*. The latter was written to mark the coronation of Franz Josef I and the Empress Elisabeth as King and Queen of Hungary, which marked the beginning of the period known in Hungarian history as the 'Compromise', signifying a greater degree of national autonomy with a few of the freedoms that had been fought for in 1848–9. Liszt was not officially invited to the ceremony on 8 June 1867 at the Matthias Church in Buda: a plan for him to conduct his Mass and for Reményi to play the violin solo of the Benedictus was overruled by the Austrian authorities, no doubt as being too dangerously patriotic for comfort. Instead the orchestra was that of the Vienna Hofkapelle under Gottfried Preyer. But Liszt took his seat among the choir. As soon as the performance was over he left and walked towards the Chain Bridge that led to Pest. Janka Wohl left a vivid description of what happened next:

> An immense crowd of eager sightseers was waiting – on stands, in windows, on the roofs, and in flag-bedecked boats – to see the royal procession which was soon to cross the bridge ... When the feverish suspense grew intense, the tall figure of a priest, in a long black cassock studded with decorations, was seen to descend the broad white road leading to the Danube, which had been kept clear for the royal procession. As he walked bareheaded, his snow-white hair floated on the breeze, and his features seemed cast in brass. At his appearance a murmur arose, which swelled and deepened as he advanced and was recognised by the people. The name of Liszt flew down the serried ranks from mouth to mouth, swift as a flash of lightning. Soon a hundred thousand men and women were frantically applauding him, wild with the excitement of this whirlwind of voices. The crowd on the other side of the river naturally thought it must be the King, who was being hailed with the spontaneous acclamations of a reconciled people. It was not *the* king, but it was *a* king, to whom were addressed the sympathies of a grateful nation proud of the possession of such a son ...[24]

Returning to Rome after this brief visit to Hungary Liszt heard another première on 6 July: Sgambati conducted the first section

[24] Wohl, *François Liszt*, 20f.

of *Christus* (the Christmas Oratorio) in the Sala Dante. At the end of the month he travelled to a festival at Meiningen and from there to conduct *St Elisabeth* in the appropriate setting of the Hall of Song in the Wartburg (as part of the celebrations of the eight-hundredth anniversary of the famous castle). He spent two weeks as a guest at Wilhelmsthal and then went to Munich, ostensibly to hear Bülow conduct *Lohengrin* and *Tannhäuser*, but more urgently to assess the developments *vis à vis* his daughter, the composer and the cuckolded conductor of these works. Three years had elapsed since he last saw Wagner and the state of their relations is mirrored in the fact that Liszt avoided the *Tristan* performances of 1865. He made a discreet visit to Tribschen in October 1867. Wagner's 'Brown Book' contains the concise entry – 'Liszt's visit: dreaded but pleasant'. Whatever was discussed or concluded regarding the Bülow crisis the two friends settled down, as always on their rare meetings, to music. *Die Meistersinger* was almost complete and Liszt sight-read long passages from the manuscript of the full score, Wagner singing all the vocal parts. Richard Pohl joined them in the evening and later recalled: 'I have never heard a finer performance of the *Meistersinger* – such ravishing truth of expression, such beauty of phrasing, such clarity in every detail'.[25] Wagner told Ludwig a few days later that he and Liszt had recaptured something of the old golden days: 'he is a dear, great, unique creature'. Liszt stayed in Munich until late October; his several public appearances with Hans and Cosima perhaps being designed to show that he remained loyal to both of them.

In Rome he now lived in the old monastery of Santa Francesca Romana by the Forum. There he remained after his return from Munich and throughout the next year except for the months of July and August 1868, during which he underwent a pilgrimage with Don Antonio Solfanelli to the little Adriatic port of Grottamare, and received serious religious instruction. Apart from his devotions and daily studies of his breviary, he began work there on his books of Technical Studies for piano. Towards the end of the year he spent much time at his favourite haven, the Villa d'Este. Gounod called on him that autumn and they spent an afternoon together: their temperaments, if not their musical styles, had much in common, blending the sacred and secular.

[25] Cf. Newman, *Life of Richard Wagner*, IV, 111.

Liszt was continually bombarded with invitations to appear here and there to attend or conduct performances of his music – London, St Petersburg, annual festivals throughout Europe – but he declined them all. Apart from journeys to hear his new works, his excursions were otherwise motivated by his concern over the Bülow–Wagner affair. But two pressing invitations altered his way of life after 1868. The Grand Duke was anxious that Liszt should return to Weimar on a regular basis, and several musical compatriots in Hungary urged him to take a more active part in artistic life in Pest. It became apparent to him that Rome was not destined to be the last chapter of his life after all. In his last letter to Brendel (who died in November 1868) he wrote: 'Next year a considerable change may take place in my outward circumstances ... How this last chapter of my life will shape itself I cannot yet foresee'.[26] The shape became clear in 1869 with periods spent in Weimar, Pest and Rome. He moved with the seasons between these three centres for each of the seventeen years left to him. The image is the familiar Liszt of iconography and literature: a grand, but restless and lonely old man, a King Lear-like figure in a Latin cassock, the last survivor of an age whose legendary heroes were now passed away – Chopin, Mendelssohn, Schumann, Berlioz, Moscheles, Rossini, Delacroix, Heine and Lamennais. But the years of his *vie trifurquée*, his three-fold life, far from being spent in retrospection or nostalgic regret, were more than ever concerned with the forging of the new. His own music became even bolder and more experimental; he was passionately concerned with the latest music of French, German and Nationalist schools; in his Weimar classes he presided over a rising young generation of pianists; and in Budapest he played a vital part in shaping the musical and educational life that was to be the inheritance of Dohnányi, Bartók and Kodály. The events and enthusiasms of his remaining years brought Liszt closer to the spirit of the twentieth century than any artist of his generation.

[26] FLB, II, 121.

6

Une vie trifurquée (1869–86)

Twilight, an ambiguous word, might be the heading of this chapter as the last phase of Liszt's career was both a dusk and a dawn. The image of twilight suggests transition, and in the works of the late years there are many glimmerings of hitherto unexplored paths in music. He did not found a new 'school' with this music but many twentieth-century techniques and styles can be found prefigured in his music after 1870. His search for new images of musical expression was lifelong, but a peculiarly intermediate, transitional character hangs over his last period. Some of these twilight creations remained in shadowy obscurity until the second half of the present century.

The final stage of his life was transitional in another sense: he constantly moved between three centres, Weimar, Pest and Rome. To plot his latitude and longitude progressively throughout this chapter would be tiresome; this table shows how he divided his years:

Germany			*Italy*			*Hungary*		
JAN.	−MAR.	1869				APR.	1869	
			MAY	1869−MAR.	1870			
APR.	−JUL.	1870				AUG.	1870−APR.	1871
MAY	−AUG.	1871	SEP.	−NOV.	1871	NOV.	1871−MAR.	1872
APR.	−OCT.	1872				OCT.	1872−MAR.	1873
APR.	−SEP.	1873	OCT.	1873		OCT.	1873−MAY	1874
			MAY	1874−FEB.	1875	FEB.	−MAR.	1875
APR.	−SEP.	1875	SEP.	1875−FEB.	1876	FEB.	−MAR.	1876
APR.	−OCT.	1876				OCT.	1876−MAR.	1877
MAR.	−AUG.	1877	AUG.	−NOV.	1877	NOV.	1877−MAR.	1878
APR.	−AUG.	1878	SEP.	1878−JAN.	1879	JAN.	−MAR.	1879
APR.	−AUG.	1879	SEP.	1879−JAN.	1880	JAN.	−MAR.	1880
APR.	−AUG.	1880	AUG.	1880−JAN.	1881	JAN.	−APR.	1881
APR.	−OCT.	1881	OCT.	1881−JAN.	1882	FEB.	−APR.	1882
APR.	−NOV.	1882	NOV.	1882−JAN.	1883	JAN.	−MAR.	1883
APR. 1883	−JAN.	1884				FEB.	−APR.	1884
APR.	−OCT.	1884				NOV.	−DEC.	1884

Une vie trifurquée (1869–86)

Germany	Italy	Hungary
	DEC. 1884–JAN. 1885	JAN.–APR. 1885
APR.–OCT. 1885	OCT. 1885–JAN. 1886	JAN.–MAR. 1886
MAY–JUL. 1886		

A pattern emerges: Weimar in the spring and early summer; to Rome or the Villa d'Este for the rest of the year; and in Pest in the new year. There are variations: in 1870 he did not go to Rome for the winter and in 1872 he was not in Italy at all. Similarly Weimar saw nothing of him in 1874. But broadly he kept faith with the three stations of his self-imposed way for roughly equal parts of each year. A visit to Vienna became habitual in March or April, to stay with his cousin Eduard, and to celebrate both Easter and his name-day (the saint-day of Francis of Paola, 2 April). 'Germany' in the above table mostly implies 'Weimar', but he often left for short stays elsewhere in the country. For 'Hungary' read 'Pest', though on longer visits he spent time at the country homes of friends.

The travels of 1869–86 constitute a largely selfless pilgrimage of hard work and musical duty unique among great composers in old age. His income, small as it was, could have enabled him to remain in Rome, or to settle down almost anywhere, and see out his days in quiet creativity. For a passionate, inquiring, restless and earnest nature such as his, however, there was no choice. Critics have viewed his latter-day wanderings as the world-weariness of a forlorn, forsaken and hopeless figure, implying that the number of train tickets he bought adds up to more worth than the value of his late compositions or the service and sacrifice he gave to the young pianists and composers who flocked to him for encouragement and help. A century on, his legacy must be judged by his works and the extent to which he shaped music and its performance in the future.

The final cycle began with his Weimar visit of early 1869. Concerts of his music there and in nearby Jena saw visitors such as Rubinstein, Pauline Viardot, and the scholar Ludwig Nohl who gave a series of lectures on musical history. The Grand Duke placed at Liszt's disposal the Hofgärtnerei (the former court gardener's house) where he occupied the upper floor as his Weimar residence for the rest of his life. Liszt's apartment included a simple but spacious drawing-room – the scene of his famous masterclasses. The house had the benefit of pleasant seclusion, facing on to the ducal park, and was described by pupils and visitors as a haven of peace and culture. From 1870 his piano classes took place regularly on three afternoons of each week from 4 to 6 p.m. The method of teaching was akin to the modern masterclass: a group of students placed their pieces on a table and from this Liszt selected the music to be played and the chosen pupil stepped forward. Several rules were clear: anyone of sufficient talent was welcome, no fee was ever charged, pupils had to be punctual and technically well-prepared. He taught interpretation, not technique, and liberally illustrated his lessons with his own playing. The sternest rebuke was reserved for anyone wasting his time with inadequately prepared work. 'Wash your dirty linen at home!' he would growl and disparagingly direct them to the pedagogues in the conservatoires. Such rare outbursts of derision were understandable as his 'open house' system of teaching was inevitably abused by those who hoped to advance their careers by appending 'pupil of Liszt' to their brochures and advertisements. Life and teaching at the Hofgärtnerei were faithfully documented by several pupils, notably Morris Bagby, Amy Fay, Arthur Friedheim, August Göllerich, Carl Lachmund, Frederic Lamond, Alexander Siloti, August Stradal, Anton Strelezki and Felix Weingartner. Among the most prominent students of the 1870s were Rafael Joseffy, Berthold Kellermann, Georg Leitert, Max Pinner, Joseph Weiss, and of the ladies Adele aus der Ohe, Sophie Menter and Vera Timanoff.

Beethoven's centenary was a celebratory feature of the 1870 Weimar visit and Saint-Saëns, David, Nohl, Damrosch, Tausig and Viardot attended four days of festivities in May. Liszt's second *Beethoven Cantata*, Beethoven's songs, late chamber music, Diabelli Variations and *Missa Solemnis* were heard. He conducted in Weimar for the first time since the *Barber of Baghdad* of 1858, directing the Ninth Symphony and the E flat Concerto with Tausig as soloist. The following Weimar summer was saddened by news of Tausig's death from typhoid. He was but twenty-nine and Liszt felt his loss keenly, for through his exceptional talents, intelligence and energy he had been an outstanding pioneer of Liszt's and of Wagner's music.

Weimar days were documented not only in the memoirs of pupils but also, of course, in his regular epistles to Carolyne. And when absent from Weimar an additional source of correspondence can be drawn upon; for in 1871 he formed a close liaison with another lady, Olga, Baroness von Meyendorff (née Princess Gortschakoff), who was widowed in January of that year and settled soon after in Weimar. He had first met the Meyendorffs in Rome in 1863: Olga's husband was first secretary of the Russian legation. He re-encountered them in Weimar in 1867, the Baron having become Russian envoy there. From the first Liszt predicted a brilliant career for Felix Meyendorff and noted that his attractive wife had a 'most original pianistic talent'.[1] Shortly after the Russian couple moved to Karlsruhe, Felix suddenly died, leaving Olga in a strange town, a widow of thirty-three with four young sons. She returned to Weimar at the invitation of several friends, among them Liszt. Soon she was his closest confidante: he saw her constantly in Weimar, she travelled extensively with him and his published letters to her run to more than 400 items – the first dated January 1871, the last July 1886. As with the published letters to Agnes Street, the extent of their intimacy is enigmatic: the printed edition of his letters to Olga fails to explain the incompleteness of some of them. Liszt destroyed almost all of her letters but, according to Alan Walker,[2] the few unpublished ones extant at Weimar 'reveal her dependence on Liszt for friendship and emotional support, and they bring out the personal side of their relationship in a much more vivid way than his do'. None the less Liszt reveals between the carefully poised lines of his prose a warmth of affection and confidentiality that makes the letters to Olga as important as those to his other principal female correspondents, Marie d'Agoult, Carolyne, her daughter Marie, and Agnes Street. Like Carolyne, Olga was widely read, highly intellectual, domineering and rather eccentric. Unlike her though, she had a charm and elegance that made her attractive to men while her own sex found her disdainful and arrogant.

Liszt attended the first Vienna performance of *St Elisabeth* under Herbeck at the *Gesellschaft der Musikfreunde* on 4 April 1869. It met with immense success. At a concert in Liszt's honour given by students of the conservatoire Vladimir de Pachmann played Liszt's Concerto No. 1 and Laura Kahrer the first Mephisto Waltz. He was joined in Vienna by several prominent Hungarians: Augusz, Reményi, the pianist and composer Kornél Ábrányi and the young Count Albert Apponyi, later a distinguished statesman and close friend. These men were anxious that he should play a regular and more vigorous part in Hungarian cultural life and, at their invitation, he travelled to Pest and on 26 April conducted

[1] FLB, III, 164.
[2] *Musical Quarterly*, LXVIII/1, Jan. 1982.

his *Hungarian Coronation Mass*, Erkel conducting the *Dante Symphony* in the same programme. He repeated the Mass on the 30th, Erkel conducting *Hungaria* and Psalm 137. This short visit, coinciding with the opening of the new session of the National Assembly, was marked by popular acclaim and laid the foundations for his later association with the Hungarian capital.[3] His establishment as an active participant in the musical life of his own land was not achieved without opposition. The anti-clerical party distrusted him because of his Abbé's garb; the pro-royalist faction viewed his patriotism with disdain and, contrariwise, the more fervent nationalists objected because he could not speak Hungarian and they feared he would be a 'Germanising' influence. The ostentatious excesses of certain disciples were criticised and a few indigent musicians were jealous of Liszt's circle. Such grumblings were largely muted by the overwhelming enthusiasm of local musical societies and of the public at large; even his severest critics were silenced when it was realised that concerts associated with Liszt raised large sums of money to benefit the city's artistic life. He received invitations to patronize or participate in musical events and it was partly on account of these, and partly because of the disturbances elsewhere in Europe in 1870–1, that his next stay in Hungary of nearly nine months was his longest. He then came ever closer to local musicians, chamber groups, choirs, bands, the opera personnel; he gave musical matinées; he advised, encouraged or discouraged young singers and players; and on stays with friends like Augusz at Szekszárd or Archbishop Haynald at Kalocsa he busied himself with revising, arranging or sketching works. In 1870 Pest held Beethoven celebrations at which Liszt conducted before the royal family. Some of his pupils followed him to Pest and he acquired new students there. Distinguished artists too crossed into Hungary largely because of Liszt's presence.

His appointment in June 1871 as a Royal Hungarian Councillor, with an annual stipend of 4000 forints, consolidated his position in Pest where he spent some months every winter thereafter. Meanwhile his name had been linked with a scheme for a new National Academy of Music. The existing Conservatory in Pest had been founded with a generous donation from Liszt in 1840. Because of political upheavals it had been unable to sustain teachers of quality and there was an urgent need for a new,

[3] Liszt's growing involvement with Hungarian musical life in these years is chronicled in detail by D. Legány: *Liszt and his Country 1869–1873*.

properly-funded institution. Liszt did not put his own name forward. He was aware of existing factions for and against him, he was anxious not to tread on the toes of established academics and he doubted how useful he could be in the practical life of such an academy. But the efforts of Ábrányi and Apponyi, who felt that Liszt's reputation and guidance were vital to a scheme that would enhance Hungary's standing in the wider world, eventually prevailed. The Chamber of Deputies voted in favour of its establishment in February 1873. In November 1873 there was a triple celebration: the silver jubilee of Franz Josef's reign, the amalgamation of the twin cities on the Danube's banks into the united capital of Budapest, and Liszt's fiftieth anniversary as a concert artist, the last marked by four days of festivities.

In Italy in 1869–70 he had spent much time at the Villa d'Este, returning now and then to visit Carolyne in Rome where, in February, he was visited by Edvard Grieg, with whom he had corresponded and whose Violin Sonata op. 8 he had praised. Grieg was astonished at Liszt's sympathetic feeling for the national idioms of Scandinavia and marvelled at the way he read through the sonata at the piano, incorporating the violin part exactly, even when it lay in the middle of the piano texture: playing with breadth and total comprehension. Even more wonderful for the young Norwegian was his second visit, when he took along his Piano Concerto and Liszt sat at the piano with the manuscript before him:

> I admit that he took the first part of the concerto too fast, and the beginning consequently sounded helter-skelter; but later on, when I had a chance to indicate the tempo, he played as only he can play. It is significant that he played the cadenza, the most difficult part, best of all. His demeanour is worth any price to see. Not content with playing, he at the same time converses and makes comments, addressing a bright remark now to me, now to another of the assembled guests, nodding significantly to the right or left, particularly when something pleases him. In the adagio, and still more in the finale, he reached a climax both as to his playing and the praise he had to bestow.[4]

Another Scandinavian whose work was encouraged by Liszt in earlier Weimar years was the Swedish composer Franz Berwald. Among others who sought him out on his travels were Smetana, Saint-Saëns, and a whole generation of Frenchmen: d'Indy,

[4]Grieg to his parents. Transl. H. T. Finck, *Edvard Grieg,* London, 1906, 31–7.

Duparc, Delibes, Fauré; and Massenet who had first visited Liszt just before Christmas 1864 when staying at the Villa Medici as winner of the Prix de Rome. He fell in love with and married one of Liszt's pupils, Constance de Sainte-Marie. The most distinguished holder of the Prix de Rome after Massenet, indeed two decades later, was Debussy who played, with Paul Vidal, duets by Chabrier to Liszt. The old man in turn played to Debussy, who remarked on Liszt's sparing use of the pedal 'as a form of breathing'. Liszt was probably responsible for introducing him to the glories of Italian Renaissance choral music, and his modal effects, whole-tone harmony, pedalling and various coloristic devices greatly influenced Debussy's piano music and that of Ravel. Lalo and Dukas also exhibit debts to Liszt and, in modern times, Messiaen is not so far removed from certain aspects of Liszt. After Berlioz it was Saint-Saëns among Frenchmen who most claimed Liszt's attention and he was responsible for having *Samson et Dalila* premièred at Weimar, under Lassen, in 1877. The young man's *Danse macabre* naturally interested Liszt and, as Searle points out, his transcription of it takes a number of liberties much to the advantage of the original.

   Liszt was also a musical bridge between Russia and France. His long-standing interest in new Russian music was revitalised in the 1860s and early 1870s through figures like the critic Vladimir Stasov, champion of the St Petersburg 'Five': Balakirev, Cui, Borodin, Mussorgsky and Rimsky-Korsakov. The publisher Bessel sent Liszt parcels of their scores along with music by Dargomizhsky and Liadov. Liszt enthused over these scores and examined them eagerly, often in the presence of his French visitors. More and more he looked to Russia in the firm belief that she was yet to unfold unparalleled musical treasures compared to which most contemporary music was colourless and anaemic. In realms that the West had almost exhaustively explored he felt sure that Russia had new horizons to discover – in music, literature, the fine arts and science. While Stasov and Balakirev championed Liszt's works in Russia, he in turn introduced the music of 'the mighty handful' to his Weimar pupils. Cui visited Weimar in 1876 and 1880, and Borodin in 1877, 1881 and 1885, the latter recounting his visits in several long letters. Liszt never met Mussorgsky or Rimsky-Korsakov but expressed great admiration for the use of folk material in their scores, and astonished Mussorgsky by his understanding of the song cycle *The Nursery*, which he planned to transcribe. Equally Borodin and Glazunov (who visited Weimar in 1884) were astounded at Liszt's energetic and penetrating performances and analyses of their works. A childlike and ingenious volume of pieces particularly delighted Liszt: *Paraphrases* (1879), a collaborative venture between Borodin, Rimsky-Korsakov, Cui and Liadov, consisting of a series of piano duets (variations, dances, marches, character pieces, a fugue, even a Requiem!) through which runs a continuous ostinato melody, a version of 'Chopsticks':

Ex.3(a)

His letter of thanks for these captivating gems made it clear that he saw behind the jest 'an admirable compendium of the science of harmony, of counterpoint, of rhythms, of figuration, and of what in German is called "the Theory of Form" [Formenlehre]! I shall gladly suggest to the teachers of composition at all the conservatories in Europe and America to adopt your *Paraphrases* as a practical guide in their teaching.'[5] For the second edition of the set he sent a free variation, characteristic of his later style (see Ex. 3(b)).

He was quite out of step with current German taste in his passion for the Russian school, but his enthusiasm was of the greatest propaganda value to its composers at home, and became a passport for these pioneers abroad. They undoubtedly stimulated the music of his later years, just as Liszt's earlier output had an enormous influence on Russian music. Tchaikovsky was kind in his comments on Liszt the man, but critical and suspicious of his music, although he did not escape its influence. Liszt, on the other hand, was keenly interested in Tchaikovsky's work. Of subsequent composers, Rachmaninov, Scriabin and Medtner were greatly indebted to Liszt, and he was admired by Prokofiev, Stravinsky and Shostakovich.

Carolyne in Rome and Olga von Meyendorff in Weimar were not the only ladies to concern themselves intimately with his life and activities in the last years. Age did nothing to lessen his

[5] FLB, II, 285f.

Ex. 3(b)

attractiveness to women and he did little to discourage their attentions. Occasionally this damaged his reputation and his dignity, and never more so than in his entanglement with Olga Janina, the 'Cossack Countess', who caused scandal of a kind unknown since his long-ago association with Lola Montez. This Olga was neither Cossack nor a countess, nor was her surname Janina. Born Olga Zielinska in 1845, daughter of a maker of boot polish in Lemberg, she had married a Pole, Karol Janina Piasecki, whom she horse-whipped and drove away on their wedding night – at least according to the legends she wove around herself such as those of her pet tiger, her riding bareback on wild horses over the Steppes, her wolf-hunting and her ever-present dagger and phial of poison. Her pianistic talent was sufficient for Liszt to accept her as a pupil in Rome in 1869, and for the next year or so she followed him almost everywhere. In Szekszárd in September 1870, for example, she joined him with other pupils, and later in Kalocsa played a duet-arrangement with him from *St Elisabeth* at a concert in Archbishop Haynald's residence. Again in Szekszárd she took part in another Liszt concert and gave a dinner in his honour at a local hotel. Her name appears frequently in the matinee concerts Liszt gave in Pest in 1870–1 and in public concerts organised by Reményi. Until then her association with Liszt was unremarkable: she was one of many promising artists whom he was happy to let share the limelight at his musical appearances. Possibly he was especially concerned with her because of her emotional problems: nervousness in performance, a dependence on drugs and a proneness to thoughts of suicide. She also suffered financial distress and determined to try her luck in the USA: again characteristically, Liszt helped her with a letter of introduction to his American publisher. At what point her infatuation with Liszt became pathological, or exactly when he first saw danger signs, is unclear. But her American sojourn was a disaster and before returning she dispatched an agitated letter and a threatening telegram to Liszt. Other correspondents warned him of her thirst for 'revenge'. Nervously Liszt recalled her nightly prowling around his Roman lodgings.

The climax of the affair came on 25 November 1871 when friends called at his Pest apartment and witnessed a dramatic scene. Janina, armed with a pistol, was threatening to take Liszt's life or force him to take poison if he continued to reject her. For hours he had struggled alone with the deranged creature who eventually swallowed her own dose of poison and collapsed, apparently in spasms. She was taken to her hotel where a doctor ascertained that she had taken nothing harmful and, having surrendered her pistol, she soon left Pest for Paris, to avoid intervention by the police. Although public scandal was avoided, news of the incident spread among his circle and he was quick to write to Carolyne and quell her curiosity. The sordid affair would have ended there but for Janina's malice, when two years later a series of books appeared which sensationalised every detail of her relationship with Liszt. She adopted a pseudonym but the identities of the composer and many of his friends were only thinly disguised and it was clear that the writer had known intimate details of Liszt's life in Pest, Weimar, Vienna and Rome. The first book, *Souvenirs d'une Cosaque* by 'Robert Franz', ran into a sixth edition in Paris in 1874 and was followed by *Souvenirs d'un Pianiste:*

Réponse aux souvenirs d'une Cosaque which purported to be the pianist-lover's reply. The last drop of venom was squeezed from their relationship by still more books, now by 'Sylvia Zorelli': *Les amours d'une cosaque, par un ami de l'Abbé X* and *Le Roman du pianiste et de la cosaque*. Hell hath no fury ... was the grim reaction of Liszt, while the knowing and worldly readers of these 'souvenirs' doubtless enjoyed such a betrayal of the Abbé's already dubious reputation.

Mercifully, other pupils of the fair sex proved to be loyal, worthy and talented companions of these years. The attractive Sophie Menter, for instance, was a virtuoso of exceptional brilliance. In Rome Nadine Helbig was, alongside Sgambati, a gifted and energetic champion of Liszt. The careers of Laura Kahrer, Anna Mehlig, Martha Remmert, Adele aus der Ohe and Vera Timanoff were sufficient witness that he was not prone to encourage only the neurotic Janinas of the world.

If Marie d'Agoult failed in her mission to devote her life to loving, inspiring and protecting her chosen genius, then – by inevitable and fateful steps – her daughter Cosima succeeded in exactly that role. She left Bülow for the last time in November 1868 and joined Wagner at Tribschen where their third child, Siegfried, was born on 6 June 1869. From then, until the eve of Wagner's death, she kept a diary, first published in two bulky volumes only in 1976–7. It is invaluable not only for its illumination of herself and Wagner, but for its revelation of their feelings about Bülow and Liszt. Cosima never forgave herself for abandoning her husband as anguished entries that span the whole journal attest. She hardly refers to the unhappiness of her first marriage or to the scandal the separation evoked, but is determined to give her children the true reasons for her actions: destiny called her to love and serve 'my only friend, the guardian spirit and saviour of my soul, the revealer of all that is true and noble'.[6] An entry for 22 February 1869 notes:

> I thought of the last letter from my father, in which he said to me, 'Passion dies, but the pangs of conscience remain'. What a superficial judgement! As if my coming to R. had been an act of passion, and as if I could ever feel pangs of conscience on that account! How little my father knows me, after all![7]

[6] Cosima Wagner, *Diaries*, I, 27.
[7] ibid., 64.

Her fear was that Liszt would influence Bülow against a divorce, or act to prevent the children being raised as Protestants or, even, stop her allowance. In fact Bülow behaved with true nobility and, after the birth of Siegfried, wrote her a long, moving letter accepting her decision and his own fate. He was not inclined towards divorce but had no objection to it if Liszt thought her association with Wagner was best made official in such a way. The early diary repeatedly blames Liszt for interfering with the divorce proceedings but not a shred of evidence supports Cosima's view.

Although his personal relations with Tribschen were at their lowest, Liszt publicly displayed his interest in Wagner the composer by attending the rehearsals of *Rheingold* in Munich in August 1869. For fear of scandal neither Wagner nor Cosima dared set foot in Munich, yet Wagner tried to control the production from afar, despite his broad disapproval of the whole enterprise. He preferred no part of the *Ring* to be seen until the tetralogy was complete and under his direction. Faced with Ludwig II's determination for a performance, Wagner relied on his emissary the young conductor Richter to obey his instructions. When Richter tried to assert Wagner's authority with a threat of resignation, the puppy was dismissed. The celebrities who had crowded into the Bavarian capital were aghast. Liszt among others was urged to take the baton for the première. In the end a local musician, Wüllner, did the honours on 22 September, by which time Liszt had returned to Rome. One benefit of his Munich visit' was that Cosima learned from her friends there that Liszt felt nothing but love for her and was anxious that her divorce be speedily expedited. But personal communication between father and daughter was not resumed and the events of 1870 darkened relations further. On 2 January Liszt's son-in-law Emile Ollivier became prime minister of France at the dawn of a tragic year. Aside from the family link, Liszt was a wholehearted admirer of Napoleon III and, to the depths of his being, his sympathies were with France in the war with Prussia that began on 19 July. It was a month crowded with decisive events: on the previous day the Dogma of Papal Infallibility was declared – a development that was strongly opposed by Liszt's friend Cardinal Hohenlohe. Coincidentally on the same day (18 July) the Bülow marriage was officially dissolved. Liszt revisited Munich for *Die Walküre* that July: the couple at Tribschen had nothing to do with this production. In the ensuing months Liszt (now in Hungary) viewed events in France with sadness and horror while, in Tribschen, every French setback and German victory was greeted with positive gloating. On 25 August Wagner and Cosima married in a Protestant church in Lucerne. Liszt learned of the event from the newspapers. Cosima noted on 20 August: 'the three figures whom my father most revered are now in unenviable positions: Mazzini in prison, the Pope beset by a thousand fears and Louis Napoleon – *in the gutter* . . .' And on 6 November: 'My father is not going to Weimar, out of sympathy for the French – so the gap between us is now beyond repair.'[8]

Yet the gap *was* slowly repaired and it was the greatness of Wagner's art that redeemed human hurts and failings. Liszt was impressed with the boldness and vision of the Bayreuth *Festspielhaus* scheme and was one of the first to contribute financially. Wagner's scheme of *Patronatscheine* (patron's certificates) was intended to raise the money for building his theatre and inaugurating the festival. Although Liszt thought the arithmetic questionable for such a grandiose project he generously bought three certificates at 300 thalers each. (900 thalers was the approximate cost of a concert grand piano in 1871 and so a considerable outlay for Liszt with his modest income. Liszt's doubts also proved correct: the certificates were poorly subscribed and the overall cost of the first festival grossly outstripped income.) Letters to and from Cosima resumed in October 1871. That month Liszt celebrated his sixtieth birthday in Rome, where Bülow joined him – their first meeting for more than two years. In late December Liszt travelled from Pest to Vienna for the first performance of Part I of *Christus*, conducted by Rubinstein and with Bruckner as organist.

In May 1872 Wagner sent Liszt a warm and friendly invitation to the foundation stone-laying ceremony at Bayreuth. Liszt replied to his new son-in-law with equal warmth and respect. He could not attend, but the breach was healed. In September Richard and Cosima visited him at Weimar and a month later he made the first of many visits to Bayreuth, where he saw the building work at the theatre and at Wagner's new home 'Wahnfried'. Cosima's diary often expresses concern for her father's apparent tiredness and weariness of soul ('the sight of him fills me with melancholy'[9]) and

[8] Cosima Wagner, *Diaries*, I, 270, 293.
[9] ibid., 627.

it also reveals Wagner's ambivalent feelings toward his friend. In his company things passed off well enough, but when alone with Cosima he gave vent to his inner dislike of Liszt and often raged at her furiously if she had spent a little too much time with her father. These explosions of childish jealousy and reproach could be triggered even by a mere letter from Liszt.

The Weimar Music School was founded in 1872 with Liszt's support and encouragement and became (under the direction of Karl Müller-Hartung) a leading school of orchestral playing in Germany. At the première of *Christus* in Weimar in May 1873 several friends attended from Hungary, along with Wagner, Cosima, little Daniela, Marie Moukhanoff and Raff. Liszt conducted the three-hour performance and Wagner's reaction to the music covered 'all extremes from ravishment to immense indignation'. Cosima viewed her father's work as 'thoroughly un-German'.[10] Despite this, her love for him remained unquenched. In the autumn for example, she bitterly reproached herself for not attending his jubilee celebrations in Budapest, a journey she had declined to make from fear of upsetting Wagner. These celebrations included another hearing of *Christus*, under Richter – a performance Liszt considered far better than the May première.

Forgoing his usual Weimar visit, Liszt left Budapest for Italy in mid-May 1874 and remained there for nine months owing to his concern over the poor health of Princess Carolyne and partly from a desire to devote himself to creative work at the quiet Villa d'Este which he now made his principal Italian home. True to his intentions the months in Tivoli saw him busy with composition, revision and arrangement (especially of his symphonic poems for piano duet). On 9 February he had written to Carolyne: 'My one ambition as a musician was, and should be, to cast my lance into the unlimited future . . .'[11] In one of the kindlier judgements recorded by Cosima, Wagner described Liszt as undoubtedly 'the greatest man of originality and genius' he had ever met.[12] Originality, the striving for new means of expression in musical language and form, and the notion that he was writing not for his present world but consciously for a future age, are the hallmarks of his work after 1870. His earlier tendency towards over-expan-

[10] ibid., 640f.
[11] FLB, VII, 57f.
[12] Cosima Wagner, *Diaries*, I, 299.

sion and over-emphasis is forsaken for an often extreme conciseness and understatement. The majority of the late pieces are
small in scale. His choral-orchestral *The Bells of Strassburg
Cathedral*, a relatively 'large-scale' canvas of these years, lasts
barely thirteen minutes. The history of this dramatic cantata-in-
miniature dates from Longfellow's visit to Rome during the winter
of 1868–9 when he met Liszt and the Princess several times.
She was deeply struck by his poetry, notably by its Christian
symbolism. In February 1869 Liszt wrote that he would soon try
to set Longfellow's *Excelsior* for her. Nothing came of this, but in
letters of 1873 Carolyne urged him to set the Prologue to *The
Golden Legend* (the central part of Longfellow's epic trilogy
Christus: a Mystery). Liszt completed the casting of his *Bells* in
October 1874, prefacing the choral section with a short prelude
Excelsior. The work was performed at an historic concert jointly
given by Liszt and Wagner in Budapest on 10 March 1875 to raise
funds for Bayreuth. The motif of the prelude

Ex.4

was remembered by Wagner when he wrote the opening theme of
Parsifal. The Budapest concert included a memorable performance
of Beethoven's E flat concerto by Liszt, under Richter, and a
number of extracts from the *Ring* conducted by Wagner. Wagner
remarked to Liszt 'You have put me in the shade!' and one reviewer
said of Liszt's playing: 'Here is no decline – this sun never sets!'

In the score the text of *The Bells of Strassburg Cathedral*
appears in German and English and illustrates Liszt's scrupulous
concern over the minutiae of word-setting, with extensive musical
alternatives to suit the metre and accents of each language. In the
preparation of the English setting he may have been assisted by
his American pupil Max Pinner. In *The Legend of St Cecilia*, of
the same year, an equally meticulous and separate notation is
given for three languages: French, German and Italian. *St Cecilia*
is scored for mezzo-soprano, chorus, organ and orchestra and is

more expansive in its musical gestures: the poetic repetitions are appropriate to the meditative mood of the text. Yet, again, the work lasts less than quarter of an hour. 1874 also saw the final version of *Hymne de l'Enfant à son réveil*. At the Villa d'Este that summer and autumn Liszt also sketched parts of *The Legend of St Stanislaus*. This was an oratorio which occupied him intermittently between 1873 and the last year of his life but remained unfinished. The Princess was especially keen to encourage this project based (rather in the manner of *St Elisabeth*) on the life of the martyr from her native Poland, and one of her bitterest disappointments was Liszt's failure to make much progress with it. (A companion oratorio on the life of St Stephen of Hungary remained merely an idea.) Time and again in letters to him and to Adelheid von Schorn, who reported to her all Liszt's doings in Weimar, Carolyne criticised his seeming indolence in creative matters. Her opinion may seem justified when comparing the sporadic output of short-winded pieces in the last years with the catalogue of his 1850s creations. But this ignores the extent of his musical activities in Weimar and Budapest, his many radical revisions of previous works for new publication and the nature of the new style he was forging, which tended towards brevity and simplicity. Size and grandeur of thought were Carolyne's ideals and, while it is possible to regret Liszt's failure to write another epic work, much as Beethoven's Tenth or Sibelius' Eighth might be lamented, the achievement of his final period cannot be judged by unrealistic expectations, only by the success, or lack of it, in the works he did accomplish. *Ossa arida* may be cited as a masterly and startlingly original example among the motets; and in *Via Crucis*, the fourteen Stations of the Cross for soloists, chorus and organ, he achieved a long-cherished ambition: the creation of a new kind of church music, a blend of advanced harmony and traditional Liturgical techniques. So 'new' that the publisher to whom Liszt sent *Via Crucis* and some other devotional works rejected them out of hand. A decade or so earlier it would have been unthinkable for a publisher to reject a manuscript by Liszt: now he often did not trouble to have certain pieces published. *Via Crucis* was not heard until 1929.

Liturgical themes are shared by piano solo works such as *Sancta Dorothea* and *In festo transfigurationis Domini nostri Jesu Christi*. In 1877 he completed the set entitled *Années de pèlerinage: troisième année* which contains *Angelus*, *Sunt lacrymae rerum* and

Sursum Corda. Two pieces were inspired by the beautiful gardens of his Tivoli home, *Aux cyprès de la Villa d'Este* I and II; and in the most famous item in the collection, *Les jeux d'eaux à la Villa d'Este,* the nature of Liszt's mysticism is reflected in a quotation from St John's Gospel over one section. This transcends the aural imagery of the ceaseless play of the fountains to thoughts of the waters of everlasting life. *Weihnachtsbaum*, a set of twelve pieces, contains a similar mixture of sacred and secular subjects. Many of his piano works are elegiac, and later examples are the *Funeral Music for Mosonyi*, in memory of the Hungarian composer who died in 1870, and a similar tribute to the poet Petőfi. The *First Elegy* (in memory of Marie Moukhanoff) for cello, piano, harp and harmonium is one of Liszt's rare chamber works and also exists in versions for cello or violin and piano, and piano solo. A *Second Elegy* adds another miniature to the cello or violin repertoire and was also arranged for piano. He continued to transcribe and, in addition to his own works, he chose at this period from music by Beethoven, Bülow, Cornelius, Lassen, Mozart, Saint-Saëns, Schubert, Spohr, Verdi, Wagner and several Hungarian composers. Two sets of miniatures show well the 'new' tendencies of the old Liszt: *5 Little Piano Pieces* and *5 Hungarian Folksongs*, which are irresistibly charming, clear and concise.

In his earlier songs the best music reflected the best poetry (Hugo, Petrarch, Heine, Goethe). In the last period of song-writing the verses chosen are rarely of such high quality. Yet Liszt's response is highly imaginative and his musical symbolism at once both vivid and restrained in capturing the poetic essence of such lyrics as *Ihr Glocken von Marling*, the two perfect miniatures *Einst* and *Gebet*, an English setting *Go not, happy day* (Tennyson) and the almost expressionist intensity of another tiny song *Und wir dachten der Toten*. His interest in the melodrama continued with settings for reciter and piano of *The dead poet's love* by Maurus Jókai and *The blind singer* by Aleksey Tolstoy in 1874–5.

His fame left him little respite and as the years advanced he increasingly complained of the drudgery of correspondence:

> For the last couple of weeks I have been gloomily writing quantities of letters. I get nearly fifty a week, not counting shipments of manuscripts, pamphlets, books, dedications, and all kinds of music. The time required to peruse them, even casually, deprives me of the time needed to answer them … Some ask for concerts, for advice,

for recommendations; others for money, for jobs, for decorations, etc., etc. I don't know what will become of me in such a purgatory.[13]

Yet he continued to enjoy the social benefits of fame: the company of distinguished visitors to Budapest like Rubinstein and Sarasate, and invitations such as those of the King of Holland to stay at his residence Het Loo, near Arnhem, where he met fellow musicians, Wieniawski, Vieuxtemps, Ambroise Thomas, and notable Dutch painters. Through Vieuxtemps he met the youthful Eugène Ysaÿe and exerted some influence on the violinist's future works. A revered and long-standing friend, Marie Moukhanoff, a woman of legendary charm, wit and talent, died in 1874. In June the next year he mounted a memorial concert for her at Weimar which included the male-voice *Requiem*, and the first performances of the *Legend of St Cecilia*, *Elegy No. 1* and the revised *Hymne de l'enfant*. Cosima attended, as Marie had been a campaigner for Bayreuth, and it was there that Liszt spent three weeks that summer, an eager witness to the hurly-burly of rehearsals for the forthcoming *Ring* cycle.

On 5 March 1876 Marie d'Agoult died. Liszt remained unmoved on learning of the passing of the mother of his three children. Four years earlier he had been much more affected by the news of Caroline de St Cricq's death.

On 26 March a concert was given by the first group of Liszt's pupils at the new music academy in Budapest, of which he was president and part-time professor, and Liszt gave a recital in the city in aid of the victims of yet another disastrous flooding of the Danube. He expressed the hope that, just as the flood benefit concert of 1838 marked the beginning of his virtuoso career, this present event would be his last public performance. It was not to be: for ten more years he was occasionally tempted back to the platform. A concert at Sondershausen in July included, at Liszt's request, the symphonic poem *Hamlet*: its first performance, eighteen years after it was composed. August brought the first Bayreuth festival and he remained there for the whole month, enjoying the mighty tetralogy which but for himself and King Ludwig, as Wagner acknowledged, might never have been heard. A galaxy of friends crowded into the little town and among the visitors Liszt met Tchaikovsky.

The next major event to coax him again to the concert

[13] LLOM, 213.

platform was in March 1877: Vienna's commemoration of the fiftieth anniversary of Beethoven's death. The cream of Viennese musicians and high society gathered to hear him play the E flat concerto and the Choral Fantasia and accompany Beethoven's Scottish song arrangements. Perhaps the most avid listener of all was a boy, just short of his eleventh birthday: Ferruccio Busoni, destined to be in many senses the spiritual heir of Liszt and one of his greatest interpreters (though never his pupil). The actual performance was a disappointment to Busoni, due to Liszt having injured a finger, although it was entirely characteristic of him to fulfil his promise to play despite his damaged hand.

Generally his physical health remained robust. But he was often enveloped by a spiritual depression, fed by doubts concerning his solitary path as a composer and intensified by loneliness that occasionally engulfed him in his nomadic life. Letters of 1877 to Olga shed light on his mental state.[14] 'So long as there is work to be done,' he writes in January, 'I still feel relaxed and in fairly good form. For the rest I am overcome by indescribable depression and have reached the point where Carthusians and Trappists almost seem garrulous to me.' Later in the year he complains of physical and mental suffering and disordered nerves, yet in October he presents the face he stoically kept for the world: 'My poor brain is very tired; I almost spent these last two days in bed but I am *not* sick, and you know how I hate people worrying about my state of health, which is always good enough.' However November brings this confession:

> I am desperately sad and completely incapable of finding a single ray of happiness. I'm in a kind of mental depression accompanied by physical indisposition. I've been sleeping badly for weeks, which doesn't help to calm my nerves ... A few more leaves have been added to the cypresses[15] – no less boring and redundant than the previous ones! To tell the truth, I sense in myself a terrible lack of talent compared with what I would like to express; the notes I write are pitiful. A strange sense of the infinite makes me impersonal and uncommunicative. In 1840 M. Mignet in speaking of me said solemnly to Princess Belgiojoso: 'There is great confusion in that young man's head.' The latter is now old but not at all confused.

[14] ibid., 266, 268, 280, 295, 297.
[15] *Aux cyprès de la Villa d'Este, thrénodie.*

The critic Hanslick paid Liszt an unexpected honour at the Paris Exposition of June 1878. He represented Austria on the international jury and Liszt attended for Hungary. Declaring that Liszt was the greatest musician present from any nation Hanslick proposed him as honorary president. In Paris he saw Emile and Daniel Ollivier, Saint-Saëns, his old secretary Belloni, Ernest Renan, and had a warm re-encounter with a friend of many decades before, now returned from his long exile: Victor Hugo. Pope Pius IX died that year; Liszt had audiences of his successor Leo XIII in November and in January 1879 and wrote some pieces in his honour. In October 1879 Liszt was elected an honorary canon of Albano. The death of his cousin Eduard Liszt in February 1879 was a keenly felt loss; he missed his friendship and wise financial counsel. Some old wounds were healed and forgotten. A meeting with his ex-friend Hiller at Hanover in 1876 was cordial, as was a visit by Joachim to Budapest in 1880 and several later meetings between the two men. He encountered Brahms occasionally over the years and came to admire some of his works through Bülow's championship.

The young circle of pianists and composers who followed him everywhere greatly helped to sustain Liszt in old age. One notable teenager was Isaac Albéniz who, from his debut at the age of four, was no stranger to arduous travel, having run away from home as a mere child, toured Spain, crossed the Atlantic and tried his luck in South America and the USA. Now he followed Liszt from Budapest to Weimar and Rome as an ardent disciple. Géza Zichy, who had lost his right arm as a boy but who became an exceptional left-hand virtuoso, joined Liszt and they gave several duo concerts. Less talented, but endowed with a charm that caught the master's fancy, was Lina Schmalhausen who also joined the circle in 1879 and brought comfort and affection to his last years.

In Rome the Princess never ceased to write. In addition to the monolithic *Causes intérieures de la faiblesse extérieure de l'Église*, she produced *Petits entretiens pratiques à l'usage des femmes du grand monde pour la durée d'une retraite spirituelle* (a mere eight volumes) and she achieved about a dozen other religious books. They are unread, perhaps unreadable, and virtually unobtainable. Their interest lies, from the gist of their content that can be gleaned from contemporary opinions and letters, in their unorthodoxy. For this most fervent of Catholics was to see her books placed on the Index by both Popes Pius and Leo. She envisaged a militant, revolutionary Church in the modern world. No doubt this was the tenor of much of the conversation when Liszt visited her each autumn. His view of the Church remained close to Lamennais, his friend Cardinal Hohenlohe was opposed to Rome on several matters and, whatever Liszt's soutane symbolised, he was never unthinkingly orthodox. Yet in the last decade his 300 or so letters to Carolyne reveal a growing weariness with her nagging criticisms of his way of life, her dislike of the Wagners, and the continual bombardment of high-flown attacks on the inner workings of the Church. 'I should like to see her wonderful intelligence and great knowledge employ themselves in less arduous regions than that of transcendental theology,' he confessed to her daughter Marie in 1877.[16]

Meanwhile another lady's pen had been busy on Liszt's behalf. Volume one of Lina Ramann's biography appeared in 1880. Her book has been much maligned and condemned as the source of confusion and error. The criticism has been overstated. Certainly Ramann is often factually wrong, especially concerning the early years; and her treatment of Princess Wittgenstein and Marie d'Agoult is grossly biased respectively for and against. But by the standards of the age her work is thoroughly objective and the recent and belated publication of her letters, diaries and documents relating to Liszt[17] largely exonerates her from the frequent charge that she was excessively manipulated. Liszt lived only to see the first volume and Carolyne, too, was in her grave when volumes two and three appeared in print (1887, 1894). A serious calumny made by some critics was that Liszt attempted to whitewash his reputation through Ramann's book. However, Liszt's copy of Volume one (in the Weimar archives) contains marginal notes made *after* publication which indicate that he had taken no trouble to correct the book even at proof stage. Ramann's biographical industry is outstripped only by another contemporary female admirer of Liszt, La Mara, a vastly prolific writer among whose output about twenty-five volumes concern aspects of Liszt.

Books bedevilled Liszt. The confusions spawned by biographers only match the problems strewn along the path by his own writings. His well-meaning studies of the Weimar years, *Chopin* and *The Gypsies and their music in Hungary*, caused him

[16] *The Letters of Franz Liszt to Marie zu Sayn-Wittgenstein*, 213.
[17] *Lisztiana*, 1983.

many subsequent headaches.[18] Breitkopf suggested a new edition of *Chopin* in 1874, and Liszt naturally consulted his former collaborator, Carolyne, about the revision. This was a move he came bitterly to regret. Her interference in the revised book seriously delayed its appearance and encumbered it with needless expansions. A fierce quarrel ensued over this, all traces of which La Mara edited out of the published letters to Carolyne. After many a long wrangle she won the day and her version was published. A consequence of these difficulties over *Chopin* was that when a new edition of the *Gypsies* book was begun, he was too old and weary to try to wrest the work from her hands. The unfortunate result of this was more serious than just a bloated and embroiled prose style. The *Gypsies* aroused controversy on its 1859 appearance and still does today. Liszt's ideas on gypsy music and his erroneous concept of its place in Hungary will be examined in Chapter 11. In the 1860s, as the country was struggling towards a degree of autonomy, many native artists and scholars were enraged that the greatest Hungarian musician had effectively declared that Hungary had no national voice in music. The 1881 reprint, greatly enlarged by Carolyne, added sections with a vein of anti-Semitism that is counter to all we know of Liszt's views. He admired the music of the Jewish rite and no hint of anti-Semitism is evinced in his letters or his friendships with many Jews. Carolyne's 'transcendental' thoughts again embarrassed the aged Liszt who had to write tactful disclaimers of the implications of his book to the press.

Bülow's occasional visits to Weimar put the less talented students there into a state of alarm. He determined to put to flight those who took unfair advantage of the master's time: to clean out the Augean Stable, as he put it. In June 1880 he found '15 she- and 13 tom-pianists now infecting the rather pure air ... I need hardly mention that the terror the news of my arrival cast on the heads (if such there be) and fingers of these wretches, is at its utmost height.'[19] When one unfortunate Fräulein played the *Mazeppa* study in a frightful manner he told her that she had only one qualification for performing this piece – she had the soul of a horse.[20] The pupils quailed as Bülow attempted to perform for Liszt 'the same service I do for my dog – ridding him of his fleas'. If Bülow's pejorative imagery of the menagerie is appropriate, then

[18] See Chapter 2, n. 27.
[19] Bülow, *Briefe*, VI, 21.
[20] Newman, *The Man Liszt*, 243, quoting Berthold Kellermann.

it is but one aspect of the masterclasses, for Weimar released some creatures of the finest pedigree and some of the tom-pianists were lions. The outstanding pupils of the 'eighties include d'Albert, Arthur de Greef, Martin Krause, Weingartner and (on his 1882 visit to Liszt) the American composer Edward MacDowell. Göllerich (who studied at Weimar in the summers from 1884 to 1886, and in Rome and Budapest too) kept a diary[21] which records the complete repertoire of the classes and many of Liszt's detailed comments. He mentions eighty pupils in that two-year period and some had distinguished careers: Conrad Ansorge, Richard Burmeister, Friedheim, Lamond, Georg Liebling, José Vianna da Motta, Alfred Reisenauer, Moritz Rosenthal, Max Sandt, Emil Sauer, Siloti, Bernhard Stavenhagen, Stradal and István Thomán.

In Budapest Liszt stayed, from January 1881, in a specially provided apartment on the top floor of the Music Academy. Several cities celebrated the year of his seventieth birthday. In February Bülow visited Budapest for two concerts. The orchestral *Second Mephisto Waltz* was premièred under Sándor Erkel in March. In April Liszt played in Pressburg and Oedenburg, and visited his birthplace (for the unveiling of a commemorative plaque which is still to be seen) en route to Vienna and another concert. At Magdeburg the honours were provided by, among others, the young Arthur Nikisch. Berlin witnessed a series of 'Liszt evenings' and a performance of *Christus*. He was similarly fêted in May at Freiburg, Baden-Baden, Antwerp and Brussels. In July he had a serious fall downstairs at the Hofgärtnerei which had lasting effects. During two months of recovery his grand-daughter Daniela stayed at Weimar to cheer him. He was able to visit Bayreuth for three weeks in September and then travelled to Rome with Daniela to spend his birthday quietly.

A Brussels performance of *St Elisabeth* in May 1882 led to further meetings with Massenet and Saint-Saëns, and with the pianist Francis Planté, one of the few great artists outside Liszt's circle to promote his works (prior to Busoni and Paderewski). He attended Massenet's new opera *Hérodiade*. But the operatic event of that year was the première of *Parsifal* on 26 July at Bayreuth. Liszt wrote: 'During and after yesterday's performance the general feeling was that there is nothing that can be said about this miraculous work. Silence is surely the only response to so deeply moving a work; the solemn beat of its pendulum is from the

[21] First published 1975 as *Franz Liszts Klavierunterricht*.

156

sublime to the most sublime.'[22] While in Bayreuth he came to know Humperdinck and witnessed the marriage of his grand-daughter Blandine to Count Biagio Gravina.

The Wagners wintered in Venice in the sumptuous Palazzo Vendramin on the Grand Canal. Liszt joined them on 19 November and stayed until 13 January 1883. *La lugubre gondola* (see page 254) dates from this time. Inspired by the striking sight of funeral gondolas it has a mysterious and prophetic quality as, only a month after Liszt's departure, Wagner's body was borne on such a vessel from his last home. News of his death on 13 February reached Budapest the following day. At first Liszt refused to believe it but as telegram after telegram began to arrive he could no longer doubt the truth. His offer to accompany Cosima from Venice to the funeral in Bayreuth was declined. She had hoped to die with her husband and for a long while she retreated into absolute solitude and grief. Even her father was forbidden to break the seclusion, a rebuff he felt sorely. When he went to Bayreuth in 1884 for the *Parsifal* performances he was not offered the hospitality of Wahnfried. More than three years passed after Wagner's death before he saw his daughter again.

Another death which distressed Liszt was that of Smetana whose career he had followed intently. But as some talents departed, new ones appeared. In April 1883 he met an admirer eager to carry the banner of Wagner and Liszt: Hugo Wolf.

On 22 May, the seventieth anniversary of Wagner's birth, Liszt conducted a memorial concert in Weimar. *Am Grabe Richard Wagners*, a short piece for harp and string quartet, commemorates that date and quotes their shared 'Excelsior-Parsifal' motif. A piano miniature *R.W. – Venezia* also belongs to 1883. The genre of late pieces in elegiac mood includes evocative titles: Elegy, Threnody, *Recueillement, Resignazione, Sospiri, Nuages gris, La lugubre gondola, Schlaflos!: Frage und Antwort, Abschied, Unstern/Sinistre/Disastro, Trauermarsch*. The late piano pieces can be divided simply into two groups: elegies and dances. The dazzling series of 'dance-fantasies' are a truly extrovert foil to the meditational, introverted 'elegy' works, and none of these pieces suggests a tired old man: the *Valses oubliées*, the three *Czárdás*, the last *Mephisto Waltzes*, the *Mephisto Polka*, the dance-like *Bagatelle sans tonalité* and a final four Hungarian Rhapsodies.

[22] Letter to H. v. Wolzogen, quoted in *Wagner: a Documentary Study*, ed. Barth, etc., London, 1975, 241.

Transcriptions of the Polonaise from Tchaikovsky's *Eugene Onegin* and of *Tarantelles* by Cui and Dargomizhsky belong to this group, while the *Sarabande and Chaconne from Handel's 'Almira'* is a more measured dance. The *Carousel de Madame Pelet-Narbonne* is a rare example of a musical joke in Liszt's output. It depicts Olga von Meyendorff's landlady, a plump and greedy lady negotiating a merry-go-round at a Weimar carnival: the musical instruction is *intrepido*!

The symphonic poem *Von der Wiege bis zum Grabe* ('From the cradle to the grave') was inspired by a drawing by Mihály Zichy in which the grave is seen as the cradle of a future life. Searle rightly points to the curiously transitional quality of the final section,[23] appropriate to the subject, and characteristic of the last period generally. Of sacred choral works, the last psalm setting, *De profundis*, the *St Christopher Legend* and the motet *Qui seminant in lacrimis* are particularly vivid in harmonic imagery.

His generally sound health slowly declined from early in 1884. He began to tire easily and had increasing trouble with his eyes. Reading and writing became progressively more difficult and towards the end he required an amanuensis (except for letters to Olga, Carolyne and Lina Schmalhausen). Despite his weakened physical state his final months were full of valiant activity. In January 1886 he left Rome for the last time and proceeded to Budapest for his round of teaching and concerts. On the horizon, in addition to his Weimar summer stay and an intended visit to Bayreuth, were invitations to Liège, Paris, London and St Petersburg for festivals of his work in this, his seventy-fifth year. Except for St Petersburg he fulfilled all these plans. That he should return to London after forty-five years delighted the small group of his British admirers, notably Walter Bache, who had long hoped and planned for such a visit, and the composer Alexander Mackenzie, who met Liszt again in Florence in January 1885: 'The lapse of 20 years since I had seen him had changed the slim, erect figure to that of a bent, round-shouldered, stoutish old man, while the broadened features, with heavy bushy eyebrows, still retained the keen, alert look of former years.'[24] (Borodin also noted, later in 1885, that Liszt seemed to have grown 'a little shorter and had put on weight; his grey mane had grown; it had become thicker and longer. He speaks with the same animation and humour, but is a

[23] *The Music of Liszt*, 116.
[24] *A Musician's Narrative*, 125.

little bit short of breath; he's become a little hard of hearing and his eyes are weaker . . .'[25]) On playing through Mackenzie's music Liszt drew attention to a passage of particularly Scottish folk flavour and remarked, 'I've done much of this sort of thing, but not that!' Another Scot, Frederic Lamond, also played a prominent role in the London visit.

The steps from Budapest to London were via Vienna, Liège, Antwerp and Paris. In the French capital his *Missa Solennis* was heard at St Eustache, where it had suffered such a debacle twenty years before: now its reception was more enthusiastic. He also heard Saint-Saëns give a performance of his *Carnival of the Animals* in Pauline Viardot's drawing room. The two weeks in England exceeded the hopes of all with their success. London was gripped with 'Liszt-fever', from the cabmen who talked excitedly of the 'Habby Liszt' to the Queen-Empress who received him at Windsor, as George IV had done sixty-two years previously. Victoria noted that Liszt 'having been a very wild, phantastic looking man, was now a quiet benevolent-looking old priest, with long white hair and scarcely any teeth'.[26] Not only did Liszt play to the Queen but he delighted the students of the Royal Academy of Music by playing for them after the inauguration of a Liszt scholarship. Mackenzie conducted performances of *St Elisabeth* at St James's Hall and at the Crystal Palace. Among the notables who met Liszt were the Prince and Princess of Wales, Robert Browning, Henry Irving, Ellen Terry, Bram Stoker, Max Müller, Alma-Tadema, Lord Leighton, George Grove, Hallé, Parry, Sullivan, Joachim, de Pachmann and Alfred Hollins.

Three weeks after returning to Weimar he was on the move again – to Sondershausen for a meeting of the *Allgemeiner Deutscher Musikverein* whose annual festivals over twenty-five years had provided an important platform for his music. Four of his *Historical Hungarian Portraits* in orchestrations by Friedheim were performed at this gathering. After another brief stay in Weimar he arrived in Bayreuth for the wedding of Daniela to Dr Henry Thode on 2 July. From there he travelled to Luxembourg

[25] Letter of 4/16 Aug. 1885, transl. G. Seaman: *Musical Quarterly*, LXX/4, 1984, 492ff.
[26] Queen Victoria's Diary, 7 April 1886; quoted in LSJ, IX, 1984, 63. For a compendium of eyewitness accounts of Liszt's 1886 London visit see LSJ, V, 1980, 15–27; and *cf.* SAE, 33, 29–56; and Adrian Williams: 'The Last Visit to London: April 1886' in NHQ, XXVII/103, Autumn 1986, 131–8.

at the invitation of the painter Mihály von Munkácsy at Schloss Colpach. Fellow guests were his faithful pupil Stavenhagen (who had also taken part in the London visit) and Cardinal Haynald. On the 19th he played at a concert in the casino in Luxembourg. La Mara tells that with this rendering of 'the first *Liebestraum*, the *Chant Polonais* from the *Glanes de Woronince* and the sixth of the *Soirées de Vienne*, Liszt's magic playing fell silent for ever'.[27]

He had suffered recently from a hacking cough, day and night. When he returned to Bayreuth on 21 July he was a sick man. Seemingly Cosima had no idea of the desperate condition of her father, who was to be lodged in a house close to Wahnfried. She had much else on her mind, having emerged from her seclusion to supervise a festival which included the first Bayreuth *Tristan*. Liszt struggled to *Parsifal* on the 23rd and *Tristan* two days later, and sat huddled in the Wagner family box, half asleep, clutching a handkerchief to his mouth. The next day he was able to sit up in his bedroom and play some hands of his beloved whist. Weingartner, Adelheid von Schorn, Stradal, Sophie Menter and others gathered to express their concern at the master's illness. Lina, Göllerich and Stavenhagen tended him. On 27 July Cosima took charge and forbade visitors: she, Isolde and Eva would nurse the old man who was in a high fever which the physicians could do nothing to abate. On the 29th Lina stole into the room, when everyone else had gone to the theatre, and took her farewell. He was delirious most of Friday 30th when, late at night, a doctor diagnosed pneumonia and gave little hope of recovery. At 10.30 p.m. on Saturday 31st, according to some accounts, he was heard to mutter 'Tristan' and not long afterwards he died without pain.

The Abbé Liszt, Canon of Albano, was not given extreme unction. No performance was cancelled at the Wagner theatre. On the day of his funeral the town was bedecked with festive flags to welcome the Crown Prince Friedrich of Germany. He was buried on 3 August in the municipal cemetery of the town where he happened to die (as he had wished to be the case). Bruckner improvised on themes from *Parsifal* at a Requiem the next day. Olga von Meyendorff arived with the intention of joining Liszt for the festival and, instead, joined Cosima in his funeral procession.

[27] La Mara, *Liszt und die Frauen*, Leipzig, 1919, 327.

Lina Schmalhausen and the other pupils left quietly the next day. In Rome the Princess completed the twenty-fourth volume of her *Causes intérieures* on 23 February 1887 and died two weeks later. Cosima Liszt-Bülow-Wagner lived for forty-four more years.

7

The man Liszt

In his biography of Sir Henry Irving, Edward Gordon Craig quotes the actor's son Laurence: 'I wish they wouldn't make such a white-winged angel of father. He was never that.' Craig comments,

> Laurence Irving's wish is a good one. He hates the white wings of sentimentality. So do we all, but though I would clip the wings, I wouldn't add to the figure a beak and claws. How to satisfy this son is the question – how to do it without making the father seem demonic? Not to make him out to be a saint is easier said than done, and, for the life of me, I can't make him out to be anything else.[1]

Craig's dilemma confronts the student of Liszt's life. On the one hand there is an abundance of literature (especially among the earlier books of the reminiscence or memoir variety) which lays stress on the saintly, not to say Christ-like:

> But I cannot attempt to enumerate the sufferings which were allevi-ated by the foresight of his good heart. His hand was truly that blessed hand in which the five loaves of the Gospel fed five thousand! A portion of the letters he received during the time I was his unsalaried secretary has remained in my possession. I consider them a testimony a thousand times more precious than the grandeur of Liszt, than the crowns of laurels with which he was covered at his concerts, the leaves of which we used to vie with one another to possess.[2]

The opposite viewpoint – Liszt as demon – is amply illustrated in the study by Ernest Newman, who dredged up every unflattering description of Liszt to be found in the muddy waters of nineteenth-century gossip and jealous innuendo. His justification was the laudable one of setting right the falsities abounding in earlier over-pious biographies. Unfortunately, through over-selective

[1] Craig, *Henry Irving*, London, 1930.
[2] Wohl, *François Liszt*, 221f.

quotation, occasional mis-quotation and mis-translation, and by stressing the evidence of dubious and discredited writers (notably 'Olga Janina') Newman created an equally false portrait. His central thesis of Liszt's life as 'the tragi-comedy of a soul divided against itself' is far too simplistic a view of this exceedingly complex personality. Newman's study and the life of the composer by Sacheverell Sitwell both appeared in 1934 and have been described aptly as counsels for the prosecution and the defence respectively. Despite its factual errors, Sitwell's book remains a classic of biography and he splendidly evokes his subject's era and its ethos.

In any assessment of Liszt's character an almost over-whelming number of witnesses can be cited. The mass of material haphazardly published in many languages and over a century and a half is unwieldy. The greatest danger is that the profusion of facts can lead to almost any psychological explanation of the man, his divine or demonic character, being credibly postulated. Liszt's Scottish pupil Frederic Lamond has no doubt concerning his master's goodness:

> Liszt never charged a fee from any of his pupils, and we all looked upon him with a feeling akin to adoration. Felix Weingartner ... once said to me 'Liszt was the decentest of them all'. The word decent seems a strange one to apply to this extraordinary person-ality, but the more I think of it, the more I realise it's the right epithet for Liszt. Indeed I go further than that. Liszt was the good Samaritan of his day and generation.[3]

In a 1978 interview Blandine Ollivier de Prévaux, the composer's great-grand-daughter, described him as 'the last functional model of what a Christian ought to be',[4] and extended this idea to view Liszt as being above divisions of Church and creed just as he was above national boundaries: a pan-European, a true internationalist in music.

Here we come closer to what may be called the 'natural resonance' of the man and his music than in the image of 'half Zigeuner and half Franciscan' – a phrase actually coined by Liszt himself. Writing to Franz Brendel in September 1863 he remarked:

> A clever man, some twenty years ago, made the not inapplicable remark to me: 'You really have three individuals to deal with in

[3] *The Memoirs of Frederic Lamond*, 74.
[4] JALS XII, Dec. 1982, 14–27.

yourself, and they all run against each other; the social salon-individual, the virtuoso and the thoughtfully creative composer. If you can manage to come to terms with one of them you may count yourself lucky.' Well, we shall see![5]

Citing this quotation, Newman doubts whether Liszt even remotely harmonised these three elements of his being. Be that as it may, and whether Liszt's soul was divided once, twice, or indeed thirty-fold, it is the multi-faceted aspect of his nature that is the real key to his 'natural resonance'. He was not, of course, a 'Zigeuner', but in spirit he shared with the gypsy an absorbing internationalism. He was a great traveller, a ceaseless explorer in the geographical and cultural senses. He also shared the gypsy genius for improvisation, both as a gifted extemporiser and in the shape and nature of much of his printed work.

Restlessness, travel and absorption of a wide culture are contributory facets of his character. In one sense he was a perpetual exile, having no one home. Like Lord Byron, his internationalism gave rise to his heroic and legendary status. In Liszt's case, however, he had to live long with the legend – a Mazeppa, a Don Juan, a Manfred, a Faust on a soul-searching quest, or, in the words of Gregorovius, 'Mephistopheles disguised as an Abbé'. Liszt was well aware of the romantic image he conjured up as a traveller. When the Viennese artist Kreihuber drew him wearing his travelling cloak in 1840, Liszt wrote these lines of Byron as a motto below the picture:

> Here's a sigh to those who love me,
> And a smile to those who hate;
> And whatever sky's above me,
> Here's a heart for every fate.

He felt tormented as a young man by his lack of early formal education. His efforts to remedy this were strenuous, and in his published writings and letters there is evidence not just of his success in absorbing ideas of culture, philosophy, politics and religion (in several languages) but of his well-rounded grasp and highly original response to the fruits of his self-education. Adam had prepared him with French and English studies when the boy was in Vienna, with future tours in mind. From 1823 he spoke mainly French for twenty years and later had to re-learn his native German.

[5] *Briefe*, II, 51.

For a quarter of a century, from his Vienna debut in 1822 until his retirement as a virtuoso in 1847 at the age of thirty-five, he was a public idol, the recipient of unparalleled attention, superlative praise and sensational acclaim. Such experiences undoubtedly affect a personality. What is remarkable is that Liszt was not entirely vain, hardened and self-centred as a result. Striking a grand pose when sitting for a painter on one occasion he was abruptly told not to assume such airs. 'I beg your pardon,' Liszt responded. 'But to have been a child prodigy, you have no idea how it spoils one!' The price of being one of Europe's most famous men inevitably brought envy in its wake. He was vilified by some as a poseur, a charlatan, morally weak, and creatively either bankrupt or in some way pernicious to the development of music. His wizardry was all too easily misconstrued as sorcery. Of course he had weaknesses: he smoked (mostly cheap cigars), he drank (Carolyne regularly counselled him against over-indulgence in cognac), he enjoyed dressing up (poetically as well as sartorially), fashionable society held an irresistible fascination for him (and he for society), he was flattered by honours bestowed upon him by heads of state and he proudly treasured the many costly gifts showered on him (most of which are now in public museums). Newman actually indexes his supposed faults: cruelty, vindictiveness, delight in applause and flattery, playing pranks with music, lack of discrimination, extravagance, insincerity, uncontrollable temper, arrogance, jealousy, indolence, lack of application, wasting time answering letters, overpraising of mediocrity, his amours, his fascination for women, and his dependence on women.

Women: they adored him and he adored them. At the height of Lisztomania girls wore bracelets of piano strings snapped by him, phials were carried containing the dregs of his coffee, his cigar butts were revered as relics. He was endowed with handsome good looks, he was charismatic, he was a temptation and much temptation was put in his way. Sometimes he succumbed. But he was not a seducer of virgins or a destroyer of marriages. Nor, apart from the three children by Marie d'Agoult, did he father illegitimate offspring: several claims that he did so have proved far-fetched and false. And the four closest attachments he made were with married women who were either separated from their husbands or widowed: Marie, Carolyne, Agnes Street and Olga von Meyendorff. He faced the disapproving gaze of society with dignity. (In tiny Weimar his scandalous association with the Catholic Carolyne was viewed in a very poor light by the Protestant populace of a duchy where adultery was still a criminal offence.)

His detractors have delighted in juxtaposing his carnal nature with his religious calling. There seems to be an untidy mixture of the sacred and secular in his life and music. But rather than viewing this as a shallow type of idealism, it should be seen as his personal and close application of his religion to every part of human life and art. That his spiritual beliefs have been called into question and his taking of minor orders mocked as more evidence of self-glorification is a sad reflection on critical misanthropy. Liszt's avowed motto was *Caritas*. He believed that art is the centre of the soul's aspiration to the divine. For all his devotion and obedience to the Catholic faith he was a modern, freethinking believer. He set Protestant texts as well as the Latin liturgy. He embraced Freemasonry as a philosophy of enlightened humanitarianism. The anti-Semitism of his closest family, Cosima, Bülow, Wagner and Carolyne, found no echo in Liszt. Tolerance and respect for nations, creeds and races is not always appreciated:

> Everyone is against me. Catholics, because they find my church music profane, Protestants because to them my music is Catholic, Freemasons because they think my music too clerical; to conservatives I am a revolutionary, to the 'Futurists' an old Jacobin. As for the Italians ... if they support Garibaldi they detest me as a hypocrite; if they are on the Vatican side, I am accused of bringing Venus's grotto into the Church. To Bayreuth I am not a composer but a publicity agent. Germans reject my music as French, the French as German, to the Austrians I write Gypsy music, to the Hungarians foreign music. And the Jews loathe me, my music and myself, for no reason at all.[6]

Heine would not have been surprised by this. As early as 1837 he wrote of Liszt:

> He is without doubt the artist who finds in Paris the most unreserved enthusiasm, as well as the keenest opposition. It is significant that no one speaks of him with indifference. A man who lacks positive stature cannot in this world arouse either favourable or antagonistic passions. It takes fire to enkindle men, whether to hate or to love. What speaks most for Liszt is the respect with which even his

---

[6] Letter to Ödön Mihalovich from the late years. NHQ, XXVII/103, Autumn 1986, 92.

enemies recognise his personal merits. He is a man of unruly but noble character, unself-seeking and without falseness.[7]

He was actively concerned with the well-being of poorer artists, he favoured the emancipation of women (a Saint-Simonian tenet), he was generous with money and, above all, tireless in his efforts on behalf of other composers – even for those who were cool or actually hostile to his own works. Hugo Wolf spoke of his 'proverbial largesse'. Anyone who reads the correspondence of his last twenty-five years or so will be forcibly struck by the modest, self-effacing attitude he adopted to his own compositions. He discouraged and even forbade artists to risk their reputations with them.

He was the valued friend of fellow musicians, performers and composers, writers, artists, politicians, princes of the Church and temporal rulers, dukes, kings and emperors. There are vivid accounts of his magnetic personality, his natural courtesy, his wit and diplomacy in conversation. Fortunately his brilliance and tendency towards self-dramatisation were balanced by a genuine humility and a strong sense of responsibility, of service, of a mission to devote himself to the callings of art, fellow artists and the public.

The music reflects the man in its range from the ascetic to the sumptuous, from the trivial and profane to the sublime and spiritual.

In old age he suffered from an acute sense of failure, of disappointment that whatever he had achieved in Paris, Weimar or Rome was inadequate. The many tragedies of his personal life and of his children weighed upon him. But this was confined to a few pages of his intimate correspondence. He had the strength to face the world with composure, to encourage and to inspire optimism in his colleagues and pupils. He once wrote to Richard Pohl:

> Courage is the mainspring of our best qualities; where it is lacking they wither, and without courage one is not even sufficiently prudent. One must, of course, consider, reflect, calculate, weigh the pros and cons. But after that one must make up one's mind and act, without paying undue attention to the direction of the wind or to any passing clouds ...[8]

[7] *Letters on the French Stage*. Quoted and transl. by Barzun in *Pleasures of Music*, London, 1952.
[8] 7 Nov. 1868. Quoted by Gal, *The Musician's World*, London, 1965, 218.

Liszt's activities ranged over such wide territory, there are so many aspects of his life's work that have until recently been neglected or misunderstood, and so many calumnies and myths were encrusted upon his legend: these are the reasons why only now – more than a century after his death – is it possible to begin to see him in perspective, to re-assess and evaluate his character in totality. Even so, he will probably always remain something of an enigma, a challenge. He was certainly no saint, but few such great human beings can be counted in the firmament of musical stars.

8

The piano: technique and teaching

'The piano is the microcosm of music,' Liszt wrote to Princess Carolyne in December 1877, echoing a sentiment from his open letter to Pictet of four decades previously. A century before, in 1777, Sébastian Erard began manufacturing his pianos in France and, in London, Adam Beyer introduced the sustaining pedal, a device patented by Broadwood in that city in 1783. Broadwoods, the favourites of Clementi and Beethoven, had a larger, rounder tone and a heavier touch than Viennese instruments, which were renowned for their light, pearly, easy touch. According to Broadwood's records[1] 1783 was also the year in which demand for pianos outstripped that for harpsichords. From that time the piano, invented early in the century, came more and more into its own. It was pre-eminently *the* instrument of the nineteenth century.

Its mechanism underwent great changes between Liszt's childhood and his last years, when it became in all important respects the instrument we know today. The improvements in the piano's structure and capabilities, the instruments Liszt favoured, and the connections between developments in mechanical possibility and Liszt's advancement of manual technique in his composition are of great interest.[2] When he arrived in Paris late in 1823 he had the advantage of Erard instruments with wide range of tone, an expanded keyboard of seven octaves and the double-escapement device, patented by Erard in 1822, which for the first time allowed very rapid repetition of notes and enhanced responsiveness to touch. During the 1830s piano frames were strengthened, heavier hammers and heavier tension on the strings were introduced. The increasing use of metal framing and the development of cross-stringing further transformed pianos over the next two or three decades. Liszt's preference was for Erard, but on his virtuoso

[1] David Wainwright, *Broadwood By Appointment: A History*, London, 1982, 60.
[2] *Cf.* Geraldine Keeling, 'The Liszt Pianos – some aspects of preference and technology', NHQ, XXVII/104, Winter 1986, 220–32.

tours he used instruments by all the leading manufacturers. When Erard's position as the leading innovator in piano construction began to wane, firms such as Bösendorfer, Bechstein, Chickering and Steinway supplied the composer with increasingly refined models. His last pianos were powerful instruments with a range of up to seven-and-a-half octaves, overstrung and metal-framed.

Throughout his career Liszt composed for pianos with two pedals: the 'damper' and the 'una corda'. His scores are carefully pedal-marked: special care should be taken to observe his longer markings, even where the harmony seems to imply a pedal change. In legato pedalling the asterisk marking is not exact, but the musical player will understand the sense of Liszt's intentions. His 'una corda' marking is always noteworthy as he carefully reserved it for particular effect. In 1883 he was introduced to Steinway's middle, 'sostenuto' pedal. His immediate reaction was to suggest several pieces of his own from previous decades which would benefit from the new pedal.[3] Undoubtedly Liszt had envisaged this invention and his enthusiasm was characteristic of a lifelong search for new possibilities of sonority.

This search for novelty in keyboard sound is seen also in his preoccupation with various devices and hybrid instruments which have (so far) remained cul-de-sac curiosities of keyboard history. Two further types of 'third pedal' interested Liszt: one a device allowing a string to sound an octave lower, the other a 'tremolo' pedal which allowed a second set of hammers to maintain a vibration on the strings, creating a sustained effect. He was enthusiastic about the possibilities of an eight-octave keyboard. And in his open letter to Pictet of 1837 he spoke of pianos with a pedal-manual of bass-notes and envisaged the natural evolution of pianos with two or three keyboards. Historically the most successful double-keyboard piano is the Moór-Duplex, introduced in 1921 by Liszt's Hungarian pupil Emanuel Moór (1863–1931). Liszt certainly would have shared the enthusiasm of players like Tovey and Max Pirani and the firms Bechstein and Bösendorfer (who built some models) had he lived to see this refinement of one of his dreams. He possessed his own 'monster keyboard' in the Alexandre-Erard harmonium-piano delivered to him at Weimar in 1854 – the result of an idea he had had twelve years before. Built to Liszt's specifications it consisted of three keyboard manuals, sixteen registers and pedal-board. It was put into store

[3] *Cf.* Joseph Banowetz, *The Pianist's Guide to Pedalling*, New York, 1985, 216ff.

when he left the Altenburg, and Liszt missed it so much that he had a smaller version built for his use in Rome and later in Budapest. These unusual instruments undoubtedly affected his experiments in multi-stave notation.

Innovation, with Liszt, is always the servant of expression. Technique is refinement. He long out-lived and far out-stripped his immediate pianist-composer predecessors and his contemporaries in advancement of technique. Of his predecessors there were Cramer, Hummel, Field, Kalkbrenner, Weber, Czerny, Herz, Ries, Pixis and Moscheles; of his contemporaries, Alkan, Chopin, Mendelssohn, Schumann and Thalberg. Liszt learned from all of them: notably from Weber, Mendelssohn, Chopin and, of course, Beethoven.

Liszt gradually imposed his own ideals on the curiously haphazard concert world of the 1830s and 1840s. Entertainments, which seem to the modern mind to have been an unpalatable succession of party pieces, contained items of tawdry display alongside works that merited serious interpretation and appreciation. Liszt often appeared in these circus-like circumstances, but he gradually achieved his aim of making public performance a direct and expressive communication of the deepest emotional experiences, and he helped lay the foundations of modern concert practice. He invented the solo recital; he was the first person to play extensively from memory; he always insisted on the piano being turned at a right angle to the stage with the lid reflecting the sound to the auditorium; and his repertoire included pieces from Bach, Handel and Scarlatti to the music of his contemporaries.[4]

Liszt's attitude towards technique was that it should be transcended: the mechanics of music are secondary to the interpretation of its content, and the conveying of that content to the feelings of the listener. Technical display should not be seen as an important end in itself. That is not to say that a thoroughly sound technique is not essential, or that the fruits of that technique should not be displayed. Liszt was by nature a great showman. Drama and passion were very much part of his poetry. But even the most advanced technique remains the servant of expression in Liszt's aesthetic ideal. Along with Schumann and Chopin he effectively rescued piano music from the fate of showy brilliance for its own sake, as found in the output of Dreyschok, Herz,

[4]Liszt's repertoire for 1838–48 is given in Raabe, *Leben*, 271–3; trans. in Walker, 445–8.

Hünten and others. That Liszt despised mere virtuosity all his life is clear from his published opinions of Thalberg and Paganini and in many remarks recorded by pupils in his late years.

Technically Liszt's music is not intrinsically 'difficult'; on the contrary, pianists at various degrees of competence may approach a variety of works and find the music, at whatever level, laid out in a congenial and gratifying way for the ten fingers. A huge stretch is *not* required: examples from his virtuoso period where Liszt writes chords of a demanding span are adapted in later revisions to ease playability. As a general rule the revised versions always simplify in texture and technical difficulty. Liszt had slender hands with unusually long second, third and fourth fingers. His overall stretch was large but apparently not exceptional (an easy 10th on white notes with other notes included in the chord; a maximum stretch on black notes of F sharp–C sharp–A sharp, without breaking the chord). The tissue between the fingers was low-lying and the palm of the hand was not thick or muscular. The tips of his fingers were broad, allowing great control of a mellow, singing touch.

The evidence of what Liszt achieved on the keyboard lies in his scores. Possibly more can be learned from them as to how he himself played than from the countless diverse reports of those who heard him. The descriptions of his playing range from awestruck generalisations and hyperbole to detailed and factual observation. Some of the evidence is contradictory, which is unsurprising over a span of seven decades. Similarly the accounts of his teaching range from the objectively specific (the Boissier and Göllerich diaries) to the subjectively anecdotal. A neat combination of informed observation and personal memoir is the charm of Miss Amy Fay's book. On one occasion a fellow pupil was playing rather feebly when

> Liszt suddenly took his seat at the piano and said, 'When *I* play, I always play for the people in the gallery ... so that those persons who pay only five groschens for their seats also hear something.' Then he began, and I wish you could have heard him! The sound didn't seem to be very *loud*, but it was penetrating and far-reaching. When he had finished, he raised one hand in the air, and you seemed to see all the people in the gallery drinking in the sound. That is the way Liszt teaches you. He presents an *idea* to you, and it takes fast hold of your mind and sticks there. Music is such a real, visible thing to him, that he always has a symbol, instantly, in the material world to express his idea. One day, when I was playing, I made too

much movement with my hand in a rotary sort of a passage where it was difficult to avoid it. 'Keep your hand still, Fräulein,' said Liszt; *'don't make omelette.'* I couldn't help laughing, it hit me on the head so nicely ... How he can bear to hear *us* play, I cannot imagine. It must grate on his ear terribly, I think, because everything *must* sound expressionless to him in comparison to his own marvellous conception. I assure you, no matter how beautifully we play any piece, the minute Liszt plays it, you would scarcely recognise it! His touch and his peculiar use of the pedal are two secrets of his playing, and then he seems to dive down in the most hidden thoughts of the composer, and fetch them up to the surface, so that they gleam out at you one by one, like stars!

Rosenthal observed:

In spite of a sometimes surprising pedantry as to pianistic cleanness and accuracy, he saw all with the eye of the composer and made us feel the same way.

Another pupil of the later years, Stradal, recorded:

Liszt demanded, of course, the greatest plasticity, cleanliness and clarity in a performance, and required the pupil to sing on the keys; that is, to play the piano in as song-like a manner as possible. To produce this beautiful singing tone he demanded an artistic use of the pedal going into the smallest detail, and allowed the *una corda* pedal, since it 'thins' and prevents a singing tone, to be employed only in exceptional cases, preferring a greater *pianissimo* to be produced without it ... Since in our time new theories about arm movement are being put forward, let it be emphasised that, were he alive today, Liszt would keep his distance from them, since, along with that of the fingers, his entire technique was that of the wrist.[5]

Liszt's principal periods of teaching were in Paris, 1827–35; Geneva, 1835–6; at Weimar in the 1850s; to a lesser extent at Rome in the 1860s; and at Weimar, Budapest and Rome, 1869–86. Valuable accounts exist by Boissier and Lenz of the early Paris years. Most pupils of that time (some hundreds) were from fashionable society and few embarked on musical careers. One young lady was Catherine Glynne, the future Mrs. W. E. Gladstone, who was in Paris at finishing school in 1829. The multi-talented Pauline Viardot-García took piano lessons from Liszt in the 1840s. Of the 1849–61 Weimar years descriptions of Liszt's lessons can be found in the letters and writings of Bülow, Cornelius, Klindworth, Mason

[5] LSJ, XI, 1986, 86; transl. A. Williams.

and Weissheimer. Constance Bache's biography of her brother Walter gives details of the Roman period. The pupils who left accounts of the last period of teaching were d'Albert, Bagby, Fay, Friedheim, Göllerich, Jaëll, Kellermann, Lachmund, Lamond, da Motta, Rosenthal, Sauer, Siloti, Stradal, Strelezki and Zichy. Pupils of the final years who lived to make acoustic or electric recordings were d'Albert, Ansorge, Friedheim, de Greef, Lamond, da Motta, Rosenthal, Sauer and Josef Weiss. Liszt invented the concept of the masterclass. But beyond compiling his colossal series of *Technical Studies*, he bequeathed no system of teaching. Nor did he demand a single style of playing. Rather he dispensed wisdom to those of sufficient pianistic merit to understand and benefit from it among the assembled groups. The students played anything they chose; only two works were forbidden, as Liszt felt they were played too frequently: his own Hungarian Rhapsody No. 2 and Chopin's B flat minor Scherzo.

Although not students of Liszt in the strict sense, Smetana and Saint-Saëns benefited through correspondence from Liszt's suggestions and corrections to their works; similarly Borodin, MacDowell and Weingartner were on the fringes of Liszt's group of pupils and wrote lively memoirs of his teaching life at Weimar. Liszt's influence was also transmitted through the teaching and travels of his most important pupils. Tausig was an influential teacher during his short life. Many of the greatest players of Liszt's Weimar summers later taught on their extensive travels. Mason and Burmeister were important figures in the development of music in the U.S.A. Klindworth, Menter and Siloti (the last both a cousin and the teacher of Rakhmaninov) in Russia; Sgambati in Italy; Szendy and Thomán in Hungary; Jaëll in France and Belgium; da Motta in Portugal and South America – the list might be expanded through other pupils and 'grand-pupils' across the globe.

Yet despite this impressive list of names and places, there was no such thing as a 'Liszt tradition' of piano-playing. Liszt taught no single 'method', he appeared only very rarely as an interpreter of his own works after 1847, and the abilities and temperaments of his latter-day pupils varied widely. In keeping with the general view of Liszt's artistry in the earlier twentieth century, it was even possible to speak pejoratively of a 'Liszt tradition', with reference to the breed of posturing, long-haired virtuosi who used his works to show off their fingers. Players and critics mistakenly viewed his advanced technical demands as an end in themselves. But the universality of his pianism was the quality that attracted great players from diverse traditions and backgrounds far beyond the Liszt circle such as Busoni, Paderewski, Cortot, Godowsky, Horowitz, Hofmann, Cherkassky, Earl Wild and Jorge Bolet. Claudio Arrau (a pupil of Krause) has spoken illuminatingly about Liszt's music,[6] and Alfred Brendel has written with insight:

> Anyone who cannot tell sentimentality from true feeling, or false pathos from the genuine kind, will ruin Liszt's music, even if he does not ruin his own reputation. Anyone who does not play Liszt with nobility passes sentence on himself. An overwhelming majority of observers bear witness to the fact that as both man and artist Liszt had nobility. There are modern chroniclers of piano-playing who describe Liszt's virtuosity as 'show'. This is a misunderstanding. Liszt was the first to leave the salon behind. To the displeasure of many of his contemporaries, he democratized the concert, occasionally appearing in large halls before thousands. That demanded a different kind of projection in piano-playing, a sort of mass-suggestion which involved a physically freer and more demonstrative treatment of the instrument . . .[7]

Saint-Saëns wrote that

> power, delicacy, charm, along with a rightly-accented rhythm, were his, in addition to unusual warmth of feeling, impeccable precision and that gift of suggestion which creates the great orator, the leader of the masses. When interpreting the classics he did not substitute his own personality for the author's, as do so many performers; he seemed rather to endeavour to get at the heart of the music and find out its real meaning . . .[8]

Liszt's piano notation is always precise and designed to facilitate the desired interpretative effect. His earlier works contain some novel symbols and original note-distributions to guide the player to the closest possible simulation of what the composer imagined in sound. Clarity and precision of effect also led him to notate on three, and occasionally four staves. He often had filigree cascades of notes printed in a lighter, smaller typeface, with a marking like *dolce, armonioso* to prevent too precipitate an intrusion into the texture. 'Quasi arpa' passages are another

[6] Joseph Horowitz, *Conversations with Arrau*, London, 1982.
[7] *The Times*, 3 Nov. 1986. See also Brendel's *Musical Thoughts and Afterthoughts*, Princeton, 1976.
[8] Quoted in F. Bonavia, *Musicians on Music*, London, 1956, 85.

characteristic Lisztian effect. His cadenza-like passagework is rigorously worked out and falls into a number of logical and symmetrical patterns. To the end of his life he probably felt the frustrating lack of a means of communicating in exact metronomic terms all the agogic and dynamic subtleties that true interpretation demands: 'Time and rhythm must be adapted to and identified with the melody, the harmony, the accent and the poetry ... But how to indicate all this? I shudder at the thought ...'[9] An important point to observe is his careful marking of fingering, which is often unorthodox but always meticulously notated with a view to capturing the exact effect of phrasing and attack. Variety of fingering in scale passages and in trills is especially noteworthy. His fingerings may seem at first wilfully devious, but on closer inspection the intrinsic reasoning will be discerned. Use of interlocking hands was a favourite device and famously exploited in the technique known as 'Liszt octaves': double octaves played with alternating hands:

Ex. 5

(Fantasy on Halévy's *La Juive*)

From the evidence preserved in the scores we can hear Liszt's other favourite devices. The possibilities of octave playing are extended to their farthest limits. A technical device such as a trill or tremolo acquires considerable expressive power with varied application of speed, dynamics and fingering. The simple concept of the broken chord or arpeggio is approached in a free assortment of ways – upwards, downwards, quickly, slowly, with accelerando, rallentando, rubato and in a range of dynamics. Common features are rapid note re-iteration; extended passages of fast, wide leaps; colour effects dependent on the pedal; new scale patterns; endless variations in laying out cantilena and accompaniment; crossing of

[9] *Briefe*, II. 10 Jan. 1870.

hands; new techniques in sequences of tenths – and, above all, the perfection of a legato line.

Liszt went beyond Chopin in his exploration of the sonorous, coloristic and orchestral possibilities of the piano. He re-created in piano terms many of the bowing techniques exploited by Paganini, and orchestral effects such as triple-tonguing and varied brass and woodwind combinations explored by Berlioz. He made extensive use of the extremes, high and low, of the keyboard, to enhance an orchestral effect. He wished his players to have an orchestrally-attuned imagination.

From the evidence of his pupils we learn of his detestation of a mechanical, soulless approach to performance; of his wonderful variety of nuance; of his phenomenal ability as a score-reader; of his analysis of the phrase-by-phrase structure of music in performance; of his breadth of interest in the general repertoire. Insight and involvement were his aspirations; anonymity and detachment he disdained. In Budapest he insisted that all the Academy piano students learn to compose, and that all the composition students learn the piano. He desired to foster a 'composer's view'. He placed considerable emphasis on improvisation as an academic discipline. (Most of Liszt's piano pupils were composers, albeit in a minor way.) He also laid stress on the importance of a thorough general and cultural education for young musicians – remembering, perhaps, his own early handicap in that direction. Truth – fidelity in performance – was another watchword. His own editions of Weber, Beethoven, Schubert and Chopin, while not approaching the standards of a modern *Urtext*, are models of their time and take remarkably few liberties.

He lived to make no recordings, and so Liszt's playing passed into legend. As Friedheim remarked, legends are not the most trustworthy sources of information.

> Liszt's technique has been the subject of much discussion and conjecture on the part of those who never heard him. Was it so prodigious, and has it been equalled since? The answer is that it was truly prodigious but that in certain respects it has not only been equalled since, but also surpassed. Moritz Rosenthal and Leopold Godowsky went beyond Liszt in specialized phases of *mécanisme*. However while Godowsky's chief *métier* was dexterity of fingers and Rosenthal concentrated on brilliance and power, Liszt shone in every department of technique and probably never has been approached as a builder of 'orchestral' climaxes, overwhelming masses of sound and exciting effects ... How little the thought of

177

empty display actuated Liszt, is best proved by a remark he made on one occasion to his pupils: 'To be able to play Beethoven, a little more technique is required than he demands.'[10]

That Liszt learned from his juniors is made amusingly apparent by Weissheimer, who recalls Tausig bringing to the Altenburg his latest composition, *Das Geisterschiff*. It contained

> an incredible passage which caused even Liszt a little trouble. It was an ascending chromatic glissando ending shrilly on a top black note! After a few vain attempts, Liszt finally said to Tausig: *Junge, wie machst du das?* Tausig sat down, performed a glissando on the white keys with the middle finger of his right hand, while at the same time making the fingers of his left hand fly so cleverly over the black keys that a chromatic scale could clearly be heard streaking like lightning up the whole length of the keyboard, ending on high with a shrill 'bip'. Now Liszt addressed himself to the problem again, and after some half a dozen practice-runs he too finally achieved the desired high 'bip' without accident.[11]

The Boissier diary describes his physical posture at the keyboard:

> His hand is never unwieldy, for he moves it with grace according to his fancy, but he does not play with his arms or shoulders. He insists that the body be straight and the head pushed more backward rather than bent forward; this he demands categorically ... As for the finger technique, he never wants striking on the extremity of the finger or the nail, but instead on the ball of the finger, which flattens the finger, of course, and allows it freedom. By these means the sound is pure, full, round and complete, not strangulated or coarse. He wants one to play, without exception, entirely with a wrist action ... with each note he wants the hand to fall from the wrist on the key in a rebounding movement ... His fingers have neither a definite position or form. They bend soft and pliant in all directions; the fingers, extended and recumbent, move in a weighty manner from one key to the next.[12]

More than forty years later Stanford was struck by Liszt's composure and seemingly effortless ease in performance:

> The moment his fingers touched the keys, I realised the immense gap between him and all other pianists. He was the very reverse of all my anticipations, which inclined me, perhaps from the caricatures

[10] *Remembering Franz Liszt*, 160f.
[11] 'With Liszt at the Altenburg' (transl. A. Williams), *Musical Opinion*, Jan. 1977, 168.
[12] Mach, *The Liszt Studies* pp. xii, xvii, xxv.

familiar to me in my boyhood, to expect to see an inspired acrobat, with high-action arms, and wild locks falling on the keys. I saw instead a dignified, composed figure, who sat like a rock, never indulging in a theatrical gesture, or helping out his amazingly full tone with the splashes and crashes of a charlatan, producing all his effects with the simplest means, and giving the impression of such ease that the most difficult passages sounded like child's play . . .[13]

Hallé remembered that

one of the transcendent merits of his playing was the crystal-like clearness which never failed for a moment even in the most complicated and, to anybody else, impossible passages; it was as if he had photographed them in their minutest detail upon the ear of the listener. The power he drew from his instrument was such as I have never heard since, but never harsh, never suggesting 'thumping'.[14]

Heine, who also wrote acidly of Liszt's gladiatorial conquests of the *Glanzperiode*, was never more generously aphoristic than when he said of Liszt's playing: 'the piano vanishes and – music appears'.

[13] Quoted by Gerald Norris, *Stanford, The Cambridge Jubilee and Tchaikovsky*, London, 1980.
[14] Hallé, quoted in Beckett, *Liszt*, 132.

9

Musical language: technique and transformation

Liszt's absorption of musical styles in his youth and early maturity is as wide as the map of his travels. The list of composers from whom he made transcriptions is long, and includes some who shaped his own musical language. He had a thorough grounding in Bach and the Viennese classics. His teacher Czerny, the revered Beethoven and, later, Schubert were primary influences. Beethoven of the *Waldstein* and *Hammerklavier* sonatas and Schubert of the *Wanderer Fantasy* and the *Lieder* profoundly affected his views of form, as did several works by Weber. An influence of equal strength to this Austro-German tradition was that of Italian operatic *bel canto*. In France his teacher Reicha and later his friends Berlioz and Chopin were, together with the virtuosity of Paganini, the principal forces to excite his imagination. To all these must be added the quality of improvisation inherent in much of his later art: as a child prodigy he was noted for his extemporisation, and the improvisatory quality of gypsy music exerted a huge influence on him from his earliest years.

A criticism often levelled at Liszt is that he was over-receptive to the ideas of others, to the resulting detriment and unevenness of his output. That his enormous output of works is uneven cannot be denied; but a full knowledge of his original works in all their varied manifestations shows that whatever he took from his models, he sought to expand and develop in new, highly personal ways. His interest in experiment was lifelong and always allied to furthering the means of expression. There is a danger of over-simplification in viewing his career as a progress from the indulgence of youth to the idealism of old age. In his musical language he constantly and consistently applied new ideas of rhythm, melody, harmony, form and instrumental sonority: in each of these elements of music he can be shown to be a pioneer.

'In general I am not ready to compromise when it comes to *rhythm* or stress, since that is the nerve of music itself', he wrote in 1855.[1] His use of rhythm again invokes the concept of improvisation: his attraction towards the freedom of the fantasy, the rhapsody. He expressed an abhorrence of mechanical regularity of beat and aimed for more flexibility and an understanding of the expressive use of rhythm. In some early piano pieces he attempted to convey subtleties of accent and rhythm by inventing a new notation for altering tempo, highlighting individual stresses, differing lengths of fermata, and occasionally he wrote without time signature.

Lisztian melody can be analysed in several characteristic categories: (a) lyrical, often ornamented, Romantic *bel canto*; (b) declamatory phrases, with a tendency towards unusual intervals; (c) melodic use of the monotone (in which we can trace his lineage from Beethoven); (d) short epigrammatic gestures (also Beethovenian); (e) fanfares; (f) a fondness for downward gestures; see Ex. 6, overleaf.

Among the many other examples of these types which could be cited are: (a) in the famous *Liebestraum No. 3*, themes in *Prometheus* (bar 129), *Orpheus* (bar 72), *Héroïde Funèbre* (bar 153), and see also Exs. 40 and 55 (a3); (b) the b1 and b2 figures of Ex. 59; (c) *Prometheus* (bar 38), the opening of the choral section of the *Faust Symphony*, and see Exs. 24 and 39; (d) *Tasso* (bar 27), *Inferno* of the *Dante Symphony* (bar 87) and see Ex. 53; (e) *Mazeppa* (bar 36) and see Ex. 55 (a7); (f) *Funérailles* (bar 24), the opening of the first piano concerto, *Inferno* (bars 22 and 311) and Ex. 36 (a).

In addition to this selection of thematic types there is an important element often described as the 'chorale': either a slow, broad, harmonised lyric cantilena or an actual liturgical melody. There are other themes that depend intrinsically on their implied or actual harmonisation to create an atmosphere of magic or to portray the unconscious: the opening of the *Faust Symphony* for example. Another category is the group of bucolic, *pastorale* themes. These generalisations already embrace descriptive ideas and it is impossible to discuss Lisztian melody in the abstract, without reference to the emotional context. In the subsequent discussion of works the aim is to strike a balance between the emotional and structural content, as the two are inseparable in Liszt. Nor can the harmonic implications of the various melodic types be ignored.

[1] 'Lettres inédites de Liszt à Alfred Jaëll', *La Revue Musicale*, 4 (1904), 53.

Liszt

Ex. 6

(a)

Lento placido

Consolation No. 3

(b)

Sursum Corda

(c)

Lento

mf

Il Penseroso

(d)

Allegro energico

Prometheus

(e)

Hunnenschlacht

182

Lento assai

(f)

quasi Cello
espr.

Vallée d'Obermann

Liszt's use of scales outside the classical major-minor system is mainly in one of four ways: pentatony, modality, the 'gypsy scale' and the whole-tone scale. Examples of pentatony can be found in the opening melody of *Au lac de Wallenstadt*, the first motif of *Sposalizio*, at several moments in *Les Préludes*, as well as in the late music. In referring to earlier piano pieces and later symphonic poems the link between the two must be stressed: a character-study such as *Chapelle de Guillaume Tell* or a darkness-to-light mood picture like *Vallée d'Obermann* clearly foreshadow concepts found in the orchestral works. The first of these pieces opens with a striking passage of modal harmony. Modal melody is found in the plainchant themes of *Totentanz*, *Hunnenschlacht* and *Der nächtliche Zug*. Many of the sacred choral works have pervasive use of modality, notably *Christus*, the *Missa Solennis*, the *Te Deum* of 1867, *Salve Regina*, *Cantantibus organis* and *Via Crucis*. From the chant *Crux fidelis* and the *Magnificat* Liszt derived a motif symbolising the cross:

Ex. 7

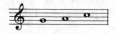

In a footnote to *St. Elisabeth*, where he made considerable use of this motto idea, he referred to its appearance in the *Missa Solennis*, the *Dante Symphony* and *Hunnenschlacht*. Other important occurrences of the symbol are in *Via Crucis* and the *B minor Sonata* (see Ex. 38).

Another rich stratum running through Liszt's output mainly from 1840 is gypsy music. The impressions he began to notate on his return to his homeland influenced all the elements of his art – rhythm, melody, harmony, form, sonority – and not only in the works bearing a 'Hungarian' title. The 'gypsy scale':

Ex. 8

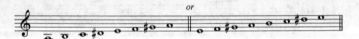

with its two augmented seconds is found, naturally, throughout the pieces 'in Hungarian style' from 1840 onwards, until the late works where its harmonic implications are exploited most boldly and it appears in many altered versions. (In the late music several modes can be discerned with tetrachordal variants often derived from folk sources.) In addition to the Rhapsodies, the gypsy mode is especially prominent in *Hunnenschlacht* (the first main theme), *Die drei Zigeuner*, the *Hungarian Coronation Mass* (at 'Qui tollis peccata mundi'), *Aux cyprès de la Villa d'Este I, Nuages gris*, the *B minor Sonata* (bars 5–7) and in several other works.

Use of the whole-tone scale, and harmonies and harmonic sequences derived from it, can be found in several pieces from the mid-1830s onwards. That Liszt well appreciated its novelty is clear from his good-humoured letter of 1860 to Ingebord Stark, which gives a remarkable insight upon his attitude to modernity. He is referring to an overture by a Russian baron (Vietinghoff, who wrote under the pseudonym Boris Scheel) which included use of the whole-tone scale:

> It is nothing but a very simple development of the scale, terrifying for all the long and protruding ears … Tausig makes pretty fine use of it in his *Geisterschiff* and in the classes of the conservatoire, in which the high art of the *mad dog* is duly taught. The existing elementary exercises of the piano methods,

Ex. 9(a)

which are of a sonorousness as disagreeable as they are incomplete, ought to be replaced by this one [see Ex. 9(b)], which will then form the unique basis of the method of harmony – all the other chords in use or not, being unable to be employed except by the arbitrary curtailment of such and such an interval. In fact it will soon be necessary to complete the system by the admission of quarter and

Ex. 9(b)

half-quarter tones until something better turns up! Behold the abyss of progress into which abominable Musicians of the Future precipitate us!

The 12-note chord quoted above was also referred to by the violinist Nándor Plotenyi who quoted Liszt's comment that 'the 12 notes of the chromatic scale struck together is the basis and principle of the new harmony – all other chords can be formed by omitting any one or more of the intervals'.[2] From the whole-tone scale to dodecaphony to microtones was a path foreseen, if not actually followed by Liszt.

Liszt's universality, which transcended the bounds of nationalism, led him to a concept of ideal Romanticism in which mythic and symbolic ideas were expressed in music. But his approach was quite different from that of the Wagnerian myth-drama and in his use of programmatic elements he radically departed from Berlioz. Each of the hero-mythical characters portrayed (Orpheus, Prometheus, Tasso, Hamlet, Mazeppa and Faust) he treats as abstract spiritual personalities who embody and symbolise some profound, universal human idea or aspiration. The ideas can be entirely abstract as in *Die Ideale* or *Les Préludes*. Christian myth-symbolism is abundant in many works: *Ce qu'on entend, Hunnenschlacht*, the *Dante Symphony*, *Der nächtliche Zug*, the *Deux Légendes*, *Die Glocken des Strassburger Münsters*, to name but a few. Liszt's use of metamorphosis of a limited number of themes in one movement to depict the symbols of his music drama (e.g. defeat, despair, youth, struggle, victory, etc.) functions through transformation, modulation and re-orchestration in a quite different way from the Wagnerian *Leitmotif* system. Berlioz had shown his *idée fixe* changing its personality at its various appearances, just as Liszt gives a work's principal themes many different characters. 'Metamorphosis' or 'trans-

[2] Buchner, *Franz Liszt in Bohemia*, 128.

formation' of themes is an advanced form of thematic development, prefigured in much earlier music in melodic ornamentation, augmentation and diminution. Liszt's application of it is most radical and vigorous, more so than in Berlioz or in Wagner. He was not fundamentally interested in describing extra-musical scenes or objects, but rather in translating into music the emotions and sentiments attached to the subjects of his symphonic poems. In his concern with the universal rather than the particular, with the contemplation of passive or poetic ideas rather than depiction of external events, Liszt is markedly different from the narrative style of Berlioz or the tone-painting of Strauss.

In his essay on Berlioz' *Harold* Symphony, Liszt discusses the ancient Homeric epic in which a hero is vividly evoked in his actions and speech, and contrasts this with his view of the 'modern epic' in which action and external events lose their importance, but what remains – the vital mythic core of the epic – can be conveyed in a new poetic way. 'The marvellous gives way to the fantastic. Entirely detached from the laws of probability, compressed and modified, the action acquires a symbolic lustre, a mythical basis.'[3] The essence of the legend, myth or dramatic story becomes therefore not the hero's deeds but his inner state of mind, which has a universal, symbolic application.[4] Thus the 'programme' may be seen as a bridge to help the audience to an understanding of the content of the work. The programme is merely a pointer, a verbal amplification of largely abstract ideas, and is hardly a guide to musical structure. Thus, as in all great music, the programme is ultimately dispensable, although Liszt, with his Romantic philosophy, thought it indispensable.

He scorned the idea that music could be in any way analogous to the art of the painter's brush:

> It is obvious that things which can appear only objectively to perception can in no way furnish connecting points to music; the poorest of apprentice landscape painters could give with a few chalk strokes a much more faithful picture than a musician operating with all the resources of the best orchestra. But if these same things are subjected to dreaming, to contemplation, to emotional uplift, have they then not a peculiar kinship with music, and should not music be able to translate them into its mysterious language?[5]

[3] GS, IV, 54.
[4] For a discussion of the semiotic aspects of myth in Liszt's works, see Eero Tarasti, *Myth and Music*, Helsinki, 1978.
[5] GS II, 104.

More than Berlioz or Wagner, Liszt was the interpreter of Beethoven's remark regarding the programme of his *Pastoral* Symphony: 'More the expression of sentiment than painting'. When Liszt took works of art as points of inspiration (either the exquisite as in Raphael, Michelangelo, an Etruscan vase, or, to most modern eyes, the nineteenth century in its ugliest brand of sentimental religiosity as in Kaulbach and Zichy) it was his interpretation of the symbolic content of the original that gave rise to musical ideas. Yet, with reference to his remark quoted above, Liszt proved himself wrong; for he actually achieved in the musical equivalent of 'a few chalk strokes' the depiction of a character or situation with extraordinary ability and exactness in the finest of his more descriptive passages.

Unlike Wagner's mainly homogeneous orchestration, Liszt's instrumental textures are fluid and ever-changing, giving emphasis to the individual timbre of every instrumental group. He prefers light textures, 'chamber' scoring, avoids obvious doublings and makes much use of solo writing. Clarity is his watchword. Colour is his memorable imprint: the use of bass clarinet accompanied by pizzicato strings, horns and harp at the main theme in *Tasso* for instance. In the E flat Piano Concerto solo instruments such as clarinet and viola play important roles. His innate sensitivity to scoring and texture, nurtured over the decades of his intense absorption with the keyboard and with orchestral transcription, is seen in remarkable *divisi* string passages, unusual woodwind couplings, and in instructions to players such as *gemendo* ('groaning', woodwind, *Mazeppa*, bar 138) and, in *Hamlet*, *schwankend* ('swaying', timpani, bar 2), *aufschreiend* ('screaming', brass, bar 103) and *schaurig* ('eerie', brass, bar 225). With *Hamlet* (the last Weimar symphonic poem) the use of muted horns, bass trombone and tuba is darkly effective. Most of Liszt's subsequent orchestration is found in the choral-orchestral works of the 1860s and 1870s, where it reaches especial refinement. His standard orchestra is: piccolo, 2 each of flutes, oboes, clarinets, bassoons; 4 horns, 2 or 3 trumpets, 3 trombones, tuba; 2–4 timpani; and strings. *Tasso* and the *Missa Solennis* require a fourth trumpet; *Festklänge* dispenses with piccolo; *Ce qu'on entend*, *Tasso*, *Mazeppa* and the *Dante Symphony* add bass clarinet; and the cor anglais is found in six of the thirteen symphonic poems, the *Dante Symphony*, the *Episodes from Lenau's 'Faust'* and the *Deux Légendes*. The harp plays a significant role representing a heroic poet or singer in

Tasso and *Orpheus*. The latter asks for two harps as do the *Dante Symphony*, *St. Elisabeth* and *St. Cecilia*. One harp appears in *Ce qu'on entend*, *Les Préludes*, the *Faust Symphony*, the Lenau *Episodes*, the *Légendes*, *Von der Wiege bis zum Grabe*, the *Second Mephisto Waltz*, *Missa Solennis* and *Christus*. He was the first to introduce the organ in symphonic works (*Hunnenschlacht*, the *Faust* and *Dante* symphonies). For the era, Liszt's use of percussion was adventurous, and only occasionally bombastic.

Liszt's concern was that *form* should never become *formula*: content should dictate structure. With his command of thematic transformation he acquired a new flexibility in portraying emotion; and by making economic use of motives he found the means of strengthening his form. Terse phrases and motivic fragments are developed and expanded to provide material for accompanimental and transitional passages. In the piano works ornamental figuration often becomes part of the structure; what at first sight seems to be a descriptive, colourful flourish is part of a highly organised thematic design.

The tonal design of each movement is individual, but certain patterns emerge. Introductory sections are almost always tonally ambiguous and frequently in slow tempo. The home key is implied rather than clearly stated in the first thematic group. The second thematic group is usually more stable in tonality. But the key relationship between these principal sections is unorthodox in classical terms, Liszt preferring mediant or submediant relationships, whether the home tonic be major or minor. The vagueness of the 'home' key at the opening is paralleled by delaying its resolution and confirmation until the very end of the work. Thus a sense of tension is built up and, at a dramatically late stage, Liszt gives maximum weight and effect to the long anticipated affirmation of the tonic. A formal device frequently found is the repetition of an expository section a tone or a semitone higher: this corresponds to some extent to the conventional classical repeat and Liszt felt that such repetition was justified in the interests of clarity. (The *Ballade No. 2* contains an example.)

His use of fugue is almost always programmatic and is associated with struggle and transition (e.g. the fugal passages in *Purgatorio* in the *Dante Symphony*, *Hunnenschlacht*, *Prometheus*). Similar simple symbolism can be observed in contrasted passages of extreme chromaticism and straightforward diatonicism, representing striving and resolution. In the passage from *Lamento* to

Trionfo in *Tasso*, from C minor to C major, there is a parallel with Beethoven's Fifth Symphony. Triumphal use of the key of C also occurs in *Les Préludes*. Certain keys have particular emotional associations: the Dantesque world of D minor; the mystical and meditative realm of F sharp major; nocturnal D flat major; a serene, often religious mood associated with E major; and A flat major frequently used to depict aspects of love (the three Petrarch songs, *Gretchen*, the three *Liebesträume*).

There is no better illustration of Liszt's imaginative and innovative approach to harmony than a study of his cadences. In all his harmonic writing Liszt strove to avoid cliché. An analysis of his final cadences in works from the 1830s to the 1880s shows a staggering variety of solutions: orthodox perfect or plagal (i.e. root position V-I or IV-I) proving the exception. Ex. 10 shows a few endings.[6]

The late works are sketches for a music of the future. There is pronounced economy of means. Every note is of importance and has its function; nothing is put to waste or used for mere effect. Much use is made of declamatory phrases both in vocal and instrumental writing, and floating, transparent harmonies, a sense of incompleteness, of vague atmosphere, of striving, of longing, or of fading away. Symptomatic of Liszt's ever-growing distance from the spirit of German classicism was his growing interest in East European folk music, the simplicity of Gregorian chant, pentatony and modality. Drastic shortening of melodic phrase-lengths led to an increased emphasis on the importance of short motives. In turn this put greater stress on harmonic and textural elements and, in the many passages of monody, considerable use of implied harmony. Motivic development is often through cumulative imitation, a repetition of motto-like motives either as an exact ostinato or varied to increase the tension: a process of 'repeat – crescendo – and vary'. Pedal-notes and pedal-harmonies (always favourite devices) are increasingly important. Expansion of expression is achieved through the simplest techniques, and a dramatic effect made within extreme brevity. There is an even greater emphasis on unusual intervals, e.g. the major 7th and the augmented 4th at the opening of Psalm 129 (1881); see Ex. 11.

Extreme chromaticism is, like many elements of Liszt's later music, also explored in his early works (*Grand galop chromatique;*

[6] See also Exs. 3(b), 32, 33, 49, 57.

Liszt

Ex. 10

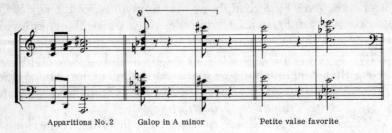

Apparitions No. 2   Galop in A minor   Petite valse favorite

Le mal du pays   Vallée d'Obermann   Tantum ergo (1869)

Einst   Go not, happy day   Des Tages laute
Stimmen schweigen

Nuages gris   Mephisto polka   Valse oubliée No. 4

190

Ex. 11

Il Penseroso) and is seen to an advanced degree in the *BACH* fantasy, the *'Weinen, Klagen' Variations* and in *Via Crucis* (1878–9):

Ex. 12

Harmonic features of the last period include parallel chords, parallel consecutive 5ths; functional and non-functional use of the augmented triad, the diminished 7th chord and the 6/4 chord; a fondness for empty 5ths, chords of superimposed 4ths and 5ths and of superimposed 3rds. Ex. 13 shows a passage from *Ossa arida*.

Ex.13

Also found are many secondary 7ths, dominant 9th chords, secondary 9ths and sometimes chords of the 11th and 13th. Chains and sequences of unusual chords are common, and there is a greatly increased use of unprepared and unresolved dissonance. This catalogue of devices must not give the impression that Liszt's later music is entirely prone to discord and angularity. He also employs very bold sequences of common chords: almost, as it were, stretching consonance to its limits.

Bartók's conclusion sums things up most aptly: 'For the future development of music Liszt's *œuvre* seems to me of far greater importance than that of Strauss or even Wagner.'

10

Transcriptions

No one knew better than Liszt that the piano in the nineteenth century had assumed the importance of the orchestra. This helps explain why the names of eighty composers will be found in section XI of Appendix B. Liszt's transcriptions and arrangements form, collectively, the most remarkable aspect of his industry – an industry unique among the great transcribers in musical history.

They fall into two types: (A) free arrangements, mainly operatic fantasias, and (B) stricter arrangements of symphonic works, songs, operatic extracts, etc., often called *partitions de piano*. The works of group (A) are found under a variety of names: *fantaisies, réminiscences, paraphrases* and *illustrations*. (Liszt also used the terms impromptu, divertissement, caprice and variations.) Eighty-three works of this genre for piano solo are listed in Searle's catalogue (nos. 383a–460). Of type (B) he lists 125 solo piano items (nos. 461–577) of which fifty-two are arrangements by Liszt of his own works.

The 'strict' arrangements may be compared in another sphere to the art of literary translation. But in using the word 'strict' it is important to understand that the art of transcription is re-creation: an adaptation to one musical medium of music originally conceived for another. The piano arrangements of Bach's organ works come closest to a note-for-note transcription. In adapting orchestral works for the piano such a literal approach is impossible if the music is to sound effective in terms of the new medium. While Liszt is faithful to the melodies, rhythms and harmonies of Beethoven's symphonies, for example, he allowed himself creative freedom in laying out the orchestral textures for the keyboard.

Categories (A) and (B) occasionally become blurred (e.g. nos 429, 555[1]), when the division between strict arrangement and freer fantasy is less clear. Early examples of type (A) in Liszt's career include the *Grande Fantaisie sur la tyrolienne* from Auber's

[1] Catalogue numbers in this paragraph refer to *The New Grove* (rev. S. Winklhofer).

opera *La fiancée* and the *Grande fantaisie de bravoure sur la Clochette* of Paganini; while a late example is the *Réminiscences* of Verdi's *Simon Boccanegra*. Of type (B) an early example is the famous arrangement of the *Symphonie fantastique*. As the years progress there is a broad tendency among the transcriptions from operas towards type (B): an evocation of a single notable episode such as the quartet from *Rigoletto*. Sometimes the chosen section is 'framed' in a dramatic way by Liszt, as in the arrangement of the Ballad from *The Flying Dutchman*. Liszt made arrangements from operas by 25 composers: more than 50 operas in total. In addition to transcriptions for piano solo, 67 works (nos. 577a–634b) are for four hands at one piano, of which 57 are arrangements of his own music and include the complete orchestral works (25 items) except for the *Faust* and *Dante* symphonies. There are also 25 transcriptions for two pianos (nos. 635–657b) including all the Weimar symphonic poems, the *Faust* and *Dante* symphonies, 5 of his concerto works; Beethoven's Ninth Symphony and Piano Concertos nos. 3–5; two-piano versions of the *Norma* and *Don Giovanni* fantasies, and an eight-hand version of the *Bülow-Marsch*. An eminently practical musician, Liszt knew that very few people possessed two pianos and so confined himself largely to realisations of his own works for study in that medium. But the exceptional four-hand Bellini and Mozart transcriptions are masterly re-creations of the solo piano versions and deserve a prominent place in the duo repertoire. He made 23 arrangements for organ (nos. 658–79); 8 items are listed under Vocal Arrangements (680–6); there are also 14 orchestral arrangements (351–64), 3 for piano and orchestra (365–7), 10 for voices and orchestra (368–77) and 10 for chamber ensemble (377a–83). To complete the statistics from the catalogue, the grand total of transcriptions is 368 items; but as there are numerous multiple entries (12 songs, 9 symphonies, etc., under one catalogue number) the true total is more than twice that number.

A vast labour, and yet one for which he has often been chastised rather than complimented. Such a long list might imply a huge series of pot-boilers produced with ready speed and mechanical facility. Not so: his re-workings of the music of others are always thoughtful and, it must be stressed, in themselves highly creative. While some of the operatic fantasies of the 1830s and 1840s can be cited as superficial, most of them are very fine indeed and often encapsulate the dramatic kernel of a particular opera in striking and original ways. As a dramatist and a performer Liszt re-created a remarkable number of works distilled from the essence of other men's flowers. A fantasy such as that on *Don Giovanni* must be listened to as Liszt and not as Mozart: it is effectively an original work in its own right in the same way as the *Paganini Variations* of Brahms are a magnificent and personal demonstration of that composer-pianist's art.

Today it is less necessary to defend the art of transcription, and arrangements are again part of the accepted repertoire. In the first half of the twentieth century the prevailing tendency to condemn them was a symptom of the new age of radio, of recording and of anti-Romanticism. The fashion became that the legacy of the past was sacred and ought not to be re-thought and sifted by latter-day standards. The purist is of course right in claiming that the *Urtext* is to be preferred to editorial excrescence. To an extent the stylistic range and historical breadth of Liszt's transcriptions were designed to provide pianists and audiences of his day with music they would otherwise have had rare opportunities to study or hear. He spans the age of Palestrina and Lassus through to a selection of his younger contemporaries. His own century was the great age of arrangement and it must be admitted that in the name of 'transcription' some of the worst crimes of musical history were committed. Conversely, Liszt is part of a distinguished pedigree. The most famous historical precedents include Mozart, and Bach with his radical re-workings of Vivaldi. It should not be forgotten that Beethoven turned his Violin Concerto into a Piano Concerto. Gustave Reese cites a keyboard intabulation of a Landini ballata *Questa fanciulla*: 'In the organ version the upper part is much embellished, coloration being as characteristic of keyboard arrangements of vocal music in the fourteenth century as it was to remain when Liszt transcribed Schubert *Lieder*.'[2] In the sixteenth and early seventeenth centuries arrangements for lute, viols or keyboard of vocal music were standard. In Arnold Schering's anthology of musical history[3] Caccini's solo madrigal *Amarilli, mia bella*, published in Florence in 1602, is followed by a transcription by Peter Philips for virginals which appeared in London in 1603. The transcription is as free as anything by Liszt, and this illustrates a view of old and new music belonging to a continuum of which Liszt is very much a part. The continuum is

[2] *Music in the Middle Ages*, New York, 1940, 367.
[3] *Geschichte der Musik in Beispielen*, Leipzig, 1931.

seen in various ways in the nineteenth century (Brahms in his left-hand piano version of Bach's D minor solo violin Chaconne, and Schumann's Bach and Paganini arrangements) and in the work of Liszt's successors: orchestral transcriptions by Ravel and by Schoenberg, and the line of virtuoso pianist-composers such as Busoni, Rakhmaninov, Godowsky and Percy Grainger.

Much of Liszt's arrangement is a homage to great pre-decessors or contemporaries. His transcriptions for piano of six of Bach's organ preludes and fugues established a tradition that was continued by Tausig, Reger and, in an even more distinguished vein (superior in many ways to Liszt himself) by Busoni and the Hungarian pianist-composer Theodor Szántó. The validity of such arrangements is again justified when it is realised that Bülow's inclusion of items from Bach's *Das wohltemperierte Klavier* was regarded in the *late* nineteenth century as grim and difficult list-ening by his audiences. Liszt's Bach transcriptions are relatively early works and it is significant that such faithful and careful renderings belong to the 1840s, his so-called 'glitter-period'. He paid further homage to Bach in his *Prelude and Fugue on BACH*, his *Prelude: Weinen, Klagen, Sorgen, Zagen* and his *Variations on 'Weinen, Klagen'*.

The vast majority of nineteenth-century arrangements for piano were of the pot-pourri variety – a level to which Liszt never descends.[4] This is noteworthy as many of his later transcriptions, as he frankly confessed, were made to eke out his modest income; and yet the quality and seriousness of approach is never com-promised. In earlier years Wagner, who desperately needed the publicity that Liszt's championship could provide, was genuinely overwhelmed with gratitude. And Meyerbeer, a composer whose success hardly required a further boost, was greatly flattered by Liszt's creative attention to his scores. Busoni praised Liszt's subtle use of contrasted sections in the operatic fantasies, his taste in selecting passages and motifs for dramatic characterisation, his use of filigree decoration as an intrinsic, formal part of the 'fanta-sy', and he acknowledged Liszt's superiority to all other con-temporary arrangers.

There were many such contemporaries; Liszt learned from them and strove to better them. His jealousy of, duelling with, and subsequent admiration for Thalberg had two results. First a lessening of the 'tinsel' in his own works, and secondly an adoption

[4] See Saint-Saëns quoted in Newman, *The Man Liszt*, 213f.

of Thalberg's technique of *sostenuto* melody in the middle piano register surrounded by arpeggiated harmonic accompaniment. Few of his virtuoso pianist-contemporaries excelled in orchestration, and Liszt's belated grasp of that art has often been commented upon. Yet it was precisely because of his involvement with the orchestral scores of others – Berlioz, Beethoven – that he delayed his own essays in the field, and meanwhile learned such a great deal from his models. His open letter to Pictet of September 1837 is a resounding manifesto, prompted by criticism of his failure to turn from the piano to 'weightier' composition:

> You do not realise that you are touching a very sensitive spot. You do not know that in suggesting that I give up the piano you are foreshadowing my day of mourning, you are taking from me the light which has illuminated the entire first half of my life and has become a part of me. For can't you see, the piano is for me what a ship is to a sailor, a horse to an Arab – even more! It has been till now my *I*, my language, my life ... Can you really want me to forsake it for the pursuit of more glittering, more resounding successes in the theatre or with the orchestra? Oh no! Even assuming that I am ready for these harmonies ... I am resolved to give up studying and developing the piano only after I have done everything that is possible, all that is now within my reach ... If I am not mistaken I have begun something quite different with my transcription of the *Symphonie fantastique* by Berlioz. I have worked on this as conscientiously as if it were a matter of transcribing the Holy Scriptures, seeking to transfer to the piano not just the general structure of the music, but all its separate parts, as well as its many harmonic and rhythmic combinations ... After my efforts I hope it will no longer be permissible to *arrange* the works of the masters as they have been before ... What I undertook in the Berlioz symphony I am now setting out to do for Beethoven. Serious study of his works, a deep appreciation of their almost limitless beauties, and on the other hand the devices with which I have become familiar owing to my constant piano practice, have made me perhaps less incapable than some others for this difficult task ... The arrangements hitherto in use have now been rendered useless; one night better call them *derangements* ...[5]

Bonn's Beethoven Monument was in large measure due to Liszt's efforts; he created his own monument to Beethoven in the symphony arrangements. Nos. 5–7 belong to the happy summer weeks of 1837 spent at George Sand's home at Nohant, and he transcribed

[5] GS, II, 151ff.

the funeral march from the *Eroica* in 1843. In 1851 his arrangement of the Ninth for two pianos was published; among its admirers were Brahms and Clara Schumann who played it together. The remaining symphonies had to wait for the calm of the Roman years for completion. For long he felt that the finale of the Ninth was an impossibility for two hands and proposed to finish his edition with the third movement. In the end even this miracle was achieved. To make the texture clearly apparent to the player, Liszt places the vocal parts above the piano part into which, however, they are fully incorporated. The complete set appeared in 1865 with a preface which ends:

> With the immense development of its harmonic power the piano seeks more and more to appropriate all orchestral compositions. In the compass of its seven octaves it can, with few exceptions, reproduce all features, all combinations, all figurations of the most thorough and profound musical creations ... My aim has been attained if I stand on a level with the intelligent engraver or the conscientious translator who comprehend the spirit of a work and thus contribute to the knowledge of great masters and to the formation of an appreciation of beauty.

As with the *Symphonie fantastique* transcription, Liszt is punctilious in indicating Beethoven's instrumentation and he reproduces the slurs and phrasing exactly. His great skill is in creating appropriate sonorities to match orchestral parts that would sound weak if merely transcribed note for note. Among many examples are the subtle redistribution of accompaniment textures in the slow movement of No. 4; the arpeggiated cluster chords deep in the bass, that effectively convey the terrifying roar of bass instruments in the thunderstorm movement of the *Pastoral*; and the frequent simultaneous combination of different textures – tremolo, sustained legato melody and staccato accompaniment as in the *Adagio* of No. 9. The clarity of the part-writing is maintained by careful notation of note-stems, either up or down. He frequently gives *ossia* passages which offer alternative solutions; and occasionally includes, on separate staves, certain parts which he could not incorporate for ten fingers. It is instructive to compare Liszt's version with the work of another transcriber who aimed at a pianistic equivalent of these symphonies (rather than a 'reduction' for study purposes). Example 14(a) is by Kalkbrenner; 14(b), on page 200, is Liszt's arrangement of the same passage from the slow movement of the *Eroica*. While (b) is far superior, Kalkbrenner must be given credit for undertaking the huge enterprise of arranging all Beethoven's symphonies earlier even than Liszt and at a time when there was hardly a comprehending public for them. Self-evidently Liszt calls for a high level of technique but much can be learned about him, about the piano and about the symphonies themselves from a study of these scores. Tovey saw in them conclusive proof 'that Liszt was by far the most wonderful interpreter of orchestral scores on the pianoforte that the world is ever likely to see'.[6]

As with Beethoven, so with Berlioz: the retention of 'the

Ex. 14

(a)

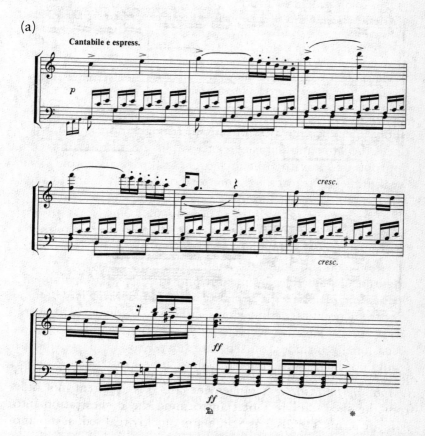

<hr />

[6] *Essays in Musical Analysis*, I, London, 1935, 193.

Ex. 14

(b)

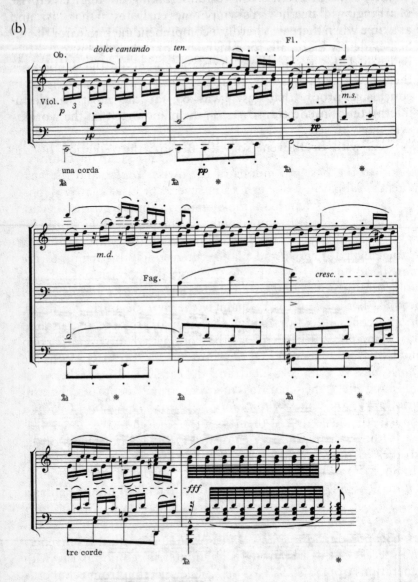

spirit of the original' is always Liszt's aim. The audacity of his *Symphonie fantastique* arrangement (1833) is apparent, not only from the successful feat of transforming the orchestration into pianistic terms, but also, as Schumann quickly realised, as a piano document in its own right:

Liszt has worked out his arrangement with so much industry and enthusiasm, that it may be regarded as an original work, a *résumé* of his profound studies, a practical pianoforte school in score-playing. This art of reproduction, so wholly different from the detail-playing of the virtuoso, the many kinds of touch that it demands, the effective use of the pedal, the clear interweaving of separate parts, the collective grasp of orchestral masses; in short the understanding of means and possibilities as yet hidden in the piano can only be the work of a master ...[7]

In several aspects the subject matter of Berlioz' symphonic vision drew a response from Liszt: the third part, 'a scene in the country', is akin to the pastoral moods of the Swiss *Année*, and the final Witches' Sabbath awoke echoes in several of Liszt's later Mephistophelean essays (compare the opening of the Berlioz finale with that of the Mephisto movement in the *Faust Symphony* for example). Fidelity is also the hallmark of the *Harold in Italy* arrangement for viola and piano (interestingly belonging to the same period as Liszt's own two substantial compositions for solo violin and piano). The *Harold* transcription marks another bond between Berlioz and Liszt – namely the Byronic spirit: the magic of landscape and wild scenery, the open air, the creative urge to travel and for spiritual quest, the contrast of introvert passion and extrovert adventure. Of the shorter Berlioz transcriptions the *Danse des Sylphes* is a lucid and delicately laid-out scherzo of charming effect; the separate *L'idée fixe* arrangement is a delightful lyric rarity; and the *Sermon and Oath from Benvenuto Cellini* a robust, stirring setting of themes all too seldom heard.

Other worthy and meticulously crafted arrangements of the 'stricter' variety include the Septets by Beethoven (Op. 20) and Hummel (Op. 74); Weber's overtures to *Oberon* and *Der Freischütz*; Rossini's *William Tell* overture; Bach's G minor Fantasia and Fugue; incidental music from Mendelssohn's *Midsummer Night's Dream*; Schubert's Marches and the lastingly and deservedly popular *Soirées de Vienne*. A measure of the attractiveness and success of this last group is its uninterrupted popularity with generations of pianists. Based on a wide selection from Schubert's dances, Liszt's aim in each of the nine numbers was to create a chain of waltzes suitable for concert performance. He achieved his aim and remained entirely within the joyous *Musikabend* spirit of the originals, confining his own creative contributions to

---

[7] From Schumann's *Neue Zeitschrift für Musik* review, 1835.

introductions and occasional cadenzas. (No. 4 of the set is a reworking of the material used in No. 3 of Liszt's *Apparitions*.)

His transcriptions of the complete set of Rossini's *Les Soirées Musicales* (eight arias and four duets composed by Rossini in the early 1830s; also famously arranged by Respighi and Britten) retain the grace, polish, wit and flamboyance of the originals. With economy and restraint Liszt allows himself only occasional graceful decoration at melodic repeats. This very approachable set is not to be confused with two extravagant fantasies Liszt also made from the *Soirées*: free and fully worked-out virtuosic treatments of, respectively, *La Serenata & L'Orgia* and *La Pastorella dell' Alpi & Li Marinari*. Such elaborations perhaps stretch the inherent content of the original material too far but, even here, Liszt soars above empty bravura and devises continually challenging piano figurations and (especially in the first of these fantasies) rhythmic intricacies. The simpler charm of the Rossini-Liszt set of twelve pieces has affinities with two other collections: *Les Soirées Italiennes*, six pieces based on melodies by Mercadante, and *Nuits d'Été à Pausilippe*, on Donizetti songs. Largely forgotten today, Mercadante (1795–1870) was a significant figure in Italian opera between Rossini and Verdi, and Liszt came to admire his work in Venice in 1838. The six 'amusements' based on his themes are indeed fun to play and, like the Rossini and Donizetti sets, are delights that deserve a hearing now and then. Such pieces may be the lollipops of the repertoire, but when confectionery is as stylish and delicately flavoured as in the Mercadante pieces (a canzonetta, galop, Tyrolean pastorale, rollicking sailors' song, brindisi and a bolero) it gives a taste of what a master of the keyboard can do with modest, unpretentious material, in a manner to be savoured from Mozart to Moszkowski.

'Whoever really wants to know what Liszt has done for the piano should study his old operatic Fantasies. They represent the classicism of piano technique.' So said Johannes Brahms to the young Arthur Friedheim.[8] Brahms significantly praised the technique rather than the form or content of the fantasies, but the last two aspects present such a varied terrain of musical topography that only an extended examination of all the operatic *réminiscences* could do the subject justice. In essence Liszt's success in these works is his variety of approach. At his best the form and content of the chosen opera dictate a personal distillation of the subject

[8] Friedheim, 'Life and Liszt' in *Remembering Franz Liszt*, 138.

in, say, ten or fifteen minutes of music which never descends into pot-pourri. Liszt's devotion to opera and his close involvement with its course in the nineteenth century is remarkable. In these fantasies lies enshrined an operatic legacy from the man who knew almost all the significant opera composers from the 1820s to the 1880s; who played, conducted and inspired some of the best works of those seven decades; and who also revered the operas of Gluck, Mozart and Weber.

Liszt's first published operatic paraphrase was an *Impromptu brillant sur des thèmes de Rossini et Spontini*, composed in 1824 around the same time as *Sept variations brillantes* on a theme from Rossini's *Ermione*, and in the same year in which he improvised a fugue on *Zitti, zitti* from *La Cenerentola* during his London visit. The *Impromptu* opens with a characteristic gesture; a precursor of the opening of his *Eroica* Transcendental Study No. 7:

Ex. 15

The 12-year-old arranger exhibits a fine grasp of transitional flow and brilliance of technique, albeit still within the confines of Czerny's idiom. Originality and a sense of dazzling assurance are more apparent in an Auber transcription of five years later, *La Fiancée*. Comparison of Liszt's rare scores from the 1820s reveals his development as an intrepid pioneer in exploring the potentials of the piano. The musical content of the 1829 Auber fantasy is hardly significant but its physical demands show Liszt pushing ahead the frontiers of technical possibility in ways that leave his contemporaries and his own previous scores far behind. Daring use of pitch and contrary-motion chromatics are seen here:

Ex. 16

Just as Liszt the player was endowed with a talent which far outstripped his child-prodigy rivals, so the evidence of his compositions marks him out for something greater. It is not just the weighty clusters of hemidemisemiquavers that distinguish the Auber piece, but also a number of felicitous touches including instructions on the use of both pedals simultaneously in *leggierissimo* passages.

The next landmark on the trail towards hitherto unheard-of effects of dexterity is the *La Clochette Fantasy* (1831–2) based on a theme from Paganini's B minor Violin Concerto. Written in the immediate wake, the delirium even, of hearing Paganini play, it consists of a fantastically difficult introduction/development of Paganini's theme, a central 'Variation à la Paganini' in which the violinist's harmonics are simulated, and a 'Finale di Bravura' of relentless virtuosity. Relentless and yet not inhuman: though rarely played today, the *Grande Fantaisie* is physically extremely demanding but not impossibly awkward (Liszt carefully notates *ossia* passages which offer an easier reading) and contains a number of ideas of lyric beauty. The version of Liszt's variations on this theme that is more commonly heard is No. 3 of the *Paganini Études*, 'La Campanella', where the transposition from the 'white-note' key (A minor) of the *Clochette* fantasy to a 'black-note' G sharp minor in itself facilitates performance, especially in octave leaps.

The finest 'old' operatic fantasies, justifying the Brahms verdict 'the classicism of piano technique', appeared in print between 1836 and the end of Liszt's career as a travelling virtuoso, eleven years later. They were very much a part of his repertoire in those years. Dates given here are of first publication:

Pacini	*Niobe* 1836
Halévy	*La Juive* 1836
Meyerbeer	*Les Huguenots* 1837
	Robert le diable (*Valse infernale*) 1841
Bellini	*I Puritani: Réminiscences* 1837
	I Puritani (*Introduction & Polonaise*) 1842
	La Sonnambula 1839
	Norma 1841
Donizetti	*Lucia di Lammermoor* (*Sextet*) 1840
	Lucia di Lammermoor (*March & Cavatina*) 1841
	Valse à capriccio sur deux motifs de Lucia et Parisina 1842
	Lucrezia Borgia (2 parts) 1841/48
	Dom Sébastien (*Funeral March*) 1845
Mozart	*Don Giovanni* 1843
	Le Nozze di Figaro (composed 1842; published 1912)
Auber	*La Muette de Portici* (*Tarantella*) 1847

The spacious virtuosic, fiery, and yet subtly organised *Don Juan* Reminiscences combine a fantasy on themes from Mozart's *Don Giovanni* with a series of variations. The introduction has symphonic grandeur, with piano writing of bold richness and variety, splendidly evoking the grim terror of the Commendatore:

stern chords associated with his appearances in Scenes 3 and 5 of Act 2. The daemonic D minor scales of Mozart's 'stone guest' are here charged with new and frightening intensity. A transition lightens the texture, preparing for a seductive elaboration of the Giovanni-Zerlina Act 1 Scene 3 duet *Là ci darem la mano*, with a cadenza added between its 2/4 and 6/8 sections. Two full variations follow; the first, marked *elegantamente*, contains a more elaborate central cadenza. The second is marked *Tempo giusto, animato* with strongly accented dotted 6/8 rhythms throughout as the libertine becomes more and more intoxicated in his enticements. At the height of the frenzy comes a dramatic return of the 'statue' music and the remainder of this increasingly free variation is a brilliant contest between the ever more alluring blandishments of the seducer and the growingly insistent chromatic scale-figures of the Commendatore. The pace increases to a *presto* 2/4 as hints of Don Giovanni's Act 2, Scene 3 'champagne' aria appear. After a long anticipatory preparation Liszt launches into a sparkling B flat major treatment of this whole aria. Hard on the heels of this reckless carousal come the tormented cries of the avenging guest, and the coda is a magnificent final tussle between Don Juan's unquenchable bravado and the inexorable chords that announce his doom.

This Romantic and dramatic re-working of Mozart's most 'Romantic' opera is doubly remarkable. Firstly for its exploitation of unusual piano textures; secondly for the extreme economy of material chosen from the original. Liszt in no way tries to tell the story of da Ponte's drama but extracts its core from three musical sections of Mozart's work – a duet, an aria and the statue music – developing, contrasting and combining the chosen material in a symphonically original way. The other Mozart fantasy, on *Figaro*, is an altogether lighter showpiece. A free introduction is based on the opening phrases of Figaro's aria *Non più andrai*. After seventy-five bars phrases from Cherubino's *Voi che sapete* appear and, after a short cadenza, the Cherubino aria is arranged in full, with an endearing aura of heart-fluttering ornamentation. There is another cadenza before the return of the theme, and twelve bars of coda. An elaboration of the middle section of Figaro's aria is followed by a stirringly martial and chromatically coloured parade of the complete *Non più andrai*. Busoni completed this Fantasy from Liszt's almost finished manuscript.

The *Reminiscences of Norma* encompass the dramatic

essence of Bellini's opera in a most imaginative way. Liszt takes seven musical ideas from the drama and arranges their appearances to depict Norma's tragic dilemma: the conflict between her human feelings of love, revenge and grief and her spiritual calling as High Priestess. The melodies of *Norma*, especially the exquisitely sculpted, slow and elegiac lines of pathos, have a simple dignity and noble grandeur that Liszt mirrors to perfection. Pianistically the *Norma* fantasy is a great study in *cantabile* playing; the soaring *legato* phrases are set against a testing variety of accompaniment figurations, including almost every permutation of broken-chord patterns, arpeggios shared between the hands (*à la Thalberg*, see Ex. 17), trills and rapid octaves. The opening G minor chords (derived from the chorus *Norma viene*, and creating a sense of tense anticipation), the beautifully expansive G major melody that follows (*Ite sul colle, O Druidi!* – the Archdruid Oroveso's plea to the people to rise against the Roman invaders) and the 'allegro deciso' march (the warlike chorus *Dell' aura tua profetica*) magnificently evoke the opera's opening setting with the druids and soldiers of Gaul. The stirring *allegro* theme is subjected to a series of brilliant free variations before the material from the Introduction returns in a dramatically heightened G sharp minor. With the free recitative passage and the modulation to B minor Liszt introduces music from the final scenes of the opera associated with Norma's fate, as well as her courage and compassion. First *Deh! non volerli vittime* and, at the wonderful transformation to B major, the duet *Qual cor tradisti*. The entire, supremely moving B major passage caused Busoni to remark that anyone who plays or listens to it and is not moved 'has not yet arrived at Liszt'. It is crowned by the melody of *Padre, tu piangi?* (see Ex. 17). The *tempestuoso* marking introduces the music from Norma's announcement that the Gods have decreed war against the Romans (*Guerra! Guerra!*) and the fantasy reaches its climax in the return of *Padre, tu piangi?*, skilfully combined at one point with the tune of *Dell' aura tua profetica* (see Ex. 18). A final glance at *Guerra! Guerra!* propels this quarter of an hour or so of *réminiscences* to a thrilling close.

The greatest of the fantasies, such as that on *Norma*, may be listened to on several levels, but should not be approached merely as catalogues of pianistic possibilities or as curiosities of a flamboyant era, just as *bel canto* opera itself is, at its best, much more than a vehicle for vocal display: the display is one part of the

Ex. 17

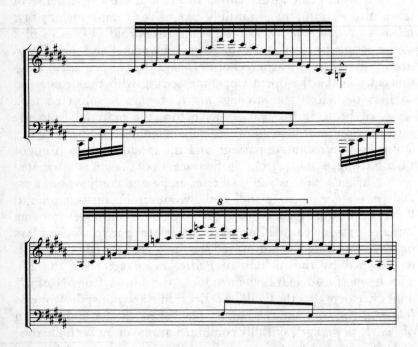

dramatic armoury, one means to an end. This supremely Italian art, with its elements of declamation, pathos, long-flowing melody, ravishing ornamentation and theatrical effect, made so deep an impression on Liszt's musical soul, both in Paris and in his Italian wanderings, that it can scarcely be overestimated. It repays both player and listener to become familiar with the finer details of

208

Ex. 18

the original operas in order to appreciate Liszt's technique of concentrating the essential foundations of the dramas and his re-expression of them in new and vivid form. His selection of 'content' from an opera, his re-arrangement of that content and, especially, his scheme of tonality, dictate the 'form' of the fantasy, and contribute to its effectiveness. With *Norma* he achieves a successful, solid structure which both summarises the 'content' of the original by judicious selection and re-arrangement, and creates an effective new 'form' through his ingenious progression of keys. The broad outline is:

Bars		
	1–27	G minor
	28–65	G major
	66–75	B major; modulation to
	89–141	G major; modulation to
	146–154	G sharp minor
	154–190	B minor
	191–239	B major; preparation for
	250–331	E flat minor
	332–372	E flat major

The scheme thus moves upward through the mediant relationships G–B–E flat. Each step follows a minor-major pattern, with the added subtlety of B major being prefigured as early as bar 66, and E flat major in the introduction (bar 21).

Just as Liszt's very different approaches can be compared in the two Mozart fantasies, so his equally contrasted methods can be seen in the context of the Bellini and Donizetti arrangements. The slight plot of *La Sonnambula* suggests a simpler design, broadly fast-slow-fast – which is also the outline of the *La Juive* reminiscences. Yet *Sonnambula* is technically a taxingly difficult and lengthy concert transcription. In the early Weimar years Liszt made a fine piano-duet version of it, redistributing and elaborating the exhilarating passage-work with superb craftsmanship. Of the three works drawn from *I Puritani*, the *Introduction et Polonaise* re-works with very slight alterations the closing section of the *Réminiscences des Puritains*. The title of the celebrated *Hexaméron* refers to the six creative minds who compiled the variations (see page 42) and the complete work is a surprisingly well-integrated sexpartite musical offering. Wagner said that mastery of the art of transition is one of the greatest gifts of a composer and Liszt, the master-of-ceremonies in this parade of the theme *Suoni la tromba* from *Puritani*, justifies that worthy maxim. His Finale, following Chopin's Variation VI, engagingly parodies the styles of his five fellow contributors. Liszt enjoyed playing *Hexaméron* on his tours and additionally performed it in an adaptation for piano and orchestra.

Lucia di Lammermoor also provided material for three piano works, although the *Sextet* and the *Funeral March & Cavatina* were intended by Liszt as one work (composed 1835–6) and were separated only by the publisher. In the *Sextet* only the short but harmonically daring introduction, two brief cadenzas and a few bars of coda are Liszt's original contributions; for the rest he lays out Donizetti's vocal parts with attentive care to range and effect. A freer approach is adopted in the *Funeral March & Cavatina*, with another short but dramatically coloured free introduction, an elaboration of the music of the Act 3 funeral procession, an exquisite exposition of Edgardo's cavatina from the same scene which itself frames a substantial central section based on the finale of Act 2. The coda, an *andante maestoso* peroration, rounds off and unifies both transcriptions by reintroducing the characteristic accompaniment figures of the *Sextet* which were so strikingly presented in the introduction to that arrangement. The third *Lucia*-based work, the *Valse à Capriccio*, a captivatingly fresh and enjoyable elaboration of the duet *Verranno a te* and a duet from Act 2 of Donizetti's *Parisina* (the two themes are combined at the climax), reached its final form in the early Weimar years as No. 3 of *Trois Caprices-Valses* (published 1852).

The variation-form operatic fantasy is a comparative rarity in Liszt, with the important exceptions of *Hexaméron* and the rigorous and spectacular variations on the *Tarantelle* from Auber's *La muette de Portici*. Later works on the variation principle include the second of the *Illustrations* from Meyerbeer's *Le Prophète* and the late *Sarabande and Chaconne from Handel's 'Almira'*. Variation technique as opposed to sets of variations is, however, an intrinsic element in the operatic elaborations of Mozart, Weber, Meyerbeer, Rossini, Bellini and Donizetti.

With the Verdi arrangements the emphasis shifts to a more direct transcription of an operatic extract – the Salve Maria from *Jérusalem* (the Paris version of *I Lombardi*), 'O sommo Carlo' from *Ernani*, the Miserere from *Il Trovatore*, the Quartet from *Rigoletto*, and two numbers each from *Don Carlos* and *Aida*. The exceptions to this are, curiously, the earliest and the last of the Verdi paraphrases: his first (unpublished) Concert Paraphrase on *Ernani* of 1847 and the *Réminiscences de [Simon] Boccanegra* of thirty-five years later. The early *Ernani* work is of the 'reminiscence' type and the final theme it uses, Don Carlo's tribute to the dead Charlemagne (*O sommo Carlo*), becomes the sole basis for Liszt's subsequent Concert Paraphrase on *Ernani*, where its treatment is much more dignified, refined and assured. This paraphrase in turn was revised in 1859 along with the *Rigoletto* and *Trovatore* extracts – all three prepared for concerts Bülow was giving in Berlin and published together as a Liszt–Verdi Album in 1860. The *Boccanegra* fantasy of December 1882 is the very last of Liszt's many operatic piano works, and his love of Italian opera is as ardent then as in the first of them, almost sixty years before. Here he returns to the reminiscence approach; elaborating an introduction and a coda from the opera's Prelude, and selecting contrasting material for the central sections – the warlike chorus *All' armi. O Liguri* and the supremely moving final ensemble of Act 3. There is no attempt to return to the *Glanzperiode* brilliance of keyboard effect, but instead a direct simplicity, as in these bars of whole-tone harmony, redolent of Liszt's late style (see Ex. 19). Such Lisztian touches are by no means confined to the later arrangements. A close study of the well-known *Bella figlia dell' amore* from *Rigoletto* and a comparison with Verdi's score, reveals how Liszt expands and develops Verdi's harmonic conception, not just in the introduction, cadenzas and coda (note the very Lisztian bars 4–6 and 16–17 of the introduction) but in a multitude of chromatic doublings, altered chords and rich appoggiaturas throughout the Quartet.

Ex. 19

With the Wagner arrangements the move towards an evocation of a particular passage from an opera is even more complete.
Of his fifteen piano adaptations from eight Wagner operas, only
the *Fantasy on themes from Rienzi* is of the old reminiscence type.
Of the most literal transcriptions there is a great divide in technical
demands, from the relatively straightforward extracts (four from
Lohengrin; the Pilgrims' Chorus, Entry of the Guests and Wolfram's Romance from *Tannhäuser*) to the truly transcendental
technique required for the Overture to *Tannhäuser* (his first
Wagner arrangement) and the pliant web of intricate textures
that comprise Isolde's *Liebestod* from *Tristan*. Of other chosen
sections: in the Spinning Chorus from *The Flying Dutchman* Liszt
confines himself to a free introduction and coda and an inter-
polation of the Dutchman's motif between verses; Senta's Ballad
from the same opera is freer still in treatment; *Walhall* from *Das
Rheingold* is a literal transcription of the orchestral transition
between Scenes 1 and 2, together with a reference to the 'sword'
motif and a final expansion of the Valhalla theme; 'Am stillen
Herd' from *Die Meistersinger* and the Solemn March to the Holy
Grail from *Parsifal* are much more personal re-workings of specific
scenes.

In addition to Wagner and Verdi, Liszt's art of operatic alchemy after 1847 was applied to a variety of composers, most significantly Meyerbeer, Mosonyi, Goldschmidt, Raff, Tchaikovsky and Gounod. In the famous paraphrase of the Waltz Scene from *Faust* Liszt develops ideas from the close of Gounod's Act 1 and additionally incorporates part of the Faust–Marguerite love duet, *O nuit d'amour!*, from Act 2, as an extended lyric central Intermezzo. Sorabji described this work as

> prodigiously ingenious, supremely elegant, exquisitely musical ... the way in which fragments from other parts of the opera are drawn upon for the Intermezzo is a model, so logical and natural a use is made of them. The modulations and harmonic twists Liszt gives to Gounod's banal tunes are a joy, and he raises and transmutes the whole thing, redeeming it from its narrow provincial Gallicism, and giving it his own spaciousness and urbanity, perfect European, citizen of the world that he was.[9]

That the Faust subject should have called forth from Liszt such a lively response is unsurprising. The bewitchingly delicate transcription of a ballet section from Gounod's *Queen of Sheba*, the Berceuse, is full of harmonic touches of novel delight:

Ex. 20

[9] *Around Music*, London, 1932, p. 197.

In studying the man who, as a youth, envisaged a grand union of theatre and church music, it is no great step to turn from dramatic transcriptions of opera to his evocations of the religious music of others. The very title 'Evocation' was used by Liszt for one of the strangest hybrids, yet most poignantly felt, among his arrangements: *À la chapelle Sixtine; Miserere d'Allegri et Ave verum corpus de Mozart* (see page 123f). The Allegri work is very freely treated, the Mozart transcribed more simply and literally. Another imposing yet neglected Mozart transcription is of the *Confutatis & Lacrymosa* from the *Requiem*. Both Palestrina's *Miserere* (No. 8 of the *Harmonies poétiques* set) and Arcadelt's *Ave Maria* are, like Allegri and (in the organ transcriptions) Lassus, treated by Liszt in a markedly nineteenth-century manner. More important than his historically coloured view of earlier church composers, however, is his enthusiasm for them.

Liszt transcribed about 150 songs, more than a third of them by his beloved Schubert. His response to poetic imagery, his conviction that purely musical images of poetic ideas are capable of projection to the listener and his belief that he could illustrate such imagery without words, are keys to understanding Liszt's lifelong aesthetic. The musical *image* of the idea, the true *symphonic poem*, thus had its genesis in concept and form in Liszt's adoration of Schubert. Just as he conveys the instrumentation of Beethoven and Berlioz scores in his notation to the pianist, so he faithfully gives the lyrics of each song above the notes of his arrangement. The verbal poetry may be absent for the listener, but Liszt discreetly compensates for this by incorporating new touches and delicate embellishments of his own to underline the imagery.

His reasons for undertaking this great task of Schubert arrangement between 1833 and 1846 were various: admiration for the neglected Viennese master, his sheer joy in the freshness and spontaneity of the songs themselves, the provision of a large corpus of attractive pieces for his touring repertoire, and above all his fascination with what Thalberg called 'the art of singing applied to the piano'. Liszt's skill in sustaining and highlighting the glorious thread of *cantabile* melody through an astounding range of accompaniment textures is a constant source of wonder. Critics of these song arrangements object to the innocent charm and simple sensitivity of Schubert's *Lieder* being wedded to the dazzling plethora of Lisztian effects. Yet he always remains faithful to the spirit of the originals and where he does alter detail it is never merely to parade his skills but always a result of his honest response to, and desire to reinforce, the essence of the poetic meaning. Many of the arrangements call for a technique akin to that of Liszt's Études, and he must have found it irresistible to bring to bear the full range of his pianistic craft when discovering Schubert's great storehouse of lyric beauty. So he luxuriates in the purely happy glow of the music of *Die Forelle* and *Horch, horch die Lerch*, adds gleaming embellishments to the rippling brook in the first two songs of *Die schöne Müllerin*, and unleashes his full forces at the appropriate storm passages in *Die junge Nonne* and *Erlkönig*. On the other hand, with the haunting starkness of *Der Leiermann* or the lovely spring tenderness of *Frühlingsglaube* he takes gentle care to preserve the intimacy of mood. In the strophic *Auf dem Wasser zu singen* he adopts a different solution to unfolding the melody in each of the three verses and adds a fourth verse of his own as an exhilarating coda in which he allows himself freedom to create a sense of unbounded sweep and play, quite appropriate to the image of shimmering flight contained in the third stanza of Schubert's song (see Ex. 21).

Liszt also paid tribute to the genius of other songwriters, notably Beethoven (nineteen songs including *Adelaïde* and the cycle *An die ferne Geliebte*), Chopin, Robert Franz, Mendelssohn and Schumann. He also helped preserve a number of items by less well-remembered composers: Josef Dessauer, Otto Lessmann, Anton Rubinstein, Clara Schumann, Hans von Bülow and Eduard Lassen. Among the last group are some fine lyric gems; for example Lassen's setting of a Peter Cornelius poem *Löse Himmel meine Seele* and Bülow's of the Dante sonnet *Tanto gentile e tanto onesta*.

As many transcriptions are long out of print, certain rarities will remain such until a new edition appears.[10] Among curiosities too numerous to mention, the two *Tarantelles* arranged from Cui and Dargomizhsky attest to Liszt's late enthusiasm for Russian music. Two Rossini pieces not included above are the aria *Cujus animam* from the *Stabat Mater* (Liszt also arranged it for trombone and organ) and *La Charité* from the *Trois Choeurs* for female voices and piano. Four hands at one piano can rewardingly explore Liszt's versions of twelve of Field's Nocturnes, or perhaps the

[10] The NE series of transcriptions is shortly to begin publication (1988); it is expected to be issued in up to 24 volumes.

Liszt

Ex. 21

(a)

(b)

(c)

216

(d)

Glinka *Tscherkessenmarsch* from *Russlan and Ludmilla* which testifies to his earlier admiration for Russian music.

For concerto-type arrangements see Chapter 12; for organ transcriptions Chapter 14; and for Liszt's orchestral songs, Chapter 16.

11

Original piano music

Early works

Three works published in Paris in 1824–5 were principally designed
to show Liszt's grasp of keyboard technique: *Allegro di bravura*
(of which he sketched an orchestral arrangement), *Rondo di
bravura* and *Huit Variations*. They are otherwise of no great value
except for signs that show the young composer's already wide-
ranging sense of tonality and harmonic adventure. The *Allegro*,
which has an improvisatory quality, is particularly restless in key:
its 37-bar slow introduction encompasses E flat minor, G flat
major, D flat minor, D major, D minor and again E flat minor,
before reaching E flat major, the home key of the work. And in
the *Rondo* some harmonic touches are quite untamed.

To set aside these early scores and turn to the first significant
original composition of the next decade, *Harmonies poétiques et
religieuses* (1833), is to enter another world. No words could
express so succinctly the changes in Liszt's psyche in those few
years as do these opening bars:

Ex. 22

Note the lack of a time signature: bars 1–2 contain 8 crotchets,
bar 3 has 10, later we find 4 or 7 or 9. And Liszt writes *senza
tempo* at the opening. There is also no key signature or clear sense
of tonality. Note, too, the many descriptive markings: there are

detailed, evocative instructions to the player over nearly every bar
of the work. Two-thirds of the way through, the music does settle
into an *andante religioso* 2/4 section, if indeed 'settled' is an apt
word to use for this extraordinary piece:

Ex. 23

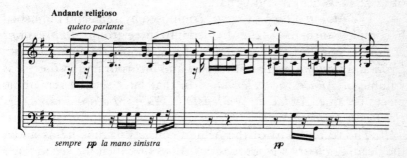

In various guises this idea pervades the whole work, thus
anticipating Liszt's later technique of 'transformation of themes'.
The final bars, like the opening, are tormented and ambiguous in
mood and tonality. The title *Harmonies poétiques et religieuses* is
derived from a set of poems by Lamartine, and Liszt prefaces his
score with Lamartine's own foreword to his collection, describing
those meditative souls 'who are invincibly raised upwards by
solitude and contemplation towards ideas of the infinite, that is
towards religion; all their thoughts converge in enthusiasm and in
prayer; their entire existence is a silent hymn to the Deity and to
hope'. At this time Liszt was imbued with the religious poetry of
Lamartine and captivated by the progressive Christian hopes of
Lamennais. He planned a set of pieces to Lamartine's *Harmonies
poétiques et religieuses* but that collection was not completed and
published for another twenty years. In it the piece under discussion
here was revised as *Pensée des morts*. Yet the first version is
important for the germs of future procedures which it contains –
the 'open' form, thematic transformation, irregular metre, augmented harmony, the audacious final cadence – and because it
marks Liszt's true emergence as an original composer. As such the
mystical quality of its conception is additionally noteworthy. It is
entirely characteristic that such a soul-searching (even if youthfully
exuberant, heart-on-the-sleeve) work comes at this early stage of
Liszt's career; it is the significant predecessor of the religious pieces

of the early Weimar years, the Roman period, and the third *Année de pèlerinage*.

Similar freedom of form, and precise, poetic verbal instructions to the player characterise the three colourful *Apparitions* (1834), a set also linked in title and spirit to Lamartine (one of whose poems is entitled *Apparition*) and perhaps to the *Auditions* of Liszt's mystical friend Urhan.

The *Album d'un Voyageur*, composed by 1838 and published in complete form in 1842, is divided into three groups. *Impressions et poésies* consists of seven items of which only the first and last, *Lyon* and *Psaume*, were not revised and incorporated in the Swiss volume of *Années de pèlerinage*. In that later set the remaining pieces became: *Au lac de Wallenstadt, Au bord d'une source, Les cloches de Genève, Vallée d'Obermann* and *Chapelle de Guillaume Tell*. The second part of the Album consists of nine items under the heading *Fleurs mélodiques des Alpes* of which the second and third were selected and rewritten as *Le mal du pays* and *Pastorale* in the Swiss *Année*. The last part of the Album consists of three *Paraphrases*. First an 'improvisation' (actually a variation set with interludes) on the *Ranz des Vaches*, a type of Swiss mountain melody sung, or played on the Alphorn, to summon the herd: this version was by the Swiss composer Ferdinand Huber (1791–1863) who also provided the theme for the third *Paraphrase*, a rondo, *Ranz de chèvres*. The middle piece *Un soir dans les montagnes* has a pastoral opening and close (on a theme by a Basel publisher, Ernst Knop), framing a dramatic mountain thunderstorm similar in character to Liszt's *Orage*. The *Paraphrases* were the earliest part of the Album to be composed and published (1836) and were reissued by Liszt in 1877 as *Trois Morceaux Suisses*.

The inspiration for *Impressions et poésies* was of course the journey Liszt made through Switzerland with the Comtesse d'Agoult in the first months of their elopement in 1835, although it would be wrong to assign the 'impression' too closely to the dates of his visits to the scenes depicted.[1] As with Wordsworth, Liszt's poetry originated as 'emotion recollected in tranquillity'; the refining of his first spontaneous feelings took place over a long span – two decades, in fact, from the Swiss travels until publication of the final versions in the Swiss *Année* (1855). In his preface to

[1] For the musical origins and the dating of the *Album d'un Voyageur* pieces see the preface to the Breitkopf Collected Edition, Piano Works, IV, p. iii; and *Liszt Studien*, II, 136–42.

the 1842 publication of the *Album d'un Voyageur* Liszt wrote of the deep sensations he experienced in travelling through 'different landscapes and places consecrated by history and poetry', the rapport he felt with 'the varied phenomena of nature' and of how, on coming to represent these in music, his 'recollections intensified'. *Les cloches de Genève* is traditionally associated with the birth of his daughter Blandine; the *Album* version contains some significant material omitted in the later revision. The early and late versions of *Vallée d'Obermann* are also rewarding to compare. The pieces in Part I of the Album are free evocations, not based on the music of others, with the exception of *Psaume* which is a simple chordal arrangement of Psalm 42 in the setting by Louis Bourgeois (1510–*c*. 61), one of the compilers of the Geneva Psalter. In Parts II and III of the Album the approach resembles that of the operatic paraphrases of the same period. Two of the *Fleurs mélodiques* (the fifth and eighth) are based on tunes by Huber, and most, if not all the others draw on Swiss folk or popular melodies, treated in a straightforward unpretentious manner.

Lyon is the most stirring and significant of the 'discarded' pieces from the set, both musically and for its political nature. Headed with the slogan of the rebelling weavers of Lyon, 'Life in work, or Death in fighting', it is dedicated to Lamennais, the insurgents' champion. Cast as an heroic march, its opening theme embraces the rhythm *and* the antithesis inherent in the workers' motto:

Ex. 24

In 1837 Liszt visited Lyon after a stay at George Sand's home:

Leaving Berry, where I had lived in the narrow circle of feelings one would be tempted to call selfish, so much contentment do they give, I betook myself to Lyons and found myself conveyed into the midst of sufferings so horrible, so cruelly distressed, that the sense of justice rose up within me and caused me inexpressible grief. What torture, my friend, is that of witnessing, with one's arms crossed over one's chest, the spectacle of an entire population struggling in vain against a misery that gnaws souls and bodies alike! of seeing old age without tranquillity, youth without hope, and childhood without joy! all crowded together in foul hovels, envying those among them who, for an insufficient wage, labour to adorn affluence and idleness! ... For, O fate's cruel mockery! he who has not a pillow to rest his head makes, with his hands, the splendid tapestries on which slumbers the rich man's indolence; he who has only rags to cover his nakedness weaves the gold brocades that array queens; and those children at whom their mothers never smile, standing near the looms over which they bend, fasten a lustreless eye on the arabesques and flowers that come into being between their fingers and go to serve as playthings for the children of the world's great. O harsh law of social fatality! whenever will thy bronze tablets be broken by the angel of wrath?[2]

This cry for social justice and freedom is mirrored in the music of *Lyon* with its violent passion, *Marseillaise*-like exhilaration, revolutionary harmony and rhetorical gestures.

An elaborate offshoot of the Swiss travels is the *Fantaisie romantique sur deux mélodies suisses* (1836), which is linked melodically with the second of the *Fleurs mélodiques* and with the later *Le mal du pays*.

Studies

The *12 Études* published in 1826 when Liszt was fourteen are of intrinsic value and interest in addition to their being the basis of the *Grandes Études* of 1837 and the further revision – *Études d'exécution transcendante* of 1851.[3] Although the boy's ambition to emulate Bach's '48' was limited to only six major and six minor key studies, he created within these tender romantic essays the basis for a pilgrimage through keyboard technique that stretches

[2] Quoted and translated by Alexander Main: 'Liszt's *Lyon* – Music and the Social Conscience' in *19th Century Music*, 1981, IV, no. 3, 228–43.

[3] Ramann quotes 1849 as the year of the last revision: *Lisztiana*, 387.

for a quarter century. The key scheme descends through the circle of 5ths and remains constant in the three versions, although the titles appeared only in the final set:

(1) C major   *Preludio*
(2) A minor   Untitled
(3) F major   *Paysage*
(4) D minor   *Mazeppa*
(5) B flat major   *Feux Follets*
(6) G minor   *Vision*
(7) E flat major   *Eroica*[4]
(8) C minor   *Wilde Jagd*
(9) A flat major   *Ricordanza*
(10) F minor   Untitled
(11) D flat major   *Harmonies du soir*[4]
(12) B flat minor   *Chasse-neige*

In the early set he contrives to make each study musically interesting as well as of technical value; each has an emotional content that he was able to intensify in the later versions. Among the many features of the 1826 group: (1) is a broken chord study with different patterns of busy semiquaver figuration; (2), broken octaves, fingering, staccato; (3), cantabile with a variety of legato broken chord accompaniment; (4), successions of parallel 3rds, accuracy in crossing and positioning hands; (5), highly ornamented rhythmic figuration, with characterful use of diminished 7th chords; (6), independence of the hands; (7), another cantabile study through rich chord textures, use of the pedal; (8), scales, strengthening the left hand; (9), a wonderful melodic study in finger equalisation, trills and filigree decoration, prefiguring Chopin – whom Liszt was not to hear until six years after publication of these Études (see Ex. 25); (10), sparkling triplets, witty use of changing hand positions; (11), the only version of this study has a delicate charm with its floating theme in the upper register, melody and accompaniment in the same hand, enhanced by chromatic touches, and pedal-notes in the left hand; (12), another cantabile study with special emphasis on tone gradation and inner passage work.

These children fathered the severe and mighty *Grandes*

[4]In the first set the E flat major study is a preliminary version of *Harmonies du soir*. The original D flat Étude was not revised, and *Eroica* first appeared as a new study in E flat major in the 1837 set.

Ex. 25

Allegro grazioso

p con leggierezza

Études, crowded with hitherto unimagined difficulties for the player to surmount. Liszt at the summit of his powers sets out to cover systematically the whole spectrum of the instrument's possibilities. He dedicated the set to his former master Czerny. In pruning the profusion of intricate effects for the Weimar version Liszt perhaps went too far and the last set loses many rhythmic subtleties that enhance the 1837 studies. A comparison of the three stages of composition provides a valuable illustration of Liszt's methods.[5] Example 26 shows *Vision* in its 1826 and 1837 versions (in the second version Liszt asks the player to take all the notes in the left hand alone!).

The union of poetic conception and technical mastery was Liszt's ultimate aim. He adopted a freer approach than Chopin had in his op. 10 and op. 25 studies. In the final version the Transcendental Studies may be briefly summarised: (1) retains its improvised, introductory character; (2), a Paganini-like display of brilliance (Louis Kentner has suggested the appropriate title

[5] The three versions are found in the Breitkopf Collected Edition. Regrettably the 1837 versions are omitted in NE.

224

Diablerie) with imitation of multiple stoppings, ricochet bowings, etc., and with the repeated pedal-note E creating some spectacular discords (bars 61–4); (3), an evocative pastoral landscape painting; (4), in fact the fourth version of this study as Liszt wrote an

Ex. 26

(continued overleaf)

intermediate version in 1840, and the material was also incorporated in the symphonic poem *Mazeppa*; (5), a shimmering and delicate *Will-o'-the-Wisp*; (6), a compound arpeggio study developed symphonically to the broadest limits of the keyboard; (7), a brilliant octave study cast as an heroic march; (8) contrasts the furious, wild chase of savage, syncopated ideas with passages of tender lyric expressiveness; 'a bundle of yellowed love-letters' was Busoni's apt description for (9), and he suggested *Appassionata* for the very fine F minor (10), whose agitated but logically expanded growth in tension demands qualities of restraint, and skill in gauging the contours of the music, lest the result descend into mere violent display; (11), the last remarks are equally pertinent to this study which has often been compared to Debussy and Rakhmaninov in its use of chords, textures, pedalling and the sustained glow of evening calm which it radiates; (12), frequently regarded as the profoundest and most impressive of the set, a masterly study in tremolo, a poetic vision of a landscape transformed slowly by the drifting snow.

The six *Grandes Études de Paganini* similarly exist in two versions: the 1851 set (most usually heard today) is a much simplified version of the *Études d'exécution transcendante d'après Paganini* of 1838–9 (published 1840). For the derivation of each item from Paganini's originals see No. 252 of Appendix B (the first study has a cadenza-prelude taken from Paganini's A minor Caprice No. 5). Throughout his Paganini Studies Liszt again displays his mastery as a transcriber: his superb skill in transferring the content and the technical aspects of a solo violin Caprice into pianistic terms, and his rigorousness in perfecting the ideal solution. In No. 4, for example, he gave two versions in his 1840 edition, each presenting a different piano reading of Paganini's original which consisted of arpeggios divided across the strings (see Ex. 27). Later in version II Liszt adds a new counterpoint in the left hand, with its own chordal accompaniment (see Ex. 28). In 1851 however, Liszt's simple solution is to present Paganini's Caprice largely as he wrote it, using a single stave, the notes divided between the hands (see Ex. 29). The 1851 version of No. 5 (Paganini's *La Chasse*) similarly returned to a closer imitation of its originator. No. 3, the popular *La Campanella*, is a study in wide leaps, rapid note re-iteration, trills and repeated octaves, with showering cascades of chromatic scales: it is most effective when the player carefully observes that the 1851 version is neither *animato* nor *fortissimo* until the last 11 bars. In the final *Étude* Liszt faithfully transcribes Paganini's variations on the famous theme elaborated by many subsequent composers, notably Brahms and Rakhmaninov.

In 1840 Liszt wrote a single study *Morceau de salon, Étude de Perfectionnement* for a publication by Fétis, *Méthode des Méthodes de piano*. In 1852 he revised it as *Ab Irato* ('in a rage'). A forceful, impetuous triplet study in E minor, both versions contain a theme (at the change to E major) which is used in *Les Préludes* (bar 346 in the symphonic poem).

Trois Études de Concert, published in 1849, were in a subsequent edition more fancifully named *Trois Caprices poétiques: Il lamento, La leggierezza, Un sospiro* – titles that have lingered to this day and certainly characterise the poetic mood of each. Chopin may be said to have invented the 'concert study' with his Études op. 10 (published in 1833 and dedicated to Liszt), although Liszt was the first to use the term. As with the 12 Études in their mature versions, these are pieces for players of well-developed technique who have transcended the schoolroom-exercise 'study'. There is a distinct echo of Chopin in No. 2 (see Ex. 30). The right hand soon teases out its material into a delicately floating thread of *leggiero* semiquavers. *Un sospiro* is one of Liszt's best-loved

Liszt

Ex. 27

(a)

(b)

Ex. 28

Ex. 29

Ex. 30

creations with its winning melodic idea, achieved at the opening by alternating hands (see Ex. 31). The last twelve bars provide a striking sequence of root position chords (see Ex. 32). In later life he suggested an even bolder alternative to the last 5 bars (see Ex. 33).[6]

Liszt's last two Concert Studies were written for Lebert and Stark's *Klavierschule* and published in 1863. Again his poetic titles

[6] Given in Ramann, *Liszt Pädagogium*, Leipzig, 1901.

Ex. 31

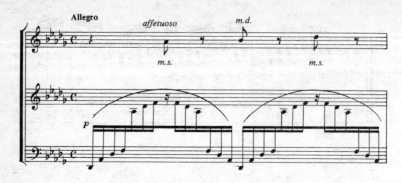

conjure up the mood of each: *Waldesrauschen* (Forest Murmurs) and *Gnomenreigen* (Dance of the Gnomes). In evoking the voices of the woodland it is the delicate nuance of the shimmering accompaniment figures (legato and carefully pedalled) that is all-important, and when the impish elemental creatures steal upon the scene in the second Puckish scherzo, the lightest and most crisp melodic staccato, with minimum pedal, will achieve the required fragile, playful effect.

From 1868 Liszt worked on a huge project of technical studies of a quite different sort from those considered above. These were exercises, a method in the pure mechanics of keyboard playing. But as the 'method' was by the most renowned pianist of the century, as it was admirably thorough and copious in length (over 450 pages in the latest edition), it was of immense significance.

Ex. 32

Ex. 33

Writing in his study of Liszt's music in 1954 Searle remarked, 'It seems extraordinary that this exposition of the technique of piano-playing, by one who was perhaps the greatest master of the art who has ever lived, has not come into general use at colleges and academies.' The reasons for the neglect of the complete set are several. Parts 1 and 2 of the Technical Exercises (divided into twelve paper-bound volumes) were first published by Liszt's pupil Alexander Winterberger shortly after the master's death in 1886. This edition (by no means free from printing errors) was never republished and scattered copies became difficult to obtain. An edition of 1910 by Martin Krause, based on the 1886 edition, was unsatisfactorily abbreviated in scope. Rumour then circulated of a missing third part, consisting of '12 grosse Etüden', which had disappeared with Liszt's notorious erstwhile pupil Olga Janina. The mystery was not resolved until 1975 when the Goethe and Schiller Archiv in Weimar purchased some Liszt manuscripts which proved to be the long-lost continuation of the Technical Exercises.[7] Thus only in 1983 was Liszt's great pedagogical work made available in a complete and reliable edition in three volumes (Editio Musica Budapest, edited by Imre Mező): volumes 1 and 2 contain six books each, corresponding to Winterberger's twelve volumes; volume 3 contains the missing '12 grosse Etüden', i.e. twelve more sections of advanced exercises. The whole set could and should at last be taken up by academies and colleges. For among the many 'methods' of the nineteenth century, and those added since to the piano-teaching repertoire, Liszt's *magnum opus* (when intelligently practised with varied rhythms, accents and the use of all dynamic ranges) ranks as an invaluable lexicon of manual devices, and can be approached at many levels of ability.

Hungarian works

In this section mention will be made of early works in Hungarian idiom (from the 1820s to the 1840s) and the sets of pieces that form the basis of the Hungarian Rhapsodies Nos. 1–15. Hungarian elements are, of course, found in many piano works and transcriptions too numerous to itemise here. Hungarian works of the late period (dances, elegies and the Rhapsodies 16–19) are included in the last section of the chapter.

Hungarian composers and characteristic national airs and dances emerged during the sixteenth century, although Turkish influence was then pervasive too. In the eighteenth century a number of picturesque national dances developed, notably the *verbunkos* (draft or recruiting dance), performed by soldiers in full uniform with swords and spurs. It consisted of 2 sections, slow

---

[7] See note 16 to the editorial preface of the 1983 edition. For a selection of the Exercises see *The Liszt Studies*, ed. Mach, Associated Music Publishers, New York, 1973. (The latter also contains the Boissier diary.)

(*lassu*) and fast, often very wild (*friss*). Haydn, Mozart, Beethoven, Weber and Schubert (and many of their contemporaries) wrote pieces in the fashionable style *All' ongarese*, and Brahms too profitably explored the *verbunkos* idiom. In Hungary the gypsies became the chief executants, propagators and developers of this musical style, but they were not its creators. Virtuoso use of the violin was a strong feature of this dance music and this was enhanced in the gypsy treatment, together with the addition of the gypsy scale (see Ex. 8) and elements of improvisation and rubato. So the style became dubbed 'Gypsy' or 'Hungarian', the use of both words becoming carelessly synonymous. A nineteenth-century style of dance and song, the *Csárdás*, was a development of the *verbunkos*. In duple time, it retained the slow and fast structure. Liszt was instinctively drawn to and captivated by the character of the gypsy; and he found many attractive features in the style of gypsy music: its intuitive, versatile and spontaneous nature, its contrasts in mood from deep melancholy to wild joy, the use of rubato, portamento, ornamentation and free cadenzas, the distinctive sound of the cimbalom and the great art of improvisation in ensemble.

Modern Hungarian scholars, such as Ervin Major and Zoltán Gárdonyi, have shown that the origins of what Liszt understood to be 'gypsy' music actually lie in fashionable pieces composed largely by members of the Hungarian middle class in the late eighteenth and early nineteenth century. These had been taken up by the gypsies and refashioned in their characteristic way – sometimes embellished beyond point of recognition. Liszt's errors on the subject of Hungarian music have caused much scholarly debate. But they are historically excusable as (not having the advantage of twentieth-century scholarship) he did not know the true source of the material that so excited him, and could not know of the existence of a quite different ethnic Hungarian music entirely beyond his experience. His sin of commission was to declare that the gypsies were the principal creators of Hungarian folk music. His sin of omission was to remain ignorant of a genuine folk tradition existing in rural Hungary, which had no connection with the gypsies. In his lifetime his theory that the gypsies represented true Hungarian music created a furore. After his death the scientific researches of Bartók and Kodály revealed the existence of an ancient, orally-transmitted Magyar tradition. For a while the romantic 'gypsy rhapsodies' fell into disrepute. Yet Kodály and

Bartók were great enough to realise the importance of Liszt's historical position in Hungarian music. Kodály made a particularly interesting observation:

> Liszt might well have become the first Hungarian folksong collector and researcher. In 1838 he writes:[8] 'It was my intention to go into the most backward districts of Hungary ... alone, on foot, with a knapsack on my back. But it came to naught.' It is startling to think where we should be today, had he carried out a task that has taken almost a century to complete! But even if his passing fancy had been transformed into reality, it is clear that he could not have been entirely successful. It was immensely difficult for persons from the cultured classes of the nineteenth century to approach the peasants.[9]

Of Bartók's two important essays on Liszt of 1911 and 1936 the latter[10] is much concerned with Liszt and Hungary and contends, like Kodály, that any true folklore research on Liszt's part would have been impossible in the prevailing social conditions; indeed

> in Liszt's time, folklore as a branch of learning did not exist at all. Nobody then had any idea that the study of problems in this field required hard work, scientific methods and the collection of facts from the widest possible first-hand experience ... All the notions of that time concerning folk music were of the most primitive kind or quite erroneous ... they knew absolutely nothing of the nature, the possibilities, and the significance of borrowed influences in folk music. This is the reason why not even Liszt could see such questions clearly, especially such a complicated one as that of the origin of gypsy music.

With regard to Liszt's taste in his more popular and brilliant piano works Bartók wrote:

> I must stress that the rhapsodies – particularly the Hungarian ones – are perfect creations of their own kind. The material that Liszt uses in them could not be treated with greater artistry and beauty. That the material itself is not always of value is quite another matter, and is obviously one reason why the general importance of the works is slight, and their popularity great.

The fact that the occasional genuine peasant song 'discovered' by Bartók had also found its way into Liszt's Rhapsodies does not alter the general position outlined above.

[8] Open letter to Massart. GS, II,225, and Chantavoine, *Pages romantiques*, 235.
[9] Kodály, *Folk Music of Hungary*, English edition, Budapest, 1982, 16. Kodály was writing in 1937.
[10] 'Liszt Problems' in Bartók, *Essays*, London, 1976, 501–10.

A Hungarian work associated with Liszt as early as his Pest performances of May 1823 is the famous *Rákóczy March*. Much later it was the basis of the Hungarian Rhapsody No. 15. Liszt also made an orchestral arrangement of it, and in turn, versions for two pianos and four hands at one piano. In the new edition of the piano works there are no less than six versions of the *Rákóczy March* for solo piano, in addition to the fifteenth Rhapsody.

His first extant Hungarian pieces are two short movements, slow and fast, based on melodies by Bihary and Csermák, dated 1828 with the title *Zum Andenken* (In memory). The Magyar cadence at bar 20 will be met with many times in later Liszt:

Ex. 34

These pieces were not published in Liszt's lifetime; nor were two incomplete ones 'in Hungarian style' of *c*. 1840, of which the first is an extended fragment in B flat minor, in several sections, which runs to 229 bars: it was published by the Liszt Society in 1954 with a concert ending by Louis Kentner. To 1840 belongs a *Heroic March in Hungarian Style*, later expanded in the symphonic poem *Hungaria*.

The antecedents of the Hungarian Rhapsodies Nos. 1–15 are eleven pieces published in Vienna in 1840 and 1843 under the title *Magyar Dallok* (Hungarian National Melodies). The series was continued with six more works (Nos. 12–17) published in 1847, now with the title *Magyar Rapszódiák* (Hungarian Rhapsodies). Four more pieces of this series (Nos. 18–21) were not published in Liszt's lifetime. In 1847 another piece, *Pester Karneval*, appeared.

Liszt then withdrew these twenty-two pieces and incorporated most of their material in the later series of Hungarian Rhapsodies, of which Nos. 1, 2 and 15 were published in 1851 and Nos. 3–14 in 1853. (For the connections between the earlier pieces and the definitive Hungarian Rhapsodies, see Nos. 255 and 287 of Appendix B. Of *Magyar Dallok*, Nos. 1–3, 6 and 8–10, were not re-used and have been republished in recent years.)

Liszt's aim in the Hungarian Rhapsodies Nos. 1–15 was to reproduce the style of gypsy bands, details of whose playing he had noted in his sketchbooks on visits to Hungary. He was particularly anxious to capture specific qualities of metre, rhythm, rubato, nuance, as well as melody, ornamentation and harmonic structure. The frequent marking *a capriccio* in the rhapsodies denotes metrical irregularity. Liszt devised numerous ways of notating free note-values, and he frequently departs from the given time signature in order to accommodate irregular note-patterns (e.g. bars 12 and 24 of No. 13). A typical cimbalom effect, together with the use of the gypsy scale and a hint of violin cadenza, are contained in 3 bars from the third Rhapsody:

Ex. 35

The origins, evolution and varied forms of these works are a complex but fascinating separate study. The signs are that, after excessive popularity and extreme misunderstanding, the Hungarian Rhapsodies are again being regarded as legitimate works in which Liszt, through the piano, interpreted a valuable legacy known to him and which – were it not for him – would otherwise be lost to us.

The Weimar period

The set of ten *Harmonies poétiques et religieuses*, published in 1853 and dedicated to Princess Sayn-Wittgenstein, consists mainly of pieces evolved over a long period or conceived originally for another medium. The general mood is of resignation and meditation and echoes the Lamartine verses which inspired Liszt. The first piece, *Invocation*, written in 1847 and later considerably expanded, is headed by two verses of Lamartine which begin: 'Arise, voice of my soul/With the dawn, with the night'. Its main ascending idea is akin to several melodies of aspiration in Liszt's religious works, such as the often-used 'cross' motif. Nos. 2, 5, 6 and 8 are transcriptions of sacred choral pieces. No. 3, *Bénédiction de Dieu dans la solitude*, No. 4, *Pensée des morts*, and No. 7, *Funérailles*, are the most interesting pieces in the collection. In No. 3 Liszt creates a remarkable sense of sustained tranquillity over a lengthy ABA + coda structure. Its Lamartine preface begins, 'Whence comes, O God, this peace which overwhelms me?/Whence comes this faith with which my heart overflows?' The musical response to these lines has been compared to later evocations of mystical serenity by Franck and Messiaen. No. 4 is an expanded and more conventional treatment of the 1833 piece (discussed earlier) whose title is now given to the whole set; it also incorporates material from an unpublished composition for piano and orchestra, *De profundis*. No. 7 bears the subtitle 'October 1849' and is a threnody, akin in spirit to his later elegiac works. Like many of those subsequent funeral pieces, the monumental *Funérailles* has a Hungarian connection: on 6 October 1849 the Austrian General Haynau executed thirteen generals who fought for the cause of Hungarian independence; also shot was the moderate minister Batthyány. The date was forever blackly imprinted on the national mind. At the start of his elegy Liszt creates the impression of deep, clamorous bells. After the introduction three main sections follow: a moving minor lament followed by a poignantly contrasted major section (bar 56), and a noble fanfare idea over repeated triplet patterns (bar 109) that reaches a huge climax with no sense of bombast. The three sections are then recapitulated in a much shortened form. October 1849 also saw Chopin's death, and some commentators have associated the work with that event, too, citing the strong resemblance of the section beginning at bar 109 to the famous central part of Chopin's A flat Polonaise, with its repeated left-hand octave patterns.

Whether or not this work was conceived partly as a tribute to Chopin, it is certainly true that some of Liszt's piano music of this time adopts characteristics and even forms used by his friend. No. 2 of *Glanes de Woronince* (published 1849) uses Chopin's song *Życzenie* (1829) as its central section, and for introduction and coda a Polish tune which Liszt had also incorporated in his Chopin-based Duo-Sonata for violin and piano and which has recently surfaced in a Chopin autograph.[11] The Chopinesque quality of the concert study *La leggierezza* has already been noted. Of the *Ballades*, the first predates Chopin's death, the second (and greater) one belongs to 1853: neither is particularly in the mould of Chopin. Nor in Liszt's two *Polonaises* (1851) is the Pole's influence evident beyond use of rhythm and form.[12] The second polonaise in E major is the more brilliant and popular of the two, but the C minor piece has many beautiful touches, especially in its major key sections. A *Mazurka brillante* of 1850 is nearer to Chopin in spirit, and with the first version of the *Berceuse* (1854; radically revised, 1862) Chopin's own example in the same key of D flat is a clear model. An earlier D flat major piece linked in style with the nocturnes of Chopin is No. 3 of Liszt's *Consolations*. The title of these six short pieces was suggested by a cycle of poems by Sainte-Beuve. Their easy approachability and fragile lyricism has ensured their enduring popularity.

Of several dances and marches of this period the *Valse Impromptu*, with its playful, sparkling triplets and unpretentious melodic flow is a joyous and successful miniature. On a larger scale the rarely heard *Scherzo and March* looks forward to the macabre and mocking Mephisto atmosphere of many later pieces, and in its use of form shows Liszt's concern with remoulding sonata structure: development within the scherzo's sonata exposition, extended fugato treatment of the second subject in the

---

[11] Dates of the Duo-Sonata and the Chopin autograph are uncertain. See F. L. M. Pattison, 'A Folk Tune associated with Chopin and Liszt', JALS XX, Dec. 1986, 38–40.

[12] Liszt's involvement with his Polish princess at this period also explains these Polish-inspired forms.

development section, varied recapitulation, integration of the introduction figures throughout the scherzo and march, and (at bar 478, after the march) a recapitulation that reviews all that has gone before in an excitingly re-vitalised 142 bars. The neglect of this undoubtedly stirring, substantial work is perhaps because its overall striving for a new type of one-movement form is at the expense of its melodic interest. The *Grosses Konzertsolo*, written for an 1850 piano competition at the Paris conservatoire and dedicated to Adolf Henselt, also shows him wrestling with a new type of one-movement form. From 1849 he was preoccupied in various sonata-type works with alternatives to the classical sonata form: incorporating the concept of a three- or four-movement form within one continuous structure, in which the characteristics of each movement correspond to the principal sections of sonata form. Vital to this scheme of telescoping several movements into one is his cyclical treatment of themes – thematic 'transformation' or 'metamorphosis'. The *Konzertsolo* was also arranged for piano and orchestra, and later for two pianos as the *Concerto pathétique*. It repays study as in both melody and form it anticipates the B minor sonata. Indeed a close examination of Liszt's different procedures in all the one-movement structures of the early Weimar years is rewarding and revealing. These integrated forms had a profound effect on the course of musical history. The main works are: *Bénédiction de Dieu, Pensée des morts, Funérailles, Ballade No. 2, Dante Sonata, Scherzo and March,* the *Konzertsolo* and the *Concerto Pathétique,* the two piano concertos, Schubert's 'Wanderer' Fantasy arranged for piano and orchestra, the *Ad nos* fantasy for organ and the early symphonic poems, especially *Prometheus* and *Tasso.* The finest example of one-movement form, and one which must be considered here, is Liszt's greatest large-scale piano work: the *Sonata in B minor.*

This historic musical landmark was the first nineteenth-century sonata in one movement, and the boldest, most significant advance in sonata form since Beethoven. The first seventeen bars of Liszt's masterpiece present three ideas (see Ex. 36). These motifs then combine in a constantly changing yet logical and coherent contrapuntal web, forming a main idea (entirely derived from Ex. 36 (b) and (c)) at bar 32 (see Ex. 37). Unfolding with increasingly dramatic momentum the energy at last propels itself to a dominant preparation of D major (bar 81) and the descending figures of Ex. 36(a) return, eventually heralding a new idea (see Ex. 38). Further gentle

Liszt

Ex. 36

(a)

Lento assai

p sotto voce

(b)

Allegro energico

f

(c)

f 3

unfolding of variants of Ex. 36(b) and (c) leads to another D major theme of exquisite expressive beauty (bar 153) (see Ex. 39). This sounds like, and functions as, a new 'second subject' idea, but is another metamorphosis of Ex. 36(c). An exciting development section commences at bar 205 in which all the themes stated so far are further expanded, merged anew and sculpted into fresh shapes. At bar 331, with the wonderful transition to F sharp major, the fifth and final theme of the sonata appears (see Ex. 40) and introduces a complete slow movement, which unfolds over a ravishing 130 bars. The development resumes with a scherzo-like fugato (bar 460). After seemingly inexhaustible permutations of Ex. 36(b) and (c) the recapitulation commences at bar 531 and Exs. 38 and 39 appear in the tonic B major (bars 600 and 616). This entire recapitulation, although compressed, is really another heightened development, with ideas arranged in new juxtapositions and the piano writing unfolding an ever richer and more wonderful web of textures and motivic strands. As the ultimate climax approaches the marking increases to Presto, and with the falling figures of bar 673 (from Ex. 36(a)) the coda begins.

Ex. 37

Ex. 38

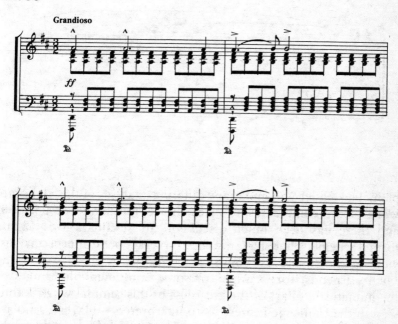

In a new guise, Ex. 36(b) blazes out in fiery intoxication (bar 682). After a tremendous statement of Ex. 38 a silence ensues and (at bar 711) the soft benediction of Ex. 40 ushers in a *sotto voce* review of all the elements that have been heard in the preceding drama. The final, gentle fifty bars are among the most haunting in all piano literature.

This bald outline is in no sense an analysis and takes little account of the complex thematic subdivisions and the subtle tonal

Ex. 39

plan. The reader will find many differing analyses of this elaborate work (some commentators place the recapitulation at bar 460) and there has been much discussion and evaluation of Liszt's formal scheme. There have also been several poetic interpretations, viewing the sonata as a musical treatment of the Faust or the Lucifer legends, for example, or some other symbolic drama of the human soul. Part of the greatness of this seminal work is thus seen in the challenge it presents to interpreters – players, scholars and listeners. But greater still is Liszt's art in unfolding such epoch-making sounds from the simplicity of his five basic cellular ideas. They have launched an unending quest for an understanding of the creative miracle. Without the B minor sonata many subsequent works of music might never have come to fruition.

The sonata was completed in February 1853. A remarkable extension of his thoughts in the same key of B minor is found in the Ballade No. 2 of the spring of that year. Again a poetic image has become associated with it: in this case the story of Hero and Leander. On a different level of approach the B minor Ballade is

Ex. 40

yet another one-movement drama which re-shapes sonata-form concepts.

Books I and II of the *Années de pèlerinage* contain some of the finest and most rewarding pieces of Romantic piano writing. The first year of pilgrimage – Switzerland – is based on pieces from the *Album d'un voyageur*, with the exceptions of *Églogue* and *Orage*. Refined and re-thought with maturity and perspective, they yet retain the freshness of the original conception and enshrine some central features of Romanticism: the desire to wander, the sense of not belonging to any one place, the search for the ideal landscape and, as well as outward roaming, the idea of the inward pilgrimage. Liszt's models are both visual and literary; a blend of descriptive pictorialism and personal, poetic response. In *The Chapel of William Tell* the Swiss struggle for liberation is recalled and Schiller's motto 'One for all – and all for one' heads the piece. A grand introduction presents the heroic main melody before an Alphorn sounds the signal for revolt which is echoed down through the valleys. From the 'allegro vivace' the mood recalls Liszt's *Lyon*, another illustration of his liberal sympathies. Nos. 2 and 4 are differing water-studies flanking a delightful vignette of pastoral life. *Au lac de Wallenstadt* (like Nos. 5, 6 and 9) bears a quotation from Byron:

> ... thy contrasted lake
> With the wild world I dwell in, is a thing
> Which warns me, with its stillness, to forsake
> Earth's troubled waters for a purer spring.

In her *Mémoires* Marie d'Agoult recalled that

> the shores of the lake of Wallenstadt kept us for a long time. Franz wrote for me there a melancholy harmony, imitative of the sigh of the waves and the cadence of oars, which I have never been able to hear without weeping.

Lines by Schiller preface *Au bord d'une source*: 'In murmuring coolness the play of young nature begins'. Cascades of gently sparkling major and minor seconds conjure up an effect of a magical water-scene. *Orage*, the central piece of the Swiss set, is an Alpine thunderstorm: a torrential octave study, full of Lisztian characteristics, both technical and melodic. (The opening is similar to that of *Malédiction* for piano and orchestra.) The greatest piece of Book I is *Vallée d'Obermann* which refers to the eponymous hero of Senancour's novel *Obermann*, a book that is set in Switzerland. The descending idea at the outset undergoes a series of transformations in the manner of a symphonic poem. For Obermann nature is overwhelming and impenetrable; for him all emotions are profound, all courses hidden, all purposes deceptive. The opening depicts this solitary abandon and wonderment. The increasingly radiant E major final section reflects Senancour's tenet that the only real truth lies in our inner feelings. Harmonically the piece is extremely interesting and bold. In complete contrast to this dark nocturnal confession of the soul, *Églogue* paints a picture of the freshness of dawn in the countryside, as Byron's lines proclaim:

> The morn is up again, the dewy morn,
> With breath all incense, and with cheek all bloom;
> Laughing the clouds away with playful scorn
> And living as if Earth contain'd no tomb!

A Swiss shepherd song is invoked to lead us into an untroubled, bucolic landscape. Similarly in *Le mal du pays* Liszt introduces a Ranz des Vaches to depict unspoiled country scenes, hidden sanctuaries, as Liszt remarks in a footnote, which are the last refuge of a free and simple mind. The sad, wistful tone of homesickness is a reflection of J. J. Rousseau's remark that the feared impact of the Ranz des Vaches upon Swiss mercenaries was so great that its playing was forbidden upon pain of death. The minor key tune gives way to brief major passages like glimpses of an unattainable realm of happiness. Another Byron motto prefaces *Les cloches de Genève*:

> I live not in myself, but I become
> Portion of that around me.

Again this gentle carillon complements perfectly the previous piece in the collection; its main melody is also similar in shape to that of the first piece; and it may not be too fanciful to hear in its echoes of Bellini a link with the second *Année*. Liszt never played the *Années* as continuous sets, but in design, patterns of contrast and key sequence, they suggest such an ideal approach.

The Italian *Année* (published 1858) has its origins in Liszt's further peregrinations with the Comtesse d'Agoult in the late 1830s. *Sposalizio* (1839), after Raphael's *Lo sposalizio della Vergine*, has a simple yet exalted quality. The pentatonic line of the first two bars becomes a vital element in the structure of the piece, and the sonorities look ahead to Debussy and Richard Strauss. *Il Penseroso* of the same year, after Michelangelo's famous statue in the Medici chapel, has these lines of Michelangelo as preface: 'I am thankful to sleep, and even more that I am made of stone, while injustice and shame still exist. My great fortune is not to see, not to feel; so do not wake me – speak softly!' The mood of tragic resignation is magnificently conveyed by the insistent use of monotone accompanied by extremely chromatic harmony. Towards the end some Wagnerian magical sleep-music is prefigured:

Ex. 41

The *Canzonetta del Salvator Rosa* is a robust and carefree
marching song based on a poem ascribed to the seventeenth-
century painter and adventurer; the tune is by Giovanni Bononcini
(1670–1747). Nos. 4–6, the *3 Petrarch Sonnets*, are transcriptions
of songs written by Liszt in 1844–5. In 1846 a piano arrangement
of the songs was published; the Italian *Année* contains the revised
versions of *c.* 1854. As always, Liszt quotes the poem with the
piano version. The three pieces are of intense poetic beauty and
rank among the finest lyric works of Liszt.

The key scheme of the pieces of the first two volumes of
Années de pèlerinage is, *Suisse*: C–A flat–E–A flat–C minor–E
minor/major–A flat–E minor–B; *Italie*: E–C sharp minor–A–D
flat–E–A flat–D minor. The sequence seems logical until the last
step: a tritone relationship. But it is this very interval that characterises the seventh and longest piece of the Italian book, whose
opening is a tritonal denial of its own tonality (see Ex. 42).

Après une lecture du Dante: Fantasia quasi sonata is Liszt's
title for the work familiarly referred to as the 'Dante Sonata'. The
French title is borrowed from a Victor Hugo poem. In Vienna on
5 December 1839 Liszt played a 'Fragment nach Dante' which may
have been the earliest form of the fantasia. Whatever its evolution,

Ex. 42

in the final result the invocation of Hugo appears to distance us from too specific a portrayal of Dante's world. A broad but vivid impression of *Inferno* is achieved through breathtaking use of keyboard effect and structural use of the tritone. (Note the use of that interval in the bass from bar 29 as the key of D minor is at last established.) Bar 25 ushers in the first subject, an agitated chromatic wailing of the shades, their outline blurred by Liszt's instruction of a sustained five-bar pedal. At bar 54 the lamentation intensifies (see Ex. 43). Two further themes grow from this idea: a mighty chorale decorated with precipitous double octaves (bar 103) and a more reflective expansion (bar 136). The repeated note idea common to both Exs. 42 and 43 re-occurs in the exquisite Francesca da Rimini episode (bar 157; and note the tritone relationship again with bar 163).

The revised version of *Venezia e Napoli* was published as a supplement to the Italian *Année*. The three pieces, *Gondoliera*, *Canzone* and *Tarantella*, are concert paraphrases of melodies by, respectively, Peruccini, Rossini (the gondolier's song from *Otello*, Act 3) and Cottrau. The first is a gentle barcarolle, the second is

247

Ex. 43

Liszt's last Rossini transcription and the third has deservedly become a popular virtuoso showpiece. The original *Venezia e Napoli* of *c.* 1840 consisted of four items of which Nos. 3 and 4 became the first and last of the revised set. The first piece of the original versions treated yet another gondolier's song, later used as the main theme of the symphonic poem *Tasso*.

The Roman years

In 1863 Liszt published a short *Prelude: Weinen, Klagen, Sorgen, Zagen,* and in the following year a set of *Variations* on the same theme from Bach. The two works were composed in 1859 and 1862. The theme comes from Bach's cantata *Weinen, Klagen* (BWV 12) where it appears as a poignant chromatic ground bass; Bach used the theme again for the 'Crucifixus' of the B minor Mass. As a ground bass it was a common musical device long before Bach (used famously by Purcell, for example), see Ex. 44(a). After a bold introduction based on the theme, Liszt begins his variations in the manner of a passacaglia but grows ever freer, both tonally and metrically. Their character is of intense inward suffering and anguish:

Ex. 44

(a)

(b)

The relief and firm hope of the final section, based on the chorale *Was Gott tut, das ist wohlgetan* (which also ends Bach's cantata), is achieved through the simple but effective return to solid diatonicism.

Liszt transcribed the *Weinen, Klagen* variations for organ. With another Bach-related fantasy involving extreme chromaticism the process was reversed. The *Prelude and Fugue on B–A–C–H* (B flat–A–C–B natural in German notation; a musical cryptonym used by Bach in *The Art of Fugue*, also used by Schumann, Reger and Busoni) was composed for organ in 1855. The piano version followed soon after and was later revised. It is chiefly remarkable for its effective transference of spectacular organ sonorities into the radically different sound world of the piano.

The most significant religious piano works of the Roman years are the *Deux Légendes*: (1) St Francis of Assisi preaching to the birds; (2) St Francis of Paola walking on the waves. They were known only as piano works for 120 years. In Berlin in October 1982 the première of the orchestral versions was given and internal evidence from the recently discovered scores suggested that the piano pieces were written shortly after the orchestral ones. The first Legend is more effective in its orchestral form, which may explain Liszt's apologetic preface to his piano score, with reference to his 'lack of ingenuity' and to the piano as 'an instrument so lacking in variety and tone colour' for the task in hand. John Ogdon has drawn attention to Liszt as precursor of Messiaen in notating birdsong in keyboard terms, and to the resemblance between this Legend and Messiaen's *Regard des Hauteurs*. In prefaces to the piano edition Liszt quotes the incidents from the lives of the saints depicted. St Francis of Assisi, beholding the multitude of birds by the wayside, marvelled and told his companions to wait while he went into the field, where 'he began to preach to the birds that were on the ground; and forthwith those which were in the trees came around him, and not one moved during the whole sermon; nor would they fly away until the saint had given them his blessing.' In this Legend Liszt uses a theme from his setting of St Francis' *Cantico del Sol*.

The second legend tells of St Francis of Paola, who was refused a crossing of the Straits of Messina by a ferryman who declared, 'If he is a saint, let him walk on the water'. Whereupon St Francis stepped upon the sea and crossed safely to the other side. Musically this is one of Liszt's finest pieces of descriptive writing and, in a similar way to the *Weinen, Klagen* variations, depicts the triumph of faith over seemingly overwhelming odds:

symbolised by the chromatic roar of the sea and the victorious quality of the diatonic chorale that develops from the opening bars.

Late works

In Chapter 6 the piano works cited were divided into two types – elegies and fantastic dances: a seemingly incongruous grouping and yet quite in keeping with the enigmatic Liszt of the last eighteen years of his life. Clearly not every work falls neatly into one or other category, and the eighty or so original piano pieces after 1868 can also be grouped as national works (pre-eminently Hungarian), descriptive 'nature' pieces, works of religious inspiration, nocturnes, purely 'abstract' rhythmic or harmonic studies, and so on. But the broad division of elegy- and dance-types is a helpful guide; and it is no more incongruous in the later years than it was in Liszt's twenties, when meditational, intensely mystical and death-laden piano scores were written alongside carefree waltzes and galops.

The *Années de pèlerinage: Troisième Année* consists of seven religious and elegiac pieces written between 1867 and 1877; it was published in 1883. This 'year' of pilgrimage is in great contrast to the earlier two: the path is now entirely reflective and inward. A simple, haunting evocation of the ringing of the *Angelus* prefaces the set. The next three pieces are impressionist paintings of the gardens of Liszt's favourite home in old age, the Villa d'Este. Two are entitled *Aux cyprès de la Villa d'Este: Thrénodie* and the third (the most famous piece of the collection) *Les jeux d'eaux à la Villa d'Este*. The first threnody is forbidding and stark; the second (originally inspired by the cypresses of Sta. Maria degli Angeli in Rome) seems to inhabit the realm of *Tristan*, Act 3. Liszt's most celebrated water-study, *The Fountains of the Villa d'Este*, opens with spectacular jets of water shooting upward, the distinctive colour of the harmonies creating impressionistic imagery that anticipates Debussy and Ravel (*cf.* the latter's own *Jeux d'eau*). Over the passage beginning at bar 144 Liszt quotes Christ's words from St John's Gospel, 4, 14: '... the water that I shall give him shall be in him a well of water springing up into everlasting life'. *Sunt lacrymae rerum* ('The source of tears in mortal things' – Matthew Arnold) takes its title from Virgil, where it refers to the fall of Troy. Liszt applies it to his native Hungary (the subtitle reads 'in Hungarian style') thinking especially of the 1849 defeat for independence. Considerable use is made of the scale with two augmented seconds, and the main melody is characterised by declamatory falling fourths. The *Marche funèbre* for Emperor Maximilian of Mexico is, until the F sharp major peroration, extremely bold harmonically. Dating from 1867 (the year of Maximilian's execution) it is the earliest piece in the set and a striking forerunner of the highly experimental use of ambiguous tonality and spare textures (frequently reduced to a single line of recitative) that characterise Liszt's music for the next two decades. The final piece, *Sursum Corda* ('Lift up your hearts') is chiefly remarkable for its musical symbolism: the rising 7th, some audacious whole-tone harmony and the prolonged use of a pedal-note E.

Weinachtsbaum (or 'Christmas Tree Suite') consists of twelve pieces. Nos. 1–9 are specifically associated with Christmas: transcriptions of old carols including *In dulci jubilo* and *Adeste Fideles*, two bell-studies *Carillon* and *Evening Bells* and a tiny scherzo, *Lighting the Candles on the Tree*. The last three pieces of this uneven set are, according to Humphrey Searle,[13] associated with Liszt and the princess. A nostalgic slow waltz, No. 10, *Jadis*, is a recollection of their first meeting; No. 11, *Ungarisch* (a march in Hungarian style), is a self-portrait; and No. 12, *Polnisch* (a mazurka), portrays Carolyne. Economy and simplicity are the hallmarks of the whole collection, which Liszt dedicated to his grand-daughter Daniela von Bülow.

5 Little Piano Pieces (dedicated to Olga von Meyendorff, composed 1865–1879 but not published in Liszt's lifetime) are all charming miniatures, easily accessible in their simplicity. No. 1 is a facilitated version of the second *Liebestraum*. Nos. 3 and 4 are particularly delightful microcosmic studies of 3rds and 6ths; their conciseness is akin to the *Kleines Klavierstück* Op. 19 No. 2 by Schoenberg. The last of the set, *Sospiri!*, which begins and ends on a diminished seventh chord, is entirely derived from the cellular ideas of its first three bars.

The *Historical Hungarian Portraits* are elegies in tribute to seven of Liszt's greatest contemporary compatriots:

---

[13] *The Music of Liszt*, 110.

1. Stephan Széchenyi, politician
2. Joseph Eötvös, politician
3. Michael Vörösmarty, poet
4. Ladislaus Teleki, politician
5. Franz Deák, politician
6. Alexander Petőfi, poet
7. Michael Mosonyi, composer

The last piece is the finest and one of Liszt's best essays in heroic oratory. Nos. 1–5 are characteristic of his late Hungarian style. No. 4 contains the second part of the *Trauervorspiel und Trauermarsch* in which an ostinato bass (F sharp–G–B flat–C sharp), relentlessly repeated in what would now be termed 'minimalist' style, creates some amazing and violent effects.

The last four *Hungarian Rhapsodies*, unlike the earlier fifteen, are not based on pre-existing Hungarian material, but are a synthesis of Liszt's own perception of Hungarian styles. The exception to this is No. 19 which is based on melodies by Ábrányi. Rhapsodies 16–19 do, however, retain the slow-fast structure that was the general feature of the group composed three decades earlier. (No. 16 has a fast introduction.) No. 17 is especially daring harmonically, with much use of augmented chords, chords built in fourths, chords of the ninth, etc. Liszt sets out the concise and polished material of his *5 Hungarian Folksongs* in a vein of straightforward simplicity that anticipates Bartók. Bartók is also foreshadowed in Liszt's inclusion of the texts of Nos. 2–5.

Use of ostinato and rigorously developed units of a very few notes are features of all the *Csárdás* pieces of the 1880s. The opening of *Csárdás obstiné* also employs a favourite late device of major and minor thirds juxtaposed (see Ex. 45). The *Csárdás macabre* plays with sequences of bare parallel fifths for 27 consecutive bars (see Ex. 46). Ironically aware of the reaction this novelty would provoke, Liszt wrote on his score, 'Is one permitted to write such a thing, or to listen to it?' (The piece was not published until 1950.) The theme at bar 163 is based on a popular folk-style melody of the time. The other dance fantasies of the last years are the four *Valses oubliées*, the *Mephisto Waltzes* Nos. 3 and 4, the *Mephisto Polka* and the *Bagatelle without tonality*. All these pieces are rich in examples of Liszt's late harmonic, melodic and rhythmic experiments as described in Chapter 9. The first *Valse oubliée* has attained some popularity, but No. 4 literally

Ex. 45

Ex. 46

remained a 'forgotten waltz' until its publication in 1954. Although Scriabin cannot have known this piece the prolongation of unresolved harmony from bar 105 is markedly prophetic of him. The second *Valse oubliée* is the most fascinating in terms of rhythm. The third *Mephisto Waltz* is also Scriabinesque, and looks beyond him in its chordal constructions of fourths (see Ex. 47).

The *Bagatelle*, it can be argued, does stay within the confines of functional tonality. But the curious, ambivalent, rootless and suspended quality Liszt aims for is effectively conjured up by his use of the diminished fifth, the diminished seventh chord, augmented triads and the 'cancelling-out' effect of, for example, the F and F sharp in the last two bars of Ex. 48. The closing sequence is an ascending series of diminished triads, and the piece ends in mid-air (see Ex. 49).

The remaining nocturnal and elegiac pieces of the final years have evocative titles. The first version of *La lugubre gondola* (again a water study, but of quite a different order from *Les jeux d'eaux* or the second Francis Legend) was a remarkable premonition of Wagner's death in Venice. Its second version belongs to 1885 and Liszt's reworking of the idea of waters gently lapping against the funeral gondola makes a fascinating study. These pieces have a disturbing and sometimes bizarre effect. Two contrasted nocturnes, *En rêve* and *Schlaflos: Frage und Antwort* explore different aspects of the night, consciousness and the unconscious.

Ex. 47

Unstern! is a Mephistophelean miniature with structural use of the 'diabolic' augmented 4th and some cataclysmic dissonance (see Ex. 50). *Nuages gris* is the masterpiece of this group. It progresses from a bleak and angular first phrase and, after an impression of mist through shifting augmented harmonies, drifts along gloomily (see Ex. 51) and then dreamily, to its final floating 'cadence' (see Ex. 10).

Liszt

Ex. 48

Ex. 49

256

Ex. 50

Ex. 51

12

Concertos

Two piano concertos of *c.* 1825 mentioned in Adam Liszt's correspondence have not survived, so their content and connection with any later works is unknown. It is unsurprising that the prodigy-composer had such concertos in his repertoire. What may surprise is that Liszt did not publish any concerto-type works until the 1850s, some years after ending his virtuoso career. But, as with much of the piano output already discussed, the works known as the Concerto No. 1 in E flat and the Concerto No. 2 in A were evolved over many years (sketches exist for them at Weimar from the early 1830s) before eventual publication in their final form: No. 1 in 1857 and No. 2 in 1863.

Apart from a few piano transcriptions which Liszt is known to have played in versions with piano and orchestra (*Hexaméron* for example) the other concerto works consist of five arrangements (of Berlioz, Beethoven, Weber, Schubert and one on Hungarian themes) and two items which fall into the category of the fantastic and macabre (i.e. related in mood to the various 'Mephisto' essays for piano or orchestra): *Malédiction* and *Totentanz*. Two unfinished and unpublished compositions complete the list of piano-concerto works: *De Profundis: Psaume instrumental* (which is so nearly complete that Searle considered that 'with a little ingenuity it might be possible to complete the score'[1]) and the version for piano and orchestra of the *Grosses Konzertsolo* (which Searle and Gustave de Mauny edited for performance in 1949).

All Liszt's piano-concerto works are continuous, effectively one-movement structures. They again demonstrate his fascination with formal variety within the sonata and variation principles. In an essay on Schumann's piano works (1837)[2] Liszt made special

---

[1] *The Music of Liszt*, 13. The work is described by P. Merrick in *Revolution and Religion in the Music of Liszt*, 20ff, and analysed by K.T. Johns in JALS, XV, June 1984, 96–104.
[2] GS, II, 99–107.

note of the title of Schumann's *Concert sans orchestre* op. 14 (later known as the Sonata in F minor) and its formal implications. He also cited novelties in concerto construction by Field (the introduction of an Adagio in the first movement of his last Concerto in C minor), Moscheles (the unity of three movements as one in his *Concert fantastique* op. 90), Weber, Mendelssohn and Herz.

Malédiction for piano and string orchestra was discovered in manuscript, and without title, after Liszt's death, and published in 1915. The word *malédiction* was written by Liszt over the opening bars for piano solo:

Ex. 52

This astonishingly bold 'curse' motif was used again in *Prometheus Unbound* (Liszt's choruses for Herder's drama) at the moment where the female chorus of Oceanides call down curses upon Prometheus (*cf.* also the opening of the symphonic poem *Prometheus* and of the piano piece *Orage*). The tritone which is implicit in the first two bars (the notes F and B) is exploited in bars 7–15, which startlingly juxtapose the chords of F major and B major. Over the theme at bar 16 Liszt wrote *orgueil*:

Ex. 53

This 'pride' motif occurs again in the 'Mephisto' movement of the

Faust Symphony (bar 188) where it is the only theme that is not a parody of Faust's themes from the first movement. Other programmatic markings by Liszt are the words *Pleurs-angoisse-songes* (tears, fears, dreams) over the passage beginning at bar 68, and *raillerie* (jesting, mocking) at bar 118. The profuse and evocative expression markings are further evidence that he had a programme in view when composing this piece. Its broad progress is a steady darkness-into-light, E minor into E major, through several episodes contrasted in mood. Despite the rather primitive scoring for strings this earliest extant concerto by Liszt is highly effective in performance.

In *Totentanz*, an altogether more tightly constructed work, we meet another important musical symbol for Liszt: the melody of the *Dies Irae* plainchant, on which this 'dance of death' is an elaborate set of free and most imaginative variations. He wrote it in 1849, although its conception dates from ten years before; it was revised prior to publication in 1865, and he also arranged it for two pianos and for piano solo. (For the possible sources of its inspiration see page 46, and for details of premières of all the Weimar period concerto works see page 103.) The opening statement of the theme by clarinets, bassoons, trombones, tuba and lower strings, accompanied by a grim, relentless, percussive tread of chords deep in the piano's bass register and reinforced by timpani, is followed (as in *Malédiction*) by a cadenza of startling dissonance and power – a truly fiendish flourish. After an orchestral introduction based on the theme and a statement of the melody by the piano alone, Liszt proceeds with a set of five numbered variations from bar 51. The fifth is a fugato which is extended into an increasingly free series of variations. About three-quarters of the way through the work (at letter H) a new eight-note theme is introduced, similar in shape to the *Dies Irae* melody, and this inaugurates a fresh set of variations which fall into more or less regular sixteen-bar patterns. After a final cadenza the original melody returns in a *tutti* passage. *Totentanz* is one of Liszt's most colourful works, ranging in hue from the sinister and grotesque to the light, disembodied and fantastical. It is a *tour-de-force* of piano writing and well matched in quality of instrumentation, especially for woodwind and brass.

Among Liszt's earliest works for piano and orchestra is the *Grande Fantaisie Symphonique* on themes from Berlioz' *Lélio* (1834), as yet published only in two-piano reduction. It is based on two themes from *Lélio*: the setting of Goethe's *Der Fischer* and the 'Chorus of Brigands'. The orchestration is competent but timid; the piano writing (especially in the later stages) is, conversely, advanced almost to excess. As with *Malédiction*, it must be regretted that Liszt did not revise this score, for it contains much that is enjoyable and lyrically effective. It deserves occasional revival especially, perhaps, as the peculiar demands of the Berlioz original have prohibited *its* regular performance.

Another work of the 1830s (but revised in 1849 and for publication in 1865) merits an occasional hearing for similar reasons: the *Fantasy on Beethoven's 'Ruins of Athens'*. (In 1846 Liszt also made a transcription for piano solo, *Capriccio alla turca*, from Beethoven's incidental music to Kotzebue's play; this is an entirely different work.) Apart from the Overture and the Turkish March, little is heard of Beethoven's score today. Liszt's delightful adaptation incorporates the priests' chorus *Schmückt die Altäre* and the 'Chorus of Dervishes' as well as the Turkish March, which is cleverly combined towards the close with the priests' chorus.

With the two adaptations for piano and orchestra of piano solo works by Weber and Schubert (both transcribed in the early Weimar years) Liszt took care to preserve the piano style of the original composers. Even the orchestration of the *Polonaise brillante* seems to evoke Weber in character. This arrangement is based on Weber's *Polacca brillante: 'L'Hilarité'*, op. 72, with a Largo introduction which Liszt took from the *Grande Polonaise* Op. 21. In other Weber works the use of thematic transformation interested Liszt, and in particular the programmatic element and novelty of form in the *Konzertstück* for piano and orchestra, a work he often played on his tours.

He also played Schubert's *Fantasy in C major* for piano solo (known as *Der Wanderer* because Schubert's song of that name is the source of the Adagio variations section). The twofold attraction of this work was its virtuoso nature, unusual in Schubert's piano writing, and its form: a combination of sonata allegro, slow movement, scherzo and finale, in one continuous structure, linked by thematic transformation. In his essay on the arrangement of the *Wanderer-Fantasy* for piano and orchestra,[3] Tovey praises Liszt's insight upon the orchestral quality of Schubert's original,

---

[3] *Essays in Musical Analysis* IV, London, 1937. See also the Eulenburg miniature score, ed. Searle, 1980, which prints Schubert's original alongside Liszt's version.

his taste and ingenuity in dividing the material between piano and orchestra, and the fidelity to Schubert's formal construction.

The *Fantasia on Hungarian Folk Themes* (1852) is an extended version for piano and orchestra of the Hungarian Rhapsody No. 14. The word 'folk' in the title must be understood in the context of popular melodies as played to Liszt by gypsy bands. The opening melody, a popular song called *The Crane flies high*, appears first slowly and sadly with horns and bassoons, in minor key, and then in a major transformation for piano alone. It recurs in the middle and at the end of this brilliant showpiece.

The 2 *Piano Concertos* have important features in common: both are continuous works and contain much thematic cross-reference between their sections; in both there are long stretches of delicate, chamber-like orchestration; and in each the piano enters after only a few bars of introduction. The E flat concerto incorporates the traditional layout of four symphonic movements in a brief span. Much of the succeeding development derives from the descending string figures of the opening *Allegro maestoso*. A nocturnal *Quasi Adagio* of Bellini-like ravishment and an *Allegro vivace*, with the piano part marked 'capriccioso scherzando', and with a triangle part which caused much offence at the time, are followed by a short cadenza and sixty bars of free development based on material from the first 'movement'. The finale, *Allegro marziale*, contains no new themes, but much metamorphosis of earlier ideas. This concerto has frequently been attacked for its glitter and vulgarity. An unfortunate tendency has developed of playing it much too fast: the recording made by Liszt's pupil Sauer and conducted by Liszt's disciple Weingartner in 1938 is a model of dignity and delicate beauty.

That the A major concerto is more poetic and its ideas more finely developed is clear from the opening expansion of its first theme (see Ex. 54). The well-gauged dramatic contrast that starts with the violent ostinato passage at bar 72, is followed at bar 115 by a 'scherzo' section. The new idea at bar 148 becomes, at bar 213, the expressive prelude to a 'slow movement' passage, Italianate and nocturnal. By now it is clear that this concerto is more subtly episodic than its E flat major predecessor, and a free development of ideas begins at bar 290. The 'finale' begins with a recapitulation of Ex. 54 in march tempo and, even if this is too banal a transformation for some ears, much ensuing play with the

Ex. 54

major and minor seconds inherent in the opening theme provides
interest and excitement before the close.

13

Orchestral music

The majority of the symphonic works date from Liszt's years at Weimar (1848–61): the *Faust* and *Dante* symphonies, twelve symphonic poems, two *Episodes from Lenau's 'Faust'*, six festive marches, and *Les Morts*. This is a prodigious output when considered along with Liszt's many other Weimar activities. *Les Morts* became the first of his *Trois Odes Funèbres*, a set completed during the Roman years. The remainder of the orchestral music consists of the *Deux Légendes*; an interlude from the incomplete oratorio *St Stanislaus*; a thirteenth symphonic poem; orchestral versions of the *Rákóczy March* and the second *Mephisto Waltz*, and two more marches (one of which, the *Hungarian Battle March*, a transcription of an earlier piano piece, is one of Liszt's most enjoyable works in this genre – and, most unusually, it has a part for cimbalom).

Liszt regarded his first few years at the ducal court of Weimar as his orchestral apprenticeship and he relied upon the help of amanuenses in scoring the first drafts of the earlier symphonic poems.[1] From 1853 he dispensed completely with such outside aid: *Festklänge* was the first work scored entirely by Liszt, and from that time he set about the re-orchestration of all the earlier symphonic poems in his own terms.

The Weimar symphonic poems, as numbered on publication, are:

1. *Ce qu'on entend sur la montagne*
2. *Tasso: Lamento e Trionfo*
3. *Les Préludes*
4. *Orpheus*
5. *Prometheus*

---

[1] Raff and Conradi, see Chapter 4. The extent to which the flautist Franz Doppler assisted in the orchestration of six of the Hungarian Rhapsodies is debatable. See Searle, *The Music of Liszt*, 45.

6. *Mazeppa*
7. *Festklänge*
8. *Héroïde Funèbre*
9. *Hungaria*
10. *Hamlet*
11. *Hunnenschlacht*
12. *Die Ideale*

The various versions and dates of composition are listed in Appendix B, although a complete chronology of all the drafts and revisions still awaits research (*cf.* the outline history of *Tasso* on page 98).

The sources of the programmatic titles fall into various categories: poetic and literary models, character studies, visual inspiration and more personal or national themes. Those based on poems are *Ce qu'on entend sur la montagne* after Victor Hugo (often encountered in its German title, *Bergsinfonie*, 'Mountain Symphony'), *Die Ideale* after Schiller, and *Mazeppa* after both Hugo and Byron. *Mazeppa* began musical life as No. 4 of Liszt's early set of *12 Études*. In revised and expanded form it appeared, still untitled, as No. 4 of the *Grandes Études* (1837). This study then appeared separately in 1840 under the title *Mazeppa* (dedicated to Hugo) with a new ending portraying Mazeppa's collapse and triumph, and it in turn was revised as No. 4 of the final version of the studies, *Études d'exécution transcendante* (1851). The symphonic poem thus has a four-fold genesis: the piano study, the poetic imagery of Hugo, that of Byron, and as Liszt's own musical character study. *Les Préludes* has an even more complex history. The final score (1854) is headed *Les Préludes* (*d'après Lamartine*), indicating that the poetic inspiration of the work is the lengthy Lamartine poem from *Nouvelles méditations poétiques*, consisting of a series of contrasted warlike and pastoral episodes. A vaguely-worded programme by Liszt, issued with the score, further linked the music to the essence of Lamartine's verses. However it is now certain that Liszt first conceived this piece as an overture to his choral settings of four poems by Joseph Autran depicting Mediterranean scenes, *Les Quatres Éléments*. This overture was written in the period 1845–9; at the same time Liszt planned an orchestral work on *Les Préludes*. The latter was never written. Instead, when finally discarding the Autran choruses (which remain unpublished) he revised the overture to them. This went through several drafts, was laid aside for a time, was later revised further and first associated with Lamartine in 1853, prior to its performance early in the next year.[2] Critics have thus accused Liszt of distortion, artificiality and arbitrariness in his switch of identity from Autran to Lamartine. But, having rejected the Autran choruses, he presumably felt that any reference in his overture to these obscure texts would be unsatisfactory. He therefore found in *Les Préludes* a poetic model that parallels, often very exactly, the moods and atmosphere of his music, and his final re-touchings of the score may have tried to make the musical and poetic links closer still.

Herein lies a lesson as to how the 'programmes' of the symphonic poems may be approached. If the musical essence occurred to Liszt without reference to the final poetic title, or even with reference to a different image, then clearly the programme is not a guide to musical form or content. *Les Préludes* is the most contentious case of all, but even here Liszt's final poetical association of his score with Lamartine may serve as a helpful, subjective description of the work's mood. Certainly his programmatic titles were never hastily arrived at and, far from being a distortion, were meant sincerely as a guide to the listener: at the very least a signpost to Liszt's aesthetic view that music and extra-musical stimuli are intertwined. With the more overtly descriptive pieces such as *Mazeppa* and *Hunnenschlacht* the programmatic references are unmistakable. In the view of many commentators Liszt is most successful when he is less specific; the very vagueness of *Les Préludes* or *Orpheus* may contribute to their success as orchestral works. Liszt's own view may be paraphrased in one sentence from his most important essay on programme music:[3] 'The programme has no other end than to make some preliminary allusion to the psychological motives that have impelled the composer to create his work and that he has sought to embody in it.'

In addition to *Mazeppa*, four other symphonic poems can be categorised as character studies: *Prometheus, Tasso, Orpheus* and *Hamlet*. The first three were written as overtures to performances of plays or operas at Weimar. The idea of an overture to a dramatic work having independent life as a musical work has famous

[2] The complex history of the evolution of *Les Préludes* is admirably summed up by Andrew Bonner, 'Liszt's *Les Préludes* and *Les Quatre Éléments*: A Re-investigation', *19th Century Music*, IX, no. 1, 1986, 95–107.
[3] *Berlioz und seine 'Harold-Symphonie'*, GS, IV, 1–102.

parallels in Beethoven, Berlioz and Mendelssohn. With *Orpheus*
Liszt had in mind an Etruscan vase in the Louvre depicting the
poet-musician with his lyre. *Hunnenschlacht* similarly evokes a
work of art: Kaulbach's fresco 'The Battle of the Huns'. With
Héroïde Funèbre and *Hungaria* Liszt responds to battles and
national struggles of his own time, specifically of 1848. *Festklänge*
(literally 'Festive Sounds') appeared without any programmatic
preface, but is associated with the (never solemnised) union of
Liszt and Princess Carolyne.

Although the twelve Weimar symphonic poems were published as a group, they are obviously very diverse in motivation,
programmatic content and form. This is to be expected as there
is no such entity as a 'symphonic poem form': it is a *genre* pioneered
by Liszt, which takes a general idea or broad subject, usually of
wide symbolic relevance, and expresses it in expansive musical
form. The form varies from work to work; the twelve symphonic
poems and the first movements of the *Faust* and *Dante* symphonies
exhibit many possibilities of tonal and thematic organisation
within a one-movement structure. As with analyses of the B minor
Sonata, Liszt's unconventionality is reflected in differing interpretations of the formal designs of these fourteen movements by
various writers. Sonata form, in varying degrees of orthodoxy, is
found in *Prometheus, Les Préludes, Tasso* and the *Faust* first
movement. *Orpheus* is akin to the classical slow-movement sonata-
without-development. *Ce qu'on entend* and *Die Ideale* follow their
poetic models in a broad programmatic sense; both are in very
loosely constructed sonata form, *Die Ideale* also incorporating a
three-movement structure. *Mazeppa, Hunnenschlacht* and *Hungaria* may aptly be described as corresponding to 'struggle and
apotheosis' in form. *Héroïde Funèbre* is a large-scale funeral
march. *Hamlet* is a series of mood-pictures constituting a portrait
of Shakespeare's hero and is most original in form. *Festklänge* is
also too episodic to be categorised in an orthodox way. Nor does
the opening *Inferno* movement of the *Dante Symphony* fit any
obvious model, although it contains references to elements of
sonata form.

Some of the symphonic poems have not withstood the test of
time, and yet the contemporary impact even of a work as banal
as *Mazeppa* was considerable. Questions of taste are unanswerable
here. Suffice to say that the oft-maligned *Les Préludes* still has its
many admirers. More importantly, the best examples of this group

are still too rarely heard. A short discussion of the main features of each of the symphonic works follows.

Ce qu'on entend sur la montagne is based on a poem from Hugo's *Feuilles d'Automne*. The opening reflects what the poet in the mountains heard from the ocean far below: 'At first it was a sound, large, immense, confused/Vaguer than the wind in the forest trees ...' An introduction of mysterious bass drum rolls and swaying string figures, characteristically slow and vague in tonality, conjures up the scene. The home key of E flat is established at bar 33 and in the ensuing Allegro two melodic ideas emerge (bars 38 and 61), while the tonality shifts once more. The Hugo poem distinguishes two separate voices amid the sounds: that of the ocean, the waves blissfully calling to each other, and that of mankind, troubled and sad. Liszt introduces the first of these ideas at bar 95 (F sharp major) and, after four bars of string transition full of wonderment and expectancy, the second at bar 135 – woeful in its repeated use of falling semitones. The antithesis of nature and humanity implicit in the poem is made explicit by Liszt in his lengthy exposition and development of these ideas (and another dolorous idea at bar 205). The poem's third principal image is a vision of the Deity, and at bar 477 Liszt introduces a religious 'chorale' symbol, the 'Song of the Anchorites'. This *Andante religioso* serves as a slow movement; it divides the further development and recapitulation of the earlier ideas; and finally it provides Liszt with an effective, meditational Coda to his long, rather diffuse work. Hugo's poem ends with a series of questions about the purpose of life, the meaning behind nature and humanity. Liszt ends with a quiet meditation on the Deity. The conflict and resolution, the struggle and apotheosis, within very loose sonata structure, add up to an unsatisfactory whole. The overall weakness is unfortunate, for *Ce qu'on entend* contains some very bold and attractive passages.

Les Préludes presents a series of diffuse poetic images in an altogether more successful musical way. This is largely due to its pervasive use of thematic metamorphosis (see Ex. 55). Theme (b) has important variants at bars 91 and 370. One other figure appears at bar 160; and the important bucolic idea (Liszt midway between Weber and Strauss) at bar 200 is also combined with (b), e.g. at bar 280. The C major recapitulatory section (bar 296) recalls (b) and the pastoral idea simultaneously before returning to the (a) thematic group.

Ex. 55

(a1)

Andante

bar 3

(a2)

Andante maestoso

bar 35

(a3)

L'istesso tempo

bar 47

(a4)

Allegro ma non troppo

bar 109

(a5)

Allegro tempestuoso

bar 131

(a6)

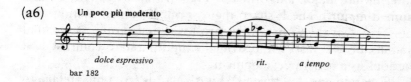

Un poco più moderato

dolce espressivo   *rit.*   *a tempo*

bar 182

(a7)

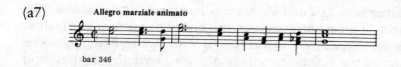

Allegro marziale animato

bar 346

(b)

Andante maestoso

bar 69

Tasso, like *Les Préludes*, was first designed as an overture. It was originally performed to mark the centenary of Goethe's birth at a performance of *Torquato Tasso*, 28 August 1849, and afterwards was much revised. Liszt admitted that Byron's *Lament of Tasso*, a poem inspired by a sight of the prison in Ferrara where Tasso was long confined, was a more immediate inspiration. Thus Liszt's full title, *Tasso, Lamento e Trionfo*, indicating the hero's suffering of earthly injustice and his glorious fame in death. The first main theme (in C minor) Liszt heard sung by a Venetian gondolier to words taken from Tasso's *Gerusalemme Liberata*:

Ex. 56

The triplet group (*x*) is used as a basic motivic device from the first bars. An E major statement of the gondolier's theme at bar 131 is akin in key-relationship to the *Faust Symphony* opening movement (C minor–E major), and *Prometheus* has a similar A minor–D flat major axis. (In *Les Préludes* and *Orpheus* it is C major–E major.) The F sharp major central minuet section (bar 165 – 'Tasso at the Court of Ferrara') was added only in the final revisions of the work; it provides a light, festive contrast and functions as a sonata development.

'Suffering and Apotheosis', Liszt's words from his preface to *Prometheus*, are as applicable to *Tasso*. The concept is broadly the same as in *Tod und Verklärung* by Strauss. In *Prometheus* the outlines of sonata form are clearer, though by no means orthodox. After an introduction (which opens with tritone harmony and a variant of the violent 'malediction' motif, see Exs. 9 and 52) and a recitative passage, the main allegro in A minor is launched at bar 48 (compare the string figures with bar 71 of *Faust*) and an exposition of the torments of Prometheus ensues. The contrasting group (bar 129) brings hope of his deliverance. A fugue (bar 161) with a subject built of falling and rising thirds takes over the function of a stormy development. The opening motif is restated at bar 237 and the A minor allegro at bar 269. The theme of hope returns in the tonic major, joyfully animated at bar 304 (with further references to the fugue and to the opening theme, bars 322 and 385).

Grief as a persistent presence in the life and history of mankind, the seemingly endless succession of wars and struggles – these thoughts occupy Liszt in his preface to *Héroïde Funèbre*. He thus raises a symphonic elegy of grand proportions from the particular to the universal, although topical references are present in this score, which was originally intended as the first movement of a huge Revolutionary Symphony. There is a distinct Hungarian character to the motif that enters in bar 7; and a phrase of the *Marseillaise* makes some striking appearances (bars 169, 201, 261). The handling of the melodies is economic and restrained: other important motivic ideas are first heard at bars 44, 72, 122 and 152. The last of these ushers in a D flat major Trio (or, viewing this F minor structure in sonata terms, a second subject group). A short transition (or development) leads to the return of the elegiac march at bar 249. This final section contains some bold and breathtaking modulations, effective use of percussion and new expansion of the earlier themes. The moving and remarkable progression of the final bars draws a veil over this solemn review of heroic and tragic endeavour.

Debussy wrote of *Mazeppa*,

> This symphonic poem is full of the worst faults; sometimes it is even vulgar. Yet all that tumultuous passion ... exerts such force that you find yourself liking it, without quite knowing why ... The fire and abandon which Liszt's genius frequently attains are much preferable to white-gloved perfection.[4]

Liszt depicts the legend of Mazeppa: his wild ride across the steppes tied naked to his horse, his fall, his recovery and final triumph as leader of the Cossacks.

There is much to commend in *Festklänge*: its radiantly happy mood, playful use of tonal ambiguity and utter lack of pomposity. On its undeservedly rare hearings it is usually given in the version Liszt published in 1856. However, five years later he issued a series of four 'Variants' to the score. Two of these alternative passages

[4] *Gil Blas*, 16 Feb. 1903.

lay more emphasis on the polonaise rhythms; one of the Variants entails a substantial cut of 282 bars, which could be used in presenting the work as a short festive overture.

If Liszt failed, with all his Variants, to find a solution to the exuberant yet ramblingly episodic form of *Festklänge*, then with *Orpheus* he succeeded splendidly. There could be no thought of cuts or alternatives in this restrained, poetic masterpiece, a hymn in praise of the spirit of music. *Orpheus* achieves nobility and expressive poise through delicacy of scoring, luminous, suspended harmonic effects, and unforced, graceful lyricism of melody. Its final sequence of chords magically suggest the phrase from Liszt's preface – 'Tones rising gradually like clouds of incense':

Ex. 57

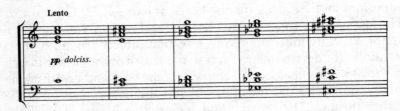

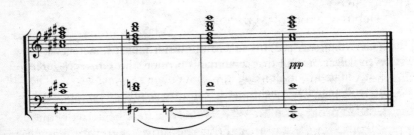

Hungaria has no preface, but is evidently a large national canvas. Along with *Funérailles* and the *Hungaria Cantata* Liszt regarded it as a patriotic reply to Vörösmarty's ode (1840) placing the nation's trust and hopes in him. Two themes (bars 19 and 207) come from his *Heroic March in Hungarian Style* (1840); use is also made of gypsy violin figurations. The contrast between dolorous, funereal passages and the vigorous jubilation of the last section perhaps symbolises the fall of Hungary's aspirations in

1848–9 and the hope for her future renewal and liberation. Alas, Liszt's form is particularly sectional and rambling: his own dissatisfaction with it is seen in his suggestions for two alternative cuts.

Hunnenschlacht has a lengthy preface describing Kaulbach's artistic vision of the battle of Attila the Hun's forces with those of Theodoric, leader of the Christian peoples, in 451. In 1879 Liszt sent August Manns a more concise explanation:

> Kaulbach's world-renowned picture presents two battles – the one on earth, the other in the air, according to the legend that warriors, after their death, continue fighting incessantly as spirits. In the middle of the picture appears the *Cross* and its mystic light; on this my 'Symphonic Poem' is founded. The [Gregorian chant] *Crux fidelis*, which is gradually developed, illustrates the final victory of Christianity in its effectual love to God and man.[5]

The work is in two halves: first a depiction of the fierce battle, earthly and spiritual, between the forces of good and evil; secondly a lengthy meditation (with an important organ part) on the triumphant 'cross' motif. At the time Liszt envisaged a series of symphonic works based on Kaulbach's other frescoes in the Altes Museum, Berlin. This grandiose project, which remained merely an idea, was to be called 'The History of the World in Pictures and Music', and was to have a literary counterpart provided by Dingelstedt.

In September 1857 Weimar celebrated the centenary of Grand Duke Carl August, patron of Goethe and Schiller, with two new works by Liszt paying homage to each poet: the *Faust Symphony* and the symphonic poem *Die Ideale*. As in *Ce qu'on entend*, Liszt depicts the elements of Schiller's poem in a broad manner, not in any detailed programmatic way. However, here he actually quotes verses from *Die Ideale* throughout the score, therefore placing a close emphasis on his poetic source. At the same time he altered the order of these verses to suit his musical purpose and added an 'apotheosis' which has no counterpart in Schiller's work. Knowledge of the verses is of doubtful value to the general listener, but the broad sequence of moods is:

Bars   1–25:   *Slow introduction*: youthful joys and ideals have vanished.

[5] *Briefe*, II, letter 246.

26–452:	*Allegro spiritoso*: the joys and aspirations of youth recalled; ideals of love, truth, fortune and fame.
453–567:	*Andante*: disillusionment, the burdens of life, weariness and loneliness; the ideal of friendship brings new hope.
568–679:	[*Allegretto-Allegro spirito molto*]: fulfilment and purpose found in employment and labour.
680–872:	'Faith in the Ideal, and moreover the unstoppable urge to realise it, is Life's highest aim. Therefore I have allowed myself to add to Schiller's poem, by repeating the motifs heard in the first section [26–452], a joyful and assertive final apotheosis. F. Liszt.'

The scheme that unfolds is therefore: aspiration, struggle, achievement, fulfilment. Musically the various sections combine a three-movement form in one continuous modified sonata structure. Unity is achieved both through motivic transformation and a pervasive thematic and harmonic use of the interval of the third. *Die Ideale* has been criticised for its excessive length: this problem is solved by adopting Liszt's suggestion of a substantial cut in the recapitulation-apotheosis section.

The last Weimar symphonic poem, *Hamlet*, is one of the finest and most concise. Liszt wrote no preface. It is a character study of Shakespeare's hero, 'pale, fevered, suspended between heaven and earth, prisoner of his doubt and lack of resolve',[6] with two contrasted sixteen-bar interludes depicting Ophelia. These quiet 'shadowy portraits, hinting at Ophelia' (Liszt's words) were later additions to the score. The opening has a quality of indecision and brooding. An ascending figure at bar 9 is linked to the motivic shapes in the Ophelia section (*cf*. bars 171–4). After a while the clock of Elsinore is heard to strike. Hamlet has two related *allegro* themes (see Ex. 58). A stormy development of (b) continues until bar 156 when, after a dramatic pause, Ophelia first appears. Her two passages are separated by a return of Hamlet's themes, marked *ironico*. After her second interlude his raging determination

---

[6] *Briefe*, III, 111.

Ex. 58

(a)

Allegro appassionato ed agitato assai

(b)

resumes anew, reaches a violent climax and then dramatically breaks up, destroyed by its own volition. The recapitulation/coda is a sombre review of his tragic themes in a dark funeral march.

If *Orpheus* and *Hamlet*, and, to some extent, *Tasso* and *Prometheus*, display Liszt's mastery in the art of character-study, then the *Faust Symphony* shows his orchestral genius and symphonic ability at their very best. The work is subtitled 'three character pictures: Faust, Gretchen and Mephistopheles, after Goethe'.[7] In the first movement Liszt's imaginative re-shaping of sonata form is seen working with its greatest power. In general outline it presents a slow introduction, lengthy exposition (with much development), short development section, condensed recapitulation and coda. Ex. 59 shows the five *Faust* themes. (a) is famous for embracing a 12-note row (formed by a descending sequence of four augmented triads): commentators have associated it with the mystical and magical aspects of Faust's character, just as (b1) may be seen as Faust's emotions and longings, (b2) as Faust the lover, (c) his ceaseless striving and (e) his heroism and his words 'Im Anfang war der Tat' (In the beginning was the deed). The yearning figure (d) plays an important part in the second movement. All the Ex. 59 themes appear in the introduction and exposition, and other significant figures are heard at bars 28, 83, 229, and a new sequential development of (a) at bar 147. The key of the main allegro (bar 71) is C minor, and of the second group (bar 179) E major. The music surges on into the development (bar 297) with seamless, energetic flow based on figures from (c) and canonic treatment of (a). The introductory phrases return at bar

[7] Liszt has been accused of an ambivalent attitude towards Goethe and the Faust subject. For a discussion of the falsity of this notion see my article 'Liszt and Goethe', LSJ, 10, 1985.

Liszt

Ex. 59

(a)

Lento assai

ff > p

(b1)

Ob.

p dolente

Vl.

(b2)

mf cantando

pp

3 3

(c)

Allegro agitato ed appassionato

molto rinf.

sf — sf — p — p —

359 and (a) appears in a remarkably adventurous harmonisation at bar 400: a passage of visionary scoring – Faust the alchemist, the summoner of spirits. In the reprise (b2) appears again in E major (bar 450) and then in the tonic major, C, at bar 472. The last bars of the coda, a monodic statement of (b1), turn the music again to the minor.

The logic and natural impulse of this opening movement give the impression that it was conceived at white heat. The first draft of the whole symphony was written in the amazingly short span of two months, August to October 1854. That version was based on some earlier sketches; parts of it were radically different in

276

Ex. 59 continued

(d)

(e)

shape (figure (c) opposite appeared in 7/8 time, for example –
extraordinarily novel for the era); and it was scored for a small
orchestra without trumpets, trombones, harp or timpani. An idea
of its orchestral style can be gained from the *Gretchen* movement,
scored entirely for small orchestra, except for the passage at bar
163 where full orchestra enters but with the utmost delicacy. The
main A flat major *Gretchen* theme (bar 15) is a lovely bel canto
song for oboe and solo viola. A pictorial episode (bars 51–6)
evokes the scene where she plucks petals from a flower, and
murmurs 'He loves me, he loves me not, he loves me!' Her second
main theme (bar 83) is marked *dolce amoroso*. In the central part
of the movement (from bar 111) the Faust themes are developed
in a new web of metamorphosis; none is more ravishing than the
return of (c), *soave con amore*, at bar 188. Gretchen's themes are
then recapitulated in new scoring (without the flower episode) and
a final section recalls (e) in a gentle transformation, showing
Faust's fulfilment in happiness, peace and contentment.

 Mephistopheles is one of Liszt's most remarkable feats of
form, variation and dramatic irony. Mephisto is sterile and Liszt
thus creates no new theme for this spirit of negation. Instead the
Faust motives are parodied, twisted, mocked and mutilated in a
scherzo of audacious and sinister power. Ex. 60 shows the diabolic
versions of (c) and (e). The only new element (bar 188) is a
quotation of the 'pride' motif from Liszt's *Malediction Concerto*
(see Ex. 53). Shortly after, a fantastic fugue is launched, based on

Ex. 60

(a)

(b)

Ex. 61

Ex. 61, a vicious distortion of (b). At bar 420 Gretchen's main theme appears – pure and uncorrupted: Mephisto has no power over her. The mighty struggle commences once more and grows ever wilder until an enormous climax is reached and with the 'pride' motif descending and disintegrating through an astonishing progression (bars 655–674) Mephisto returns to eternal emptiness. At the reappearance of Gretchen's theme, Liszt's 1854 version of the symphony came to a close with a final glance at Faust's triumphant Ex. 59 (e). The addition in 1857 of the C major finale with male chorus enormously enhanced the work, providing a most effective summing-up and a greater sense of solemnity and uplift. Trombones intone the rhythm of the choral theme and, after a pause, the unison male voices sing the 'Chorus Mysticus' that ends Goethe's *Faust* Part II. The words 'Das Ewig-Weibliche' are taken up by a tenor soloist, to the Gretchen melody, and rise ever-higher in soaring phrases.

While sketching ideas for *A Symphony on Dante's 'Divine Comedy'* in 1847, Liszt anticipated Scriabin in considering the use of lantern slides projected through some form of diorama, so that the work would be an audio-visual experience. He also anticipated Ravel and Strauss by proposing the creation of a wind-machine for the *Inferno* movement. Although he abandoned these ideas, the symphony can still be described as scenic in the vividness of its effects. On commencing serious work on the score in 1855, he planned a three-movement work corresponding to the sections of Dante's great poem: *Inferno–Purgatorio–Paradiso*. Later he decided not to represent the third part in music, a move usually attributed to the influence of Wagner, who wrote him a long letter criticising the *Paradiso* section of Dante, and arguing that no human being could adequately portray the joys of Paradise. Possibly this only confirmed what Liszt felt instinctively, and his final scheme fell into two parts: the descent into the Inferno and the ascent through Purgatory. In the poet's ascent to the Heavenly Paradise he is led by his own *Ewig-Weibliche*, Beatrice. In Canto I of *Paradiso*, as Dante gazes upon her, he hears the music of the heavenly spheres. This is an appropriate image for the conclusion of Liszt's *Purgatorio* movement, to which he appends a setting for high voices of the *Magnificat*. The first movement has an introduction in which trombones, tuba and lower strings declaim the first three lines of the inscription over the gates of Hell:

> Per me si va nella città dolente,
> per me si va nell'eterno dolore,
> per me si va tra la perduta gente …
> Lasciate ogni speranza, voi ch'entrate!
>
> (Through me is the way to the city of woe,
> through me is the way to eternal sorrow,
> through me is the way among the lost …
> Abandon all hope, ye that enter!)

The last line, which is a recurring refrain throughout the movement, is given to horns and trumpets and ends on a diminished 7th chord, a significant symbol of two interlocking tritones. A vivid depiction of descent leads to the main part of the movement, the pattern of which is ABA + Coda. 'B' illustrates the episode of Paolo and Francesca in the whirlwind of the lustful, and over a cor anglais melody Liszt quotes the lines of Francesca da Rimini:

> Nessun maggior dolore
> che ricordarsi del tempo felice
> nella miseria

> (There is no greater sorrow than to recall a time of happiness in misery.)

The lovers' past happiness is recalled with most effective use of 7/4 time. With the return of the sinister and diabolic themes of the 'A' section (bar 395) Liszt indicates in a footnote that the entire passage is intended to sound like 'blasphemous mocking laughter'.

After the grotesquerie, plangent cries and atmosphere of fearful alarm created by dissonance and chromaticism in the opening movement, the tranquil, meditative mood of *Purgatorio* stands in utter contrast. Its tonal construction conveys a sense of upward movement, of darkness giving way to light, which is carried through to the final, ethereal *Magnificat*. Despite its many beauties the movement suffers from several longueurs; its choral ending is undeniably effective, however, and – as with the *Faust Symphony* – Liszt wished the chorus to remain unseen.

Of the *Two Episodes from Lenau's 'Faust'* the second, *The Dance in the Village Inn*, is by far the better known both in its orchestral and piano versions as the *Mephisto Waltz No. 1*. The first episode, *Der nächtliche Zug* (The Procession by Night), deserves more frequent performance, for it is a very fine piece of orchestral tone-painting and Liszt was keen that the two contrasted pieces be played together. *The Procession* opens with a sombre portrayal of deep darkness, and sensations of a warm spring night in the forest. Faust becomes aware of the approach of distant lights and voices, and withdraws to witness a religious procession pass by. Liszt introduces phrases of the plainsong melody *Pange lingua gloriosi*. After they have marched into the distance, Faust, left alone once more, weeps bitterly as he reflects on his own lost happiness. The music's structure closely follows the sequence of events in the poem and falls naturally into a long crescendo and diminuendo. In the second episode Mephistopheles takes Faust to a village tavern. The tuning-up of rustic fiddlers is illustrated by the superimposed 5ths of the opening:

Ex. 62

Mephisto himself takes up the fiddle (bar 77) with a rousing, increasingly frenzied dance. A second theme shows Faust in amorous pursuit of a dark-eyed local beauty; its ecstatic voluptuousness foreshadows Scriabin, who learned much from this score (see Ex. 63).

As Faust pursues his passion in the depths of the wood, nightingales sing (bar 427). The climax of the orgiastic dance begins with a combination of the two main themes at bar 668. Liszt wrote two alternative endings for the orchestral version; the more familiar one (with a final whirl of the dance) is that found in the piano solo version. The piano-duet version also offers the

Ex. 63

alternative and subtler conclusion which sensuously depicts the sated lovers and ends *pianissimo*.

With the *Three Funeral Odes* we again encounter the elegiac mood that characterises so much of Liszt's later (and some of his earlier) output. All three pieces also exist in versions for piano solo and piano duet. *Les Morts*, written after the death of his son Daniel, was also arranged for organ. *La Notte*, written after the death of his daughter Blandine, is in its outer sections a reworking of the piano piece *Il Penseroso*, and was additionally arranged for violin and piano. As in the earlier piece Michelangelo's quatrain 'The Speech of Night' is quoted at the head of the score (see page 245). Over the new central section appears a line from Virgil's *Aeneid* where Antores, in death, thinks fondly of his distant homeland: 'Dulces moriens reminiscitur Argos' (Dying, he remembers sweet Argos). That Liszt was thinking of his own homeland is clear from the prominent use of a 'Hungarian cadence' (bars 60–2, etc.). The third piece *Le Triomphe funèbre du Tasse* was conceived as an epilogue to the symphonic poem *Tasso*. The *Odes* are thus intensely personal and autobiographical: No. 3 enshrines Liszt's belief that his work, like Tasso's, would be appreciated only after his death. Ironically, these three interesting orchestral pieces have only rarely been performed. Liszt expressed a wish that *La Notte* and *Les Morts* be performed at his funeral, but they were not heard until 1912, and the piano solo version of *La Notte* appeared only in 1979.[8] *Les Morts* is described as an 'oration for orchestra, after Lamennais' whose lines, reflecting on the dead, are written into the score (see page 115). In 1866 Liszt added an important part for male chorus: they sing lines from the psalms, the *Te Deum* and the Sanctus and Benedictus of the Mass. Just before the first choral entry there is a significant theme based on Liszt's 'cross motif'. The central section of *Le Triomphe funèbre du Tasse* is based on Ex. 56. All three *Odes* show Liszt harmonically at his most original and formally at his most inventive and unpredictable.

Just as the *Odes* exist in separate versions for piano solo and for orchestra, the same is true of all the other orchestral works Liszt was to write. In some cases it is uncertain which came first, the piano or the orchestral piece. Liszt's habit of making three or four performing versions of his works increased in later years: of the earlier Weimar period orchestral works only the marches and the *Gretchen* movement were arranged for piano solo.

Salve Polonia (intended as an interlude for the oratorio *St Stanislaus*) was published for orchestra in 1883, for piano a year later, but composed in 1863 and based on ideas sketched early in his relationship with Princess Carolyne. It incorporates two Polish patriotic melodies: a song, *Boże ooś Polskę* sung by Polish rebels in the early nineteenth century and the *Dąbrowski-Mazurek*, the revolutionary song of Dąbrowski's Polish legionaries who fought Napoleon in Italy. Since 1927 the latter has been the national anthem of Poland.

Of the *Deux Légendes* (see page 250) special mention must be made of the wonderfully delicate orchestral texture in the first movement for the song of the birds: a light, shimmering, floating effect created by 3 flutes, 2 oboes, 2 clarinets, harp and solo and divisi upper strings. This imaginative, impressionistic scoring frames the sermon of St Francis who is portrayed by a cor-anglais recitative and a chorale theme based on the 'cross motif'.

The second *Mephisto Waltz*, if less dazzling in brilliance and energy than No. 1, is still startlingly effective and exciting. It opens with the 'diabolic' tritone B–F, and it ends with a most arresting cadence on those notes, just as the music seems to be approaching a final peroration in E flat major.

[8] NE, XI.

The thirteenth symphonic poem, *Von der Wiege bis zum Grabe* (From the Cradle to the Grave), inspired by a drawing by Mihály Zichy, is cast in three sections which are played without a break: *The cradle – The struggle for existence – To the grave, the cradle of the future life*. It is a restrained, modest yet searching and unsentimental last orchestral essay. The first section sets up a gentle rocking motion in thirds and is scored throughout for two flutes, harp and muted violins and violas. The thematic material is extremely concise. The central section brings the full orchestra into play. Its violent, fragmented first theme incorporates a triplet figure from bar 32 of the opening part. A theme marked *nobilmente cantando* enters at bar 149 and the climax of the section is a struggle between the two themes. The final section uses only motives already heard, but now presented in altered form. Its opening is in stark, whole-tone monody, stressing unorthodox intervals and leading to a passage of remarkable, expressive dissonance (bar 313). The quiet ending is based symbolically on the opening 'cradle' figures.

14

Organ and chamber music

The Margittay edition of the complete organ works[1] contains forty-seven items. Of these eleven are transcriptions from other composers – Arcadelt, Bach, Chopin, Lassus, Mozart, Nicolai, Verdi and Wagner. Twenty are arrangements by Liszt of his own compositions: *Am Grabe Richard Wagners, Andante maestoso* (from the hymn for male chorus and organ *Slavimo Slavno, Slaveni!*), *Angelus* (from the third *Année*), *Ave Maria* (see Appendix B No. 36), *Ave maris stella, Nun danket alle Gott, Consolation in D flat, Évocation à la Chapelle Sixtine, Excelsior, Hosanna* and *San Francesco* (the last two from the *Cantico del Sol*), the *Offertorium* from the *Hungarian Coronation Mass, Preludium* (from *In domum Domini ibimus*), *Requiem for organ* (from the male voice *Requiem*), *Rosario, Trauerode* (from *Les Morts*), *Ungarns Gott, Weimars Volkslied, Zur Trauung* (from *Sposalizio*) and – the most important of all these self-transcriptions – the Variations on *Weinen, Klagen*.

The edition also contains arrangements for organ by Gottschalg of Liszt works, which were corrected and altered to such an extent by Liszt himself that they may be regarded as authorised transcriptions: *Consolation in E major, Dante* (an abbreviation of *Purgatorio* and the *Magnificat* from the symphony), *Gebet* (from an *Ave Maria, cf.* Appendix B No. 5), *Orpheus*; also the organ movements from *Via Crucis*, the first four pieces of *Weihnachtsbaum* (laid out with a pedal part); and the Introduction to *St. Elisabeth* (arranged by Müller-Hartung, with Liszt's corrections).

This leaves nine works originally conceived for organ: *Ad nos, ad salutarem undam, Prelude and Fugue on BACH*, a *Missa pro organo*, and six short pieces: *Andante religioso* (on the 'Song of the Anchorites' from *Ce qu'on entend sur la montagne*), *Introitus, Ora pro nobis, Salve Regina, Der Papst-Hymnus* (later arranged as *Tu es Petrus* and incorporated in *Christus*), and

[1] See Appendix B: the note following no. 392.

Resignazione (a simple miniature on two staves for harmonium or piano).

While many of these pieces enrich and expand the organist's repertoire, for both church and recital use, the three largest and by far the finest works are *Ad nos, BACH* and *Weinen, Klagen*. They are of such significance that, because of them, Liszt can be regarded as the most important composer for the organ since J. S. Bach, and the key mid-nineteenth-century composer in paving the way for the organ works of Reubke and Reger in Germany, Franck, Saint-Saëns, Widor and the succeeding French schools through to Messiaen.

Between J. S. Bach and Liszt, C. P. E. Bach, Mozart, Mendelssohn and Schumann added significantly to the organ repertory, but did not advance the nature of that repertory in any substantial way. Because Liszt was not an organist and (apart from a few sacred choral works written prior to *Ad nos*) was not from a background of ecclesiastical composition, he approached the instrument with a new versatility and in a completely free way, uninhibited by conventions of form or keyboard technique. He utilised the fullest range of the manuals and pedal-board. He was indebted to four organist-composers resident in Weimar for increasing his awareness of the technical possibilities of the 'king of instruments': Gottschalg, Müller-Hartung, Sulze and Töpfer.[2] Another important figure was his pupil Alexander Winterberger, who played *Ad nos* at the inauguration of the new Ladegast organ in Merseburg Cathedral in 1855 and, a few months later, first performed *BACH* there.

The Merseburg instrument, with eighty-one stops, four manuals and pedals, was entirely characteristic of larger instruments of its time.[3] Mid-century organs emphasised eight-foot registers; mixtures were reserved for *tutti* passages. Special importance was attached to colour effects – 'string' sounds, solo reeds and tremulants. Much expressive use was made of the swell-boxes for crescendo and diminuendo. Stops such as *vox humana*, *voix céleste* and *Unda-Maris* incorporated a slightly false tuning to create 'beats', i.e. an impression of vibrato. The expressive use of colour and a huge range of dynamics are essentials of Liszt's organ writing.

[2] See M. Sutter, 'Liszt and the Weimar Organist-Composers', *Liszt Studien* I, 203–13.
[3] Its registration is given in the preface to each volume of the Margittay edition.

The *Fantasy and Fugue on the chorale 'Ad nos, ad salutarem undam'*, Meyerbeer's 'sermon' for the three Anabaptists in Act 1 of his opera *Le Prophète*, is not only an historic milestone in Romantic organ composition, but is also a seminal work in Liszt's Weimar-period creations which attempted to solve the problem of one-movement form in new ways (see also the *Grosses Konzert-solo*, the *Scherzo and March*, the B minor Sonata and the Symphonic Poems). The basic outline of *Ad nos* is Fantasy, Adagio,

Ex. 64

Introduction and Fugue. Meyerbeer's melody (see Ex. 64) is never presented in its original form. Instead Liszt takes its constituent

287

parts and builds up a monumental structure, a great monothematic mosaic, free and rhapsodic, through wide-ranging use of metamorphosis, fragmentation, rhythmic variation and melodic alteration. The opening of the C minor fantasy is concerned mainly with the first four bars of the theme. The melodic tritone at bars 3–4 is the first of Liszt's significant changes to Meyerbeer's tune. At bar 141 a fanfare-like development of the second phrase begins. A short cadenza and recitative herald the central Adagio, which begins with a monodic statement in the meditative key of F sharp major of the whole theme, and then a harmonised variant. A more elaborate cadenza serves as introduction to the double fugue. Like the fugue in *BACH*, this one is strictly fugal only for a short time; its textures soon freshly expand into another fantasy. A grand C major chordal statement of the theme brings to a close one of the largest, most brilliant and impressive single movements written for the organ. Busoni made a fine transcription of *Ad nos* for piano solo.

The *Prelude and Fugue on BACH* is really another free fantasia; a powerful showpiece, smaller in scale than *Ad nos*, but with several thrilling effects. To some ears it suffers from an over-reliance on the chord of the diminished 7th, and its extreme chromaticism is carried even further in the *Variations on 'Weinen, Klagen'*, a most effective organ transcription of the piano work described in Chapter 11.

Among other transcriptions for organ the *Trauerode*, the Allegri-Mozart *Évocation*, the arrangement of Otto Nicolai's Sacred Festival Overture *Ein feste Burg ist unser Gott* and three pieces from Bach (an Adagio from a violin sonata and two extracts from the Cantatas) all make fine recital pieces.

Although Liszt wrote little chamber music, it should be remembered that one of the greatest features of his orchestral works is his tendency towards 'chamber scoring'. His output of actual chamber works may be small, but it too enhances the repertoire, particularly that for violin and piano for which he composed:

(1) *Duo-Sonata* (on Chopin's Mazurka in C sharp minor, Op. 6 No. 2)
(2) *Grand duo Concertant* (on Lafont's *Le Marin*)
(3) *Epithalam*
(4) *Benedictus* and *Offertorium* (from the *Hungarian Coronation Mass*)
(5) *La Notte*

(6) *Elegy No. 1*
(7) *Elegy No. 2*
(8) *Romance oubliée*
(9) *La lugubre gondola*

The first three were composed specifically for violin and piano. (4) above was also arranged for violin and organ, and for violin and orchestra. (5) is a substantial piece, an arrangement of the second of his *Trois Odes Funèbres* for orchestra. Nos. 3 to 9 all exist in piano solo versions. No. 6 was first written for the remarkable combination of harp, harmonium, cello and piano – a blend of plucked, reed, bowed and keyboard sounds that foreshadows the chamber music of the Second Viennese School. Liszt also made versions for cello and piano of 6, 7, and 9. No. 8. was originally written for viola, specifically for the *viola alta*, an instrument of larger than usual size invented by Hermann Ritter, with whom Liszt had contact. No. 3 and Nos. 5 to 9 are all late works and their spare, linear style is much enhanced by the colour of a solo string instrument. The sombre No. 9 is well-suited to its cello and piano adaptation.

Nos. 1 and 2 are astonishing works to have emerged in France in the 1830s, especially from the pen of Franz Liszt, and both are far superior in conception and style to the general level of fashionable contemporary pieces based on popular melodies. The *Duo-Sonata* (first published 1963) is of particular interest in that the seemingly endless succession of variations to which the sections of Chopin's mazurka are treated looks forward to Liszt's technique of motivic transformation in monothematic works like *Ad nos* and other cyclical works of the Weimar period. The Sonata is cast in four movements: Moderato (in free sonata form), followed without a break by Tema con Variationi (increasingly demanding in its piano writing); Allegretto (in which the violin assumes the virtuoso role); and Allegro con brio (a strongly rhythmic rondo).

The French violinist and composer Charles Philippe Lafont (1781–1839) was for a time a rival of Paganini; he wrote some 200 romances, one of which Liszt selected for his *Grand duo concertant*. After a dramatic, declamatory introduction the fifty-bar theme is presented, followed by four brilliantly ornamented Variations (the fourth is a Tarantella) and a spectacular Finale which gradually increases in energy and excitement. Liszt revised the *Grand duo* in 1849 and had it published in 1852.

He wrote the solo violin passages in his *Hungarian Coronation Mass* with the Hungarian virtuoso Eduard Reményi in mind. Early in 1872 he composed a piece in celebration of the violinist's wedding: *Epithalam*, a simple, elegant and lyrically graceful tribute. All these violin works make it a cause for regret that Liszt never composed his planned violin concerto for Reményi.

Apart from the curious exception of the First Elegy, larger chamber combinations than the duo never seem to have interested Liszt. There are three late arrangements: *Angelus* (from the third book of *Années de Pèlerinage*) for string quartet; the short valedictory piece *Am Grabe Richard Wagners* (At Wagner's Grave) for string quartet and harp; and *Die Wiege* (The Cradle) for the very unusual combination of four violins (it is related to the opening section of the last symphonic poem *From the Cradle to the Grave*). In his last years he arranged *Vallée d'Obermann* for piano trio. One other unfinished, unpublished curiosity for string quartet is *Die vier Jahreszeiten* (The Four Seasons) of which a sketch for the first movement 'Winter' is complete, and part of 'Spring'.

15

Choral works

Part-songs for male voices were popular in mid-nineteenth century Germany and contributions to this aspect of Romanticism were made by Schubert, Schumann, Mendelssohn, Bruckner and Cornelius. From 1839 until the mid-1850s Liszt composed over thirty male voice choruses, either unaccompanied or with piano. Most have German texts and five are settings of Goethe, to which he added trumpet and timpani parts for the *Soldiers' Song* from *Faust*, and two horns to *Über allen Gipfeln ist Ruh*. (In 1849 he set the *Chorus of Angels* from *Faust* for mixed voices and harp.) Many of the choruses are in traditional vein: songs in praise of nature, hunting songs, serenades, patriotic choruses. But some reveal his social ideas and hopes for a spiritually enlightened and united brotherhood of mankind. Both *Wir sind nicht Mumien* and *Licht, mehr Licht* are calls to action, for the forward march of the masses in new strength, as a day of light dawns for them. In *Le Forgeron* Lamennais's lines describe those whose servile fate is to toil in darkness and polluted air to feed their families, yet who long for the light and the open country. Hunger, cold, ragged clothes and fear of eviction are their lot. But,

> Take courage, brothers, do not give up;
> Struggle, yes, struggle as men!
> God will be with us, He watches from above.
> Today there is pain, tomorrow peace –
> For our sons a better future dawns.
> The iron is hard, strike it! strike it!

The image of a watchful, protecting Deity occurs again in the *Arbeiterchor* where all who labour, with tools, swords or the pen, are urged to rally in brotherhood and freedom.

Struggle against oppression and the victory of the human spirit is the symbolic theme of Liszt's most important large-scale secular choral work, the set of eight choruses to Herder's *Der entfesselte Prometheus* (Prometheus Unbound). The first version

(1850) was conceived as part of a theatrical performance but Liszt always intended it for the concert hall, and that was the aim of its revision in 1855 for which Richard Pohl wrote a linking text. The work thus calls for narrator, soprano, alto, solo male voice quartet, double chorus and large orchestra. In view of its length, tableaux form, the forces required and the need for a concise yet lucid connecting narrative (especially for non-German-speaking audiences) it has rarely been performed. The character of each chorus is coloured musically by the various groups that comment on the sufferings and liberation of Prometheus: Oceanides, Tritons, Dryads, Reapers, Vintners, Shades of the Underworld, Invisible Spirits and the Muses. There is a well-balanced contrast of atmosphere in the succession of moods from grief and torment to final enlightenment and triumph. Choruses 4 and 5 depict the joy and gratitude of humanity in a way that gives a firm centre to the work, and the gradual sense of upliftment from No. 6 onwards is well-managed (and enhanced by bold harmonic sequences in the final chorus[1]).

The lack of performing standards in Catholic church music of the nineteenth century led to a dearth of good liturgical composition. Despite Liszt's association with the Vatican hierarchy from the 1860s and his interest in the Cecilian movement (founded in 1867 by Franz Witt), the plight of ecclesiastical music was much the same at the time of his death as it had been more than half a century earlier when he wrote his heady, impassioned essay *On the Future of Church Music*. That article called for the creation of a new kind of sacred music, both popular and universal. In the enormous breadth of his choral works, oratorios, masses, psalm settings and many shorter pieces, as well as in the abundant wealth of Christian symbolism already observed in his instrumental music, Liszt strove to fulfil his early idealism. His achievement is equalled among his contemporaries only by the motets and masses of Bruckner. Whereas Bruckner had a closer affinity with Baroque ecclesiastical practice and the Viennese classical tradition of the festive Mass, Liszt brought to his sacred works a range of styles, from the theatrically dramatic to the austerely Gregorian, and embraced national elements, symphonic development, the Lutheran chorale, attempts at the revival of a Palestrina-style (significantly long before the foundation of the Cecilian movement

[1] The bass line of which is the basis of the fugue subject in the symphonic poem *Prometheus*.

which had that aim) and he also incorporated some of the most daring harmonic and melodic weapons from the armoury of his late, experimental period.

There is, therefore, an enormous diversity in his religious works. But there is also unity of purpose: to apply to sacred choral-instrumental writing the highest standards and the widest range of expression that the age could offer. That he failed to convince the musical public with his large-scale choral works is because it was generally disinclined to adapt to a new kind of sacred music and probably expected from the Liszt of popular legend a blend of profanity and religiosity. That his smaller liturgical works failed to find a home within the church is the fault, not of Liszt, but of the church itself. Of these shorter pieces there are about twenty published motets for mixed chorus, about a dozen for male chorus and a few for female chorus. Enumeration is complex as many of the small choral works exist in more than one version, for high, low or mixed groups. Most are with organ accompaniment but on the whole this is very discreet, judiciously employed to maintain pitch, especially in very chromatic passages. As well as motets and offertories, there are groups of chorale settings, responses and antiphons and a few *pièces de circonstance* such as *Domine salvum fac regem* for the accession of Grand Duke Carl Alexander of Weimar. A number of the short works were also arranged for solo voice and organ, e.g. the simple and effective *Ave maris stella* and the tender 1869 setting of the *Ave Maria*.

In 1822 Liszt composed a *Tantum ergo* while he was studying with Salieri. This piece is lost, but he told Ramann that his 1869 *Tantum ergo* (in two versions, one for male, the other for female voices) was similar in mood to his recollection of the early work. From among his first published sacred choruses, the free, expressive movement of the parts in the bars of the *Ave Maria* (1852 version) gives a good idea of Liszt's approach to choral layout (see Ex. 65). The cadence of this delightful, atmospheric setting is typically original: VI-II-I. Fine examples among the later motets include the first setting of *Anima Christi sanctifica me* for male voices and organ, and *Salve Regina* for *a cappella* mixed voices. *Ossa arida* (see Ex. 13) sets words from Ezekiel 37, 4: 'O ye dry bones, hear the word of the Lord'. It is one of the most dramatic instances of Liszt's symbolic use of dissonance followed by consonance to highlight a text (another illustration of this is in *Qui seminant in lacrimis*).

Liszt

Ex. 65

294

There are four settings of the Mass, and one of the Requiem Mass. The earliest is for male choir and organ (1848). It was revised in 1869 and is called the *Szekszárd Mass*, as the revision was conceived for the dedication of a church in Szekszárd. Parts of this Mass are markedly austere and there could be no better proof of how far Liszt was removed from the cloying sentimentality of so much religious music of the time, nor of how far he was in advance of the Cecilian reforms. The Mass utilises plainsong, the declamatory choral writing is laid out with skill and variety, and there are two effective passages of fugato – early in the Gloria and at 'Crucifixus'.

Conceived on the grandest scale, the *Missa Solennis* ranks high among the choral-orchestral masterpieces of the nineteenth century. Its natural symphonic flow, exciting use of choral and orchestral colour, inventive and prominent use of the quartet of soloists, vivid, daring realization of the text in both homophonic and polyphonic sections, all combine to show Liszt (in his mid-Weimar years) working at the zenith of his inspiration and imaginative powers. A unifying feature is his use of thematic reminiscence and metamorphosis: the opening motif of the 'Christe eleison' and the fanfares that announce the Gloria prove especially fruitful in this regard. Among the most telling moments in the score are the fugue on the 'cross motif' at 'Cum sancto spiritu', the brass writing at 'judicare' and, just after the dark opening orchestral phrases, the entry of 'Kyrie' to an empty fifth chord. If the work benefits from a sideways glance to Berlioz (the French-style six-part division of the choir at bar 309 of the Gloria), it also confidently gazes to the future, to Bruckner and to the Verdi of the *Requiem*.

In utter contrast the *Missa choralis* returns to the austere idiom of the male-voice Mass. It is laid out for SATB (the organ is reserved almost entirely for subtle reinforcement of the choral parts) but the voices sometimes divide into eight parts and solo sections are indicated. This worthy Mass, over which he took extreme care, shows Liszt of the Roman years consciously aiming for a purity and directness akin to sixteenth-century vocal music, although his language is entirely that of the 1860s.

The content and proportions of the *Hungarian Coronation Mass* were dictated by the nature of the ceremony for which it was composed (see Chapter 5). Following the première Liszt added a Graduale and an Offertorium. This choral-orchestral Mass makes appropriate use of 'Hungarian' modes and rhythms (especially in the Gloria, the Offertorium and the declamatory phrases that open the Sanctus). The Credo is taken from the *Messe royale* by Henri Dumont (*c.* 1610–84): it is sung mostly in unison with occasional chords added, and accompanied throughout only by organ. Conciseness (the royal ceremony must not be too long), the need to keep the music simple, and the necessary sense of solemnity were Liszt's general aims in the *Coronation Mass*. The forces are smaller than in the *Missa Solennis* and there is a complete lack of contrapuntal writing. It gains, however, from rhythmic vitality, the incorporation of Hungarian elements, the addition of the Graduale (a stirring, jubilant setting of Psalm 116 *Laudate Dominum omnes gentes*) and the truly impressive Sanctus, to which the Benedictus with its hovering, graceful violin solo (bestowing a similar benediction to that found in Beethoven's Mass in D) adds a perfect foil. The overall work is not as well-knit or as sustained in inspiration as the other orchestral Mass, but it has many virtues, it proved very popular in Liszt's lifetime and is certainly worth revival.

The *Requiem* for male voices (TTBB plus four soloists) and organ has optional parts in the Dies Irae and Sanctus for two trumpets, two trombones and timpani. It has an air of intimacy, of restraint, and was intended for church, not concert performance. Its extreme chromaticism and intensely expressed emotion look forward to *Via Crucis* of more than a decade later. The *Requiem*, for all its dissonance, darkness and deep inward reflection, is a work of exceptional and often haunting beauty, and balances its anguish with the hope of consolation.

With the psalm settings we meet a diverse array of instrumental possibilities. They are

Psalm 13	(How long, O Lord, wilt Thou forget me?) Tenor solo, mixed chorus and orchestra
Psalm 23	(The Lord is my Shepherd) Tenor *or* soprano solo, harp *or* piano, and organ *or* harmonium
Psalm 137	(By the rivers of Babylon) Mezzo-soprano solo, female chorus, violin, harp and organ
Psalm 18[2]	(The Heavens tell out the glory of God) Male chorus and orchestra, *or* organ, *or* woodwind/brass
Psalm 116[2]	(Praise the Lord, all nations) Male chorus and

[2] One number higher in the Protestant numbering, i.e. Psalm 18 = Psalm 19, etc.

piano (arranged for mixed chorus and orchestra as a Graduale for the *Hungarian Coronation Mass*)

Psalm 129[2]   (*De profundis*, Out of the depths have I called unto Thee) Baritone solo, male chorus and organ; *or* Baritone *or* alto solo and organ *or* piano.

In addition Liszt set parts of

Psalm 72[2]   (*Mihi autem adhaerere*, But it is good for me to draw near to God; an Offertory for the Mass in celebration of St. Francis of Assisi) Male chorus and organ

Psalm 122   (*In domum Domini ibimus*, Let us go into the House of the Lord) Mixed chorus, organ, brass and drums

Psalm 125[2]   (*Qui seminant in lacrimis*, They that sow in tears shall reap in joy) Mixed chorus and organ.

Psalm 13 is perhaps the best known of all Liszt's choral works. The orchestral phrases at the opening, which are immediately taken up by the tenor, undergo a number of transformations in the manner of the symphonic poems. The work contains two fugues; the first, orchestral one is a good example of Liszt using this device to express suffering and yearning (see Ex. 66). A glorious transformation of the opening theme in A flat major occurs at the words 'Schaue doch', and another stormy one at 'dass nicht mein Feind rühme'. The resolution and reassurance of hope is brought with a radiant melody, which is related to the main theme and also incorporates the 'cross' idea (see Ex. 67). After a recapitulation of the 'Schaue doch' motif, the second, choral fugue is launched triumphantly and trustingly in A major (its subject is derived from the first motto phrases). This long progress from the troubled, chromatically disturbed A minor of the opening to the final major key optimism, this passage from darkness to light, was conceived by Liszt in a passionate, heartfelt outburst of creation. He wrote to Agnes Street on 28 July 1855: 'I have left off scoring my *Prometheus* choruses to compose this psalm which welled up from the depths of my heart.'[3] Years later he told Brendel, 'The tenor

[3] *Briefe*, III 37.

297

Liszt

Ex. 66

Ex. 67

part is a very important one. I have made myself sing it, and thus
had King David's feelings poured into me in flesh and blood!'[4]

A similar minor to major transformation, from doubt and
despair to hope and transfiguration, occurs in the lovely *Psalm
137*, with its unique combination of instruments. Liszt introduces
elements of the 'gypsy scale' to identify his thoughts of home with

[4] *Briefe*, II, letter 8.

298

the psalmist's thoughts of Zion. He described the orchestral *Psalm 18* as 'very simple and massive – like a *monolith*'.[5] It is indeed majestic and monumental in effect, with bold use of monody and virtually no choral polyphony until the final Hosannas. Both the lyrically melodic *Psalm 23* and the extraordinary late *Psalm 129* (see Ex. 11) can be performed effectively by solo voice and piano.

The oratorio *The Legend of St. Elisabeth* is cast in two parts, each containing three scenes which correspond to the six frescoes of von Schwind at the Wartburg. The shape and musical style of the work have been described as operatic. This is only true to a limited extent. The series of scenes from the life of the saint lack the necessary connecting narrative or any fundamental dramatic driving force to make a stage version effective. *St. Elisabeth* has been performed as an opera; the first occasion was at Weimar in 1881, but Liszt dissociated himself from the enterprise. Lack of dramatic unity matters less on the concert platform and it is the oratorio's strength that through a disciplined series of thematic transformations, musical unity is secured. The orchestral introduction, a marvel of delicate scoring, opens with a plainsong-derived theme, which represents Elisabeth (see Ex. 68). Other traditional and Hungarian themes are used in the work.

In the first scene the child Elisabeth, daughter of the King of Hungary, arrives at the Wartburg and meets her husband-to-be, Ludwig, son of the Landgrave of Thuringia. There is a children's chorus and a recapitulation of the opening chorus of welcome. With the second scene, years have passed: the children have grown up, Ludwig is Landgrave, his wife has become renowned for her religious devotion and works of charity, but he has forbidden her to give so freely to the poor. On returning from hunting one day, he encounters her leaving the castle with a covered basket. When questioned she says she has been gathering roses. No sooner is the lie told than she confesses the truth: she is laden with bread and wine for the poor. But Ludwig looks and, to his great wonder, sees a host of roses. The scoring of this 'rose miracle' section is of great beauty. As the chorus exclaim 'The Lord has worked a miracle', Ludwig sees the light of the cross shining over her head, and the 'cross motif' rings out decisively. In the last scene of Part I Ludwig, his conversion now complete, prepares to depart on a crusade to the Holy Land. In the Crusaders' Chorus and March

---

[5] *Briefe*, II, letter 66.

Ex. 68

the 'cross' theme is further developed. Elisabeth has a presentiment that she has bade farewell to her husband forever.

In Part II Ludwig's death in Palestine is confirmed. Elisabeth is now persecuted by her mother-in-law, the Landgravine Sophie, who is characterised musically by the 'diabolic' augmented fourth. The saint is driven out of the Wartburg but, as soon as Sophie appears to have triumphed in her evil, a tremendous storm arises and her castle is struck by lightning. Years elapse, and Elisabeth is depicted in the penultimate scene, alone and homeless, wandering among the poor. A long soliloquy presents her prayer, her dreams of home and her dying vision of Ludwig in Paradise. Her soul is carried aloft by a Chorus of Angels. The finale is introduced by an orchestral interlude which recalls the main themes of the work. The Emperor Friedrich II of Hohenstaufen, a procession of crusaders, a funeral chorus of the people and the poor, and the bishops of Hungary and Germany participate in her solemn burial.

Christus is regarded by many as Liszt's choral masterpiece. The huge structure is divided thus:

Part I   *Christmas Oratorio*
1. Introduction: *Rorate coeli*
2. The Annunciation: *Angelus Domini*
3. *Stabat Mater speciosa*

4. Shepherds' song at the manger: Pastorale
5. The three Holy Kings

Part II *After Epiphany*
6. The Beatitudes
7. *Pater Noster* (The Lord's Prayer)
8. The Founding of the Church: *Tu es Petrus*
9. The Miracle
10. The Entry into Jerusalem

Part III *Passion and Resurrection*
11. *Tristis est anima mea*
12. *Stabat Mater dolorosa*
13. Easter Hymn: *O Filii et Filiae*
14. *Resurrexit*

The composer Edmund Rubbra wrote perceptively about the style, scale and language of the oratorio:

The coupling of Liszt with Wagner has had an unfortunate effect on relative judgements, giving to the former a kind of John the Baptist role that is quite contrary to actuality. Language similarities must not blind us to the fact that Liszt's is far more inventive and more prophetic, and if his sense of form had been generally more acute and less given to impulsive side-trackings, such a work as *Christus* would have received as much acclaim as *Parsifal*, which by comparison is far less deeply involved in the mysteries of faith, and moves, as it were, on the periphery of religious experience. *Christus* suggests a natural involvement with subject-matter born of the faith that Liszt undoubtedly possessed, even if it was often overlaid with the rich patina of Romanticism. Such a faith had lifted the unaffected simplicities of material largely grounded in plain-song to the expressive certainty of a Giotto fresco. The Prelude to the first part of *Christus*, with a limpid string texture based on the plain-song setting of *Rorate coeli*, has a fresh beauty with no intrusive romantic ingredients, and this kind of approach is duplicated in the following choral setting of the words from Luke describing the appearance of the angels to the shepherds. Here some of the ultra-triadic writing, with sharp changes of the harmonic centres, recalls Monteverdi and spills over into the lovely block-harmonic setting of *Stabat Mater speciosa*. Two enchantingly scored orchestral vignettes complete the first part of *Christus* (Song of the Shepherds and March of the Three Kings), the silvery splendour of the middle section of the latter a supreme example of Liszt's orchestral mastery and imagination. (*The Listener*, London, 28 Jan. 1971.)

Part II is even more impressive. The first two sections show Liszt at his most assured as composer for choir and organ. No. 8 begins with an awesome declamation by unison male chorus of the everlastingly steadfast Rock upon which the Church is founded; then in an E major section of beguiling tenderness the full chorus sing Christ's words 'Simon, son of Jonas, lovest thou me? Feed my sheep, feed my lambs'. Liszt, the unrivalled master of storm effects, excelled even himself in the description of the storm on the lake from Matthew, Chapter 8, and the moment of the calming of the waters is as breathtaking as anything in the furious crescendo that has gone before. The last number of the second part is a great musical portrait of public joy, while the first section of Part III is a profound expression of the darkness of a soul in deepest grief. These immensely contrasted scenes of Christ's earthly triumph and his agony show Liszt's versatile command of emotional effect over a wide range. Paul Merrick[6] sees No. 12 as 'the dramatic and musical apex of the oratorio ... a huge set of variations for soloists, choir and orchestra' on this plainsong, later used in *Via Crucis*:

Ex. 69

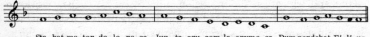

Sta-bat ma-ter do-lo-ro-sa, Jux-ta cru-cem la-crymo-sa. Dum pendebat Fi-li-us.

The Easter Hymn, which follows with refreshing simplicity, is a harmonisation of another plainsong melody. Motives from earlier in the work are recalled in the exultant, upward-striving finale. Throughout *Christus* Liszt succeeds, where Gounod and Franck failed, in blending medieval elements, plainsong and polyphony, with an advanced symphonic technique; and whereas Wagner tried to take the church into the theatre, Liszt succeeded in revitalising sacred music with true drama.

St Francis of Assisi and St Francis of Paola are linked in Liszt's well-known *Legends*. The two saints are also celebrated in works for male chorus. *An den heiligen Franziskus von Paula* is a dramatic invocation, with an accompaniment for organ, three trombones and timpani. It utilizes a theme from the second *Legend*. The *Cantico del Sol* (Hymn to the Sun) is a setting of lines by St

---

[6] Merrick, *Revolution and Religion in the Music of Liszt*, 204–8.

Francis of Assisi: the final version is scored for baritone, male chorus, organ and orchestra, but it can be performed adequately by solo voice and organ alone. The backbone of the work is the tune *In dulci jubilo*, over which a variety of rhythmic figures reflect Francis's praise of the myriad wonders of creation. Liszt was extremely fond of this work which he considered to be among his finest. He celebrated the legends of two other saints in his music. In *St Cecilia* the legend tells of her pious life and martyrdom but, more importantly, Liszt views the patron saint of music as a divine symbol of the higher power of art, in much the same way as Orpheus was portrayed in the symphonic poem. The music is based on a Gregorian chant for the Feast of St Cecilia, *Cantantibus organis*. Another work for chorus and orchestra bears that very title, and is thus also linked to St Cecilia; it was written for a Palestrina Festival in Rome in 1880. To complete Liszt's hagiography, there is the *Legend of St Christopher*, depicting the story of the immensely strong man – the Christian Atlas – in the manner of a dramatic ballad of powerful force, with a final seraphic chorus of female voices.

The Bells of Strassburg Cathedral, a short but splendidly evocative and exciting work, has a symbolism similar to *Hunnenschlacht*. Lucifer (a darkly agitated Klingsor-like baritone role) and his demons of the air attempt to tear down the cross from the spire of the cathedral in a night of storm and lightning. But the sound of the bells, represented by the basses of the choir (who sing the plainchant *Te Deum*), five deep orchestral bells and trombones, finally repel the forces of evil who sweep away defeated. There is a final radiant chorus of *Laudamus Deum verum*.

One of the projects that absorbed Liszt most deeply in the later years was *Via Crucis*, which consists of a prelude, *Vexilla regis prodeunt*, and fourteen movements representing the Stations of the Cross. It can be performed by mixed chorus with organ, piano or harmonium. The keyboard dominates much of the work and four of the Stations are for keyboard alone. No. VI is a harmonisation of the Passion chorale *O Sacred Head sore wounded*, another chorale, *O Traurigkeit*, is used in Station XII, and Liszt employs the plainchant *Crux fidelis* and the *Stabat mater* (see Ex. 69 above). This profoundly affecting work is almost a compendium of the most unusual features of Liszt's late style and it is rich in the symbols of music and religion that meant most to him.

16

Songs

Liszt's importance as a song composer has been re-appraised in recent years. Apart from a handful of popular items, his songs suffered long neglect: quite unjustly, for the best of them are very good indeed. Liszt had a natural lyric gift, his vivid imagination was often fired by literature, and when he succeeded in finding music of poetic appropriateness and sensitivity then his settings rank among the finest of the nineteenth century. An encouraging sign is the number of distinguished international singers who have recorded his songs in the last decade.[1] Scarcity of scores and lack of modern reprints have hindered the dissemination of his songs. A new complete edition, with all the versions, is urgently necessary. The composer himself, of course, did much to discourage performances of his own music over the last thirty years of his life, so disillusioned was he by public and professional criticism. But many of the songs were brought out in collected volumes under his supervision and there are several evidences of the pleasure it gave him to know of singers adding them to their repertoire.

His motivation towards song writing must include his many transcriptions of Schubert *Lieder*, his friendship with Schumann, and the great impetus he received from poetry. His literary friends were numerous and his passion for reading insatiable. The first songs number amongst the poets Goethe, Heine and Hugo (of each of whom he made seven settings), Freiligrath, Dingelstedt, Herwegh, Rellstab, Schiller, Uhland, de Musset, Dumas and Petrarch. In the Weimar years he set verses by his friends Franz von Schober and Hoffmann von Fallersleben. Song was in many ways the ideal medium for the expression of Liszt's dramatic nature, revealed through his use of violent contrast, brilliant colour, unrestrained bursts of emotion (in which Heine's texts

---

[1] Among them Janet Baker, Hildegard Behrens, Brigitte Fassbaender, Dietrich Fischer-Dieskau, Hermann Prey, Margaret Price, Sylvia Sass, Elisabeth Söderström, Frederica von Stade and Bernd Weikl.

suited him well) and orchestral treatment of the piano. The more he is in control of these elements, the better the song. Liszt had at his disposal and made full use of a spectrum of musical techniques – strophic setting, aria, arioso, measured and unmeasured recitative, 'speech-song' and actual speech.

Of the eighty-two songs listed in Appendix B there are 58 German settings, 14 French, 5 Italian, 3 Hungarian, 1 Russian and 1 English. The many versions greatly increase the actual number of published songs: Liszt revised 30 of the songs written up to 1848, another 4 exist in 3 versions, and he transcribed 8 of his songs for voice and orchestra.

His comments on his songs in his letters reveal the importance he attached to them. He implied that extremes were to be avoided: the most vehement song is still melodious and the most restrained remains expressive. He told Brendel in 1859:

> The songs in their present form can stand on their own feet ... and if some singers, neither coarse nor superficial, find the necessary courage to sing songs by the notorious non-composer Franz Liszt, then probably they too will find their public ... A couple of them made a *furore* in certain salons which are very much set against me, as *posthumous songs of Schubert* and were encored! Of course I have begged the singer to carry the joke on further.[2]

In 1862 he was gratified to hear that Schnorr von Carolsfeld (the first Tristan) had taken an interest in his 'orphaned songs'. In a sense these works are a link between the *Lieder* of Schubert and Schumann and those of Wolf and Strauss. But despite the preponderance of German settings, Liszt can never completely be considered a German song writer. His musical style remained essentially cosmopolitan. There are no especially French traits in his *mélodies*. Instead, in responding to the spirit of French and German poetry he united the Romantic souls of two nations. The language of Italian opera affected him deeply in early years and in his settings of Italian, French and German its influence is to be found. He was also intensely interested in the national music of many groups and peoples. Two of the songs have a prominent Spanish quality, *Gastibelza* and (with its guitar-like accompaniment) *Comment, disaient-ils. Die drei Zigeuner* directly reflects his gypsy ethnic interests and is akin to the Hungarian Rhapsodies in style. Significantly it is a setting of Lenau who was, like Liszt,

[2] *Briefe*, I, letter 227.

a Hungarian expatriate and who wrote in a foreign language with nostalgic memories of the country in which they were both born. Bartók's early songs have affinities with Liszt, and Kodály's songs occasionally reveal Lisztian virtuosity and harmonic effects. Liszt's songs also influenced the Balakirev circle, including Tchaikovsky.

A cosmopolitan composer of songs has certain language problems to face: firstly the obvious one of faults in stress and, secondly, misunderstanding of words or subtleties of poetic emphasis. In the first version of the Petrarch sonnet *I vidi in terra* the word *soglia* is mistakenly set as three syllables, corrected in the later version. In an Italian setting of the late years, *La Perla*, the mistake of treating the diphthong as two syllables occurs again with the word *mia*. The first version of *Mignons Lied* has a notorious, unnatural opening with stresses on *du* and *die*, which are carefully put right in the revision. In the Hungarian setting *Isten veled!* the word *szerelmed* has the accent placed mistakenly on the second syllable. There is often a struggle between music and words in the earlier songs. As his later music became simpler in texture, so his treatment of words grew more cautious, modest and respectful. When he settled in Weimar he realised that most of his earlier songs were 'too inflated and sentimental'. Then, and in the late period of song writing, he showed that he could be sensitive to textual subtleties, and that his musical imagination was equal to them. He achieved new intimacy of words and music, bringing himself near at times to Wolf's transformation into sound of the finer shades of poetic meaning. At Weimar his fidelity to speech-rhythm became very conscious, as we learn from his correspondence with a musician friend Louis Köhler, who had theories on the subject:

> Probably Schlesinger will bring out several volumes of my songs next winter, in which you will perhaps find much that is in sympathy with your ideas of '*the melody of speech*'.[3]

It is fascinating to follow Liszt's songs in chronological order, as he finds new solutions to his problems, and corrects the mistakes of earlier years, when he had occasionally done violence to a text and failed to grasp the delicate poise of a song. The early settings, which sometimes try to express the words in terms too drastic, were of an experimental order; most of them were later rewritten with fastidious care. He is at his best when he avoids over-vivid word-painting and over-emphasis of dramatic gesture. *Es war ein*

[3] 9 July 1856. *Briefe*, I, letter 154.

König in Thule is a fine song, slightly marred by the outburst of descriptive writing as the goblet sinks beneath the waves. He gradually learned that the pictorial use of accompaniment is subservient to the images of the text. His successive refinement of the flowing accompaniment of the 'river' in *Im Rhein* is a characteristic example: in the final version the majestic sweep of the river is under full control.

The three songs from Schiller's *Wilhelm Tell* capture the feeling of Alpine freshness in a way that matches the Swiss book of *Années de pèlerinage*. In these the pictorialism of the busy piano part is entirely justified. In some songs he makes a virtue of limiting his thematic figures to those derived from a short primary motif, capable of expressing the varying moods in a poem and yet retaining unity: *Es war ein König in Thule, Ich möchte hingehn* and *Die Fischerstochter*. The piano part of *Ich möchte hingehn* is of the 'symphonic' type that is so much a feature of Wolf's songs, and in stylistic mood this song foreshadows Mahler.

The moods of the chosen texts vary widely. There is possibly a predilection for poems expressing poignant grief, and there is certainly a lack of humour of the Schumann or Wolf type. Now and then there is a glimmer of that Mephistophelean quality Liszt explores so well in other works. With poems of very dramatic quality he often broke away from all previous notions of song writing and followed solely the poetic programme of the verses. This was a risky path to take in extended songs, but where he retains unity he often creates a fine result, e.g. in the ballads *Die Lorelei* and *Die drei Zigeuner*.

His occasionally operatic approach to song is perhaps seen at its most successful in the early Petrarch settings. Both *Pace non trovo* and *Benedetto sia'l giorno* have optional top D flats! The Petrarch songs and their very fine piano transcriptions represent all the romantic exuberance of Liszt's youth with great warmth and elegance. Other songs display operatic conception in terms of recitative and aria, with contrasting sections: *Die Lorelei* and *Jeanne d'Arc au bûcher* for example. Recitative-like elements abound throughout the songs, even where there are no operatic tendencies. There are many instructions like 'deklamiert', 'gesprochen' and so on. *Wo weilt er?* (a dramatic song which works well) and *Gestorben war ich* contain instances of Liszt aiming at a spoken effect. There is also an increasing tendency to leave the voice unaccompanied both at 'speech-song' moments and at points

of emphasis. *Vergiftet sind meine Lieder* calls forth Liszt's finest
declamatory and dramatic powers to make a song of extraordinary
power and harmonic boldness for its date. The vengefulness and
passion of the text are caught exactly, while Liszt at the same time
retains pity and despair.

Among the lyrical songs *Es muss sein Wunderbares sein*
justifies its popularity as a simple love lyric. He composed it
between lunch and supper for Princess Augusta of Prussia at
Ettersburg near Weimar. Likewise *Du bist wie eine Blume*, perhaps
because it too avoids any dramatic striving, retains a pure, dreamy
quality, preferable in many respects to Schumann's setting. The
final cadence, submediant to tonic, is a favourite of Liszt's. Songs
similar in mood to the *Liebesträume* group are *Kling leise, mein
Lied* and *Oh pourquoi donc*, both eloquently melodic. *Jugend-
glück*, to words by the composer's friend Richard Pohl, is exceptional among the songs for its mood of rare joyousness, owing
something to Schubert. The strophic songs range from the grandiose *Jeanne d'Arc* to the simple cradle-song for Liszt's daughter
Blandine, *Angiolin dal biondo crin*. *S'il est un charmant gazon* is
a tender evocation of the Hugo poem, and *Wieder möcht ich dir
begegnen* a fine setting of a love-lyric by Cornelius.

There are many *ossia* passages which, apart from offering
choices of difficulty or alternatives in vocal range, show yet again
the fecundity of Liszt's compositional approach. He is being
neither uncertain nor lazy in these instances but, rather, generous,
practical and deep-thinking as a creator and craftsman. Such
passages illustrate his continual striving towards a more perfect
form of expression. An excellent comparison of Liszt's approach
in his three periods of song composition can be made with the
three versions of the short *Was Liebe sei?*

Other outstanding songs which were revised or written in the
1850s include the final versions of the Goethe settings *Der du von
dem Himmel bist,* and *Über allen Gipfeln ist Ruh*, which mirror
exactly the enchantment and simplicity of the poetry, with unhur-
ried, pictorially effective chords. Similar economy and concen-
tration, and a finely gauged independence of voice and piano,
distinguish *Mignons Lied* and *Wer nie sein Brot mit Tränen ass*
in their last revisions. Again it is in the final setting of *Freudvoll
und leidvoll* that Liszt penetrates Goethe's verse most beautifully,
creating a bitter-sweet charm through lucid, uncomplicated means.
In Hebbel's *Blume und Duft* the fragrance 'that touches innermost

depths and gives promise of the Eternal' is delicately suggested by gentle syncopations and intangibly shifting harmonies. With spare, cruelly stripped plainness the accompaniment underlines the closing thought of how quickly the flower will wither. This contrast of beauty and grace with a bitter strain of melancholy is caught with equal sensitivity in Heine's *Ein Fichtenbaum steht einsam* with its contrast of the frost-bound pine and the luxuriant, oriental palm. The best of Liszt's Hugo settings, probably the masterpiece among his French songs, is *O quand je dors*, the haunting final bars of which are given in Ex. 70. Frits Noske rightly praises it as 'one of the most beautiful *mélodies* written before Duparc ... Hugo's language, so rich in imagery, has only rarely found such a worthy musical equivalent.'[4]

The songs after 1871 display in abundance the experimental, pioneering characteristics of Liszt's late style. De Musset's *J'ai perdu ma force et ma vie* has been seen as a symbol of Liszt's last period: it is a sad, affecting reflection on the weariness and resignation of an old man. But the old Liszt did not lack sincerity or a burning necessity to express new thoughts in music. The poetry he selected is of mixed quality; little of it is profound but most of it is highly successful in making its effect. This could almost be a judgement of the music itself, so much does it reflect the texts. Prominent features are atmospheric use of (sometimes startling) harmony and long passages of unaccompanied (sometimes unbarred) vocal declamation. In the exquisite *Des Tages laute Stimmen schweigen* the last sentence, 'I hear you sigh softly still, then night kisses you softly and gently', is left to the whispering voice alone, supported before and after by pianissimo piano chords. Cadences are all unorthodox, floating, longing, 'unfinished' in effect. Expressionist directness and extreme brevity, subtle and carefully calculated touches of just the right accompanimental or reflective piano gesture, add up to a style where every single note (perhaps more importantly every single *rest*) counts for much, to an extent unprecedented before Webern. *Einst* and *Gebet* are good examples. *Ihr Glocken von Marling* is more impressionistic with its clusters of bell-chords. In his Tennyson setting *Go not, happy day* the image of roses drew from Liszt a self-quotation from the 'rose miracle' section of his *St Elisabeth*.

The melodrama form appealed considerably to Liszt, although it has never become a favourite device either in the

[4] *French Song from Berlioz to Duparc*, New York, 1970, 127–36.

Liszt

Ex. 70

concert hall, where it had only a period of fashionability, or in the theatre, where its use was also limited. Liszt gave the first performance of Schumann's *Manfred*; other important works of the melodrama type in his day include Berlioz' *Lélio* and Grieg's

Bergliot. Later, Strauss provided music for the recitation of Tennyson's *Enoch Arden* and Uhland's *Das Schloss am Meer*, both of which recall Liszt. Of his own melodramas four are with piano and one with orchestra. They are all remarkably atmospheric, and *Der traurige Mönch* is harmonically the most extraordinary (see Ex. 2).

Liszt's orchestrations of his songs are all too rarely performed and yet, historically, they are landmarks between the orchestral songs of Berlioz and those of Mahler and Strauss. The only French orchestral song, *Jeanne d'Arc au bûcher*, was a favourite of the Wagnerian soprano Marianne Brandt. *Die Lorelei,* which is like a miniature symphonic poem, benefits from instrumentation, making particular use of solo violin (also a feature of the arrangement of *Die drei Zigeuner*). Varied timbres and original layout of textures add colour and lustre to Mignon's vision of Italy, *Kennst du das Land?* In the three Schiller songs from *Wilhelm Tell* the orchestra contributes significant touches to what are, in their original form, pictorial and evocative settings. Another orchestration of one of Liszt's Goethe songs was made by Tchaikovsky in 1874: *Es war ein König in Thule*. Liszt himself made tasteful and perceptive arrangements of six of Schubert's songs.

His last song orchestration, indeed the last composition on which he worked, was Uhland's *Die Vätergruft* (1886) – a poem he had first set in 1844 when he was only thirty-two. It can thus be said to have accompanied him throughout his song-writing career. The words of this sombre ballad are uncannily apposite: an old warrior comes to take his place in the tomb of his ancestors. Liszt, the old warrior, had fought his last battle throwing open the gates to the twentieth century.

Appendix A

Calendar

Year	Age	Life	Contemporary musicians and events
1811		Adam Liszt (34), an employee on the Esterházy estates, and Maria Anna Lager (22) marry, 11 Jan., in Raiding (Doborján) near Oedenburg (Sopron) – a predominantly German-speaking part of Hungary. Their son Franz is born there, 22 Oct.	Ambroise Thomas born, 5 Aug. Ferdinand Hiller born, 24 Oct. Adolphe Adam aged 8; Auber 29; Balfe 3; Beethoven 40; Bellini 9; Berlioz 7; Berwald 15; Boieldieu 35; Cherubini 51; Chopin 1; Clementi 59; Cramer 40; Czerny 20; Diabelli 30; Donizetti 13; Dussek 51; Erkel 1; Field 29; Glinka 7; Gossec 77; Grétry 70; Halévy 12; Hérold 20; Herz 8; Hummel 32; Kalkbrenner 25; Kalliwoda 11; Kuhlau 25; Loewe 14; Lortzing 9; Marschner 16; Méhul 48; Mendelssohn 2; Mercadante 16; Meyerbeer 20; Moscheles 17; Nicolai 1; Paer 40; Paganini 28; Reicha 41; Ries 26; Rossini 19; Salieri 61; Schubert 14; Schumann 1; Spohr 27; Spontini 36; Tomášek 37; Weber 24.
1812	1		Thalberg born, 8 Jan. Vincent Wallace born, 11 Mar. Dussek (52) dies, 20 Mar. Flotow born, 27 Apr. Beethoven (42) completes Symphonies 7 and 8. Napoleon retreats from Moscow.
1813	2		Dargomizhsky born, 14 Feb. Heller born, 15 May. Wagner born 22 May. Grétry (72) dies 24 Sep. Verdi born, 10 Oct.

Year	Age	Life	Contemporary musicians and events
			Alkan born, 30 Nov.
1814	3		John Field (32): first *Nocturnes* pub. Schubert (17): *Gretchen am Spinnrade*. Stephenson constructs the first steam locomotive. Mälzel invents the metronome.
1815	4		Robert Franz born, 28 June. Mosonyi born, 4 Sep.
1816	5		Sterndale Bennett born, 13 April. Rossini (24): *The Barber of Seville*. Carl August of Saxe-Weimar grants the first German constitution.
1817	6	Shows interest in his father's piano playing, music of gypsies and of the Church.	Méhul (54) dies, 18 Oct. Clementi (65): *Gradus ad Parnassum*. Lamennais (35): *Essai sur l'indifférence*.
1818	7	Piano lessons from his father result in remarkably quick progress.	Karl Marx born, 5 May. Gounod born, 17 June.
1819	8	Fluent in sight-reading, extemporisation; repertory from Bach to Hummel. Plays to Czerny (27).	Offenbach born, 20 June. Abt born, 22 Dec. Beethoven (49): Sonata op. 106. Byron (31): *Mazeppa*.
1820	9	Gives his first concert, Oct., Oedenburg. Another concert in Pressburg (Bratislava) results in an award from various Hungarian aristocrats, enabling him to study in Vienna.	Lamartine (30): *Méditations poétiques*. Britain: George IV ascends the throne.
1821	10	Further lessons from Adam, who requests his employer to grant permission to leave Hungary.	Weber (34): *Der Freischütz*. Comte de Saint-Simon (61): *Du Système industriel*. Napoleon I (52) dies, 5 May. Erard patents double-escapement piano action.
1822	11	The family moves to Vienna. Liszt studies piano with Czerny (30) and composition with Salieri (71). Writes	Raff born, 27 May. Franck born, 10 Dec. Schubert (25): *Unfinished Symphony*.

Year	Age	Life	Contemporary musicians and events
		Variation on a Waltz by Diabelli. Vienna debut, 1 Dec.	
1823	12	Further Vienna concerts; meets Beethoven. Plays in Pest, May; and in various German towns en route for Paris, where the family arrives, 11 Dec. Cherubini (63) refuses Liszt admission to the conservatoire.	Lalo born, 27 Jan. Beethoven (53): *Choral Symphony, Diabelli Variations.*
1824	13	Writes several bravura piano works. Paris debut, 7 Mar., causes a sensation. Befriended by Erard who arranges an English tour. Liszt's mother leaves Paris for Austria, while Adam and Franz leave for London. Debut there, 21 June. Appears at Windsor before George IV, and plays in Manchester, Aug. Begins composition lessons with Paer (52) in Paris.	Smetana born, 2 Mar. Bruckner born, 4 Sep. Cornelius born, 24 Dec. France: Charles X crowned. Byron (36) dies at Missolonghi.
1825	14	Tours southern France. Second English tour. His opera *Don Sanche* produced, Paris, Oct.	Salieri (74) dies, 7 May. Hanslick born, 11 Sep. Johann Strauss II born, 25 Oct. Beethoven (55): Quartets opp. 127, 130, 132, *Grosse Fuge.* Saint-Simon (65): *Nouveau Christianisme.* The Hungarian Diet is reopened after 13 years and the Hungarian Academy of Sciences founded.
1826	15	Second tour of French provinces. Studies with Reicha (56). Publishes *Études en douze exercices.* Tour of Switzerland.	Weber (39) dies, 5 June. Mendelssohn (17): *Midsummer Night's Dream* music.
1827	16	3rd visit to England; performs an early piano concerto. Composes Scherzo in G minor. Father and son go to Boulogne for a rest cure and Adam Liszt (50) dies there, 28 Aug. Liszt	Beethoven (56) dies, 26 Mar. Heine (30): *Buch der Lieder.* Schubert (30): *Winterreise.*

Year	Age	Life	Contemporary musicians and events
		returns to Paris and commences teaching; his mother joins him.	
1828	17	Affair with his pupil Caroline de Saint-Cricq, whose father intervenes and separates the pair. Liszt suffers acute melancholy and various illnesses. Seeks consolation in religion and Romantic literature.	Schubert (31) dies, 19 Nov. Goethe's *Faust* Part I, first perf.
1829	18	Continuing depression and disillusionment with the virtuoso's lifestyle. Reads literature imbued with *le mal du siècle*: Chateaubriand, Constant, Senancour. Continues teaching.	Gossec (95) dies, 16 Feb. Gottschalk born, 8 May. Anton Rubinstein born, 28 Nov. Berlioz (25): *Symphonie Fantastique* (–1830). Rossini (37): *William Tell*. Victor Hugo (27): *Les Orientales*.
1830	19	Events in Paris awaken Liszt to a positive philosophy of life. He sketches a *Revolutionary Symphony*; soon makes the acquaintance of Lamartine, Hugo and Heine; is attracted to Saint-Simonism; meets Berlioz (26) and attends the première of his *Symphonie Fantastique*, 5 Dec.	von Bülow born, 8 Jan. Goldmark born, 18 May. Leschetitzky born, 22 June. Mendelssohn (21): first *Songs without Words*. July revolution in France: Louis Philippe elected King. Lamennais advocates a free press and religious toleration. Britain: William IV succeeds to the throne.
1831	20	Paris debut of Paganini (48), 9 Mar. Liszt spends some time in Geneva. Friendship with Mendelssohn and Hiller.	Joachim born, 28 June. Jadassohn born, 13 Aug. Bellini (30): *La Sonnambula, Norma*. Schumann (21): *Papillons*. Meyerbeer (40): *Robert le diable*. Hugo (29): *Notre Dame de Paris*.
1832	21	Chopin's Paris debut, 26 Feb. Liszt befriends him. Paganini's performances spur him on to attain a new virtuosity and further the possibilities of piano technique; writes Fantasy on Paganini's *La Clochette*. Attends lectures by	Clementi (80) dies, 10 Mar. Kuhlau (45) dies, 12 Mar. Goethe (82) dies, 22 Mar. Chopin (22): *Mazurkas* opps. 6 and 7. G. Sand (28): *Indiana*. Hugo (30): *Le Roi s'amuse*.

Year	Age	Life	Contemporary musicians and events
		Fétis (48) on the philosophy of music.	
1833	22	Affair with Comtesse Marie d'Agoult (27) begins. Plays with Chopin at a benefit concert for Harriet Smithson, Apr.; in Oct. acts as witness at her marriage to Berlioz. Makes piano arrangement of the *Symphonie Fantastique,* and his first Schubert song transcription.	Hérold (41) dies, 19 Jan. Brahms born, 7 May. Borodin born, 12 Nov. Mendelssohn (24): *Italian Symphony.* Chopin (23): *Études* op. 10. G. Sand (29): *Lélia.*
1834	23	Stays with Lamennais at La Chênaie, autumn. Piano works: *Harmonies poétiques et religieuses* (single piece; 1833, revised 1835); *Apparitions.* Essay: *On the future of Church music.* First performance of *Lélio Fantasy* for piano and orchestra (Berlioz conducting), 24 Nov. de Musset (24) introduces Liszt to George Sand (30).	Reubke born, 23 Mar. Ponchielli born, 31 Aug. Boieldieu (58) dies, 8 Oct. Wagner (21): *Die Feen.* Berlioz (31): *Harold in Italy.* Schumann (24) founds *Neue Zeitschrift für Musik.* Revolt of silk workers in Lyon, Apr. Republican riots in Paris crushed. Lamennais (52): *Paroles d'un croyant.*
1835	24	Writes *Réminiscences de La Juive* – based on the new opera by Halévy (35). After concerts in Paris elopes to Switzerland with Marie d'Agoult, early June. Here Liszt finds inspiration for his *Album d'un voyageur* and teaches at the Geneva Conservatoire. Their daughter Blandine born, 18 Dec. Essay: *On the Position of Artists.*	Cui born, 18 Jan. Bellini (33) dies, 24 Sep. Saint-Saëns born, 9 Oct. Donizetti (38): *Lucia di Lammermoor.*
1836	25	Many piano arrangements especially of Bellini, Donizetti and Meyerbeer. Concerts in Lyon, Apr.; visits Paris, May; plays in Lausanne and Dijon, June–July. Rejoins Marie in Geneva, where George Sand visits them, Aug.–Oct. The	Delibes born, 21 Feb. Reicha (66) dies, 28 May. Meyerbeer (45): *Les Huguenots.* Glinka (32): *A Life for the Czar.* Chopin (26): *Ballade in G minor.* France: Louis Napoleon (28) exiled after attempted coup. Arc de

Year	Age	Life	Contemporary musicians and events
		trio then settle in Paris and Liszt introduces Sand to Chopin, Nov.	Triomphe, Paris, completed. Communist League founded, Paris.
1837	26	Rivalry between Thalberg (25) and Liszt who takes part in a series of distinguished chamber concerts, hires the Opéra for a concert, 19 Mar. and faces Thalberg in the famous 'duel' at the salon of Princess Belgiojoso, 31 Mar. At Nohant with George Sand and Marie, May–July. Transcribes Schubert songs and Beethoven symphonies. To Italy with Marie, autumn. *12 Grand Études* written. Their second daughter, Cosima, born at Como, 24 Dec.	Balakirev born, 2 Jan. Jensen born, 12 Jan. Field (54) dies, 23 Jan. Hummel (58) dies, 17 Oct. Berlioz (34): *Benvenuto Cellini*. Britain: Queen Victoria crowned.
1838	27	In Milan and Venice. Learns of flood disaster in Pest and plays in Vienna in aid of the victims, Apr.–May. The remainder of the year in Italy, where work includes *Études d'après Paganini* and the *Grand galop chromatique*.	Bruch born, 6 Jan. Ries (53) dies, 13 Jan. Bizet born, 25 Oct. Schumann (28): *Kinderszenen, Kreisleriana*.
1839	28	First six months in Rome: friendship with Ingres (58); Liszt gives the first solo 'recital'; his son Daniel born, 9 May. Offers to pay the balance for the proposed Beethoven monument in Bonn. Relations deteriorate with Marie, who returns to France, Oct. Liszt's years as a touring virtuoso begin with concerts in Vienna, Nov. Returns to Hungary for first time since childhood. Commences *Magyar Dallok* (–1847). Writes first songs and sketches pieces for Italian book of *Années de pèlerinage*.	Mussorgsky born, 21 Mar. Paer (57) dies, 3 May. Chopin (29): *Preludes* Op 28. Berlioz (36): *Romeo and Juliet*. Balzac (40): *Béatrix*. W. H. Fox Talbot (37) prints a photographic negative and Daguerre (49) produces his first images.

317

Year	Age	Life	Contemporary musicians and events
1840	29	Great acclaim in Pest where he is presented with the sword of honour, and conducts for the first time. Further concerts in Brno, Vienna, Prague, Dresden and Leipzig. Meets Schumann, Mar., and Wagner, in Paris, Apr., for the first time. Visits London, May–June, and plays before Queen Victoria. After tours of Rhineland towns returns to England, Aug.–Sep. 6 concerts in Hamburg are followed by his 3rd visit to England this year, the tour continuing in Ireland from 17 Dec.	Tchaikovsky born, 7 May. Paganini (57) dies, 27 May. Svendsen born, 30 Sep. Schumann (30): many *Lieder*. Louis Napoleon (32) imprisoned after attempted rising at Boulogne. Sainte-Beuve (36) begins *Histoire de Port-Royal*.
1841	30	Concerts in Ireland and Scotland, Jan., then in Brussels, Liège and (during a 6-week stay) Paris. Another London visit, May–early July, and subsequent concerts in Hamburg, Kiel and Copenhagen, followed by a holiday on the Rhine island of Nonnenwerth, which he visits with Marie for the following 2 summers. Concert tour of Germany begins in autumn. Many transcriptions including those based on *Don Giovanni*, *Norma* and *Robert le diable*; also songs and secular choruses.	Chabrier born, 18 Jan. Sgambati born, 28 May. Dvořák born, 8 Sep. Tausig born, 4 Nov. Wagner (28): *The Flying Dutchman*.
1842	31	Sensational success in Berlin with 21 public and additional private concerts. First visit to Russia. Concerts in Paris and Belgium; meets Franck (19). Appointed honorary Kapellmeister at Weimar, Oct., but continues touring Holland and Germany to end of year.	Boito born, 24 Feb. Cherubini (81) dies, 15 Mar. Massenet born, 12 May. Glinka (38): *Russlan and Ludmilla*.

Year	Age	Life	Contemporary musicians and events
1843	32	Concerts in Berlin and Breslau (where he conducts opera for the first time). Visits to Poland and Russia, where he meets Glinka (39) and Dargomizhsky (30). After a stay in Hamburg holidays for the last time with Marie on Nonnenwerth, and once more spends the autumn and winter touring Germany. Publishes his first songs, including settings of Heine, Goethe and Hugo.	Grieg born, 15 June.
1844	33	In Weimar, Jan.–Feb. Attends performance of *Rienzi* in Dresden. Liaison with Lola Montez (24). Final break with Marie, although correspondence continues. Concerts in Germany, Paris, Provence, Languedoc and Spain.	Rimsky-Korsakov born, 18 Mar. Erkel (34): *Hunyady László*. Verdi (31): *Ernani*. London debut of Joachim (13).
1845	34	Early year in Spain and Portugal. Writes *Le Forgeron*. First *Beethoven Cantata* performed at unveiling of the Beethoven monument in Bonn, Aug. Concerts in Germany and eastern France, autumn.	Fauré born, 12 May. Wagner (32): *Tannhäuser*.
1846	35	In France, Frankfurt and Weimar. Concerts in Vienna, Brno and Prague, Mar.–Apr. The summer and autumn in Hungary and Romania. Renewed interest in gypsy music: *First Hungarian Rhapsody*.	Korbay born, 8 May. Berlioz (43): *The Damnation of Faust*. Marie d'Agoult (40): *Nélida*. Pope Pius IX elected.
1847	36	From Bucharest to the Ukraine. Meets Princess Carolyne zu Sayn-Wittgenstein (28) in Kiev, Feb., and spends some time at her	Mackenzie born, 22 Aug. Mendelssohn (38) dies, 4 Nov.

Year	Age	Life	Contemporary musicians and events
		estate at Woronince. Then in Lemberg, Czernovtsy, Jassi and Constantinople, June–July. Final concerts at Odessa and Elisabetgrad, 14 Sep., ending Liszt's virtuoso career. He never again accepts a fee for public performance. At Woronince to end of year. Works: *Glanes de Woronince; Harmonies poétiques et religieuses* (–1852).	
1848	37	In Weimar, Feb. To Prince Lichnowsky's castle at Křižanovice to await the arrival of Carolyne and her daughter from Russia. (Lichnowsky (34) assassinated outside the Frankfurt parliament, Sep.) Assists Smetana (24) publish his op. 1. To Vienna with Carolyne, May; they visit Eisenstadt and his birthplace, Raiding. Settles permanently in Weimar, June, after visiting Wagner in Dresden; Wagner in turn visits Weimar, Aug. *Consolations, Arbeiterchor* and *Mass for male chorus* written, and first versions symphonic poems *Les Préludes* and *Ce qu'on entend sur la montagne* (–1849).	Duparc born, 21 Jan. Parry born, 27 Feb. Donizetti (50) dies, 8 Apr. Wagner (35): *Lohengrin*. Marx (30) and Engels (28): *Communist Manifesto*. Revolt in Paris, republican government proclaimed under Lamartine (58). Further risings during year; Louis Napoleon (50) elected president, Dec. Uprisings in Vienna, Prague, Poland, Italian States, Danubian provinces. Kossuth (46) proclaimed president of committee for national defence of Hungary, Sep.
1849	38	Conducts *Tannhäuser*, 16 Feb. Wagner flees to Weimar from the unsuccessful Dresden revolt, May, and Liszt aids his escape to Switzerland. *Tasso* (1st version) premièred Weimar, 28 Aug. Visits north Germany, autumn. *Années de pèlerinage II (Italy)* completed.	Nicolai (38) dies, 11 May. Kalkbrenner (64) dies, 10 June. Chopin (39) dies, 17 Oct. Meyerbeer (58): *Le Prophète*. Schumann (39): *Manfred*. Prussia, Austria and Russia crush revolts in Germany, Italy and Hungary. Kossuth flees his short-lived independent republic. The French overthrow the Rome republic

Year	Age	Life	Contemporary musicians and events
			of Mazzini and Garibaldi and restore Pius IX who, in an encyclical, condemns socialism.
1850	39	Première of *Prometheus* (1st version), 24 Aug. Conducts première of Wagner's *Lohengrin*, 28 Aug. Joachim (19) becomes leader of Weimar orchestra; Raff (28) and Liszt's mother also in Weimar. Completes *Heroïde funèbre* (1st version); organ fantasia and fugue *Ad nos, ad salutarem undam*.	Tomášek (75) dies, 3 Apr. Fibich born, 21 Dec. Balzac (51) dies, 17 Aug.
1851	40	Première of symphonic arrangements of Weber's *Polonaise brillante*, Weimar 14 Apr., and of Schubert's *Wanderer Fantasia*, Vienna 14 Dec. Bülow (21) at Weimar as Liszt's pupil. Completes symphonic poem *Mazeppa* (1st version); *Scherzo and March; Deux Polonaises;* final versions of *Études d'exécution transcendante* and *Grandes Études de Paganini*. Articles (assisted by Carolyne) including book *F. Chopin*.	Lortzing (49) dies, 21 Jan. Spontini (76) dies, 24 Jan. d'Indy born, 27 Mar. Verdi (38): *Rigoletto*. Longfellow (44): *The Golden Legend*. Wagner (38): *Opera and Drama*. The Great Exhibition, London.
1852	41	Conducts premières of *Benvenuto Cellini* (Berlioz, revised version), Weimar 20 Mar., and *Manfred* (Schumann) 13 June. Cornelius (27) in Weimar. Liszt mounts a Berlioz week in Weimar, Nov., attended by the composer. Writes Fantasia for piano and orchestra on Hungarian Folk Themes. Joachim (21) leaves Weimar, Dec.	The Second Empire proclaimed in France under Napoleon III (54), Dec.

Year	Age	Life	Contemporary musicians and events
1853	42	Completes *Sonata in B minor; Festklänge; Ballade No 2.* Brahms and Reményi (25) visit Weimar, June. Liszt visits Wagner in Zurich, July; they meet again in Basel, Oct., and together make a short visit with Carolyne to Paris, where Liszt sees his children.	Messager born, 30 Dec. Brahms (20): Piano Sonata in C, op. 1. Haussmann begins reconstruction of Paris. Verdi (40): *Il Trovatore, La Traviata.* Vienna-Trieste railway built through the Alps. Russia invades Danubian provinces, precipitating the Crimean War.
1854	43	Premières of symphonic poems *Orpheus, Festklänge* and (in final versions) *Les Préludes, Mazeppa, Tasso; Hungaria* composed. *Faust Symphony* complete (except final chorus), Oct. Liszt premières Schubert's opera *Alfonso and Estrella,* June. Conducts many other operas and concerts. Visits Holland, Belgium and north Germany, July. Affair with Agnes Street begins. George Eliot (44) in Weimar. Liszt collaborates with Carolyne in many prose articles.	Janáček born, 3 July. Moszkowski born, 23 Aug. Humperdinck born, 1 Sep. Lamennais (71) dies, 27 Feb. Harriet Smithson (54) dies, 3 Mar. Berlioz (51): *L'enfance du Christ.* Pius IX declares the dogma of the Immaculate Conception of the Blessed Virgin Mary to be an article of faith. Moritz von Schwind (50) paints frescoes at Wartburg Castle depicting the life of St Elizabeth of Hungary.
1855	44	*Piano Concerto in E flat* premièred, Liszt as soloist, Berlioz conducting, during a second Berlioz festival at Weimar. *Missa Solennis* and *Prelude and Fugue on BACH* for organ composed. Attends first perf. of *Ad Nos* (A. Winterberger, organ) Merseburg. Conducts *Prometheus* (final version), Brunswick 18 Oct., and *Psalm 13* Berlin 6 Dec. Second major phase of song-writing (–1860). *Années de pèlerinage I* (*Switzerland*) pub. Tausig becomes Liszt's pupil.	Chausson born, 20 Jan. Liadov born, 11 May. Russia: Alexander II succeeds as Czar. Paris World Fair. Steinway of New York manufacture pianos with cross-stringing.

Year	Age	Life	Contemporary musicians and events
1856	45	Conducts at Mozart Centenary Festival, Vienna, 3 Jan. Berlioz week at Weimar, Feb. *Dante Symphony* completed, July. To Hungary for premières of *Missa Solennis*, Esztergom 31 Aug., and *Hungaria*, Pest 8 Sep. Carolyne and Liszt visit Wagner in Zurich, Oct., and the two composers jointly conduct a concert at St Gallen, 23 Nov.	Heine (58) dies, 17 Feb. Adam (52) dies, 3 May. Schumann (46) dies, 29 July. Dargomizhsky (43): *Russalka*. Austria declares amnesty for Hungarian rebels of 1848–9.
1857	46	First perfs of *Piano Concerto in A major* (soloist Bronsart) and *Ce qu'on entend sur la montagne* (final version), Weimar 7 Jan.; *Sonata in B minor* (soloist Bülow), Berlin 22 Jan.; *Faust Symphony* and *Die Ideale*, Weimar 5 Sep.; *Dante Symphony*, Dresden 7 Nov.; *Heroïde funèbre* (final version), Breslau 10 Nov.; *Hunnenschlacht*, Weimar 29 Dec. Smetana (33) visits Weimar (and in 1859). Liszt's concerts in Leipzig Feb., Aachen, May–June, and Dresden, Nov., provoke much opposition and in Weimar his position is weakening. Both Liszt's daughters are married: Cosima (19) to Hans von Bülow (27), 18 Aug.; Blandine (21) to Emile Ollivier (32), 22 Oct.	Kienzl born, 17 Jan. Glinka (52) dies, 15 Feb. Elgar born, 2 June. Czerny (66) dies, 15 July. Wagner (44) interrupts composition of *The Ring* after *Siegfried* Act 2, and commences *Tristan*. Baudelaire (36): *Les Fleurs du Mal*.
1858	47	Visits Prague and Pest, Mar.–Apr. *Hamlet* composed. Growing disillusionment with criticism of his works and aims. The première of *The Barber of Baghdad* by Cornelius (34) at Weimar, 15 Dec., provokes a hostile	Matthay born, 19 Feb. Diabelli (76) dies, 7 Apr. Leoncavallo born, 8 Mar. Cramer (87) dies, 16 Apr. Reubke (24) dies, 3 June. Puccini born, 23 Dec. Berlioz (54) completes *Les Troyens*. Covent Garden Opera House built.

Year	Age	Life	Contemporary musicians and events
		demonstration against Liszt, who resigns his post.	
1859	48	Cooling of relations with Wagner. Work includes *Psalms 23* and *137; Venezia e Napoli* (final version); Verdi arrangements from *Ernani, Il Trovatore, Rigoletto;* article *John Field and his Nocturnes* and book *The Gypsies and their music in Hungary. The Beatitudes* (part of *Christus*) performed, Weimar 2 Oct. Liszt's son becomes critically ill in Berlin; Liszt hastens there, but Daniel (20) dies, 13 Dec.	Spohr (75) dies, 22 Oct. Gounod (41): *Faust.* Darwin (50): *The Origin of Species.* Franco-Austrian War: Austria defeated in Italy.
1860	49	Joachim (29), Brahms (27) and others publish a *Manifesto* attacking Liszt and other 'New German' composers. Carolyne leaves Weimar for Rome, May. Liszt makes his Will. His first grandchild Daniela von Bülow born, 12 Oct. Writes *Psalm 18; Two Episodes from Lenau's 'Faust'; Les Morts.*	Wolf born, 13 Mar. Albéniz born, 29 May. Charpentier born, 25 June. Mahler born, 7 July. Paderewski born, 6 Nov. Garibaldi proclaims Victor Emmanuel King of Italy.
1861	50	Visits Paris, May. Plays to Napoleon III; sees many acquaintances; meets Bizet (22), Marie d'Agoult (55) and Wagner (48). After the inaugural festival of the *Allgemeiner Deutscher Musikverein*, Weimar, Aug., Liszt leaves Weimar. Visits Löwenberg and Berlin; travels to Marseilles and sets sail for Italy. The planned marriage to Carolyne in Rome on his fiftieth birthday, 22 Oct., does not, however, take place. They continue to live in Rome in separate apartments.	Arensky born, 12 July. Marschner (66) dies, 14 Dec. Paris: Wagner's *Tannhäuser* fiasco, Mar. Outbreak of American Civil War.

Year	Age	Life	Contemporary musicians and events
1862	51	A son, Daniel, born to Liszt's daughter Blandine Ollivier (26), 3 July, but she dies in Sep. Oratorio *St Elisabeth* completed. Also writes *Cantico del sol di S. Francesco d'Assisi* and the piano variations *Weinen, Klagen*.	Delius born, 29 Jan. Halévy (62) dies, 17 Mar. Debussy born, 22 Aug. Hugo (60): *Les Misérables*. Helmholtz (41): *Sensations of Tones*. Bismarck (47) premier of Prussia.
1863	52	Liszt enters the monastery of the Madonna del Rosario, June, where the pope visits him, 11 July, and hears him play.	Mascagni born, 7 Dec. Delacroix (64) dies, 13 Aug. de Vigny (66) dies, 17 Sep. Bizet (25): *The Pearl Fishers*.
1864	53	First visit, June, to Villa d'Este, Tivoli, where he is to stay frequently as a guest of Archbishop Hohenlohe. Visits music festival at Carlsruhe with Cosima, Aug., and sees Wagner at Starnberg and Munich where he is under the patronage of Ludwig II, and where his adulterous relations with Cosima have commenced. In Paris with Cosima, Oct.; sees his mother and Marie d'Agoult. *La Notte* composed.	d'Albert born, 10 Apr. Meyerbeer (72) dies, 2 May. R. Strauss born, 11 June; Grechaninov born, 25 Oct. Bruckner (40): Mass in D minor. Schleswig-Holstein conflict. Ludwig II (18) ascends the Bavarian throne.
1865	54	Cosima gives birth to Isolde (Wagner's daughter) 12 Apr. Bülow premières Liszt's *Totentanz*, The Hague, 15 Apr. Liszt gives a recital in the Palazzo Barberini, 20 Apr.; and on 25th receives the tonsure from Hohenlohe and enters the Vatican. Receives further minor orders of the Church, Villa d'Este, 30 July. To Pest for the première of *St Elisabeth*, 15 Aug. Bülow and Cosima present. Liszt plays his *Deux Légendes* in public for first time, 29 Aug. Returns to	Nielsen born, 9 June. Glazunov born, 10 Aug. Dukas born, 1 Oct. V. Wallace (53) dies, 12 Oct. Sibelius born, 8 Dec. U.S. Civil War ends.

Year	Age	Life	Contemporary musicians and events
		the Vatican, Sep. *Missa choralis* written.	
1866	55	His mother dies, Paris, 6 Feb. Liszt visits her grave, Mar., and hears his *Missa Solennis* at the church of St Eustache: poor reception. Hears Franck (43) play the organ, and Saint-Saëns (30) take part in a 4-hand arrangement of the *Dante Symphony* at the home of Gustave Doré (34). Last meeting with Marie d'Agoult. Returns to Rome, May. Composes *Le Triomphe funèbre du Tasse.*	Busoni born, 1 Apr. Satie born, 17 May. Kalliwoda (65) dies, 3 Dec. Smetana (42): *The Bartered Bride.* Seven Weeks War among German States and Austria. War between Austria and Italy.
1867	56	Visits Pest for première of *Hungarian Coronation Mass,* 8 June, at the coronation of Franz Joseph as king of Hungary. *Christus* now complete, and the *Christmas Oratorio* from it is heard in Rome, 6 July. In Weimar for *St Elisabeth* performance, 28 Aug. In Munich, Sep.–Oct.; visits Wagner at Tribschen. Returns to Rome and remains in Italy until end of 1868.	Granados born, 27 July. Koechlin born, 27 Nov. Verdi (54): *Don Carlos.* Wagner (54): *Die Meistersinger.* Ingres (87) dies, 17 Jan. Baudelaire (46) dies, 31 Aug. Hungary achieves a compromise degree of independence: the Diet reopened, dual monarchy with Austria. Garibaldi's march on Rome defeated by French and Papal troops, Nov.
1868	57	*Requiem* completed. At Grottamare, near Ancona July–Aug., for theological instruction. Cosima leaves Bülow forever, to live with Wagner, Nov.	Berwald (71) dies, 3 Apr. Rossini (76) dies, 13 Nov. Grieg (25) *Piano Concerto.* Brahms (35): *A German Requiem.*
1869	58	Longfellow (61) visits Liszt, Rome, Jan. To Weimar, 12 Jan.; visit from Duparc (21). To Vienna, Mar. In Pest, late April. Returns to Rome early May. Thus begins his 'Vie trifurquée' in which almost every year till his death he spends some months (usually	Dargomizhsky (55) dies, 17 Jan. Berlioz (65) dies, 8 Mar. Loewe (73) dies, 20 Apr. Pfitzner born, 5 May. Gottschalk (40) dies, 18 Dec. Lamartine (79) dies, 28 Feb. Sainte-Beuve (65) dies, 13 Oct. The Suez Canal opened. First Vatican Council.

Year	Age	Life	Contemporary musicians and events
		the summer) teaching and working in Weimar; some months (usually the winter and spring) in Budapest, and some months (usually the autumn and winter) in Rome and Tivoli. Acquaintance with Olga Janina begins. Attends rehearsal of Wagner's *Rheingold*, Munich, Aug. Writes several sacred choral works.	
1870	59	At Villa d'Este and in Rome, where Grieg (26) visits him, until late Mar. Conducts 2nd *Beethoven Cantata*, as part of centenary celebrations, Weimar, 29 May. Attends première of Wagner's *Die Walküre*, Munich, July. Bülow and Cosima granted divorce, and she marries Wagner 25 Aug. Liszt in Hungary from Aug. (–April 1871). Writes *Funeral Music for Mosonyi*.	Godowsky born, 13 Feb. Moscheles (75) dies, 10 Mar. Lehár born, 30 Apr. Balfe (62) dies, 20 Oct. Mosonyi (55) dies, 31 Oct. Mercadante (75) dies, 17 Dec. Mussorgsky (31): *Boris Godunov*. Lenin born, 9 Apr. Emile Ollivier (44) becomes French premier, 2 Jan. Franco-Prussian War begins, July. Napoleon III (62) capitulates at Sedan, Sep. Dogma of Papal Infallibility declared. Rome becomes the capital of Italy.
1871	60	Close friendship and correspondence with Baroness Olga von Meyendorff (33) begins. Last phase of song writing (–1880). Bülow with Liszt in Rome, Oct. Olga Janina's attempt to kill Liszt and herself, Pest, Nov.	Thalberg (59) dies, 27 Apr. Auber (89) dies, 13 May. Tausig (29) dies, 17 July. Verdi (58): *Aida*. Wilhelm I proclaimed German Emperor at Versailles. The days of the commune in Paris.
1872	61	Relations with the Wagners improve: they visit Weimar, Sep., and Liszt goes to Bayreuth, Oct. Visits his birthplace, Raiding, Nov.	Scriabin born, 6 Jan. Vaughan Williams born, 12 Oct. Franck (50): *Les Béatitudes*. Nietzsche (28): *The Birth of Tragedy*.
1873	62	Charity concerts in Pest, Mar. Conducts première of *Christus*, Weimar 29 May.	Reger born, 19 Mar. Rakhmaninov born, 1 Apr. Bruckner (49): Symphony No

Year	Age	Life	Contemporary musicians and events
		d'Indy (22) and Amy Fay (29) in Weimar. Jubilee celebrations of Liszt's career as an artist, Budapest, 8–11 Nov. *Five Hungarian Folksongs* published.	3. The cities of Buda and Pest are united to form the capital of Hungary.
1874	63	Charity concerts in Vienna, Jan., and Oedenburg, Feb. Makes final version of *Hymne de l'enfant à son réveil*. In Rome from mid-May: writes sacred choral works including *The Legend of St Cecilia*, *The Bells of Strassburg Cathedral* and part of the oratorio *St Stanislaus*. Also *Elegy No 1*, revisions of transcriptions and 4-hand arrangements of symphonic poems.	Schoenberg born, 13 Sep. Holst born, 21 Sep. Ives born, 20 Oct. Cornelius (49) dies, 26 Oct. Smetana (50): *Ma Vlast* (–1879). Verdi (60): *Requiem*. Wagner (61): finishes full score of *Götterdämmerung* and thus completes *The Ring*. First Impressionist exhibition, Paris.
1875	64	Liszt and Wagner give a joint concert, Budapest, 10 Mar.: *The Bells of Strassburg Cathedral* premièred; Liszt plays Beethoven's E flat Concerto. Appointed president of the Budapest Music Academy. Attends summer rehearsals, Bayreuth.	Glière born, 11 Jan. Sterndale Bennett (58) dies, 1 Feb. Ravel born, 7 Mar. Bizet (36) dies, 3 June. Tovey born, 17 July. Hahn born, 9 Aug. Coleridge-Taylor born, 15 Aug. Bizet: *Carmen*.
1876	65	Completes *Weihnachtsbaum* and transcribes *Danse macabre* (Saint-Saëns). Charity concert for flood disaster, Budapest, 20 Mar. Première of *Hamlet*, Sondershausen, 2 July. Cui (41) visits Weimar. Attends first Bayreuth festival, Aug.; meets Tchaikovsky (36) there.	Havergal Brian born, 29 Jan. Falla born, 23 Nov. Marie d'Agoult (70) dies, 5 Mar. George Sand (71) dies, 8 June. Borodin (43): Symphony No 2. Edison invents the phonograph.
1877	66	Despite an injured finger, plays in Vienna (50th anniversary of Beethoven's death): E flat concerto and the Choral Fantasia, 16 Mar. Busoni (10) present. *Le Triomphe funèbre*	Dohnányi born, 27 July. Saint-Saëns (42): *Samson et Dalila* (première at Weimar due to Liszt).

Year	Age	Life	Contemporary musicians and events
		du Tasse premièred, New York. Saint-Saëns, Fauré and Borodin visit Weimar. Carolyne's book *Causes intérieures* placed on the Index. To Italy mid-Aug.; writes *Angelus, Aux cyprès de la Villa d'Este, Les Jeux d'eaux à la Villa d'Este, Sursum corda,* and so completes the 3rd book of *Années de pèlerinage; Elegy No 2; In Memory of Petőfi; Recueillement.*	
1878	67	Albéniz (18) with Liszt in Budapest. Visits Paris and Erfurt, June. Writes *Septem Sacramenta, Chorales* and *Via Crucis* (–1879).	Boughton born, 23 Jan. Schreker born, 23 Mar. Dvořák (37): *Three Slavonic Rhapsodies,* op. 45. Humbert I succeeds as King of Italy, and Leo XIII as pope.
1879	68	Gives charity concerts, Klausenburg, Budapest, Vienna, Mar.–Apr. Attends performances of his works in Vienna, Frankfurt and Wiesbaden. Lina Schmalhausen (15) joins the Weimar pupils. Liszt made an honorary canon of Albano, 12 Oct. Writes *Ossa arida; Rosario; Missa pro organo; Sarabande and Chaconne from Handel's 'Almira';* transcribes Dargomizhsky's *Tarantella* and the *Polonaise* from *Eugene Onegin.*	Jensen (42) dies, 23 Jan. Respighi born, 9 July. Tchaikovsky (39): *Eugene Onegin.* Grove (59): *Dictionary of Music and Musicians.* Stalin born, 21 Dec.
1880	69	From Rome to Florence, Venice and Budapest. Concerts of his music, Vienna, Mar., Baden, Apr. Continues work on *St Stanislaus* during summer at Weimar and writes variation on *Chopsticks.* With the Wagners at Siena, Sep.	Medtner born, 5 Jan. Bloch born, 24 July. Offenbach (61) dies, 5 Oct. Rimsky-Korsakov (36): *May Night.*

Year	Age	Life	Contemporary musicians and events
1881	70	Writes *Nuages gris, Valse oubliée No 1* and *Csárdás macabre*. Première of *Second Mephisto Waltz*, Budapest, 9 Mar. Concert in Pressburg, Apr. Visits Raiding; in Vienna, Nuremberg, Weimar and Berlin, 23–28 Apr., for various performances; the German Emperor receives him. Further Liszt concerts in Freiburg, Baden, Cologne, Antwerp, Brussels, Magdeburg. Serious fall down stairs at Weimar, July, from which he never fully recovers. His grand-daughter Daniela joins him in Weimar and accompanies him to Rome, Oct., where his 70th birthday is celebrated. Writes *Psalm 129, Legend of St Christopher* and revises *Cantico del Sol*.	Bartók born, 25 Mar. Mussorgsky (42) dies, 28 Mar. Verdi (68): *Simon Boccanegra* (revised). Russia: Czar Alexander III succeeds.
1882	71	Composes 16th *Hungarian Rhapsody*, Budapest. Attends performances in Brussels and Antwerp, May; Freiburg, Baden and Zurich, July; 2nd Bayreuth Festival, July–Aug., première of *Parsifal*: makes arrangement of the *Solemn March to the Holy Grail*. Last symphonic poem, *From the Cradle to the Grave*, completed Oct. Last Verdi transcription, from *Simon Boccanegra*. d'Albert (18) plays Liszt's E flat concerto, Weimar, on the eve of Liszt's birthday. Nikisch (27) and Rubinstein (52) visit him. With the Wagners in Venice, from 19 Nov. Writes *La lugubre gondola*.	G. F. Malipiero born, 18 Mar. Stravinsky born, 17 June. Raff (60) dies, 25 June. Grainger born, 8 July. Szymanowski born, 6 Oct. Kodály born, 16 Dec. Balakirev (45): *Tamara*.
1883	72	Leaves Venice for Budapest, 13	Flotow (70) dies, 24 Jan.

Year	Age	Life	Contemporary musicians and events
		Jan. In Weimar, Apr. to end of year. Conducts memorial concert for Wagner, 22 May. Composes: *R. W.-Venezia; Am Grabe Richard Wagners; Schlaflos!; Mephisto polka; Mephisto waltz No 3; Valse oubliée No 3; Zur Trauung.*	Wagner (69) dies, 13 Feb. Bax born, 8 Nov. Webern born, 3 Dec. Varèse born, 22 Dec. Karl Marx (65) dies, 14 Mar. Mussolini born, 19 Jul. Bruckner (59): Symphony No 7. R. Strauss (19): Horn Concerto No 1.
1884	73	*Allgemeiner Deutscher Musikverein* meets in Weimar, May: *Salve Polonia* performed. Visits *Parsifal* performances, Bayreuth, July–Aug. Writes 2 *Csárdás; Qui seminant in lacrimis* and other religious pieces.	Smetana (60) dies, 12 May. Massenet (42): *Manon.* Franck (62): *Les Djinns.*
1885	74	Last works: *Hungarian Rhapsodies* 18 and 19; *Historical Hungarian Portraits; Trauer-vorspiel und -marsch; Mephisto waltz No 4; En rêve; Bagatelle sans tonalité: Valse oubliée No 4;* motets. Attends concerts, May–June, in Mannheim, Karlsruhe, Strassburg, Antwerp, Aachen; and Leipzig, Sep. Debussy (23) meets Liszt in Rome, Nov.	Berg born, 9 Feb. Abt (65) dies, 31 Mar. Hiller (73) dies, 11 May. Victor Hugo (83) dies, 22 May. Brahms (52): Symphony No 4. Wolf (25): *Penthesilea.*
1886	74	Leaves Rome for Budapest, Jan. Farewell concert there, 10 Mar. Hears *Missa Solennis,* Liège, 17 Mar. and Paris, 25 Mar. To London, 3 Apr., for many concerts and receptions; meets Queen Victoria. Further concerts: Antwerp and Paris. In poor health on reaching Weimar, 17 May: partial blindness and dropsy. Attends concerts Sondershausen 3–6 June, and Daniela's wedding, Bayreuth, 3 July. Stays 2 weeks at Castle Colpach, Luxembourg: plays for last	Ponchielli (51) dies, 17 Jan. Albéniz aged 26; d'Albert 22; Alkan 72; Arensky 25; Balakirev 49; Bartók 6; Bax 2; Berg 1; Bloch 6; Boito 44; Borodin 52; Boughton 6; Brahms 53; Havergal Brian 10; Bruch 48; Bruckner 61; Bülow 56; Busoni 20; Chabrier 45; Charpentier 26; Chausson 31; Coleridge-Taylor 10; Cui 51; Debussy 23; Delibes 50; Delius 24; Dohnányi 9; Dukas 20; Duparc 38; Dvořák 44; Elgar 39; Erkel 75; Falla 9; Fauré 41; Fibich 35; Franck 63; Franz 71;

Year	Age	Life	Contemporary musicians and events

time, Luxembourg, 19 July.
To Bayreuth where he attends
Parsifal, 23rd, and *Tristan*,
25th. His illness develops into
pneumonia and Liszt dies, 31
July. Several pupils attend his
burial, Bayreuth, 3 Aug.;
Bruckner plays the organ at
the requiem service. 8 months
later, having finished the 24th
volume of her *Causes
intérieures*, Carolyne (68) dies
in Rome.

Glazunov 20; Glière 11;
Godowski 16; Goldmark 56;
Gounod 68; Grainger 4;
Granados 19; Grechaninov 21;
Grieg 43; Hahn 10; Hanslick
60; Heller 73; Herz 83; Holst
11; Humperdinck 31; d'Indy
35; Ives 11; Jadassohn 54;
Janáček 32; Joachim 55;
Kienzl 29; Kodály 3; Koechlin
18; Korbay 40; Lalo 63; Lehár
16; Leoncavallo 29;
Leschetitzky 56; Liadov 31;
Mackenzie 38; Mahler 26;
G. F. Malipiero 4; Mascagni
22; Massenet 44; Matthay 28;
Medtner 6; Messager 32;
Moszkowski 31; Nielsen 21;
Paderewski 25; Parry 38;
Pfitzner 17; Puccini 27;
Rakhmaninov 13; Ravel 11;
Reger 13; Respighi 7; Rimsky-
Korsakov 42; A. Rubinstein
56; Saint-Saëns 50; Satie 20;
Schoenberg 11; Schreker 8;
Scriabin 14; Sgambati 45;
Sibelius 20; J. Strauss II 60; R.
Strauss 22; Stravinsky 4;
Svendsen 45; Szymanowski 3;
Tchaikovsky 46; Thomas 74;
Tovey 11; Varèse 2; Vaughan
Williams 13; Verdi 72; Webern
2; Wolf 26.

Appendix B

List of works

In cataloguing the complete works of Liszt I have aimed for simplicity. Within each section the items are placed (as far as possible) in chronological order. In section XI both the strict transcriptions and the freer arrangements appear under the (alphabetically listed) names of the original composers. The catalogue numbers are intended to facilitate cross-reference. It is not wished to foist yet another set of catalogue numbers upon the Liszt scholar (there are already three: Raabe, Searle and Milstein) and the present numbering is for the convenience of the user of this book alone. The order of the sections is:

I	Opera, page 335	
II	Sacred choral works, 335	
III	Secular choral works, 340	
IV	Songs, 343	
V	Miscellaneous vocal works; recitations, 347	
VI	Orchestral works, 348	
VII	Pianoforte and orchestra, 351	
VIII	Original pianoforte works, 352	
(A)	For 2 hands, 352	
(B)	For 4 hands, 362	
(C)	For 2 pianofortes, 362	
IX	Organ works, 362	
X	Chamber music, 363	
XI	Transcriptions and arrangements, 364	
XII	Works edited by Liszt, 377	
XIII	Literary works, 378	

The many arrangements Liszt made of his own works are referred to alongside the original composition in each case and are not listed separately. Liszt's literary works appear at the end of the catalogue.

Each work is cross-referenced to Humphrey Searle's catalogue (*Grove's Dictionary of Music and Musicians*, 5th and 6th editions) with a 'G' number. In the Searle catalogue, to which I am principally indebted, can be found groupings of works into various types, dates of publication, whereabouts of manuscripts and Raabe catalogue numbers. In the re-publication of the New Grove article in book form, the catalogue was thoroughly revised and updated by Sharon Winklhofer: *Early Romantic Masters I*, London, 1985.

All works are published unless otherwise stated; the date of first publication is given only when even the approximate date of composition is uncertain. Some lost, unfinished and projected works are included where it was felt they might cast light on Liszt's principal creative phases.

In the right-hand column is a reference to the edition and volume number of Liszt's works in which certain items can be found. (There is as yet no actual *complete* edition.) The abbreviations for publications are:

BH – *F. Liszt: musikalische Werke*, ed. F. Busoni, Bartók, da Motta, P. Raabe, etc. Breitkopf und Härtel, Leipzig, 1907–36.

LS – *Liszt Society Publications*, Vols 1–7. Schott, London, 1950–78.

NE – *Franz Liszt. New Edition of the Complete Works*, ed. Gárdonyi, Sulyok, Szelényi and Mező. Bärenreiter, Kassel, 1970– .

RS – *Gosudarstvennoe musïkal'noe izlatel'stvo*, ed. Below and Sorokin. Moscow, 1958– .

The LS and NE volumes are easily available. BH is long out of print, but parts of it have been reprinted by various publishers. There are many other publishers of Liszt's music and a complete list would be impractical here. The reader should consult the catalogues of the following in particular: Belwin-Mills Music Ltd.; Dover Publications Inc.; Edition Eulenburg Ltd.; and Peters Edition Ltd.

Other abbreviations used in this appendix are:

A	: alto
arr	: arranged/arrangement
B	: bass
Bar	: baritone
c	: *circa*
cf	: *confer*, compare
ed	: edited by

G	: Searle catalogue number in *The New Grove*
harm	: harmonium
ma	: major
mi	: minor
orch	: orchestra/orchestrated
pf	: pianoforte
pf 4 hands	: pianoforte duet (4 hands)
2 pf	: two pianofortes
rev	: revised
S	: soprano
T	: tenor
unacc	: unaccompanied

I OPERA

1   1824–5   *Don Sanche, ou le Château de l'Amour* (Mme Théaulon & de Rancé, after Claris de Florian) G1. (Composed with Paer's help; unpublished).
Liszt wrote no other operas but planned to compose several at various dates; for details see Chapter 4. Many sketches for *Sardanapale* (Rotondi?, after Byron; G687) are preserved in Weimar.

II SACRED CHORAL WORKS

2   1822   *Tantum ergo* G702 (lost).

3   in 1840s   *Five Choruses with French texts* G18 (unpublished).

4   1846   *Pater Noster* G21. 1st version, unacc male chorus.
2nd version, *c* 1848, male chorus + organ.   BHv/6
cf 291(5).

5   1846   *Ave Maria* G20. Mixed chorus + organ (B flat ma).   BHv/6
2nd version (A ma), 1852.   BHv/6
cf 291(2).

6   1847   *Hymne de l'enfant à son réveil* (Lamartine) G19. 1st version: female chorus, harm (or pf) + harp (ad lib.).
2nd version, 1862; revised 1865.
3rd version, 1874.   BHv/5
cf 291(6).

7	1848	*Mass for 4-part male chorus + organ* (*Szekszárd Mass*) G8. 1st version, revised 1859.	
		2nd version, 1869.	BHv/3
8	1850	*Pater Noster* G22. Mixed chorus + organ (C ma) (unpublished).	
9	1853	*Domine salvum fac regem* G23. T, male chorus + organ or orch.	BHv/5
10	?1853	*Te Deum* G24. Male chorus + organ.	BHv/7
11	1855	*Missa Solennis* (*Gran Mass*) G9. SATB, chorus + orch.	
		Revised 1857–8.	
12	1855	*Psalm 13* (*Lord, how long?*) G13. T, chorus + orch.	
		Revised 1858, 1862.	
13	1855–9	*The Beatitudes* G25. Bar, mixed chorus + organ (ad lib.). Later added to 31.	BHv/6
14	1857–62	*The Legend of St Elisabeth*. Oratorio (Otto Roquette) G2. SA, Bar, B, chorus, orch + organ. (Planned 1855).	
		Arr pf 4 hands, 1862: *4 pieces from St Elisabeth* (G578).	
		Arr pf: *3 pieces from St Elisabeth* (published 1873).	NExvi
15	1858	*Festgesang zur Eröffnung der zehnten allgemeinen deutschen Lehrerversammlung* (Hoffmann von Fallersleben) G26. Male chorus + organ (ad lib.).	BHv/6
16	1859	*Psalm 23* (*The Lord is my Shepherd*) G15. T (or S), harp (or pf) + organ (or harm).	
		Rev 1862 (unpublished), adds male chorus (ad lib.).	
17	1859	*Psalm 137* (*By the rivers of Babylon*) G17. S, female chorus, violin, harp + organ.	
		Revised 1862.	
18	by 1860	*An der heiligen Franziskus von Paula. Gebet* G28. Solo male voices, male chorus, organ (or harm), 3 trombones + timpani (ad lib.).	BHv/5
		cf 320(2).	
		Revised version *c* 1874.	
19	by 1860	*Pater Noster* G29. 7-part mixed chorus + organ. (A flat ma) Later added to 31.	BHv/6
20	1860	*Psalm 18* (*Coeli enarrant*) G14. Male chorus + orch or organ or woodwind/brass.	
21	1860	Responses and Antiphons G30. Mixed chorus (+ organ?).	BHv/7
22	1862	*Cantico del sol di San Francesco d'Assisi* G4. Bar, male chorus, orch + organ.	
		Revised 1880–1.	BHv/5

		Arr (from the first version): *Hosanna* for organ and bass trombone, 1862 (G677).	
		Arr (from the revised version):	
		(1) *San Francesco. Preludio* for organ and for pf, 1880 (G665).	NExvii
		(2) *Cantico del sol di San Francesco* for pf, 1881 (G499).	NExvii
		cf 320(1) and 406.	
23	?1863	*Christus ist geboren* I (Landmesser) G31.	BHv/6
		(1) Mixed chorus + organ.	
		(2) Male chorus + organ.	
24	?1863	*Christus ist geboren* II (Landmesser) G32.	BHv/6
		(1) Mixed chorus + organ.	
		(2) Male chorus unacc; organ postlude.	
		(3) Female chorus unacc.	
		Arr pf, 1864, as *Weihnachtslied* (G502).	NExv
25	1863	*Slavimo Slavno Slaveni!* (Count Urso Pucić) G33. Male chorus + organ; revised 1866.	BHv/6
		Arr pf, *c* 1863 (G503).	NExi
		Arr organ, 1863 (*Andante maestoso*, G668).	
26	1865	*Missa Choralis* G10. Mixed chorus + organ.	BHv/3
27	1865	*Crux! Sailors' Hymn* (Guichon de Grandpont) G35.	BHv/6
		(1) Male chorus unacc.	
		(2) Female or children's chorus + pf.	
28	1865 or 6	*Ave Maris Stella* G34.	BHv/6
		(1) Mixed chorus + organ.	
		(2) Male chorus + organ or harm.	
		Arr voice + pf or harm, 1868 (G680).	
		Arr pf, published 1871 (G506).	NExvi
		Arr organ, as no. 2 of *Zwei Kirchenhymnen* (G669), published 1880. *cf* 388.	
29	1866–7	*Hungarian Coronation Mass* G11. SATB, chorus + orch.	
		The Benedictus and Offertorium from this Mass were arr for:	
		(1) pf, 1867 (G501).	NExvi
		(2) violin + pf, 1869 (G381).	
		(3) pf 4 hands, 1869 (G581).	
		(4) violin + organ, 1869 (G678).	
		(5) violin + orch, 1875 (G362).	
		The Offertorium also arr for harm or pedal-pf, 1867 or later (G667).	
30	1866	*Dall' alma Roma* G36. From 31 (section 8). 2-part chorus + organ. Unpublished.	
31	by 1867	*Christus. Oratorio* (On texts from Holy Scripture and the Liturgy) G3. SAT, Bar, B, chorus, orch + organ.	
		Incorporates 13, 19 and an arr of 386.	

		See also 30. The 4th and 5th sections of the oratorio arr for pf, published 1873; and for pf 4 hands, published 1873 (G579). The 8th section arr organ as *Tu es Petrus*, 1867 or later (G664).	NExvi
32	1867	*Te Deum* G27. Mixed chorus, organ, brass + timpani (ad lib.).	BHv/7
33	1867–8	*Requiem* G12. TTBB, male chorus + organ + brass (ad lib.). Arr organ, 1883 (G266), *cf* **42**.	BHv/3
34	1868	*Mihi autem adhaerere* G37. From Psalm 73. Male chorus + organ.	BHv/6
35	1869	*Pater Noster* G41. (1) Mixed chorus + organ (F ma). (2) Male chorus + organ or harm or pf (B flat ma).	BHv/6
36	1869	*Ave Maria* G38. Mixed chorus + organ. *cf* **390**. Arr voice + organ or harm, 1869 (G681). Arr twice for pf (G504): (1) 1871, D ma, pf or harm. (2) 1873, D flat ma.	BHv/6 BHv/6 NExii
37	1869	*Tantum ergo* G42. (1) Male chorus + organ. (2) Female chorus + organ.	BHv/6
38	1869	*Inno a Maria Vergine* G39. Mixed chorus, harp, organ (or pf 4 hands) + harm.	BHv/5
39	1869	*Psalm 116* (*Laudate Dominum*) G15a. Graduale for **29**. Male chorus + pf.	
40	?1869	*O salutaris hostia* G40. Female chorus + organ.	BHv/6
41	?1870	*O salutaris hostia* G43. Mixed chorus + organ.	BHv/6
42	1870	*Libera me* G45. Male chorus + organ. Added to **33**.	
43	1871	*Ave verum corpus* G44. Mixed chorus + organ (ad lib.).	BHv/6
44	1873–85	*The Legend of St Stanislaus. Oratorio* (Libretto after L. Siemienski by Princess C. Sayn-Wittgenstein, P. Cornelius and K. E. Edler) G688. Sketched earlier. First scene completed, the rest unfinished. *cf* **59, 215**. Arr from this: *Deux Polonaises* for pf, in the 1870s (G519).	NExvii
45	1874	*St Cecilia. Legend* (de Girardin) G5. Mezzo- S, chorus (ad lib.) + orch or pf or harp or harmonium. (Two earlier settings, 1845 and 1868/9, lost.)	

46	1874	*Anima Christi sanctifica me* G46. Male chorus + organ. 2 versions.	BHv/6
47	1874	*The Bells of Strassburg Cathedral* (Longfellow) G6. Mezzo-S, Bar, chorus + orch. (1) Prelude: *Excelsior* (*cf* **360**). (2) *The Bells*. Arrs of Prelude, *c* 1875: for pf (G500), for pf 4 hands (G580), for organ (G666).	
48	1875	*Der Herr bewahret die Seelen seiner Heiligen: Festgesang zur Enthüllung des Carl-August Denkmals in Weimar* G48. Mixed chorus, organ + wind.	BHv/6
49	after 1876	*Weihnachtslied* (*O heilige Nacht*) G49. From 338(2). T, female chorus + organ or harm.	BHv/6
50	1878	*Septem Sacramenta* G52. Mezzo-S, Bar, mixed chorus + organ.	BHv/7
51	1878–9	*Via Crucis* (*The 14 Stations of the Cross*) G53. Sketched earlier. SATB, chorus + organ (or pf). *cf* **52**. Arr pf (G504a). Arr pf 4 hands (G583, unpublished). Arr organ (G674a).	BHv/7 NEx
52	*c* 1878–9	*Twelve Old German Sacred Tunes* (*Chorales*) G50. (1) for mixed chorus + organ. (2–12) unison chorus + pf (1) *Es segne uns Gott* (2) *Meine Seel' erhebt den Herrn* (*Gott sei uns gnädig*), see **53**. (3) *Nun ruhen alle Wälder*. (4) *O Haupt voll Blut und Wunden*, used in **51**. (5) *O Lamm Gottes*, also arr for pf 4 hands, 1878–9 (G582, unpublished). (6) *Was Gott tut, das ist wohl getan*. (7) *Wer nun den lieben Gott lässt walten*. (8) *Vexilla regis*, used in **51**. (9) *Crux ave benedicta*, used in **51**. (10) *O Traurigkeit*, used in **51**. (11) *Nun danket alle Gott*, see **61**. (12) *Jesu Christe pro nobis crucifixe*.	BHv/7 (nos. 1–7) NEx (nos 2–12)
53	1878	*Gott sei uns gnädig* (*Meine Seel' erhebt den Herrn*) G51. Extended version of 52(2).	
54	1879	*Ossa arida* G55. Unison male chorus + organ (two players) or pf 4 hands.	BHv/6
55	1879	*Rosario* G56. (1) *Mysteria gaudiosa* (2) *Mysteria dolorosa* (3) *Mysteria gloriosa* (4) *Pater Noster*. (1–3): Mixed chorus + organ or harm. (4): Bar or male chorus (unison) + organ or harm. Nos. 1–3 arr organ, 1879 (G670).	BHv/7
56	1879	*O Roma nobilis* G54. Mixed chorus + organ	

		(ad lib), or solo voice + organ.	BHv/7
		Arr harm or pf, 1879? (G546a).	NExvii
57	1879	*Cantantibus organis* G7. Antiphon for St Cecilia's Day. Soloists, chorus + orch.	BHv/5
58	c 1880	*Pro Papa* G59.	BHv/6
		(1) *Dominus conservet eum*. Mixed chorus + organ.	
		(2) *Tu es Petrus*. Male chorus (unison) + organ.	
59	1880–3	*Psalm 129* (*De Profundis*) G16. Intended for **44**.	
		(1) Bar, male chorus + organ (1882–3).	
		(2) B or A + organ or pf (1880–1).	
60	1881	*St Christopher. Legend* G47. Unpublished. Bar, female chorus, pf, harm + harp (ad lib.).	
61	1883	*Nun danket alle Gott* G61. Expansion of 52(11).	BHv/7
		Mixed or male chorus, organ, brass + drums (ad lib.).	
62	1883	*Zur Trauung* G60. Setting of Ave Maria; from 296(1). Female chorus (unison) + organ or harm. (Voices ad lib.)	BHv/6
63	1884	*Qui seminant in lacrimis* G63. From Psalm 125. Mixed chorus + organ.	BHv/6
64	by 1884	*Mariengarten* (*Quasi cedrus!*) G62. SSAT + organ.	BHv/6
65	?1884	*In domum Domini ibimus* G57. Mixed chorus, organ, brass + drums.	BHv/5
		Prelude arr organ (G671).	
		Prelude arr pf (G505).	NExvii
66	?1884	*O sacrum convivium* G58. A, female chorus (ad lib.) + organ or harm.	BHv/6
67	1885	*Pax vobiscum!* G64. Male chorus + organ.	BHv/6
68	1885	*Qui Mariam absolvisti* G65. Bar, mixed chorus (unison) + organ or harm.	BHv/6
69	1885	*Salve Regina* G66. Mixed chorus unacc.	BHv/6

III SECULAR CHORAL WORKS

N.B. Unless otherwise stated all works are for 4-part unaccompanied male-voice chorus.

70	1839	*Das deutsche Vaterland* (Arndt) G74. 2 versions, the 2nd probably unpublished.
71	1841	*Four-part male choruses* G72.

(1) *Rheinweinlied* (Herwegh), with pf.
(2) *Students' Song* from Goethe's 'Faust'.
(3) *Reiterlied* (Herwegh), with pf. (4)
Reiterlied (another version, unacc.).

72	1842	*Gottes ist der Orient* (Goethe) G90(12). No. 12 of *Für Männergesang*.[1]
73	1842	*Wir sind nicht Mumien* (Hoffmann von Fallersleben) G90(3). Originally with pf. No. 3 of *Für Männergesang*.
74	1842	*Das düstre Meer umrauscht mich* G76. With pf.
75	1842	*Über allen Gipfeln ist Ruh* (Goethe) G75. 2nd version, 1849, with 2 horns.
76	1842	*Titan* (Schober) G79. Bar, male chorus + pf. Unpublished. Revised 1845 and 1847.
77	1843	*Trinkspruch* G78. With pf.
78	1844	*Soldiers' Song* from Goethe's 'Faust' G90(7). Trumpets + timpani ad lib. No. 7 of *Für Männergesang*.
79	1845	*Les Quatre Éléments* (Autran) G80. With pf. Unpublished. *cf* 197. (1) *La Terre* (2) *Les Aquilons* (1839) (3) *Les Flots* (4) *Les Astres*.
80	1845	*Es war einmal ein König* (Goethe, 'Faust') G73. B, male chorus + pf. Unpublished.
81	1845	*Le Forgeron* (de Lamennais) G81. With pf (3 other Lamennais settings planned as companion pieces).
82	1845	*Geharnischte Lieder* (Th. Meyer) G90(4–6). With pf. Nos 4–6 of *Für Männergesang*. 2nd version, 1860, unacc (published 1861 with text ascribed to Carl Götze). (1) *Vor der Schlacht* (2) *Nicht gezagt* (3) *Es rufet Gott uns mahnend*. Arr pf, published 1861 (G511). NExv
83	?1845	*Die alten Sagen kunden* G90(8). With solo 4tet. No. 8 of *Für Männergesang*.
84	?1845	*Saatengrünn* (Uhland) G90(9). No. 9 of *Für Männergesang*.
85	?1845	*Der Gang um Mitternacht* (Herwegh) G90(10). With T solo. No. 10 of *Für Männergesang*.
86	1845	*Beethoven Cantata No. 1* (O.L.B. Wolff) G67. SSTTBB, choruses + orch. Unpublished. Arr pf 4 hands, 1845 (G584). Arr pf as *70 bars on themes from the first Beethoven Cantata, c* 1847 (G507). NExi

[1] *Für Männergesang*: a set of 12 male-voice choruses, published 1861.

87	1846	*Die lustige Legion* (A. Buchheim) G77. With pf.	
		Arr T, pf + chorus, published 1848.	
88	1846	*A patakhoz. To the Brook* (János Garay) G81a.	
89	?1847	*Singe, wem Gesang gegeben* G689.	
		Unfinished. (Orchestrated by Conradi.)	
90	1848	*Hungaria 1848. Cantata* (Schober) G83. STB, male chorus + pf.	
91	1848	*Arbeiterchor* (de Lamennais?) G82. Theme used in **202**. B, male 4tet, male chorus + pf.	
		Arr pf, *Marche héroïque* (G510).	NExv
		Arr pf 4 hands (G587), unpublished.	
92	1849	*Licht, mehr Licht* (Schober?) G84. With brass.	
93	1849	*Chorus of Angels* from Goethe's 'Faust' G85. Mixed chorus + harp or pf.	
94	1850	*Festchor zur Enthüllung des Herder-Denkmals in Weimar* (A. Schöll) G86. With pf.	
95	1850	*Choruses for Herder's 'Prometheus Unbound'* G69. SATTBB, double chorus + orch.	
		1st version orch Raff. Revised with Liszt's own orchestration, 1855.	
		Pastorale (Schnitterchor) arr pf, 1861 (G508).	NExv
		Pastorale arr pf 4 hands, 1861 (G585).	
96	1853	*An die Künstler* (Schiller) G70. TTBB, male chorus + orch. 1st version orch Raff.	
		2nd and 3rd versions orch Liszt and published 1854 and 1856. Organ part added 1859. *cf* **209**.	
97	1856	*Vereinslied* (Hoffmann von Fallersleben) G90(1). No. 1 of *Für Männergesang*.	
98	by 1857	*Ständchen* (Rückert) G90(2). With T solo. No. 2 of *Für Männergesang*.	
99	1857	*Weimars Volkslied* (Cornelius) G87. From trio of **310** (orch version).	
		6 versions: (1) + wind. (2) + pf. (3) male chorus unacc. (4) + organ. (5) SA or TB. (6) 3-part chorus.	
		Arr twice for pf, 1857 (and later?), G542.	NExv
		Arr pf 4 hands, 1857 (G588).	
		Arr organ, 1865 (G672). *cf* **159**.	
100	1859	*Festlied zu Schillers Jubelfeier* (Dingelstedt) G90(11). With Bar solo. No. 11 of *Für Männergesang*.	
101	1859	*Morgenlied* (Hoffmann von Fallersleben) G88. Female chorus unacc.	
102	?1859	*Mit klingendem Spiel* G89. Children's voices.	
	1862	Planned choral work on *Manfred* (Byron).	

103	1869	*Gaudeamus igitur. Humoreske* G71. Soli (ad lib.), mixed or male chorus + orch. *cf* 276.	
		Arr pf, *c*1870 (G509).	NExvi
		Arr pf 4 hands, *c* 1870 (G586).	
104	1869–70	*Beethoven Cantata No 2* (Adolf Stern; F. Gregorovius) G68. SATB, double chorus + orch.	
105	1871	*Das Lied der Begeisterung. A lelkesedés dala* G91.	
		Revised 1874.	
106	1875	*Carl August weilt mit uns. Festgesang zur Enthüllung des Carl-August-Denkmals in Weimar* G92. Male chorus, brass, drums + organ (ad lib.).	
107	1883	*Ungarisches Königslied. Magyar Király-dal* (Ábrányi) G93. (1) Male chorus unacc. (2) Mixed chorus unacc. (3) Male chorus + pf. (4) Mixed chorus + pf. (5) Male or mixed chorus + orch; or orch alone. (6) Children's chorus.	
		Arr pf, *c* 1883 (G544).	NExvii
		Arr pf 4 hands, *c* 1883 (G626).	
		cf 183.	
108	?1885	*Gruss* G94.	

IV SONGS

109	1839	*Angiolin dal biondo crin* (Marchese C. Bocella) G269. 1st version. Arr pf, published 1844 (G531, 6).	NExv
		2nd version, published 1856.	BHvii/2 & LSvi
110	*c* 1840	*Il m'aimait tant* (Delphine Gay) G271.	BHvii/1
		Arr pf, published 1843 (G533).	NExv
111	*c* 1840	*Im Rhein* (Heine) G272. 1st version.	BHvii/1
		Arr pf, published 1844 (G531, 2).	NExv
		2nd version, 1854.	BHvii/2
112	1841	*Die Lorelei* (Heine) G273. 1st version. Arr pf, published 1844 (G531,1).	NExv
		2nd version, published 1856.	BHvii/2
		Arr pf, 1861 (G532).	NExv
		Arr voice + orch, 1860 (G369).	
113	by 1841	*Die Zelle in Nonnenwerth* (Lichnowsky) G274.	
		cf 133 and 277 1st version. Arr pf as *Élégie*,	

		published 1843 (G534); several later arrs, the last in 1880.	LSvii & NExvii
		2nd version, 1857; revised and published 1862. Arr violin or cello + pf (G382) and for pf 4 hands, both unpublished.	BHvii/3
114	1842	*Mignons Lied* (*Kennst du das Land*) (Goethe) G275.	
		1st version. Arr pf, published 1844 (G531,3).	NExv
		2nd version, 1854	BHvii/2
		3rd version, 1860.	BHvii/2
		Arr voice + orch, 1860 (G370).	
115	1842	*Der du von dem Himmel bist* (Goethe) G279.	
		1st version.	BHvii/1
		Arr pf, published 1844 (G531,5).	NExv
		2nd version, published 1856.	BHvii/2
		3rd version, 1860.	BHvii/2
		Fragment of another version, published 1918.	BHvii/1
116	1842	*Es war ein König in Thule* (Goethe) G278.	
		Arr pf, published 1844 (G531,4).	NExv
		2nd version, published 1856.	BHvii/2
117	1842	*O quand je dors* (Hugo) G282. 1st version.	BHvii/1
		Arr pf, ?1847 (G536).	NExviii
		2nd version, published 1859.	BHvii/2
118	1842	*Comment, disaient-ils* (Hugo) G276. 1st version.	BHvii/1
		Arr pf, ?1845 (G535).	NExviii
		2nd version, published 1859.	BHvii/2
119	1842	*Vergiftet sind meine Lieder* (Heine) G289.	
		Revised version published 1859.	BHvii/2 & LSvi
120	?1843	*Du bist wie eine Blume* (Heine) G287.	BHvii/2
121	1843	*Bist du* (Prince E. Metschersky) G277.	
		Revised version, *c* 1877–8.	BHvii/3
122	?1843	*Was Liebe sei* (C. von Hagn) G288.	BHvii/1
		2nd version, *c* 1855.	BHvii/2
		3rd version, *c* 1878–9.	BHvii/3
123	?1843	*Die tote Nachtigall* (Kaufmann) G291.	BHvii/1
		Revised version, 1878.	BHvii/3 & LSvi
124	?1843	*Morgens steh ich auf und frage* (Heine) G290.	BHvii/1
		Revised version, *c* 1855.	BHvii/2 & LSvi
125	1843	*Quand tu chantes bercée* (Hugo) G306a.	
126	1843	*Nimm einen Strahl der Sonne* (*Ihr Auge*) (Rellstab) G310.	BHvii/2
127	1843	*Oh pourquoi donc* (Mme Pavloff) G301a. *cf* 292.	RSiiiappx.
128	1844	*Freudvoll und leidvoll* (Goethe) G280.	
		1st setting, 1st version.	BHvii/1

		2nd setting, published 1848.	BHvii/1
		1st setting, 2nd version, published 1860.	BHvii/2
129	1844	*Die Vätergruft* (Uhland) G281.	BHvii/2
		Arr voice + orch, 1886 (G371).	
130	?1844	*Enfant, si j'étais roi* (Hugo) G283.	BHvii/1
		Arr pf, ?1847 (G537).	NExviii
		Revised version, published 1859.	BHvii/2
			& LSvi
131	?1844	*S'il est un charmant gazon* (Hugo) G284.	BHvii/1
		Arr pf, ?1847 (G538).	NExviii
		Revised version, published 1859.	BHvii/2
132	?1844	*La tombe et la rose* (Hugo) G285.	BHvii/1
		Arr pf, ?1847 (G539).	NExviii
133	?1844	*Gastibelza, Bolero* (Hugo) G286.	BHvii/1
		Arr pf, ?1847 (G540).	NExviii
134	1844	*En ces lieux. Élégie* (E. Monnier) G301b. (New text to the music of **113**.)	
135	1844	*Wo weilt er?* (Rellstab) G295.	BHvii/2
136	1844–5	*Three Petrarch Sonnets* G270.	BHvii/1
		(1) *Pace non trovo* (no. 104). (2) *Benedetto sia 'l giorno* (no. 47). (3) *I vidi in terra angelica costumi* (no. 123).	
		Arr pf, *cf* **282**.	
		All three songs revised, 1854.	BHvii/3
			& LSvi
		cf **296**(4–6). In this second version, (1) and (2) are in reverse order.	
137	?c 1845	*Es rauschen die Winde* (Rellstab) G294.	
		Revised before 1856.	BHvii/2
		2nd version, published 1860.	BHvii/2
138	?1845	*Songs from Schiller's 'Wilhelm Tell'* G292.	BHvii/1
		Revised version, published 1859.	BHvii/2
		(1) *Der Fischerknabe* (2) *Der Hirt* (3) *Der Alpenjäger*.	
		Arr voice + orch, *c* 1855; later revised and published 1872 (G372).	
139	1845	*Jeanne d'Arc au bûcher* (Dumas) G293.	
		Revised version, 1874.	BHvii/3
		Arr voice + orch, 1858; revised 1874 (G373).	
140	1845	*Ich möchte hingehn* (Herwegh) G296.	BHvii/2
		Later revised, published 1860.	& LSvi
141	?c 1845	*Wer nie sein Brot mit Tränen ass* (Goethe) G297.	BHvii/2
		Revised version, published 1860.	BHvii/3
142	?1845	*O Lieb, so lang du lieben kannst* (Freiligrath) G298.	BHvii/2
		Arr pf (no. 3 of *Liebesträume. Drei Notturnos*) *c* 1850 (G541).	NExv
143	1845	*Schwebe, schwebe, blaues Auge* (Dingelstedt)	

		G 305.	BHvii/1
		Revised version, published 1860.	BHvii/2
144	*c*1845	*Ein Fichtenbaum steht einsam* (Heine) G309.	BHvii/2 & LSvi
		Revised version, 1854.	BHvii/2 & LSvi
145	1846–7	*Isten veled (Farewell)* (Horvath) G299.	
		Revised version, published 1879.	BHvii/3 &LSvi
146	?1847	*Über allen Gipfeln ist Ruh* (Goethe) G306. *cf* 75.	
		Revised version, published 1860.	BHvii/2
147	1847	*Le juif errant* (Béranger) G300. Unpublished.	
148	by 1848	*Weimars Toten. Dithyrambe* (Schober) G303.	BHvii/1
149	by 1848	*Le vieux vagabond* (Béranger) G304.	
		Foreshadows **197** and **207**.	BHvii/1
150	1848	*Kling leise, mein Lied* (Nordmann) G301.	BHvii/1
		Revised version, published 1860.	BHvii/2
151	1848–9	*Die Macht der Musik* (Duchess Helen of Orleans) G302.	BHvii/1
152	*c* 1849	*Anfangs wollt' ich fast verzagen* (Heine) G311.	BHvii/2
		Version with new ending *c* 1880.	
153	?1850	*Hohe Liebe* (Uhland) G307.	BHvii/2
		Arr pf (no. 1 of *Liebesträume. Drei Notturnos*) *c* 1850 (G541).	NExv
154	?1850	*Gestorben war ich (Seliger Tod)* (Uhland) G308. *cf* 324(1).	BHvii/2
		Arr pf (no. 2 of *Liebesträume. Drei Notturnos*), 2 versions, *c* 1850 (G541).	NExv
155	1852	*Es muss ein Wunderbares sein* (Redwitz) G314.	BHvii/2
156	1854	*Ich scheide* (Hoffmann von Fallersleben) G319.	BHvii/2 & LSvi
157	1854	*Blume und Duft* (Hebbel) G324.	BHvii/3
158	?1856	*Wie singt die Lerche schön* (Hoffmann von Fallersleben) G312.	BHvii/2
159	1857	*Weimars Volkslied* (Cornelius) G313. *cf* 99.	BHvii/2
160	1857	*Ich liebe dich* (Rückert) G315.	BHvii/3
		Arr pf (G542a).	NExv
161	1857	*Muttergottes – Strässlein zum Mai-Monate* (Müller) G316. (1) *Das Veilchen* (2) *Die Schlüsselblumen*.	BHvii/2
162	?1858	*Lasst mich ruhen* (Hoffmann von Fallersleben) G317.	BHvii/2
163	?1858	*In Liebeslust* (Hoffmann von Fallersleben) G318.	BHvii/2
164	1860	*Die drei Zigeuner* (Lenau) G320.	BHvii/3
		Arr voice + orch, 1860 (G374).	
		Arr violin + pf, 1864 (G383).	

165	1860	*Wieder möcht ich dir begegnen* (Cornelius) G322.	BHvii/3
166	?1860	*Die stille Wasserrose* (Geibel) G321.	BHvii/3
167	?1860	*Jugendglück* (Pohl) G323.	BHvii/3
168	1871	*Die Fischerstochter* (Count C. Coronini) G325.	BHvii/3
169	1872	*La Perla* (Princess Therese von Hohenlohe) G326.	BHvii/3
170	1872	*J'ai perdu ma force et ma vie. 'Tristesse'* (de Musset) G327.	BHvii/3 & LSvi
171	1874	*Ihr Glocken von Marling* (Emil Kuh) G328.	BHvii/3 & LSvi
172	1874	*Und sprich* (Biegeleben) G329. Revised 1878.	BHvii/3
173	1877	*Sei still* (Nordheim = Henriette von Schorn) G330.	BHvii/3 & LSvi
174	?1878	*An Edlitam* (Bodenstedt) G333.	BHvii/3
175	?1878	*Einst* (Bodenstedt) G332.	BHvii/3 & LSvi
176	?1878	*Gebet* (Bodenstedt) G331.	BHvii/3 & LSvi
177	?1878	*Der Glückliche* (Wilbrandt) G334.	BHvii/3
178	1879	*Go not, happy day* (Tennyson) G335.	BHvii/3 & LSvi
179	1880	*Verlassen* (G. Michell) G336.	BHvii/3
180	1880	*Des Tages laute Stimmen schweigen* (F. von Saar) G337.	BHvii/3 & LSvi
181	?1880	*Und wir dachten der Toten* (Freiligrath) G338.	BHvii/3 & LSvi
182	1881	*Ungarns Gott. A magyarok Istene* (Petőfi) G339. (With male chorus, ad lib.).	BHvii/3
		Arr pf, and for pf left hand alone, 1881 (G543).	NExvii
		Arr organ, published 1882 (G674).	
		Arr male chorus, brass + woodwind (G381a) and for Bar, male chorus, brass + woodwind, 1882, both unpublished.	
183	1883	*Ungarisches Königslied. Magyar Király-dal* (Ábrányi) G340. *cf* 107.	BHvii/3
184	1886	*Ne brani menya, moy drug. 'Do not reproach me my friend'* (Tolstoy) G340a.	

V MISCELLANEOUS VOCAL WORKS; RECITATIONS

| 185 | 1858 | *Lenore* (Bürger) G346. Recitation with pf. Planned 1857, revised 1860. | BHvii/3 |

186	1859	*Vor hundert Jahren* (F. Halm) G347. Recitation with orch. Unpublished.	
187	1860	*Der traurige Mönch* (Lenau) G348. Recitation with pf.	BHvii/3
188	1872	*Wartburg-Lieder* (from Scheffel's 'Der Braut Willkomm auf Wartburg') G345. T, 2 Bar, mixed chorus + orch or pf. (Orch version unpublished).	BHvii/3

(1) Intro and mixed chorus (2) *Wolfram von Eschenbach* (Bar) (3) *Heinrich von Ofterdingen* (T) (4) *Walther von der Vogelweide* (T; a version for T, violin + pf. unpublished) (5) *Der tugendhafte Schreiber* (Bar) (6) *Biterolf und der Schmied von Ruhla* (2 Bar) (7) *Reimar der Alte* (T).

189	1874	*Des toten Dichters Liebe. A holt költö szerelme* (Jókai) G349. Recitation with pf. *cf* 342.	BHvii/3
190	1875	*Der blinde Sänger* (Alexei Tolstoy) G350. Recitation with pf.	BHvii/3
		Arr pf, 1878 (G546).	NExvii
191	?1880	*O Meer im Abendstrahl* (Meissner) G344. Duet, SA + pf or harm.	BHvii/3
192	1881	*Ave Maria* G341. Voice + organ or harm or pf.	
		Arr pf or harm, 1881 (G545).	
193	1884	*Le crucifix* (Hugo) G342. A + pf or harm (3 versions).	BHv/6
194	1884	*Sancta Caecilia* G343. A + organ or harm.	BHv/6

VI ORCHESTRAL WORKS

195	1830	*Revolutionary Symphony* G690. Unfinished. Revised 1848. *cf* 201 and 333.	
196	1848–9	*Ce qu'on entend sur la montagne. Symphonic Poem* G95. 1st version, orch Raff.	
		2nd version, 1850, orch Raff.	
		3rd version, 1854, orch Liszt.	BHi/1
		Arr 2 pf, *c* 1854–57 (G635).	
		Arr pf 4 hands, 1874 (G589).	
		cf 385.	
197	1848	*Les Préludes. Symphonic Poem* G97. From the prelude to 79.	
		Revised before 1854. cf 149 and 259.	BHi/2
		Arr 2 pf, *c* 1854–56 (G637).	
		Arr pf 4 hands, *c* 1858 (G591).	

198	1849	*Tasso, Lamento e Trionfo. Symphonic Poem* G96.	
		1st version, orch with Conradi (sketches date from 1841–5).	
		2nd version, 1850–1, orch Raff.	
		3rd version, 1854, orch and expanded by Liszt.	
		cf 218.	BHi/1
		Arr 2 pf, *c* 1854–6 (G636).	
		Arr pf 4 hands, *c* 1858 (G590).	
199	1849	*Festmarsch zur Goethejubiläumsfeier* G115.	
		1st version, from 298, orch Conradi and later Raff.	
		2nd version, 1857, orch Liszt.	BHi/11
		Arr pf, 1857 (G521).	NExiv
		Arr pf 4 hands, *c* 1858 (G606).	(two versions)
200	1850	*Prometheus. Symphonic Poem* G99. Overture to 95. Opening comes from 224.	
		1st version orch Raff.	
		Revised version, 1855, orch Liszt.	BHi/3
		Arr 2 pf, 1855–6 (G639).	
		Arr pf 4 hands, *c* 1858 (G593).	
201	1849–50	*Héroïde funèbre. Symphonic Poem* G102. From the 1st movement of 195.	
		1st version orch Raff.	
		2nd version, *c* 1854?, orch Liszt.	BHi/4
		Arr 2 pf, *c* 1854–6 (G642).	
		Arr pf 4 hands, *c* 1877 (G596a).	
202	1851	*Mazeppa. Symphonic Poem* G100. From 240(4), 251(4), 258 and 303(4). *cf* 91.	
		1st version orch with Raff.	
		2nd version, before 1854, orch Liszt.	BHi/3
		Arr 2 pf, 1855 (G640).	
		Arr pf 4 hands, 1874 (G594).	
203	1853	*Festklänge. Symphonic Poem* G101.	BHi/4
		Revisions added to 1861 publication.	
		Arr 2 pf, *c* 1853–6 (G641).	
		Arr pf 4 hands, ?1854–61 (G595).	
204	1853–4	*Orpheus. Symphonic Poem* G98.	BHi/2
		Arr 2 pf, *c* 1854–6 (G638).	
		Arr pf 4 hands, *c* 1858 (G592).	
		(A *Postlude* on the same themes – designed for Gluck's *Orpheus* – is unpublished as is a chamber arrangement, G723a).	
205	1854	*Hungaria. Symphonic Poem* G103. Main themes from 260.	BHi/5
		Arr 2 pf, *c* 1854–61 (G643).	
		Arr pf 4 hands, *c* 1874 (G596).	

206	1854	*A Faust Symphony, in three character pictures* G108. *cf* **224**. Choral finale added 1857. Arr 2 pf, 1856, revised 1860 (G647). 2nd movement arr pf, by 1867 (G513).	BHi/8–9 NExvi
207	1855–6	*A Symphony to Dante's 'Divina Commedia'* G109. Planned 1839, 1847. Arr 2 pf, *c* 1856–9 (G648).	BHi/7
208	1856–7	*Hunnenschlacht. Symphonic Poem* G105. Arr 2 pf, 1857 (G645). Arr pf 4 hands, *c* 1877 (G596b).	BHi/6
209	1857	*Die Ideale. Symphonic Poem* G106. One theme from **96**. *cf* **210**. Arr 2 pf, 1857–58 (G646). Arr pf 4 hands, *c* 1874–7 (G596c).	BHi/6
210	1857	*Künstlerfestzug zur Schillerfeier* G114. On themes from **96** and **209**. Arr pf 4 hands, 1859 (G605). Arr pf, 1857–60; revised 1883 (G520).	BHi/11 NExv
211	1857	*Festmarsch nach Motiven von E.H.z.S.-C.-G.* G116. (Ernst, Duke of Saxe-Coburg-Gotha; from his opera 'Diana von Solange'). Arr pf, 1857 (G522). Arr pf 4 hands, *c* 1859 (G607).	 NExv
212	1858	*Hamlet. Symphonic Poem* G104. Arr 2 pf, *c*. 1858–61 (G644). Arr pf 4 hands, 1874 (G597).	BHi/5
213	1859–61	*Two Episodes from Lenau's 'Faust'* G110. (1) The Procession by Night (2) The Dance in the Village Inn (= '1st Mephisto Waltz'). Arr pf 4 hands, 1861–2 (G599). *1st Mephisto Waltz* arr pf, 1859–62 (G514).	BHi/10 NExv
214	1860	*Les Morts. Oration for full orchestra* G 112(1). (Odes Funèbres No 1) *cf* **392**. Male chorus added 1866 (text: de Lamennais). Arr pf, 1860 (G516). Arr pf 4 hands (G601), unpublished.	 BHi/12 NExi
215	1863	*Salve Polonia* G113. Interlude from **44**. Sketched 1850. Arr pf, after 1863 (G518). Arr pf 4 hands, 1863 (G604).	 NExvii
216	1863–4	*La Notte* G112(2). (Odes Funèbres No. 2) From **296**(2). Arr pf, 1863–66 (G699). Arr violin + pf, 1864–66 (G377a). Arr pf 4 hands, 1866 (G602, unpublished).	 BHi/12 NExi

217	1865	*Rákóczy March* G117. Sketched earlier. From 255(13) and 287(15).	
		For pf, *cf* 287(15) (second version).	NExiii
		Arr pf 4 hands, 1870 (G608) and for 2 pf, 1870.	
218	1866	*Le Triomphe funèbre du Tasse* G112(3). (Odes Funèbres No. 3) Epilogue to 198, with which it shares themes.	BHi/2
		Arr pf, 1866 (G517).	NExvi
		Arr pf 4 hands, 1866 and 1869 (G603 unpublished).	
219	1870	*Ungarischer Marsch zur Krönungsfeier in Ofen-Pest* G118.	BHi/12
		Arr pf, 1870 (G523).	NExvi & RSvii
		Arr pf 4 hands, 1870 (G609).	
220	1875	*Ungarischer Sturmmarsch* G119. Revised version of 279.	BHi/12
		Arr pf, 1875 (G524).	NExvi & RSvii
		Arr pf 4 hands, 1875 (G610).	
221	1880–1	*Second Mephisto Waltz* G111.	BHi/10
		Arr pf, 1881 (G515).	NExvii
		Arr pf 4 hands, 1881 (G600).	
222	1881–2	*Von der Wiege bis zum Grabe. Symphonic Poem* G107.	BHi/10
		The first part from 352. *cf* 401.	
		Arr pf, 1881 (G512).	NExvii
		Arr pf 4 hands, 1881 (G598).	

See also **310, 311, 320**.

VII PIANOFORTE AND ORCHESTRA

223	?1825	*Two concertos* G713. Lost.	
224	1833	*Malédiction* G121.	BHi/13
		One theme used in **206**. *cf* **200**.	
225	?1834	*De Profundis. Psaume instrumental* G691. Sketched earlier. Unfinished and unpublished. Partly used in **228** and **291**(4).	
226	1834	*Grande Fantaisie Symphonique on themes from Berlioz's 'Lélio'* G120. Unpublished. Arr 2 pf (published 1981).	
227	?1837	*Fantasia on themes from Beethoven's 'Ruins of Athens'* G122. Revised 1849.	
		Arr 2 pf, published 1865 (G649).	RSiv/2
		Arr pf, published 1865 (G389).	RSi/1
228	1849	*Totentanz. Paraphrase on the Dies Irae* G126.	BHi/13

		Planned 1839. Revised 1853 and 1859. *cf* **225**.	
		Arr 2 pf, after 1859 (G652).	
		Arr pf, *c* 1860–5 (G525).	NExvi
229	1849	*Concerto no. 1 in E flat* G124. Sketched 1832.	BHi/13
		1849 version orch with Raff.	
		Revised by Liszt 1853 and 1856.	
		Arr 2 pf, 1853 (G650).	
230	1849	*Concerto no. 2 in A* G125. Sketched *c* 1830.	BHi/13
		1st version, 1839; revised 1853, 1857 and 1861.	
		Arr 2 pf, 1859 (G651).	
231	1852	*Fantasia on Hungarian Folk Themes* G123.	
		From **287**(14).	

Liszt wrote no other concerto works but sketched a Violin Concerto, 1860 (G692; unpublished).

A Piano Concerto 'in the Hungarian Style' (G126a) is attributed to Liszt, *c* 1885. It is probably by Sophie Menter (perhaps based on some suggestions by Liszt); the orchestration is by Tchaikovsky, *c* 1892.

cf **530** and **575**.

VIII ORIGINAL PIANOFORTE WORKS

(A) *For 2 hands*

232	1822	*Variation on a waltz of Diabelli* G147.	BHii/7
233	1824	*Rondo and Fantasy* G724. Lost.	
234	1824	*Impromptu brillant sur des thèmes de Rossini*	
		et Spontini G150. Based on themes from 'La	RSi/1
		donna del lago', 'Armida', 'Olympie' and	
		'Fernand Cortez'. Opening bars used in	
		251(7) and **303**(7). Orchestral version	
		sketched; unpublished.	
235	1824	*Allegro di bravura* G151.	BHii/7
			& NExi
		Arr orch, *c* 1830, unfinished (G701a).	
236	1824	*Rondo di bravura* G152.	BHii/7
			& NExi
237	?1824	*Sept Variations brillantes sur un thème de G.*	
		Rossini G149. (Theme from 'Ermione'.)	
238	?1824	*Huit Variations* G148.	BHii/7
			& NEix
239	1825	*3 Sonatas* G725. Lost.	
240	1825	*Études en douze exercices dans tous les tons*	BHii/7
		majeurs et mineurs G136. *cf* **251**, **258** and **303**.	&NExviii
240a	by 1825	*Waltz in A Major* G208a, pub. 1832.	NExiii
		Version for vl and pf pub. late 1820s.	
241	1827	*Scherzo in G minor* G153.	BHii/9 &
			NExiii
242	1828	*Two Movements of Hungarian character*	

		(*Zum Andenken*) G241. Arrs of works by Bihary and Csermák.	
243	*c* 1830	*Grand Solo caractéristique à propos d'une chansonette de Panseron* (rediscovered 1987; unpub.). Central section resembles **247**(5) and **295**(1).	
244	*c* 1832	*La romanesca* G252a. Revised by 1852.	LSvii,
245	1833	*Harmonies poétiques et religieuses* G154. *cf* **291**(4).	BHii/5
		Originally conceived for pf + orch. Revised 1835.	NEix & LSii
		NB This is a single piece; compare **291**.	
246	1834	*Apparitions* G155.	BHii/5,
		(1) Senza lentezza quasi Allegretto. (2) Vivamente. (3) Molto agitato ed appassionato (on Schubert's Waltz in F, Op 9 no. 33; *cf* **531**).	LSii (nos. 1– 2) & NEix
	c 1835	A *Piano Sonata* (G692b) is listed in catalogues among 'unfinished works'.	
247	1835–8	*Album d'un Voyageur* G156. *cf* **248** and **295**.	BHii/4, LSii
		I *Impressions et poésies*	(no. 1), LSv
		(1) *Lyon* (2a) *Le Lac de Wallenstadt* (2b) *Au bord d'une source* (3) *Les cloches de G....* (4) *Vallée d'Obermann* (5) *La Chapelle de Guillaume Tell* (6) *Psaume*.	(nos. 3–4, 7–9) & NEvi (sections I– II)
		II *Fleurs mélodiques des Alpes* (7a) Allegro. C ma. (7b) Lento. E mi/G ma. (7c) Allegro pastorale. G ma. (8a) Andante con sentimento. G Ma. (8b) Andante molto espressivo. G mi. (8c) Allegro moderato. E flat ma. (9a) Allegretto. D flat ma. (9b) Allegretto. D flat ma. (9c) Andantino con molto sentimento. G ma.	
		III *Paraphrases* (10) *Improvisata sur le Ranz de Vaches* (*Aufzug auf die Alp*) de Ferd. Huber (11) *Un soir dans les montagnes. Nocturne sur le chant montagnard* (*Bergliedchen*) d'Ernest Knop (12) *Rondeau sur le Ranz de Chèvres* (*Geissreihen*) de Ferd. Huber.	
248	1835–6	*Fantaisie romantique sur deux mélodies suisses* G157. On same theme as **247**(7b) and **295**(8).	BHii/5 & LSv
249	1835	*Grande Valse di Bravura* G209.	BHii/10
		Arr pf 4 hands, 1836 (G615). 2nd version: *cf* **301**(1).	& NExiii
	1835–6	*Églogue.* cf **295**(7).	
250	1836	*Rondeau fantastique sur un thème espagnol*,	

'*El Contrabandista*' G252.

251	1837	*12 Grandes Études* G137. From **240**. Intro of no. 7 from **234**. *cf* **202** and **303**.	BHii/7
252	1838–9	*Études d'exécution transcendante d'après* 24 solo violin caprices. (3) is from his Violin Concerto. in B mi. *cf* **304**.	BHii/3

(1) G mi; tremolo study (Paganini no. 6).
(2) E flat ma; octave study (Paganini no. 17).
(3) *La Campanella*; G sharp mi. On same theme as **502**. (4) E ma; arpeggio study (Paganini no. 1). (5) *La Chasse*; E ma (Paganini no. 9).
(6) A mi; theme & variations (Paganini no. 24).

253	1838	*Grand galop chromatique* G219.	BHii/10
		Arr pf 4 hands, 1838 (G616).	& NExiii
		Simplified version arr *c* 1838.	NExiii
	1839	1st versions of **296** (*q.v.*).	
254	1839	*Valse mélancolique* G210. *cf* **265**.	BHii/10,
		Revised version: *cf* **301**(2).	LSiv & NExiii
255	1839–47	A. *Magyar Dallok* (*Hungarian National Melodies*) G242.	LS vii (nos 1–3, 6, 8–
		(1) C mi (2) C ma (3) D flat ma	10)

(4) C sharp ma *cf* **262**(2) and **287**(6)
(5) D flat ma *cf* **262**(1) *and* **287**(6)
(6) G mi (7) E flat ma. *cf* **287**(4)
(8) F mi (9) A mi (10) D ma *cf* **287**(15)
(11) B flat ma *cf* **262**(3), **287**(3 & 6)

		B. *Magyar Rapszódiák* (*Hungarian Rhapsodies*).	NExviii (nos 13, 15,
		(12) E mi *Héroïde élégiaque*. *cf* **287**(5).	17, 20)

(13) A mi *cf* **287**(15).
(14) A mi *cf* **287**(11).
(15) D mi *cf* **287**(7).
(16) E ma *cf* **287**(10).
(17 A mi *cf* **287**(13).
C. (18) C sharp mi/C ma *cf* **287**(12).
(19) F sharp mi *cf* **287**(8).
(20 G mi. Published, ed. Busoni, as *Romanian Rhapsody*, 1936. *cf* **287**(6 & 12).
(21) E mi *cf* **287**(14).

256	?1840	*Venezia e Napoli* 1st Version. G 159.	BHii/5 &
		(1) Lento (uses theme on which **198** is based).	NEvii
		(2) Allegro (3) Andante placido, *cf* **314**.	
		(4) *Tarantelles napolitaines*, *cf* **314**(3).	
257	?1840	*Fantasia on English themes* G694. Unfinished.	
258	1840	*Mazeppa* G138. Slightly altered version of **251**(4). *cf* **303**(4).	BHii/1
259	1840	*Morceau de Salon, Étude de perfectionnement*	

		G142. Contains theme of **197**. *cf* **307**.	BHii/3
260	1840	*Heroic March in Hungarian Style* G231. *cf* **205**.	RSvii & NExiii
261	1840	*Hussitenlied* G234. On a melody by J. Krov. Arr pf 4 hands, 1840 (G620).	
262	1840	*Ungarische Nationalmelodien* G243. *cf* **287**(6).	
		(1) D flat ma. From **255**(5).	
		(2) C sharp ma. From **255**(4).	
		(3) C sharp/B flat ma. From **255**(11).	
263	?1840	*Two Hungarian Piano Pieces* G693. Unfinished.	LSiii
		(1) B flat mi (2) D mi.	
264	?1840	*Galop de bal* G220.	NExiii
265	1840	*Albumblatt in E major* G164. From **254**.	NExiii
266	1841	*Paraphrase on 'God save the Queen'* G235.	
267	?1841	*Galop in A minor* G218.	BHii/10 LSiv & NExiii
268	1841	*Feuille d'album no. 1 in A flat major* G165.	BHii/10 & NExiii
269	1841	*Albumblatt in waltz form* (A ma) G166.	BHii/10 & NExiii
270	1842	*Petite valse favorite (Albumblatt)* (A flat ma) G212. *cf* **299**.	BHii/10 & NExiii
271	1842	*Deux mélodies russes. Arabesques* G250. (1) *Le Rossignol, air russe d'Alabieff* (Alyabyev) (2) *Chanson bohémienne*.	
272	1842	*Canzone Napolitana* G248.	
273	?date	*Ruhig* G167a. Unpublished.	
274	1842	*Élégie sur des motifs du Prince Louis Ferdinand de Prusse* G168. Revised *c* 1851.	NExi
275	1843	*Ländler in A flat* G211.	NExiii
276	1843	*Gaudeamus igitur. Concert paraphrase* G240. *cf* **103**.	
277	?1843	*Feuille d'album no. 2 in A minor* G167. From **113**.	NExvii
278	?1843	*Piano piece in F major* G695. Unfinished.	
279	?1843	*Ungarischer Sturmmarsch* G232. *cf* **220**.	NExvi & RSvii
280	1844	*Faribolo Pastour* and *Chanson du Béarn* G236.	
281	1844	*Madrigal* G171a. Unpublished early version of **294**(5).	
282	1844–5	*Tre Sonetti del Petrarca* G158. From **136**. Revised version: *cf* **296** (4–6). See also **380**.	BHii/5
283	1844	*Hungarian March* E flat mi G233b.	RSvii & NExiii

284	1845	*Grosse Konzertfantasie über Spanische Weisen* G253. *cf* 321.	
285	1845–8	*Ballade no. 1 in D flat major* G170.	BHii/8 & NEix
286	1845	*Piano piece in A flat major* G189a. Similar to 'andantino' section of 285.	NEix
287	from 1846	*Hungarian Rhapsodies nos 1–15* G244. (nos 3–15 published 1853; nos 16–19 *cf* 356, 371–2, 377.	BHii/12 & NEiii–iv

(1) C sharp mi. (Lento, quasi Recitativo) 1846.
(2) C sharp mi. (Lento a capriccio) 1847. Arr orch by Franz Doppler (rev. Liszt; G359) and for pf 4 hands, 1874 (G621).
(3) B flat ma. From 255(11).
(4) E flat ma. From 255(7).
(5) *Héroïde – Élégiaque*. E mi. From 255(12). Arr as for (2) above.
(6) D flat ma. From 255(4, 5, 11 and 20). *cf* 262. Arr as for (2) above.
(7) D mi. From 255(15).
(8) F sharp mi. From 255(19).
(9) *Pester Karneval*. E flat ma. Published 1847; 2nd version published 1853. Arr as for (2) above; and for violin, cello + pf (G379).
(10) *Preludio*. E ma. From 255(16) and a work by Egressy.
(11) A mi. (Lento a capriccio). From 255(14).
(12) C sharp mi. (Mesto). From 255(18 and 20). Arr as for (2) above.
(13) A mi. (Andante sostenuto). From 255(17).
(14) F mi. From 255(21). *cf* 231. Arr as for (2) above.
(15) *Rákóczy March*. A mi. 1st version; from 255(10 and 13).
Simplified version, 1852.

		2nd version, 1870. From 217.	RSvii
		Arr pf 4 hands, 1870 (G608).	
288	1847	*Hymne de la nuit; Hymne du matin* G173a. Originally intended for 291.	NEix
289	?1847	*Andante amoroso* G168a.	
290	1847–8	*Glanes de Woronince* G249. (1) *Ballade d'Ukraine* (Dumka). (2) *Mélodies polonaises cf* 442(1). One theme used in 394. (3) *Complainte* (Dumka).	
291	1847–52	*Harmonies poétiques et religieuses* G173. Sketched 1845. An unfinished piece, *Litanie de Marie*, 1847 (G695a) was intended originally for inclusion. (1) *Invocation* (Earlier version, 1845, in NEix).	BHii/7 & NEix

(2) *Ave Maria.* From 5. (3) *Bénédiction de Dieu dans la solitude.* (4) *Pensée des morts.* From 225 and 245. (5) *Pater Noster.* From 4. (6) *Hymne de l'enfant à son réveil.* From 6. (7) *Funérailles,* October 1849. (8) *Miserere, d'après Palestrina.* Arr harp, 1856. (9) Andante lagrimoso. (10) *Cantique d'amour.*

292	1848	*Romance* E minor. G169. From 127. Revised as *Romance oubliée,* 1880 (G527). *cf* 399.	LSvii & NExi
293	?1848	*3 Concert Studies* G144. (1) *Il lamento,* A flat ma. (2) *La leggierezza,* F mi. (3) *Un sospiro,* D flat ma.	BHii/3 & NEii
294	1848	*Consolations* G172. (1) Andante con moto (2) Un poco più mosso (3) Lento placido (4) Quasi adagio (on a theme of Grand Duchess Maria Pavlovna) (5) Andantino; 1844, from 281. (6) Allegretto.	BHii/8 & NEix
295	1848–55	*Années de Pèlerinage. Première Année. Suisse.* G160. (1) *Chapelle de Guillaume Tell.* From 247(5). (2) *Au lac de Wallenstadt.* From 247(2a). (3) *Pastorale.* From 247(7c). (4) *Au bord d'une source.* From 247(2b). (5) *Orage.* 1855. (6) *Vallée d'Obermann.* From 247(4). Arr. pf. trio in Liszt's late years (unpub.). (7) *Églogue* 1835–6. Revised *c* 1854. (8) *Le mal du pays.* From 247(7b). (9) *Les cloches de Genève.* From 247(3).	BHii/6 & NEvi
296	1839–49	*Années de pèlerinage. Deuxieme Année. Italie* G161. (1) *Sposalizio,* 1839. *cf* 62. (2) *Il Penseroso,* 1839; rev. 1849. *cf* 216. (3) *Canzonetta del Salvator Rosa* 1849. (4) *Sonetto 47 del Petrarca.* (5) *Sonetto 104 del Petrarca.* (6) *Sonetto 123 del Petrarca.* (4–6; from 136, second version). (7) *Après une lecture du Dante, fantasia quasi sonata,* 1st version 1839; revised 1849.	BHii/6 & NEvii
297	?1849	*Grosses Konzertsolo* G176. *cf* 382. Arr pf + orch, *c* 1850 (G365; unpublished).	BHii/8 & NEv
298	1849	*Goethe Festival March* G227. *cf* 199.	BHii/10 & NExiv
299	?1850	*Valse Impromptu* G213. From 270.	BHii/10 & NExiii
300	1850	*Mazurka brillante* G221.	BHii/10, LSv, NExiii
301	?1850	*Trois Caprices-Valses* G214.	BHii/10 (nos. 1–2)

(1) from **249** (2) from **254** (3) from **455**.

302	?1850	*La cloche sonne* G238.	
303	1851	*Études d'exécution transcendante* G139. From **251**.	BHii/2 & NEi

(1) *Preludio* (2) A mi (3) *Paysage* (4) *Mazeppa* From **258**; *cf* **202**. (5) *Feux follets* (6) *Vision* (7) *Eroica* (8) *Wilde Jagd* (9) *Ricordanza* (10) F mi (11)*Harmonies du soir* (12) *Chasse-neige*.

304	1851	*Grandes Études de Paganini* G141. From **252**.	BHii/3 & NEii
305	1851	*Scherzo and March* G177.	BHii/8 & NExiii
306	1851	*Deux Polonaises* G223. (1) C mi (2) E ma.	BHii/10 & NExiii
307	1852	*Ab Irato. Étude* G143. From **259**.	BHii/3 & NEii
308	1852–3	*Sonata in B minor* G178. Sketched 1851.	BHii/8 & NEv
309	1853	*Ballade No 2 in B minor* G171.	BHii/8 & NEix
310	1853	*Huldigungsmarsch* G228.	NExv
		Arr orch, 1853; rev. 1857 (G357) *cf* **99**.	BHi/11
311	1853–6	*Vom Fels zum Meer. Deutscher Siegesmarsch* G229.	NExv
		Arr orch, 1860 (G358).	BHi/12
		Arr pf 4 hands (G618a; unpublished).	
312	1854	*Berceuse* G174. 1st version.	BHii/9
		2nd version, 1862.	NExi
313	1856	*Festvorspiel (Preludio pomposo)* G226.	NExi
		Arr orch, 1857 (G356)	BHi/11
314	1859	*Venezia e Napoli. Supplément aux Années de Pèlerinage, 2de volume* G162. From **256**.	BHii/6 & NEvii

(1) *Gondoliera* (theme by Cavaliere Peruchini).
(2) *Canzone* (theme from Rossini's *Otello*).
(3) *Tarantella* (on themes by Guillaume Louis Cottrau).

315	1859	*Weinen, Klagen, Sorgen, Zagen. Prelude after J.S. Bach* G179.	BHii/9
316	after 1860	*Klavierstück* F sharp ma. G193.	BHii/10, LSvii & NExi
317	1862	*Variations on a theme of Bach, 'Weinen, Klagen, Sorgen, Zagen'* G180.	BHii/9
		Arr organ, 1863 (G673).	
318	1862	*Ave Maria (The Bells of Rome)* G182.	BHii/9 & NExi
	1862	*Alleluja cf* **406**.	

319	1862–3	2 Concert Studies G145. (1) *Waldesrauschen* (2) *Gnomenreigen*.	BHii/3 & NEii
320	1862–3	*Deux Légendes* G175. (1) *St François d'Assise. La Prédication aux oiseaux* (one theme from **22**). (2) *St François de Paule marchant sur les flots* (one theme from **18**). Arr orch, 1863 (G354). Simplified version of (2).	BHii/9 & NEx NEx
321	?1863	*Spanish Rhapsody (Folies d'Espagne et Jota Aragonesa)* G254. (one theme from **284**).	
322	1864	*Vexilla regis prodeunt* G185. Arr orch, 1864 (G355; unpublished).	NExii
323	1864	*Urbi et Orbi. Bénédiction papale* G184.	NExii
324	1865	Nos 1 and 2 of '5 little piano pieces' G192. No. 1 on same theme as **154**. *cf* **334**, **339** and **348**.	BHii/9, LSi & NEx
325	1866	*Piano piece. A flat ma* G189.	
	1867	*Funeral March for Maximilian of Mexico. cf* **340**(6).	
326	1868–c 80	*Technical Studies* (12 books) G146. (published 1886, ed. Winterberger). The complete set, with the addition of '12 grosse Etüden', published 1983.	
327	1868	*La Marquise de Blocqueville. Un portrait en musique* G190.	NExii
328	1870	*Ungarischer Geschwindmarsch. Magyar Gyors indulo* G233.	RSvii & NExiv
329	1870	*Mosonyis Grabgeleit. Mosonyi gyázmenete* G194. *cf* **369**(7).	LSiii
330	?date	*Siegesmarsch. Marche triomphale* G233a.	NExiv
331	?1870–80	*Vive Henri IV* G239.	LSvii
332	1872	*Impromptu (Nocturne)* G191.	BHii/9 & NExii
	1872	*Sunt lacrymae rerum cf* **340**(5).	
333	?1872	*La Marseillaise* G237 (the theme had been used in **195**).	
334	1873	No. 3 of '5 little piano pieces' G192. *cf* **324**, **339** and **348**.	BHii/9, LSi & NEx
335	1873	*5 Hungarian folk songs* G245.	LSiii
336	1874	*(First) Elegy* G196. *cf* **397**.	BHii/9, LSiii & NEx
337	?1870s	*Stabat Mater* (published 1978).	NExii
338	1875–6	*Weihnachtsbaum. Christmas Tree* G186. Sketched 1866. (1) '*Psallite*' (2) *O Holy Night cf* **49** (3) *The Shepherds at the Manger* (4) *Adeste fideles* (5) *Scherzoso* (6) *Carillon* (7) *Slumber Song*	BHii/9 & NEx

		(8) *Old Provençal Christmas Song* (9) *Evening Bells* (10) *Jadis. Old Times* (11) *Hungarian* (12) *Polish.* Arr pf 4 hands, 1876 (G613).	
339	1876	No. 4 of '5 little piano pieces' G192. *cf* **324**, **334** and **348**.	BHii/9, LSi & NEx
340	1867–77	*Années de Pèlerinage. Troisième Année.* G163.	BHii/6 & NEviii
		(1) *Angelus! Prière aux anges gardiens* (1877). Arr harm, 1877 (G378,1).	BHii/6
		Arr string 4tet, 1880 (G378,2). (2) *Aux cyprès de la Villa d'Este; Thrénodie* (3/4) (1877). (3) *Aux cyprès de la Villa d'Este; thrénodie* (4/4) (1877). (4) *Les Jeux d'eaux à la Villa d'Este* (1877). (5) *Sunt lacrymae rerum, en mode hongrois* (1872). (6) *Marche funèbre* (1867). (7) *Sursum corda* (1877).	
341	1877	*Second Elegy* G197. *cf* **398**.	BHii/9, LSiii & NEx
342	1877	*Petőfi Szellemének. In memory of Petőfi* G195. Theme from **189**. *cf* **369**(6). Arr pf 4 hands, 1877 (G614).	LSiii
343	1877	*Sancta Dorothea* G187.	BHii/9, LSvii & NExiii
344	1877	*Recueillement* G204.	BHii/9 & NExii
345	1877	*Resignazione* G187a.	NExii
346	1879–81	*Toccata* G197a.	NExii
347	*c* 1875–81	*Carousel de Mme Pelet-Narbonne* G214a.	NExii
348	1879	*Sospiri* (No. 5 of '5 little piano pieces') G192. *cf* **324**, **334** and **339**.	NEx
349	1879	*Sarabande and Chaconne from Handel's 'Almira'* G181.	RSi/1
350	1880	*Variation on 'Chopsticks'* (for a set of pieces on the theme by Borodin, Cui, Liadov and Rimsky-Korsakov) G207a.	
351	1880	*In festo transfigurationis Domini nostri Jesu Christi* G188.	BHii/9, LSvii & NExii
352	1880	*Wiegenlied (Chant du berceau)* G198. *cf* **222**.	NExii
353	1881	*Nuages gris* G199.	BHii/9, LSi & NExii
354	1881	*Valse oubliée No. 1* G215.	BHii/10 & NExiv
355	1881–2	*Csárdás macabre* G224.	LSi, RSvii & NExiv
		Arr pf 4 hands, 1882 (G617; unpublished; not by Liszt?).	

356	1882	*Hungarian Rhapsody No 16* A mi. (Allegro) G244.	BHii/12 & NEiv
		Arr pf 4 hands, 1882 (G622).	
357	1882	*La lugubre gondola* G200.	BHii/9, LSi & NExii
		1st version (6/8).	
		2nd version (4/4), 1885; from **403**.	
358	1883	*R.W. -Venezia* G201.	BHii/9, LSi & NExii
359	1883	*Schlaflos! Frage und Antwort* G203.	BHii/9, LSiii & NExii
360	1883	*Am Grabe Richard Wagners* G202.	LSii & NExii
		Uses theme from **47**(1). *cf* **391** and **402**.	
361	1883	*Valse oubliée No. 2* G215.	BHii/10, LSiv & NExiv
362	1883	*Bülow-Marsch* G230.	BHii/10 & NExiv
		Arr pf 4 hands, *c* 1883 (G619).	
		Arr pf 8 hands, 1884, unpublished (G657b).	
363	1883	*Mephisto Polka* G217.	BHii/10, LSv & NExiv
364	1883	*Mephisto Waltz No. 3* G216.	BHii/10, LSi & NExiv
365	1883	*Valse oubliée No. 3* G215.	BHii/10, LSiv & NExiv
366	1883–4	*Valse oubliée No. 4* G215.	NExiv
367	1884	*2 Csárdás* G225.	LSiii (no. 2), RSvii & NExiv
		(1) Allegro (2) *Csárdás obstiné*.	
		(2) Arr pf 4 hands, *c* 1884 (G618).	
368	?date	*Puszta-Wehmut. A Puszta Keserve* G246.	
		Published after 1884; arr of a work by Zámoyská, on a poem by Lenau.	RSvii
		Arr violin + pf (G379a; unpublished).	
369	1885	*Historical Hungarian Portraits. Magyar történelmi arcképek* G205.	RSvii, LSi (no. 4), LSiii (nos. 6–7) & NEx
		(1) *Széchenyi István* (2) *Eötvös József* (3) *Vörösmarty Mihály* (4) *Teleki László* (another version of 'Trauermarsch', **370**). (5) *Deák Ferenc* (6) *Petőfi Sándor* (*cf* **342**). (7) *Mosonyi Mihály* (*cf* **329**).	
370	1885	*Trauervorspiel und Trauermarsch* G206. *cf* **369**(4).	LSi & NExii

371	1885	*Hungarian Rhapsody No. 18* C sharp mi. (Lento) G244. Arr pf 4 hands, 1885 (G623).	BHii/12 & NEiv
372	1885	*Hungarian Rhapsody No 19.* D mi. (Lento) G244. Based on the *Csárdás nobles* of Ábrányi. Arr pf 4 hands, *c* 1885 (G623a).	BHii/12 & NEiv
373	1885	*Abschied. Russisches Volkslied* G251.	
374	1885	*Mephisto Waltz No. 4* G696.	LSii & NExiv
375	1885	*Bagatelle sans tonalité* G216a.	NExiv
376	1885	*En rêve. Nocturne* G207.	BHii/9, LSi & NExii
377	1886	*Hungarian Rhapsody No. 17* D mi. (Lento) G244.	BHii/12 & NEiv
378	?date	*Unstern! Sinistre. Disastro* G208.	BHii/9, LSi & NExii

(B) *For 4 hands*

379	1876	*Festpolonaise* G634b. Arr pf solo, 1876 (G230a).	NExvii
380	?date	*Notturno* E ma. G256a. From **282** (Sonnet 104) (not by Liszt?).	

(C) *For 2 pianofortes*

381	1834	*Grosses Konzertstück über Mendelssohns 'Lieder ohne Worte'* G257. Unpublished.
382	by 1856	*Concerto pathétique* G258. From **297**.

IX ORGAN WORKS

383	1850	*Fantasy and Fugue on the chorale 'Ad nos, ad salutarem undam'* G259. Theme from Meyerbeer's *Le Prophète*. Arr pf 4 hands (or pedal-piano), 1850 (G624).	RSiv/3
384	1855	*Prelude and Fugue on the name BACH* G260. 2nd version 1870. Arr pf, *c* 1856; revised 1870 (G529).	NEv

385 ?1861   *Andante religioso* G261a. Based on a theme
                  from **196**.

386 ?1863   *Pio IX. Der Papsthymnus* G261. Later arr as
                  31(8).
                  Arr orch, *c* 1863 (G361; unpublished).
                  Arr pf, *c* 1864 (G530).   NExv
                  Arr pf 4 hands, *c* 1865 (G625).

387 1864   *Ora pro nobis. Litanei* G262.

388 1877   *Zwei Kirchenhymnen* G669.
                  (1) *Salve Regina* (2) *cf* **28**.

389 1879   *Gebet* G265. *cf* **390**.

390 1879   *Missa pro organo* G264. The 'Graduale' from
                  389, and the 'Offertorium' from **36**.

391 1883   *Am Grabe Richard Wagners* G267. *cf* **360** and
                  402.

392 1884   *Zwei Vortragsstücke* G268.
                  (1) *Introitus* (2) *Trauerode* (1860) from **214**.

All these organ works together with Liszt's organ and harmonium arrange-ments of works by himself (see above under nos. **22, 25, 29, 31**(8), **33, 36, 47, 55, 61, 62, 65, 99, 182, 317, 340**(1), **345**) and of works by other composers (see below nos. **405, 406, 412, 414, 443, 483, 500, 554, 562**) may be found in: Ferenc Liszt, *Complete Organ Works*, edited by Sándor Margittay. 4 volumes, Editio Musica Budapest/Boosey & Hawkes, London, 1970–3.

X CHAMBER MUSIC

393 1825   *Trio* and *Quintet* G717–18. Lost.
394 *c* 1832–5   *Duo* (*Sonata*) Violin + pf G127. Based on
                  Chopin's *Mazurka* op 6 no. 2.
395 *c* 1837   *Grand duo concertant sur la Romance de M.
                  Lafont, 'Le Marin'* Violin + pf G128. Revised,
                  1849?
396 1872   *Epithalam* Violin + pf G129.
                  Arr pf, 1872 (G526).   NExii
                  Arr pf 4 hands, 1872 (G611).
397 1874   *Elegy* G130. *cf* **336**. 3 versions:
                  (1) cello, pf, harp + harm. (2) cello + pf.
                  (3) violin + pf.
                  Arr pf 4 hands, 1874 (G612).
398 1877   *Second Elegy* Pf + violin or cello. G131. *cf* **341**.
399 1880   *Romance oubliée* Pf + viola or violin or cello.
                  G132. Revised version of **292**.   LSvii &
                  Also arr pf, 1880 (G527).   NExii
400 *c* 1880   *The Four Seasons* String 4tet. G692a.
                  Unfinished.

401	?1881	*Die Wiege* 4 violins. G133. Unpublished. (Based on the first part of **222**.)
402	1883	*Am Grabe Richard Wagners* String 4tet + harp (ad lib.). G135. *cf* **360** and **391**. LSii
403	?1885	*La lugubre gondola* Pf + violin or cello. G134. *cf* **357** (2nd version).

XI TRANSCRIPTIONS AND ARRANGEMENTS

NB All works are transcribed for pianoforte solo unless otherwise stated.
Vocal arrangements are found under **458, 476, 478, 504, 505, 513, 533, 534, 579**.
Orchestral arrangements under **405, 440, 445, 460, 532, 577**.
Arrangements for piano and orchestra, **530, 575**.
4-hand piano arrangements, **405, 418, 425, 434, 452, 460, 465, 468, 490, 499, 507, 634**.
2-piano arrangements, **415, 422, 424, 427, 496, 530**.
Others, see **513, 557**.
For organ arrangements see note to Section IX above.

Ábrányi, Kornél von
404	1881	*Elaboration on Virag dál* G383a. Unpublished.

See also **372**.

Allegri, Gregorio
405	1862	*À la chapelle Sixtine. Miserere d'Allegri et Ave verum corpus de Mozart* G461. Also arr orch, *c* 1862 (G360; unpublished). Also arr organ, *Évocation à la Chapelle Sixtine, c* 1862 (G658). Also arr pf 4 hands, *c* 1865 (G633).

Alyabyev, Alexander Alexandrovich
See **271**(1) and **580**.

Arcadelt, Jacob
406	1862	*Alleluja and Ave Maria* G183. The 'Alleluja' is an original work on themes from **22** (published in NExi). The 'Ave Maria' (attributed to Arcadelt) also arr organ, 1862 (G659).

Auber, Daniel François Esprit
407	1829	*Grande fantaisie sur la tyrolienne de l'opéra 'La fiancée'* G385. Two versions. RSi/1 & RSiv/1
408		*Tyrolean Melody* G385a. Based on theme of **407**.
409	1846	*Tarantelle di bravura d'après la tarantella de*

		'La muette de Portici' G386.	RSi/1
410		3 Pieces; 2 on themes from 'La muette de Portici' G387. Unpublished.	

Bach, Johann Sebastian

411	1842–50	6 Organ Preludes and Fugues G462. (NB transcribed for piano) (1) A mi. BWV543. (2) C ma. BWV545. (3) C mi. BWV546. (4) C ma. BWV547. (5) E mi. BWV548. (6) B mi. BWV544.	
412	1860	For organ: Introduction and Fugue from the cantata 'Ich hatte viel Bekümmernis' (BWV21) and Andante from 'Aus tiefer Not' (BWV38) G660.	
413		Fantasia and Fugue in G minor (BWV542) G463. Published 1863.	
414	1864	For organ: Adagio from Violin Sonata No. 4 (BWV1017) G661.	

In 1880 Liszt planned an arr of Bach's
Chaconne in D minor.
See also **315**.

Beethoven, Ludwig van

415	1837/1863–1864	Nine Symphonies G464. (Nos 5–7, 1837; slow mvt. of no. 3, 1843; nos 1–3, 4, 8, 9 and revision of nos 5–7, 1863–4). No. 9 arr 2 pfs, 1851 at latest (G657).	BHarrs 2–3
416	1839	Adelaïde, op. 46 G466. Later revised.	
417	1840	6 Geistliche Lieder, op. 48 G467.	
418	1841	Grand Septuor op. 20 G465. Also arr pf 4 hands (not by Liszt?), 1841? (G634).	
419	1846	Capriccio alla turca from 'The Ruins of Athens' G388.	RSi/1 & RSiv/1
420	by 1849	Lieder von Goethe (from op. 75, op. 83, op. 84) G468. (1) Mignon (2) Mit einem gemalten Bande (3) Freudvoll und leidvoll (4) Es war einmal ein König (5) Wonne der Wehmut (6) Die Trommel gerühret.	RSiv/1 (nos 3 and 6)
421	1849	An die ferne Geliebte op. 98 G469.	
422	1878	For 2 pianos: Piano Concertos nos 3, 4 and 5 (with cadenzas) G657a.	

See also **227**.
Liszt also transcribed Beethoven's *Coriolan* and *Egmont* overtures; now lost. (G739–40).

Bellini, Vincenzo

423	1836	*Réminiscences des Puritains* G390.	RSii/2
424	1837	*Hexaméron, Morceau de Concert. Grandes Variations de Bravoure sur la Marche des Puritani* G392.	RSii/2
		In collaboration with Chopin, Czerny, Herz, Pixis and Thalberg.	
		Also arr 2 pfs, after 1837 (G654).	RSiv/2
425	1839	*Fantaisie sur des motifs favoris de l'opéra La Sonnambula* G393. Revised 1840–1.	RSii/2 & RSiv/1
		Also arr pf 4 hands, *c* 1852 (G627).	RSiv/3
426	1840	*I Puritani. Introduction et Polonaise* G391.(Polonaise from 423).	RSii/2
427	1841	*Réminiscences de Norma* G394.	RSii/2
		Also arr 2 pfs, after 1841 (G655).	RSiv/2

Berlioz, Hector

428	?1833	*L'idée fixe: andante amoroso* G395. Revised 1846?, and 1865.	
429	1833	*Symphonie fantastique* G470. 4th movt. revised *c* 1864–5.	
430	1833	*Ouverture des Francs-juges* G471.	
431	1836	*Harold en Italie* G472. With viola part.	
432	?1837	*Marche des pèlerins* ('Harold in Italy') G473. Revised 1862.	
433	1837	*Ouverture du Roi Lear* G474.	
434	1852	*Bénédiction et serment, deux motifs de Benvenuto Cellini* G396.	RSii/2
		Also arr pf 4 hands, 1852 (G628).	RSiv/3
435	?1860	*Danse des Sylphes de La damnation de Faust* G475.	

See also **226**.
An arr of the Overture *Le carnaval romain*
(G741) is lost.

Bertin, Louise

436	1837	*Esmeralda. Opéra en 4 actes. Accompagnement de piano* G476.
437	1837	*Air chanté par Massol* ('Esmeralda') G477.
438	?1837	*3 Pieces from 'Esmeralda'* G477a.

Bihary, János
See **242**.

Bulgakov, A.

439	1843	*Russischer Galopp* G478.

Bülow, Hans von

440	1865	For orchestra: *Mazurka Fantasie* op. 13 G351.
441	1874	*Dante's sonnet 'Tanto gentile e tanto onesta'* G479.

Chopin, Frédéric François
442 1847–60   *6 Polish Songs (from op. 74)* G480. (no. 1: *cf*
   290(2)).
443 1863   For organ:
   2 Preludes from op. 28 (nos 4 & 9) G662.
See also **394**.

Conradi, August
444 ?1847   *Le célèbre Zigeunerpolka* G481.

Cornelius, Peter
445 1877   For orchestra:
   Second Overture to 'The Barber of Baghdad'
   G352. (Completed from Cornelius's
   sketches).

Cottrau, Guglielmo Luigi
   See **314(3)**.

Csermák, Antal
   See **242**.

Cui, César
446 1885   *Tarantelle* G482.

Dargomizhsky, Alexander
447 1879   *Tarantelle* G483.   RSii/2

David, Ferdinand
448 1850   *Bunte Reihe, op. 30* G484.

Delibes, Léo
449 after 1880   *La Mandragore. Ballade de l'opéra Jean de
   Nivelle* G698. Unfinished.

Dessauer, Josef
450 1846   *3 Lieder* G485.
   (1) *Lockung* (2) *Zwei Wege* (3) *Spanisches
   Lied.*

Donizetti, Gaetano
451 1835–6   *Réminiscences de Lucia di Lammermoor*
   G397. (Sextet).   RSii/1
452 1835–6   *Marche et cavatine de Lucia di Lammermoor*
   G398.   RSii/1
   Also arr pf 4 hands, 1835–6 (G628a)   RSiv/3
453 1838   *Nuits d'Été à Pausilippe* G399.
454 1840   *Réminiscences de Lucrezia Borgia* G400.   RSii/1 &
   (1) Trio from Act 2. (2) Fantasia on themes   RSiv/1
   from the opera.   (original ver
                             of (2))
455 1842   *Valse à capriccio sur deux motifs de Lucia et*   LSiv, RSii/1

		Parisina G401. Revised version, *cf* 301(3).	& RSiv/1
456	1844	*Marche funèbre de Dom Sébastien* G402.	RSii/1
456a	1846	*'Spirito gentile' from La Favorita.* Unpublished.	

Donizetti, Giuseppe
| 457 | 1847 | *Grande paraphrase de la marche ... pour Sa Majesté le Sultan Abdul Medjid-Khan* G403. |

Draesecke, Felix
| 458 | 1860 | Song arranged as a recitation for voice + pf: *Helges Treue* G686. |
| 459 | 1870 | *Cantata, Der Schwur am Rütli, Part 1* G485a. Unpublished. |

Egressy, Béni
| 460 | 1873 | *Szózat und Ungarischer Hymnus* (Egressy and Erkel) |

3 Transcriptions: (1) For orchestra, G353.

(2) For pf, G486.   NExvi

(3) For pf 4 hands, G628b. (?by Liszt).

See 287(10).

Erkel, Franz
| 461 | 1847 | *Schwanengesang and Marsch from 'Hunyadi László'* G405. Unpublished. |

See also 460.

Ernst, Duke of Saxe-Coburg-Gotha
| 462a | 1849 | *Halloh! Jagdchor und Steyrer from the opera 'Tony'* G404. | RSiii/2 |
| 462b | 1842 | *Die Gräberinsel der Fürsten zu Gotha* (published 1985). | |

See also 211.

Festetics, Leo
| 463 | 1846 | *Spanisches Ständchen* G487. Unpublished. |
| 464 | 1858 | *Variations on Pásztor Lakodalmas* G405a. |

Field, John
| 465 | | For pf 4 hands: *Nocturnes Nos 1–9, 14, 18 and Nocturne pastorale* G577a. |

Franz, Robert
| 466 | 1848 | *Er ist gekommen in Sturm und Regen* G488. |
| 467 | 1848 | *12 Lieder* G489. |

I *Schilflieder* op. 2: (1) *Auf geheimen Waldespfaden* (2) *Drüben geht die Sonne scheiden* (3) *Trübe wird's* (4) *Sonnen-untergang* (5) *Auf dem Teich.*
II 3 Songs from op. 3 and op. 8: (6) *Der Schalk* (7) *Der Bote* (8) *Meeresstille.*

III 4 Songs from op. 3 and op. 8: (9) *Treibt der Sommer* (10) *Gewitternacht* (11) *Das ist ein Brausen und Heulen* (12) *Frühling und Liebe.*

Fuerto, Mariano Soriano
    See 540.

Glinka, Mikhail Ivanovich
468	1843	*Tscherkessenmarsch* ('Russlan and Ludmilla') G406.	RSii/2

Glinka, Mikhail Ivanovich
468 1843   *Tscherkessenmarsch* ('Russlan and Ludmilla') G406.   RSii/2
          Later revised.   RSiv/1
          Arr pf 4 hands, 1843, revised 1875 (G629).   RSiv/3

Goldschmidt, Adalbert von
469 1880   *Liebesszene und Fortunas Kugel* ('Die sieben Todsünden') G490.

Gounod, Charles
470 by 1861   *Valse de l'opéra Faust* G407. (A transcription of the Soldiers' Chorus from 'Faust', G743, is probably lost.)   RSiii/2
471   *Les Sabéennes. Berceuse de l'opéra La Reine de Saba* G408. Published 1865.   RSiii/2
472 1866   *Hymne à Ste Cécile* G491. Unpublished.
473 1867   *Les Adieux. Rêverie sur un motif de l'opéra Roméo et Juliette* G409.   RSiii/2

Halévy, Jacques François
474 1835   *Réminiscences de La Juive* G409a.   RSii/1

Handel, George Frideric
    See 349.

Herbeck, Johann
475 1869   *Tanzmomente* G492.

Hohenzollern-Hechingen, Prince F.W.C. von
476   Arr for voice + pf:
          Serbisches Lied (*Ein Mädchen sitzt am Meeresstrand*) G683. (Liszt collaborated on this arr of a traditional tune.)

Hummel, Johann Nepomuk
477 1848   *Septet op. 74* G493.

Korbay, Francis Alexander
478 1883   Arr for voice + orch:
          2 Songs G368. Unpublished?
          (1) *Le matin* (Bizet) (2) *Gebet* (Geibel).
          Arr of (2) for voice + organ (G683a; unpublished?)

Lassen, Eduard

479	1861	*Löse Himmel meine Seele* G494.
480	1872	*Ich weil in tiefer Einsamkeit* G495.
481	1878–9	*From the incidental music to Hebbel's 'Nibelungen' and Goethe's 'Faust'* G496.

I *Nibelungen:* (1) *Hagen und Krimhild* (2) *Bechlarn.*
II *Faust:* (1) *Osterhymne* (2) *Hoffest: Marsch und Polonaise.*

482	?1882–3	*Symphonisches Zwischenspiel zu Calderons Schauspiel 'Über allen Zauber Liebe'* G497.	RSiii/2

Lassus, Orlandus

483	1865	Arr for organ: *Regina coeli laetare* G663.

Lessmann, Otto

484	?1882	*3 Songs from J. Wolff's 'Tannhäuser'* G498.

(1)*Der Lenz ist gekommen* (2) *Trinklied* (3) *Du schaust mich an.*

Méhul, Étienne-Nicolas

484a	*c*1834	*Fünf Variationen über Romanze aus 'Joseph'.* Unpublished.

Massenet, Jules
See 542.

Mendelssohn, Felix

485	1840	*Lieder* (from op. 19, op. 34 & op. 47) G547.

(1) *Auf Flügeln des Gesanges* (2) *Sonntagslied* (3) *Reiselied* (4) *Neue Liebe* (5) *Frühlingslied* (6) *Winterlied* (7) *Suleika.*

486	1848	*Wasserfahrt* and *Der Jäger Abschied* (op. 50/4 and 2) G548.	
487	1849–50	*Wedding March and Dance of the Fairies from the incidental music to 'A Midsummer Night's Dream'* G410.	RSii/2

See also 381.

Mercadante, Saverio

488	1838	*Soirées italiennes. Six amusements* G411.

(1) *La primavera* (2) *Il galop* (3) *Il pastore svizzero* (4) *La serenata del marinaro* (5) *Il Brindisi* (6) *La zingarella spagnola.*

Meyerbeer, Giacomo

489	1836	*Grande Fantaisie sur des thèmes de l'opéra Les Huguenots* G412.	RSi/2 & RSiv/1 (an early version)

490	1841	*Réminiscences de Robert le Diable. Valse infernale* G413.	RSi/2
		Arr pf 4 hands (not by Liszt?), 1841–3 (G630).	
491	1841	*Le Moine* G416. (Arr of a song, with 2 other melodies by Meyerbeer).	
491a	1849	*Cavatine from Robert le Diable.* Unpublished.	
492	1849–50	*Illustrations du Prophète* G414.	RSi/2
		(1) *Prière, Hymne triomphale, Marche du sacre* (2) *Les Patineurs: Scherzo* (3) *Choeur pastoral, Appel aux armes* (4) *cf* **383**.	
493	1860	*Festmarsch zu Schillers 100-Jähriger Geburtsfeier* G549.	
494	1865	*Illustrations de l'Africaine* G415.	RSi/2
		(1) *Prière des matelots* (2) *Marche indienne.*	

Mosonyi, Mihály

495	1865	*Fantaisie sur l'opéra hongrois Szép Ilonka* G417.	RSiii/2

Mozart, Wolfgang Amadeus

496	1841	*Réminiscences de Don Juan* G418	RSi/1
		Arr 2 pfs, published 1877 (G656).	RSiv/2
497	1842	*Fantasia on themes from 'Le nozze di Figaro'* G697. Unfinished. (Published 1912, completed by Busoni.)	
498		*Confutatis and Lacrymosa from the Requiem* G550.	
		Published 1865.	
499	1875–81	Arr for pf 4 hands:	
		Adagio ('Der welcher wandelt diese Strasse') from 'Die Zauberflöte'. G634a. Unpublished.	

See also **405**.
A possible transcription of the overture to *Die Zauberflöte* (G748) is lost.

Nicolai, Otto

500	1852	Arr for organ:
		Kirchliche Festouvertüre über den Choral 'Ein feste Burg ist unser Gott' G675.

Pacini, Giovanni

501	1835–6	*Divertissement sur la cavatine 'I tuoi frequenti palpiti'* ('Niobe') G419.	RSii/1

Paganini, Niccolò

502	1831–2	*Grande Fantaisie de bravoure sur La Clochette* G420.	BHii/2
		On 'La Campanella' from the B mi Violin Concerto, op. 7. *cf* **252**(3).	
503		*Carnaval de Venise* G700. Unfinished; unpublished.	

See also **252** and **304**.

Palestrina, Giovanni Pierluigi da
See **291**(8).

Pantaleoni
504   Arr for voice + pf:
Barcarolle vénitienne G684. Published 1842.

Pavlovna, Grand Duchess Maria
505   Arr for voice + pf:
Es hat geflammt die ganze Nacht G685.
Unpublished.
See also **294**(4).

Peruccini, Cavaliere
See **314**(1).

Pezzini
506   *Una stella amica, mazurka* G551.

Prussia, Prince Louis Ferdinand of
See **274**.

Raff, Joachim
507 1853   *Andante finale and March from 'King Alfred'*
G421.
Also arr pf 4 hands, 1853 (G631).   RSiii/2

Rossini, Gioachino
508 1830   *Introduction des Variations sur une marche*
du Siège de Corinth G421a.
509 1835–6   *La serenata e L'orgia, grande fantaisie sur des*
motifs des Soirées musicales G422. *cf* **511**(10–11).
510 1835–6   *La pastorella dell' Alpi e Li marinari, 2me*
fantaisie sur des motifs des Soirées musicales
G423. *cf* **511**(6 and 12).
511 1837   *Soirées musicales* G424.
(1) *La promessa* (2) *La regata veneziana*
(3) *L'invito* (4) *La gita in gondola* (5) *Il*
rimprovero (6) *La pastorella dell' Alpi* (7) *La*
partenza (8) *La pesca* (9) *La danza* (10) *La*
serenata (11) *L'orgia* (12) *Li marinari.*
512 1838   *Ouverture de l'opéra Guillaume Tell* G552.   RSii/1
513 1847   *2 Transcriptions* G553.
(1) *Air du Stabat mater (Cujus animam)*
(2) *La charité.*
Arr of (1) also for organ + trombone,
published 1874 (G679), and for T + organ,
published 1874 (G682).   BHv/7
See also **234** and **314**(2).

Rubinstein, Anton
514 1880   *2 Songs* G554.
(1) *O! wenn es doch immer so bliebe* (2) *Der*
Asra.

515   *Introduction to Study* (*C ma*) G554a.
                      Unpublished.

Saint-Saëns, Camille
516   1876   *Danse macabre* op. 40 G555.

Schubert, Franz
517   1833   *Die Rose* G556. Revised 1833, published 1838.
518   1835–7   *12 Lieder* G558.
                      (1) *Sei mir gegrüsst* (2) *Auf dem Wasser zu singen* (3) *Du bist die Ruh* (4) *Erlkönig* (5)*Meeresstille* (6) *Die junge Nonne* (7) *Frühlingsglaube* (8) *Gretchen am Spinnrade* (9) *Ständchen* ('Horch, horch die Lerch') (10) *Rastlose Liebe* (11) *Der Wanderer* (12) *Ave Maria.*
519   1837   *Lob der Tränen* G557.
520   1838   *Der Gondelfahrer* G559.
521   1838–9   *Mélodies hongroises* G425. From the Divertissement à l'hongroise op. 54.
                      (1) Andante (2) Marcia (3) Allegretto.
                      (2) also arr for orch, cf 532.
522   1838–9   *Schwanengesang* G560. (14 songs).
523   1839   *Winterreise* G561. (12 songs).
                      (1) *Gute Nacht* (2) *Die Nebensonnen* (3) *Mut* (4) *Die Post* (5) *Erstarrung* (6) *Wasserflut* (7)*Der Lindenbaum* (8) *Der Leiermann* (9) *Täuschung* (10) *Das Wirtshaus* (11) *Der stürmische Morgen* (12) *Im Dorfe.*
524   1840   *Geistliche Lieder* G562.
                      (1) *Litaney* (2) *Himmelsfunken* (3) *Die Gestirne* (4) *Hymne.*
525   1846   *6 Melodien* G563.
                      (1) *Lebewohl* (2) *Mädchens Klage* (3) *Das Sterbeglöcklein* (4) *Trockene Blumen* (5) *Ungeduld* (1st version; cf 527) (6) *Die Forelle* (1st version; cf 526).
526   1846   *Die Forelle* (2nd version) G564.
527   1846   *Müllerlieder* G565.
                      (1) *Das Wandern* (2) *Der Müller und der Bach* (3) *Der Jäger* (4) *Die böse Farbe* (5) *Wohin?* (6) *Ungeduld* (2nd version).
528   1846   *3 Marches* (from op. 40 and op. 121) G426. Also arr for orch, cf 532.
529   1850–1   *Alfonso und Estrella*, Act 1 Piano score. G753. Probably lost.
       1850   Planned arrangement of Schubert's 'Great' C major symphony.
530   1851   For pf + orch:

Wanderer Fantasia in C major Symphonic
arrangement G366.
Also arr for 2 pfs, after 1851 (G653).

531 1852 *Soirées de Vienne. 9 Valse caprices* G427.
On Schubert's waltzes op. 9, op. 18, op. 33,
op. 50, op. 67, op. 77.
No. 4 based on same waltz as 246(3).
Cadenzas added to nos 6 and 9, 1883.

532 1859–60 Arr for orchestra:
4 Marches G363. From **521** and **528**.
Also arr for pf 4 hands, 1879 (G632).

533 1860 Arr for voice + orch:
6 Songs G375. (Nos. 5 and 6 unpublished)
(1) *Die junge Nonne* (2) *Gretchen am
Spinnrade* (3) *Lied der Mignon* (4) *Erlkönig*
(5) *Der Doppelgänger* (6) *Abschied*.

534 1871 Arr for T or S solo, male chorus + orch:
Die Allmacht G376.

Schumann, Clara
See **538**(II).

Schumann, Robert

535 1848 *Liebeslied (Widmung)* G566.

536 *2 Songs* G567. Published 1861. (1) *An den
Sonnenschein* (2) *Rotes Röslein*.

537 *Frühlingsnacht* ('*Überm Garten durch die
Lufte*') G568. Published 1872.

538 *Lieder von Robert und Clara Schumann* G569.
Published 1872.
I By Robert (from op. 79 and op. 98a):
(1) *Weihnachtslied* (2) *Die wandelnde Glocke*
(3) *Frühlings Ankunft* (4) *Des Sennen
Abschied* (5) *Er ist's* (6) *Nur wer die Sehnsucht
kennt* (7) *An die Türen will ich schleichen*.
II By Clara: (1) *Warum willst du andere
fragen?*
(2) *Ich habe in deinem Auge* (3) *Geheimes
Flüstern*.

539 1881 *Provençalisches Minnelied* G570.

Sorriano (Mariano Soriano Fuerto)

540 1844–5 *Feuille morte; Élégie d'après Sorriano* G428.

Spohr, Louis

541 1876 *Die Rose; Romanze* G571.

Spontini, Gasparo
See **234**.

Szabady, Károly
542 1879   *Revive Szegedin. Hungarian March G572.*
                   From the orchestral version by Massenet.

Széchényi, Imre
543 1872   *Bevezetés és magyar induló. Introduction and*
                   Hungarian March G573.

Tchaikovsky, Peter Ilyich
544 1879   *Polonaise from Eugene Onegin G429.*   RSiii/2

Tirindelli, P.A.
545 1880   *Seconda Mazurka variata G573a.*

Végh, János
546 1882–3   *Concert Waltz G430.* Based on the 2nd Waltz
                   Suite for pf 4 hands.

Verdi, Giuseppe
547 1847   *Concert Paraphrase on 'Ernani' G431a.*
                   Unpublished.
548 1848   *Salve Maria de Jérusalem* ('I Lombardi')
                   G431.   RSiii/2
549 by 1849   *Ernani. Paraphrase de concert G432.* Revised
                   1859.   RSiii/2
550 1859   *Miserere du Trovatore G433.*   RSiii/2
551 1859   *Rigoletto. Paraphrase de concert G434.*   RSiii/2
552 1867–8   *Don Carlos. Coro de festa e marcia funebre*
                   G435.   RSiii/2
553   *Aida. Danza sacra e duetto final*   G436.
                   Published 1879.   RSiii/2
554 1877   Arr for organ, harm or pf:
                   Agnus Dei de la Messe di Requiem G437.
555 1882   *Réminiscences de Boccanegra G438.*   LSii &
                                                                       RSiii/2

Wagner, Richard
556 1848   *Overture, 'Tannhäuser' G442.*   BHarrs/1 &
                                                                       RSiii/1
557 1849   *O du mein holder Abendstern* ('Tannhäuser')   (N.B. these
                   G444.   volumes
                   Also arr for cello + pf, 1852 (G380;   contain all
                   unpublished?).   the piano
                                                                       arrs of
                                                                       Wagner
                                                                       listed here)

558 1852   *2 Pieces from Tannhäuser and Lohengrin*
                   G445.
                   (1) Entry of the guests on the Wartburg
                   (2) Elsa's bridal procession.
559 1854   *From Lohengrin G446.* (1) Festival and Bridal

		Song (2) Elsa's Dream (3) Lohengrin's Rebuke.	
560	1859	*Fantasy on themes from Rienzi* G439.	
561	1860	*Spinning Chorus (Der fliegende Holländer)* G440.	
562	1860	Arr for organ: *Pilgrims' Chorus (Tannhäuser)* G676. Revised 1862. Also arr for pf, 1861 (G443; later revised and published 1885).	
563	1867	*Isolde's Liebestod (Tristan und Isolde)* G447. Revised edition published 1875.	
564	1871	*Am stillen Herd (Die Meistersinger)* G448.	
565	1872	*Ballad from Der fliegende Holländer* G441.	
566	1875	*Walhall (Der Ring des Nibelungen)* G449.	
567	1882	*Solemn march to the Holy Grail ('Parsifal')* G450.	

Weber, Carl Maria von

568	1840–1	*Fantasia on themes from Der Freischütz* G451. Unpublished.	
569	1843	*Overture, 'Oberon'* G574.	RSi/1
570	1846	*Overture, 'Der Freischütz'* G575.	RSi/1
571	1846	*Jübelouvertüre* G576.	
572	1848	*Leyer und Schwert* G452.	
573	1848	*Einsam bin ich, nicht alleine (La Preciosa)* G453.	RSi/1
574	1848	*Schlummerlied (mit Arabesken)* G454.	
575	1849	Arr for pf + orch: *Polonaise brillante Op 72* G367. Also arr for pf solo, *c* 1851 (G455).	

Wielhorsky, Michael (Vielgorsky, Mikhail Yuryevich)

576	1843	*Ljubila ja (I love you)*; *Romance* G577.	

See also 580.

Zámoyská, Ludmilla
See 368.

Zarembski, Jules de

577	1881	Arr for orch: *Danses galiciennes* G364.	

Zichy, Géza

578		*Valse d'Adèle* G456. Published 1877.	
579	1884	Arr for voice + orch: *Der Zaubersee. Ballad* G377. Unpublished; MS destroyed *c* 1945.	

Unknown/Anonymous

580	1842	*Mazurka pour piano composée par un*	

		amateur de St Pétersbourg (Wielhorsky? or Alyabyev?) G384.
581	1846	*Variations on Tiszántúli szép leány* G384a. Unpublished.
582		*Piece based on Italian operatic melodies* G458. Unpublished.
583		*Kavallerie-Geschwindmarsch* G460. Published 1883.

XII WORKS EDITED BY LISZT

Bach, Johann Sebastian
Kompositionen für Orgel. Revidiert und mit Beiträgen versehen von F. Liszt. (Includes **412** and **414**).
Chromatic Fantasy
3 Preludes and Fugues in C sharp minor
Das wohltemperierte Klavier. Transcription for organ. Unpublished.

Beethoven, Ludwig van
Works for piano: 2 and 4 hands (1857).
Duos for piano, with violin or cello; horn, flute or viola.
Trios for piano with violin (or clarinet) and cello.
Mass in C.
Mass in D.
Piano Quartets (1861).
Trios for string and wind instruments.
Menuet, revu par F. Liszt.

Bräunlich, A. and Gottschalg, W.
Mädchenlieder. Unter Mitwirkung von Hoffmann von Fallersleben und Franz Liszt, herausgegeben von A. Bräunlich und W. Gottschalg.

Chopin, Frédéric François
Études (published 1877).
B minor Sonata. Variant for finale. Unpublished.

Clementi, Muzio
Préludes et Exercices, corrigés et marqués au métronome par le jeune Liszt, suivis de douze de ses Études (published 1826).
cf **240**.

Field, John
18 Nocturnes, redigés et accompagnés d'une preface (1859). *cf* **464**.

Gottschalg, A.W.
Repertorium für Orgel, Harmonium oder Pedal-Flügel. Bearbeitet unter Revision und mit Beiträgen von F. Liszt.

Handel, George Frideric
Fugue in E minor.

Hummel, Johan Nepomuk
Septet, op. 74 for pf, flute, oboe, horn, viola, cello and bass.
Also as a Quintet for pf, violin, viola, cello and bass. *cf* 477.

Schubert, Franz
Selected sonatas and solo piano pieces (2 and 4 hands). (1868–80).

Scarlatti, Domenico
Cat's Fugue

Viole, Rudolf
Gartenlaube. 100 études for pf.

Weber, Carl Maria von
Selected sonatas and solo piano pieces. (1868; 1870).
Paraphrase on the *Invitation to the Dance* (1843).
6 Pages of Variants to the *Konzertstück*.

Zámoyská, Ludmilla
Songs. (Unpublished).

XIII LITERARY WORKS

(A) *Gesammelte Schriften* (Collected writings)
6 volumes, edited (with German translations) by Lina Ramann. Leipzig, 1880–83. Reprinted Wiesbaden, 1978.
Vol. I
F. Chopin (1851–52). (English translation by E.N. Waters, New York, 1963.)
Vol. II
(1) Essays from the *Revue et Gazette Musicale*: On the future of Church music (1834). On the position of artists (1835; 6 articles). On popular editions of important works (1836). On Meyerbeer's *Les Huguenots* (1837). Thalberg's *Grande Fantaisie* op. 22, and *Caprices* op. 15 and op. 19 (1837). To M. Fétis. A reply (1837). R. Schumann's piano compositions, op. 5, op. 11 and op. 14 (1837). Paganini: a Necrology (1840).
(2) Letters of a Bachelor of Music (1835–39).
(1–3) To George Sand. (4) To Adolphe Pictet. (5) To Louis de Ronchaud. (6) By Lake Como (To Louis de Ronchaud). (7) La Scala (To Moritz Schlesinger). (8) To Heinrich Heine. (9) To Lambert Massart. (10) On the position of music in Italy (To Moritz Schlesinger). (11) St Cecilia (To M. d'Ortigue). (12) To Hector Berlioz.
The second volume in the original French was published as *Pages romantiques*, ed. J. Chantavoine, Paris, 1912; reprinted with a preface by Serge Gut, Plan de la Tour (Var), 1985.
Vol. III
(1) Gluck's *Orpheus* (1854). Beethoven's *Fidelio* (1854). Weber's *Euryanthe*

(1854). On Beethoven's music to *Egmont* (1854). On Mendelssohn's music to *A Midsummer Night's Dream* (1854). Scribe and Meyerbeer's *Robert le diable* (1854). Schubert's *Alfonso and Estrella* (1854). Auber's *La Muette de Portici* (1854). Bellini's *Montecchi e Capuleti* (1854). Boieldieu's *Dame Blanche* (1854). Donizetti's *La Favorita* (1854). Pauline Viardot-García (1859). No Entr'acte Music! (1855). Mozart: on the occasion of his centenary festival in Vienna (1856).

(2) *Richard Wagner*

Tannhäuser and the Song Contest on the Wartburg (1849). *Lohengrin* and its first performance at Weimar (1850). *The Flying Dutchman* (1854). *The Rhinegold* (1855).

Vol. IV

Berlioz and his *Harold Symphony* (1855). Robert Schumann (1855). Clara Schumann (1855). Robert Franz (1855). Sobolewski's *Vinvela* (1855). John Field and his Nocturnes (1859).

Vol. V

On the Goethe Foundation (1850). Weimar's September Festival in honour of the centenary of Carl August's birth (1857). *Dornröschen*: Genast's poem and Raff's music (1856). Marx and his book *The Music of the Nineteenth Century* (1855). Criticism of criticism: Ulibishev and Serov (1858). A letter on conducting: a defence (1853).

Vol. VI

The Gypsies and their music in Hungary. (French edition 1859; German translation by Peter Cornelius, 1861; English translation by Edwin Evans, 2 vols., London, n.d.).

Vol. VII

Not published. It was to contain: Two 'letters' of 1837–8 and 1841. Illustrations to *Benvenuto Cellini* (1838). Liszt's forewords to his musical works.

(B) *Other Works. Essays published separately.*

Alkan's *Trois Morceaux dans le genre pathétique, op. 15* (1837). *Some Advice for Artists in connection with the 'Esquisses' by Kroll and the 'Esquisses mignonnes' by Ch. Reinecke for piano* (1849). *Lohengrin et Tannhäuser de Richard Wagner* (1851). *R. Schumann's Musikalische Haus- und Lebensregeln.* French translation by F. Liszt (1860).

Liszt also collaborated with Marschner, Reissiger and Spohr on articles for Eduard Bernsdorf's *Neues Universal-Lexicon der Tonkunst* (1856–65). Manuscript sketches by Liszt for a treatise on modern harmony are lost.

Appendix C

Personalia

Albéniz, Isaac (1860–1909). Spanish pianist and composer. Pupil of Liszt.

Bache, Walter (1842–88). English pianist and conductor. Pupil of Liszt.

Balzac, Honoré de (1799–1850). French novelist.

Bechstein, Carl (1826–1900). Founder of the firm of German piano manufacturers. Friend of Liszt and Bülow.

Belgiojoso, Princess Cristina (1808–71). Italian patriot and writer, resident in Paris from 1831.

Boissier, Valerie (1813–94). French pupil of Liszt. Her mother, Caroline (Mme. Auguste Boissier), kept a diary of the piano lessons, 1831–2.

Brendel, Franz (1811–68). German music critic and champion of Liszt. A founder of the *Allgemeiner Deutscher Musikverein*.

Bülow, Hans Guido, Freiherr von (1830–94). German pianist and conductor. Also teacher, composer, editor, transcriber and writer. Pupil of F. Wieck and Liszt. As player and conductor he championed Beethoven, Wagner, Liszt and, latterly, Brahms. Married Cosima Liszt 1857, and secondly the actress Marie Schanzer, 1882. Despite a vigorously active career he often suffered ill-health, and died while convalescing in Cairo.

Chorley, Henry (1808–72). English music critic, poet and librettist. Admirer of Liszt.

Clementi, Muzio (1752–1832). Italian composer, pianist and teacher; lived mainly in England. Profoundly influenced modern piano technique. Czerny learned from him; Cramer and Field were his pupils.

Cohen, Hermann (1820–71). German pianist, pupil of Liszt in 1830s, nicknamed 'Puzzi'. After a period of dissipation and gambling he became a Carmelite friar in 1850.

Conradi, August (1821–73). German organist, conductor and composer of operas and many other works. Liszt's amanuensis at Weimar 1848–9.

Cornelius, Peter (1824–74). German composer, also poet and critic.

Cramer, John Baptist (1771–1858). German pianist, composer and teacher; lived mainly in Paris and London.

Czerny, Carl (1791–1857). Viennese pianist, composer and teacher. Pupil of Beethoven. Teacher of Liszt, Döhler and Kullak. Dedicatee of Liszt's *Études d'exécution transcendante*.

Damrosch, Leopold (1832–85). German conductor, violinist and composer. Emigrated to New York in 1871 where he gave the première of *Le Triomphe funèbre du Tasse,* March 1877.

David, Ferdinand (1810–73). German violinist, composer and teacher of Joachim and Wilhelmj.

Diabelli, Anton (1781–1858). Austrian composer, teacher and music publisher.

Erard, Sébastien (1752–1831). Founder of the French firm of piano and harp manufacturers. Succeeded by his nephew Pierre (1796–1855). Patrons and friends of Liszt.

Erkel, Franz (1810–93). Hungarian composer (of patriotic operas and songs), conductor and pianist. Director of National Music Academy, Budapest.

Fay, Amy (1844–1928). American pupil of Tausig, Kullak, Deppe and Liszt, of whom she wrote memoirs. Visited Weimar several times from 1873.

Fétis, François Joseph (1784–1871). Belgian composer, music theorist and historian. Author of *Biographie Universelle des Musiciens.*

Göllerich, August (1859–1923). German pianist and biographer of his teachers Liszt and Bruckner.

Habeneck, François Antoine (1781–1849). French conductor and violinist. Pioneered Beethoven's symphonies in France.

Hallé, Sir Charles (1819–95). German pianist and conductor who settled in England. Founded the Hallé Orchestra in Manchester, 1858.

Heine, Heinrich (1797–1856). German author and poet; lived in Paris from 1831. Friend and admirer of Liszt but became critical of what he saw as the pianist's Romantic excesses.

Herz, Henri (1803–88). Pianist and composer; born in Vienna, mainly resident in Paris. Brother of the pianist Jacques Simon Herz (1794–1880).

Hiller, Ferdinand (1811–85). German pianist, composer and teacher. In Paris 1828–35.

Hugo, Victor (1802–85). French poet, dramatist and novelist. One of the greatest of the French Romantics, he lived in voluntary exile in the Channel Islands during the Second Empire, 1851–70.

Ingres, Jean Auguste Dominique (1780–1867). French painter.

Joachim, Joseph (1831–1907). Hungarian violinist and composer. After leaving Weimar, where he had been Liszt's orchestral leader, he became attached to the Schumann circle and helped Clara rebuild her career after Robert's collapse. Friend of Brahms, and dedicatee of his Violin Concerto.

Kalkbrenner, Friedrich (1785–1849). German pianist, composer and teacher. Settled in Paris, 1824.

Klindworth, Karl (1830–1916). German pianist, composer and conductor. Pupil of Liszt. Pursued his career in London, Moscow and Berlin. Noted for his piano arrangements of Wagner scores. In late life he adopted an English girl, Winifred Williams, who married Liszt's grandson Siegfried Wagner.

Köhler, Louis (1820–86). German piano teacher, writer on music, composer of pedagogic works, operas, etc.

La Mara (pseudonym of Marie Lipsius; 1837–1927). German writer. Translator of Liszt's *Chopin*; editor of many volumes of his letters and those of his circle.

Lamartine, Alphonse de (1790–1869). French poet and statesman.

Lamennais, Abbé Félicité de (1782–1854) French writer of Christian philosophy. Liszt's spiritual mentor.

Lassen, Eduard (1830–1904). Danish composer and conductor. Liszt's successor at Weimar from 1858.

Lehmann, Henri (1814–82). German portrait painter.

Lenz, Wilhelm von (1809–83). Russian state councillor. Pupil of Liszt and Chopin and author of studies of Beethoven.

Mackenzie, Sir Alexander (1847–1935). Scottish composer, conductor and teacher. Principal of the Royal Academy of Music, 1888–1924.

Massart, Joseph Lambert (1811–92). Belgian violinist. Teacher of Wieniawski and Sarasate.

Moscheles, Ignaz (1794–1870). German pianist, composer and teacher of Czech birth. Friend of Beethoven and Mendelssohn. Settled in London, 1826, and in Leipzig, 1846.

Motta, José Vianna da (1868–1948). Portuguese pianist and composer. Pupil of Liszt and editor of his works.

Musset, Alfred de (1810–57). French poet, playwright and novelist. Lover of George Sand, 1833–5.

Nerval, Gérard de (1808–55). French author and poet.

Nikisch, Arthur (1855–1922). Hungarian violinist, pianist and notable and influential conductor. Protégé of Liszt.

Nohl, Ludwig (1831–85). German writer on music, particularly of studies of Mozart, Beethoven, Liszt and Wagner.

Nourrit, Adolphe (1802–39). French tenor; leading singer at the Opéra from 1826–37. Popularised Schubert's songs. He killed himself after a period of depression and illness apparently caused by the success of his rival Duprez.

d'Ortigue, Joseph (1802–66). French music critic and historian. Earliest biographer of Liszt (*Gazette Musicale*, 1835).

Paer, Ferdinando (1771–1839). Italian opera composer. After posts in Vienna and Dresden he settled in Paris, 1807. Teacher of Liszt.

Parry, John Orlando (1810–79). English concert artist of Welsh parentage. For his many talents see page 55.

Pixis, Johann Peter (1788–1874). German pianist, teacher and composer; settled in Paris, 1825.

Pleyel, Marie (née Moke; 1811–75). French pianist; wife of the piano manufacturer Camille Pleyel. Berlioz fell in love with her.

Pohl, Richard (1826–96). German composer and journalistic champion of Liszt and Wagner. In Weimar, 1854–64.

Potter, Cipriani (1792–1871). English composer, pianist and teacher. Pupil of Beethoven.

Pruckner, Dionys (1834–96). German pianist and teacher. Pupil of Liszt.

Raabe, Peter (1872–1945). German music scholar and conductor. Director of the Liszt Museum, Weimar; editor of and biographer of Liszt. Under the Nazi regime he succeeded Strauss when the latter was forced to resign as head of the Reichsmusikkammer in 1935.

Raff, Joachim (1822–82). German composer. Liszt's assistant at Weimar in the early 1850s.

Ramann, Lina (1833–1912). German music teacher and writer; director of the Nuremberg Music School. Biographer of Liszt, editor of his collected writings and of Liszt-Pädagogium, 5 volumes of piano works with Liszt's own annotations.

Reicha, Antonín (1770–1836). Czech composer and theorist. Friend of Haydn and Beethoven. Settled in Paris, 1808, where pupils included Berlioz, Liszt and Franck. His use of counterpoint and of instrumental sonority was highly original.

Reményi, Eduard (1830–98). Hungarian violinist, composer and arranger.

Riedel, Carl (1827–88). German choral conductor, composer and editor. Succeeded Brendel as conductor of the *Allgemeiner Deutscher Musikverein.*

Ries, Ferdinand (1784–1838). German pianist, composer and conductor. Wrote eight piano concertos.

Rubinstein, Anton (1829–94). Russian pianist and prolific composer. In the wake of Liszt he was the most widely acclaimed pianist of the age. Brother of the distinguished pianist and teacher Nikolai Rubinstein (1835–81).

Saint-Simon, Claude Henri, Comte de (1760–1825). French philosopher and theorist of social reform.

Sainte-Beuve, Charles Augustin (1804–69). French literary critic, historian and poet.

Salieri, Antonio (1750–1825). Italian opera composer, mainly resident in Vienna. Rival of Mozart; friend of Haydn, Schubert and Beethoven. Teacher of Liszt.

Sand, George (1804–76). French novelist, famed for her male attire. Lover of de Musset, 1833–5, and Chopin, 1837–47.

Schober, Franz von (1796–1882). Austrian poet and writer. Friend of Schubert and Liszt. Councillor of legation at Weimar.

Schumann, Clara (née Wieck; 1819–96). Daughter of the German piano pedagogue Friedrich Wieck (1785–1873). Child prodigy pianist; also composer. In 1840 married Robert Schumann (1810–56) after whose death she resumed her concert career and taught. Noted interpreter of Chopin, Schumann, Beethoven and her close friend Brahms.

Sgambati, Giovanni (1841–1914). Italian composer, pianist, teacher and conductor. Pupil of Liszt.

Smart, Sir George (1776–1867). English conductor and organist. A founder of the Philharmonic Society.

Smithson, Harriet (1800–54). English actress of Irish descent who enjoyed great fame as Ophelia and Desdemona in Paris between 1827 and 1833. In the latter year she made her ill-judged and unhappy marriage to Berlioz.

Taubert, Wilhelm (1811–91). German pianist, conductor and composer.

Tausig, Carl (1841–71). Polish pianist, teacher, composer and transcriber. Child prodigy pupil of Liszt.

Thalberg, Sigismund von (1812–71). Swiss virtuoso pianist and composer; pupil of Hummel and Moscheles. Toured widely in Europe, North and South America. Had many pupils and published a method called *The Art of Singing as Applied to the Piano.*

Urhan, Chrétien (1790–1845). French violinist and composer of quartets, songs, piano pieces.

Viardot-García, Pauline (1821–1910). French operatic mezzo-soprano. Studied piano with Liszt and composition with Reicha. Daughter of the great Spanish tenor Manuel García; sister of Malibran and of the singing teacher Manuel García. Widely admired for her intellectual, artistic and dramatic gifts. She was the close companion of Turgenev in his last twenty years.

Vigny, Alfred Victor de (1797–1863). French poet, philosopher and dramatist.

Vörösmárty, Mihály (1800–55). Hungarian poet, dramatist and critic.

Weingartner, Felix (1863–1942). Austrian composer and conductor. Protégé of Liszt.

Weissheimer, Wendelin (1838–1910). German composer, conductor and teacher. Friend of Wagner and Liszt.

Winterberger, Alexander (1834–1914). German organist, pianist and composer. Pupil of Liszt and editor of his Technical Studies.

Wohl, Janka (1846–1901). Hungarian writer; friend of Liszt.

Appendix D

Select bibliography

A BIBLIOGRAPHIES

Koch, Lájos, *Liszt Ferenc, Bibliográfiai Kísérlet: Franz Liszt, ein biblio-graphischer Versuch*, Budapest, 1936.

Searle, Humphrey, *Liszt* in *New Grove, Dictionary of Music*, London, 1980.

Suttoni, Charles, *Franz Liszt's published correspondence: an annotated bib-liography* in 'Fontes Artis Musicae', Vol. XXVI, No. 3, Kassel, 1979.

B LETTERS

There is no complete edition of Liszt's correspondence, some of which remains unpublished; the rest is scattered in many volumes, collections and periodicals (for details see Suttoni, above). The following are the principal sources:

Hans von Bülow: Briefe und Schriften (ed. Marie von Bülow), 8 vols, Leipzig 1899–1908. There is an English selection: *Letters of Liszt and von Bülow* (transl. C. Bache), London, 1898; based in turn upon *Briefwechsel zwischen Franz Liszt und Hans von Bülow* (ed. La Mara), Leipzig, 1898.

Franz Liszts Briefe an Baron Anton Augusz (ed. Wilhelm von Csapó), Budapest, 1911.

Letters of Franz Liszt to Marie zu Sayn-Wittgenstein (ed. and transl. Howard E. Hugo), Cambridge, Mass., 1953.

Briefwechsel zwischen Wagner und Liszt (ed. Erich Kloss), 2 vols., 3rd edition, Leipzig, 1910. Earlier editions are untrustworthy because of editorial sup-pressions, and even this edition is incomplete. Unreliable also is the early English translation *Correspondence of Wagner and Liszt* (transl. Francis Hueffer) 2 vols, new rev. ed. London, 1897.

Franz Liszts Briefe (ed. La Mara), 8 vols, Leipzig, 1893–1904. (1) From Paris to Rome (2) From Rome to the End (3) Letters to a Friend [Agnes Street] (4–7) Letters to Princess Sayn-Wittgenstein (8) Additional letters to vols 1 and 2. There is an English edition of (1) and (2): *Liszt's Letters* (transl. Constance Bache), London, 1894; reprinted New York, 1969.

Briefe hervorragender Zeitgenossen an Franz Liszt (ed. La Mara), 3 vols, Leipzig, 1895–1904. Letters of his contemporaries to Liszt.

Briefwechsel zwischen Franz Liszt und Carl Alexander, Herzog von Sachsen (ed. La Mara), Leipzig, 1909.

Franz Liszts Briefe an seine Mutter (ed. and transl. La Mara), Leipzig, 1918. German translations of the unpublished originals.

Gérard de Nerval: Lettres à Franz Liszt (ed. J. Guillaume and C. Pichois), Namur, 1972.

Correspondance de Liszt et de Madame d'Agoult (ed. Daniel Ollivier), 2 vols, Paris, 1933–34.

Correspondance de Liszt et de sa fille Mme Emile Ollivier (ed. Daniel Ollivier), Paris, 1936.

Autour de Mme d'Agoult et de Liszt (ed. Daniel Ollivier), Paris, 1941.

Franz Liszt: Briefe aus ungarischen Sammlungen, 1835–86 (ed. Margit Prahács), Kassel, 1966.

Franz Liszts Briefe an Carl Gille (ed. Adolf Stern), Leipzig, 1903.

Franz Liszt: l'artiste, le clerc. Documents inédits (ed. Jacques Vier), Paris, 1950.

The Letters of Franz Liszt to Olga von Meyendorff, 1871–86 (ed. E. N. Waters; transl. W. R. Tyler), Washington D.C., 1979.

Franz Liszt und sein Kreis in Briefen und Dokumenten (ed. M. P. Eckhardt and C. Knotik), Eisenstadt, 1983.

Franz Liszt: Correspondance (Lettres choisies, présentées et annotées par Pierre-Antoine Huré et Claude Knepper), Paris, 1987.

C BIOGRAPHICAL WORKS

* Books which contain letters not found in the above collections are marked with an asterisk.

† A cross indicates that the work contains substantial discussion of the music.

* Bory, Robert, *Liszt et ses enfants Blandine, Cosima et Daniel*, Paris, 1936.

* Bory, Robert, *Une Retraite romantique en Suisse*, Geneva, 1930.

* Bory, Robert, *La vie de Franz Liszt par l'image*, Geneva, 1936.

* Buchner, Alexander, *Franz Liszt in Böhmen* (transl. Czech to German, C. and F. Kirschner), Prague, 1962. The English edition *Franz Liszt in Bohemia* (transl. R. F. Samsour), London, 1962; omits an entire section of letters but is lavishly illustrated.

Burger, Ernst *Franz Liszt: Eine Lebenschronik in Bildern und Dokumenten* Munich, 1986 (English and French translations in preparation).

Eckhardt, María *Liszt's Music Manuscripts in the National Széchényi Library*, Budapest, 1986.

Eösze, László, *119 római Liszt-dokumentum* (*Roman Liszt documents*), Budapest, 1980.

Friedheim, Arthur, *Life and Liszt* (ed. T. L. Bullock) in *Remembering Franz Liszt*, New York, 1986 [also includes Siloti's 'Memories' – see below]

Gavoty, Bernard, *Liszt. Le virtuose, 1811–1848*, Paris, 1980.

*† Göllerich, August, *Franz Liszt*, Berlin, 1908.

Göllerich, August, *Franz Liszts Klavierunterricht von 1884–1886* (ed. Wilhelm Jerger), Regensburg, 1975.

Haldane, Charlotte, *The Galley Slaves of Love*, London, 1957.

Hamburger, Klara, *Franz Liszt*, Budapest, 1966.

*† Haraszti, Émile, *Franz Liszt*, Paris, 1967.

Helm, Everett, B., *Franz Liszt in Selbstzeugnissen und Bilddokumenten*, Hamburg, 1972.

Horvath, Emmerich Karl, *Franz Liszt* (Vol. 1 *Kindheit 1811–27*; Vol. 2 *Die Jugend 1827–37*), Eisenstadt, 1978, 1982.

Huneker, James, *Liszt*, London, 1911; reprinted New York, 1971.

Kapp, Julius, *Franz Liszt*, Berlin, 1909.

*Lachmund, Carl V., *Mein Leben mit Franz Liszt. Aus dem Tagebuch eines Liszt-Schülers*, Eschwege, 1970.

László, Zsigmond and Máteka, Béla, *Franz Liszt. A biography in pictures*, London, 1968.

*Legány, Deszö, *Franz Liszt: Unbekannte Presse und Briefe aus Wien, 1822–1886*, Vienna, 1984.

Legány, Deszö, *Liszt Ferenc Magyarországon, 1869–73*, Budapest, 1976. English translation (by G. Gulyás, B. Gaster and P. Merrick): *Ferenc Liszt and His Country 1869–73*, Budapest, 1983.

Liszt, Eduard Ritter von, *Franz Liszt: Abstammung, Familie, Begebenheiten*, Vienna, 1937.

Newman, Ernest, *The Man Liszt*, London, 1934.

Perényi, Eleanor, *Liszt*, London, 1974.

Pourtalès, Guy de, *Franz Liszt, the Man of Love* (transl. E. S. Brooks), London, 1927.

*†Raabe, Peter, *Franz Liszt: Leben und Schaffen*, 2 vols, Stuttgart, 1931; revised ed. (Felix Raabe), Tutzing, 1968.

†Ramann, Lina, *Franz Liszt als Künstler und Mensch*, 3 vols, Leipzig, 1880–94. First vol. only transl. into English (E. Cowdrey), London, 1882.

*Ramann, Lina, *Lisztiana: Erinnerungen an Franz Liszt (1873–1886/87)* (ed. A. Seidl and F. Schnapp), Mainz, 1983.

†Rehberg, Paula and Nestler, Gerhard, *Franz Liszt: die Geschichte seines Lebens, Schaffens und Wirkens*, Zurich, 1961.

Rellstab, Ludwig, *Franz Liszt*, Berlin, 1842.

Schumann, Karl, *Das kleine Liszt-Buch*, Hamburg, 1981.

*Siloti, Alexander, *My Memories of Liszt*, Edinburgh, c. 1908. [See also under Friedheim, above].

Sitwell, Sacheverell, *Liszt*, London, 1934; revised ed. 1955.

*†Walker, Alan, *Franz Liszt*, 3 vols, New York and London, 1983–.

Wallace, William, *Liszt, Wagner and the Princess*, London, 1927.

*Weilguny, Hedwig and Handrick, Willy, *Franz Liszt: Biographie in Bildern*, Leipzig, 4th ed., 1980.

Wessling, Berndt W., *Franz Liszt: ein virtuoses Leben*, Munich, 1973.

Wilkinson, Anthony, *Liszt*, London, 1975.

Williams, Adrian, *Portrait of Liszt*, London, 1989.

Wohl, Janka, *François Liszt: Recollections of a compatriot* (transl. B. P. Ward), London, 1887.

D MUSICAL STUDIES

Gut, Serge, *Franz Liszt, les éléments du langage musical,* Paris, 1975.

Hamburger, Klara (ed.), *Franz Liszt: Beiträge von ungarischen Autoren,* Budapest, 1978.

Heinemann, Ernst Günter, *Franz Liszts Auseinandersetzung mit der geistlichen Musik,* Munich, 1978.

Liszt Studien I (Kongressbericht Eisenstadt 1975), ed. Wolfgang Suppan, Graz, 1977.

Liszt Studien II (Kongressbericht Eisenstadt 1978), ed. Serge Gut, Munich, 1981.

Liszt Studien III (Kongressbericht Eisenstadt, 1983), ed. Serge Gut, Munich, 1986.

Kókai, Rudolf, *Franz Liszt in seinen frühen Klavierwerken,* Leipzig, 1933; new ed., Kassel, 1968.

Mach, Elyse, *The Liszt Studies,* New York, 1973.

Merrick, Paul, *Revolution and Religion in the Music of Liszt,* Cambridge, 1987.

Metzger, Heinz-Klaus and Riehn, Rainer, *Franz Liszt* (Musik-Konzepte 12), Munich, 1980.

Montu-Berthon, Suzanne, *Un Liszt Méconnu. Mélodies et Lieder,* 2 vols (*La Revue Musicale* Nos. 342–6), Paris, 1981.

Schnapp, Friedrich, *Verschollene Kompositionen Franz Liszts,* Leipzig, 1942.

Schwartz, Peter, *Studien zur Orgelmusik Franz Liszts: ein Beitrag zur Geschichte der Orgelkomposition im 19. Jahrhundert,* Munich, 1971.

Searle, Humphrey, *The Music of Liszt,* London, 1954.

Stevenson, Ronald, *Liszt Piano Music,* BBC Music Guides, London (in preparation).

Szabolcsi, Bence, *The Twilight of Ferenc Liszt* (transl. A. Deák), Budapest, 1959.

Walker, Alan (ed.), *Franz Liszt: the man and his music,* London, 1970.

Winklhofer, Sharon, *Liszt's Sonata in B minor. A study of autograph sources and documents,* U.M.I., Michigan, 1980.

E PERIODICALS

Journal of the American Liszt Society (ed. Maurice Hinson; Michael Saffle), Louisville, Kentucky, 1977–.

Liszt Saeculum (formerly *I.L.C. Quarterly*) (ed. Lennart Rabes), Deal; Älvsjö, 1978–.

Liszt Society Journal (ed. Eunice Mistarz; Adrian Williams), London, 1975–.

Musical Opinion Franz Liszt Issue, London, Jan., 1977.

New Hungarian Quarterly Liszt-Bartók Issue, Budapest, 1962.

19th Century Music (ed. Joseph Kerman) University of California, 1977–.

Revue Musicale Paris: Special Liszt Issue, May 1928. Double Issue (nos. 292–3), 1973. Double Issue (nos. 342–6), 1981.

Studia Musicologica Academiae Scientarium Hungaricae, Budapest, 1961–.

F RELATED LITERATURE

d'Agoult, Marie, *Mémoires 1833–54* (ed. Daniel Ollivier), Paris, 1927.

d'Agoult, Marie, *Nélida,* Paris, 1846.

d'Agoult, Marie, *Mes Souvenirs 1806–33*, Paris, 1877.

Balzac, Honoré de, *Béatrix* (transl. R. and S. Harcourt-Smith), London, 1957.

Bartók, Béla, *Essays* (ed. B. Suchoff), London, 1976.

Berlioz, Hector, *Memoirs* (transl. David Cairns), London, 1969.

Brombert, Beth Archer, *Cristina. Portraits of a Princess,* London, 1978.

Cornelius, Peter, *Literarische Werke; Ausgewählte Briefe,* 4 vols, Leipzig, 1904–5.

Fay, Amy, *Music Study in Germany*, London, 1885; reprinted New York, 1965.

Hallé, Sir Charles, *The autobiography: with correspondence and diaries* (ed. Michael Kennedy), London, 1972.

Lamond, Frederic, *The Memoirs of Frederic Lamond,* Glasgow, 1949.

Lenz, Wilhelm von, *Great Piano Virtuosos of Our Time,* New York, 1973; and London, 1983 (reprint of 1899 transl. by M. R. Baker).

Mason, William, *Memories of a Musical Life,* New York, 1901; reprinted New York, 1970.

Roës, Paul, *Music, the Mystery and the Reality* (transl. and ed. E. D. McGray), Chevy Chase, Maryland, 1978.

Sand, George, *Journal intime*, Paris, 1926 (Various English translations).

Schorn, Adelheid von, *Das nachklassische Weimar*, 2 vols, Weimar, 1911–12.

Schorn, Adelheid von, *Zwei Menschenalter*, Berlin, 1901.

Stasov, Vladimir V., *Aleksander Porfir'yevich Borodin*, St Petersburg, 1887; rev. and enlarged 1889. The French edition (A. Habets, Paris, 1893) was transl. into English by Rosa Newmarch: *Borodin and Liszt*, London, 1895 (reprinted New York, 1977), and contains Borodin's accounts of meetings with Liszt.

Stasov, Vladimir V., *Selected Essays on Music* (intro. by Gerald Abraham; transl. F. Jonas), London, 1968.

Vier, Jacques, *La Comtesse d'Agoult et son temps,* 6 vols, Paris, 1955–63.

Wagner, Cosima, *Diaries* (ed. M. Gregor-Dellin and D. Mack; transl. Geoffrey Skelton), 2 vols, London, 1978–80.

Wagner, Richard, *Mein Leben* (ed. M. Gregor-Dellin) Munich, 1963; English transl., 2 vols, London, 1911; and (transl. A. Gray) London, 1983.

Appendix E

The Liszt Society

The Liszt Society was founded in London in 1950 on the initiative of Vernon Harrison (the current chairman) and Humphrey Searle. Its first president was Edward J. Dent and committee members were Ralph Hill, Louis Kentner, CBE, Constant Lambert, Edward Sackville-West, Sir Sacheverell Sitwell Bt. and Sir William Walton OM. Current patrons are Vladimir Ashkenazy, Alfred Brendel, France Clidat (France), Gunnar Johansen (USA), The Lord Londonderry, Sir Yehudi Menuhin, OM, Lord Rayne and Sir Georg Solti.

The society has advanced the cause of Liszt in four valuable ways: through concerts, recitals and competitions under its auspices; by answering queries concerning Liszt, the scores and recordings of his music; through its annual journal and newsletters; and by publishing unfamiliar works (first seven volumes in association with Schott and Co. Ltd.).

Many other Liszt societies exist in various parts of the world, among them the Liszt Ferenc Társaság (The Liszt Society, Budapest), The European Liszt Centre (Eisenstadt), The American Liszt Society, The French Liszt Society, The Dutch Liszt Society and The South Pacific Liszt Society (Sydney), etc. Information on these and other matters may be obtained from the London Liszt Society. Address for enquiries:

The Secretary
The Liszt Society
135 Stevenage Road
Fulham
London SW6 6PB

Another organisation which bears Liszt's name has published much of interest concerning the composer: The International Liszt Centre for 19th Century Music, based in Älvsjö, Sweden.

Index

Index

Index

Index